Joe

The Complete Plays

Entertaining Mr Sloane, Loot, What the Butler Saw,
The Ruffian on the Stair, The Erpingham Camp,
Funeral Games, The Good and Faithful Servant

This book contains everything that Orton wrote for the theatre,
radio and television in the three years between his first play in
1964 and his violent death in 1967 at the age of 34. Intro-
ducing the volume is an informative and revealing essay by John
Lahr, Orton's official biographer.

'Joe Orton deserves attention, not simply as one of our most
astute and sophisticated playwrights, but also as a sign or portent
of the times. Mr Orton deals with themes still fashionable . . .
brutality, jackboots, rape, perversion, necrophilia, all sorts of
kinkiness behind the sofa and inside the wardrobes of drab
suburban homes; he is our best example of the hole-and-corner
arty type made good as a West End success.'

Hilary Spurling, *The Spectator*

'He is the Oscar Wilde of Welfare State gentility.'

Ronald Bryden, *The Observer*.

*Joe Orton was born in Leicester in 1933 and was battered to death in
August 1967. He left school at sixteen and went to RADA two
years later. He spent six months in prison for defacing library books.
In 1964 his first play,* The Ruffian on the Stair, *was broadcast and
his first full-length piece,* Entertaining Mr Sloane, *was staged in the
West End, as was* Loot *two years later. The* Erpingham Camp
*was televised in 1966 and staged at the Royal Court in 1967 in
double-bill with* The Ruffian on the Stair. *His television plays,*
The Good and Faithful Servant *and* Funeral Games *were shown
posthumously in 1967 and 1968. His last play,* What the Butler
Saw, *was not staged until 1969, though it was successfully revived
by the Royal Court in 1975 in a season that also included important
revivals of* Loot *and* Entertaining Mr Sloane. *These last two plays
have been made into successful films. Orton also wrote a screenplay
for the Beatles which was never filmed. A novel,* Head to Toe, *was
published posthumously in 1971.*

JOE ORTON
The Complete Plays

Introduced by
JOHN LAHR

Entertaining Mr Sloane
Loot
What the Butler Saw
The Ruffian on the Stair
The Erpingham Camp
Funeral Games
The Good and Faithful Servant

Grove Press
New York

Contents

Introduction   *page* 7

THE RUFFIAN ON THE STAIR   29

ENTERTAINING MR SLOANE   63

THE GOOD AND FAITHFUL SERVANT   151

LOOT   193

THE ERPINGHAM CAMP   277

FUNERAL GAMES   321

WHAT THE BUTLER SAW   361

Introduction

All classes are criminal today. We live in an age of equality.
                                    Joe Orton, *Funeral Games*

Like all great satirists, Joe Orton was a realist. He was prepared to speak the unspeakable; and this gave his plays their joy and danger. He teased an audience with its sense of the sacred, flaunting the hard facts of life people contrived to forget. There were, for Orton, no 'basic human values'. Man was capable of every bestiality; and all moral credos were heroic daydreams, the luxury of affluence. Orton's inspired megalomaniacs depict life as a vicious and hilarious evasion of Man's death and death-dealing.

With *Loot* and *What the Butler Saw*, Orton became the master farceur of his age. His laughter was etched in the despair, isolation and violence of modern life and offered instead of stasis the more apt metaphor of frantic activity. Farce allowed Orton to make a spectacle of disintegration. He showed man dummying up a destiny in a meaningless world by making panic look like reason. 'In a world run by fools,' Orton wrote, taunting the readers of the *Radio Times* about his first play, *The Ruffian on the Stair* (1963), 'the writer can only chronicle the doings of fools or their victims. And because the world is a cruel and heartless place, he will be accused of not taking his subject seriously . . . But laughter is a serious business, and comedy a weapon more dangerous than tragedy. Which is why tyrants treat it with caution. The actual material of tragedy is equally viable in comedy – unless you happen to be writing in English, when the question of taste occurs. The English are the most tasteless nation on earth, which is why they set such store by it.'

Orton was a connoisseur of chaos, the first contemporary playwright to transform the clown's rambunctious instincts from the stage to the page. Like all pranksters, Orton was an enemy of order who adopted many protean disguises for his anarchic fun including the *noms de plume* of Edna Welthorpe (Mrs) with which he fanned the scandal of his plays by condemning them in the press and Donald H. Hartley which he used to praise himself. Orton also had a prankster's instinct for phallic mischief. 'I'm to be at King's Cross station at eleven. I'm meeting a man in the toilet,' Mike explains at the beginning of *The Ruffian on the Stair*. Joyce replies: 'You always go to such interesting places . . .' Orton's plays put sexuality back on stage in all its exuberant, amoral, and ruthless excess. He laughed away sexual categories. 'I'm a heterosexual,' protests the psychiatrist, Dr Prentice in *What the Butler Saw*. Dr Rance counters: 'I wish you wouldn't use these Chaucerian words.' A penis ('the missing parts of Sir Winston Churchill') is held aloft in the penultimate image of *What the Butler Saw*, an archetypal comic symbol of Orton's life and his art. Orton's plays goosed his public. 'Sex,' he noted in his diary reminding himself to 'hot-up' *What the Butler Saw* in the rewrite, 'is the only way to infuriate them. Much more fucking and they'll be screaming hysterics in next to no time.'

Orton's plays are a flamboyant dance with the death he found in life. He liked being 'the fly on the wall' who registered the idiom, the lives and the longings in his many anonymous subterranean encounters. Hunger and how it disguises its craving was what amused him. His sexual adventuring taught him to suspect every show of normality:

After walking for a long while I found a gent's lavatory on a patch of grass near a church. I went in. [Orton wrote in his diary about a walk in Brighton while visiting his producer Oscar Lewenstein.] It was v. dark. There was a man in there. Tall, grand, and smiling. In the gloom he looked aristocratic. When the lights were turned on (after about five minutes) I could see that he was stupid, smiling and bank-clerkish. He showed his cock. I let him feel mine. 'Oo!', he gasped, not noticing the sinister sore that had developed on the end over the last week or so, 'Oo!'. I asked if he had anywhere to go back to? 'No,' he said, 'I don't have the choice of my neighbours, you see. They're down on me and I couldn't take the risk.' He nodded to a dwarf skulking in the corner of the lavatory. 'He'll suck you off, though. I've seen him do it.' He made a motion to the dwarfish creature, rather as someone would call a taxi. The dwarf sucked me off while the other man smiled benevolently and then, I suppose, went back to his neighbours refreshed

'I'm an acquired taste,' Orton explained in 1967. 'That's a double entendre if there ever was one. Oh, the public will accept me. They've given me a licence, you see. What they'll do is say "Joe Orton can do these things" if I'm a success. But I'm a success because I've taken a hatchet to them and hacked my way in. I mean it wasn't easy. *Sloane* wasn't easy. It wasn't the enormous success that people seem to think . . It's always a fight for an original writer because any original writer will always force the world to see the world his way. The people who don't want to see the world your way will always be angry.' Long before Orton found his comic voice, he was dreaming of conquest. In *The Vision of Gombold Proval* (1961), a novel posthumously published as *Head to Toe* (1971), Orton set down a battle plan carried out by his plays:

To be destructive, words must be irrefutable. Print was less effective than the spoken word because the blast was greater; eyes could ignore, slide past, dangerous verbs and nouns. But if you could lock the enemy into a room somewhere, and fire the sentence at them you could get a sort of seismic disturbance.

Orton's comic salvos were devastating. 'It's Life that defeats the Christian Church. She's always been well-equipped to deal with Death.' (*The Erpingham Camp*) 'God is a gentleman. He prefers blondes.' (*Loot*) 'Marriage excuses no one the freak's roll-call'. (*What the Butler Saw*) 'Being a man of good will I'm well prepared for violence'. (*Funeral Games*) Orton always wanted to shine. He polished the wit of his plays with the same delighted concentration that he rubbed baby lotion on his face to make it gleam. The result, in both cases, was dazzling. Style is an expression of body as well as spirit; and Orton built up his mind and body from its skimpy and undernourished Leicester boyhood to an appealing and lethal maturity. 'The style isn't superimposed. It's me,' Orton explained. 'You can't write stylised comedy in inverted commas, because the style must ring true to the man. If you think in a certain way and you write true to yourself, which I hope I am, then you will get a style, a style will come out. You've only got to be sitting on a bus and you'll hear the most stylised lines. People think I write fantasy, but I don't; some things may be exaggerated or distorted in the same way that painters distort and alter things, but they're realistic figures. They're perfectly recognisable. I don't like the discrimination against style that some people have. Every serious writer has a style. I mean Arnold Wesker has a style, but people don't normally think of him as a stylist, in the same way they think of Wilde, Firbank or Sheridan. Style isn't camp or chi-chi. I write in a certain way because I can express things that I couldn't express in naturalistic terms. In naturalistic drama you can't do anything except discuss teacup things, you know – Mavis' new hat. In a naturalistic style I couldn't make any comment on the kind of policeman Truscott is, or on the laws of the Establishment without style. Oscar Wilde's style is much more earthy and colloquial than most people notice. When we look at Lady Bracknell, she's the most ordinary, common, direct woman. She's not an affected woman at all. People are taken in by the 'glittering style'. It's not glitter. It's just that the author can express more things by style. Sheridan is the same. *The Rivals*. If you read *The Rivals*, it's most real. Congreve too. It's a slice of life. But it's perfectly believable. There's nothing incredible about it.'

Orton, dubbed by the *Observer* 'the Oscar Wilde of Welfare State gentility', did something special with the English language. His dialogue was a collage of the popular culture. It assimilated advertising jargon, the shrill overstatement of tabloid journalism, the stilted lusciousness of B-movies and fused them into his own illuminating epigrammatic style. 'I think you should use the language of your age, and use every bit of it, not just a little bit,' Orton told the BBC in

1964. 'They always go on about poetic drama and they think that you have to sort of go into some high-flown fantasy, but it isn't poetic drama, it's everything, it's the language in use at the time. I have to be very careful in the way that I write, not to let it become sort of a mannerism, it could very easily become a mannerism.' Orton's dialogue forged a poetry from words debased and thrown away by the culture. Orton added his own brand of irony to the colloquial. 'My uterine contractions have been bogus for some time.' The pitch and roll of Mrs Prentice's declaration in *What the Butler Saw* has all the playful strut and surprise that Orton loved in language.

I read Genet's *Querelle of Brest*, an interesting book, but unformed. A first draft of rough jottings for a masterpiece. [Orton wrote in his diary.] Undoubtedly Jean Genet is the most perfect example of an unconscious humorist since Marie Corelli. I find a sentence like: 'They (homosexuals of Brest) are peace-loving citizens of irreproachable outward appearance, even though, the long day through, they may perhaps suffer from a rather timid itch for a bit of cock' irresistibly funny. A combination of elegance and crudity is always ridiculous.

'Words,' Orton wrote in *Head To Toe*, 'were more effective than actions; in the right hands verbs and nouns could create panic.' Orton's hero, Gombold, 'looked up more books, studied the propagation of idiom and found pages on the penetrative power of faulty grammar.' Orton made the same study. His notebooks from his earliest writing efforts in 1954 up to his breakthrough with *Entertaining Mr Sloane* in 1964 show him experimenting with words and analyzing idiom:

Are both, perhaps
Which is always
Remaining a
Have has what
Towards the never
All is what
Very much what
I can only say how
I cannot say where
Be no
Except for now

Orton, like Gombold, was looking for a way to 'kill' with language. The instinct is built into the comedian's language for success, a language of annihilation where laughter 'knocks them dead', 'lays them in the aisle', 'slaughters them'. Orton's laughter aspired to drive an audience crazy with pleasure. Orton offered his audience grotesques which, like the gargoyles of a medieval cathedral, forced the public to imagine Hell and redefine Heaven. He was the pure comic spirit – angry, impish, and articulate. The impact of Orton's distinctive vision in his brief literary career between 1964–1967 is seen in the word 'Ortonesque' which worked its way into the critical vocabulary as a shorthand for scenes of macabre outrageousness.

The comedian is a marginal man, someone who lives outside the boundaries of conventional life and acquires power (and danger) precisely because he can't be controlled by society. Laughter is the message sent back from his cultivated isolation. Orton was a survivor whose brutal laughter was a vindictive triumph over a drab and quietly violent working class world.

'You look very pretty in that fur coat you're wearing', Oscar [Lewenstein] said, as we stood on the corner before going our separate ways. [Orton wrote about a production meeting with his producers Lewenstein and Michael White to discuss the Broadway cast of *Loot*.] I said, 'Peggy [Ramsay] bought it me. It was thirteen pounds nineteen.' 'Very cheap,' Michael White said. 'Yes, I've discovered that I look better in cheap clothes.' 'I wonder what the significance of that is,' Oscar said. 'I'm from the gutter,' I said. 'And don't you ever forget it because I won't.'

Orton's laughter never forgot his origins. He was born John Kingsley Orton in Leicester on 1 January 1933, the first of four children. His mother, Elsie, was a machinist who, because of failing eyesight in later years, became a char. His father, William – a timid wisp of a man – was a gardener. They were an unaffectionate family. The struggle to scrape together a living left the Orton children isolated from their parents as well as each other. They lived off the scraps of life and of emotion. 'I never thought of myself as ordinary,' Orton said. Asthmatic as a child and frequently absent from school, Orton failed his 11+ and was sent at great cost by his status-conscious mother to Clark's College under the misguided impression that she was paying for a liberal education. She wasn't. The 'college' was primarily a secretarial school where Orton learned Pitman's shorthand and accounting. His teacher remembers that at fifteen 'he was semi-literate. He couldn't spell. He couldn't string a sentence together. He spoke very badly. He had a lisp.' Orton tried to educate himself. An avid reader, he also listened to classical music and took up amateur dramatics. Theatre, especially, appealed to him. It was a way to get out of a damp and gloomy council house and belong to a community where he could invent possibilities for himself that were depressingly absent from his workaday world. 'I was sacked from all the jobs I had between sixteen and eighteen because I was never interested in any of them,' he said. 'I resented having to go to work in the morning.' His adolescent diary recounts the tedium of a work routine whose deadening ethic he would skewer in *The Good and Faithful Servant*:

> Thank God it's Friday again. [Orton wrote on 14 January 1949.] I wish I belonged to one of the idle rich and didn't have to work.

Theatre and the promise of productions thrilled him. They were an antidote to his stalled life. His fantasy of theatrical success was as desperate and unfounded as the rest of his aspirations. Even before Orton had ever performed in a play (his parts were, to his never-ending annoyance, usually small) he dedicated his life to the stage:

> It's nearly 12 noon. I am writing this on paper at work. I know I am slacking but I don't feel like work. I am longing for dinner time to come because then the time whizzes by and it's soon 6-30. I will work really hard this afternoon and forget the theatre for a while at least. Last night sitting in the empty theatre watching the electricians flashing lights on and off the empty stage waiting for rehearsals to begin, I suddenly knew that my ambition is and has always been to act and act. To be connected with the stage in some way, with the magic of the Theatre and everything it means. I know now I shall always want to act and I can no more sit in an office all my life than fly. I know this sounds sentimentall [sic] and soppy but it is all perfectly true.

Orton got the idea of going to RADA. He took voice lessons to eliminate his lisp and his prominent Leicester accent. To the amazement of his voice coach, Orton won a place at RADA and a Leicester Council grant. 'It was rather extraordinary,' he recalled. 'I did a piece from Peter Pan between Captain Hook and Smee. I think I was both at the same time – a schizophrenic act. It was quite alarming. I don't know how I did it. It impressed the judges. I didn't have a very good time at RADA ... I actually expected to be taught something. It was complete rubbish. I was more enthusiastic and knew more about acting at the beginning of my first term than I did at the end. I had two years there. I completely lost my confidence and my virginity.'

A month after Orton left for RADA, he met and moved in with Kenneth Halliwell. They were a strange combination. Halliwell, seven years Orton's senior, had been a classics scholar at the Wirral Grammar School. He had given up a promising academic career for what he saw as the greater glory of the Artistic Life. Orphaned as a teenager, by 1953 when he was 25, Halliwell was bald, grave, pretentious and abrasive in his egoism. Orton provided the zest, beauty and companionship Halliwell so painfully lacked. And Halliwell offered his independent means, a literate dialogue and paternal authority which had been absent from Orton's boyhood. They became lovers, and their relationship lasted their lifetime. Neither of them were happy at RADA and neither did as well as he'd hoped. After a brief stint at Ipswich Rep ('What I learned from that was not to write in too much business with drinks or telephones because it was awfully hard on the assistant stage manager to fix all those things'), Orton returned to London to live with Halliwell and write. It had never been Orton's ambition to write; but Halliwell had written a few plays before attending RADA and was working on a novel which Orton judiciously typed while they were still at acting school. Writing was Halliwell's dream, and he invited Orton to share it.

Halliwell introduced Orton to the works of Ronald Firbank. Together, he and Orton made collages which, in time, would feed Orton's comic style. Firbank, to Orton, was the master of English comic prose. 'I've read *Black Mischief*,' Orton notes in his diary, '(patchy – Waugh isn't up to Firbank: the source).' Firbank was a conspicuous influence on the series of unpublishable novels that Orton and Halliwell wrote together: *The Silver Bucket*, *The Mechanical Womb*, *The Last Days of Sodom*, *The Boy Hairdresser*. Orton took Firbank's fluting mischievousness and brought it down to earth:

Claude's such an extremist, you know. They say that when he kissed the Pope's slipper he went on to do considerably *more*. . . .

His Hellenism once captivated me. But the *Attic* to him means nothing now but servants' bedrooms.

Have you taken up transvestism? I'd no idea our marriage teetered on the brink of fashion.

Only the last joke is Orton's (*What the Butler Saw*), the others are from Firbank's only play, *The Princess Zoubaroff*. Orton's humour was more robust and gregarious than Firbank's rarefied fantasies. He shared Firbank's obsessions and adapted many of Firbank's comic manoeuvres to a much more aggressively popular dramatic form.

The Last Days of Sodom (1955) attracted the attention of Faber and Faber. It was a recherché joke which reversed the current sexual and social norms. Although never published, Orton and Halliwell felt the gates of the literary world squeak open when Charles Monteith of Faber's and Richard Brain, then of Hamish Hamilton's, asked to meet them. 'They hardly ever met other human beings. This was the first time, they told us, they'd met strangers by arrangement,' Charles Monteith recalls. 'I had a very clear impression at that first meeting that Kenneth was the one that did the writing. Kenneth's talk, his appearance, his age vis à vis Orton certainly gave the impression that Kenneth was the literary figure. I thought that John was – quite simply – his young, pretty, and rather vivacious boyfriend.'

Orton and Halliwell lived an isolated life. They wrote in the mornings and read in the afternoons. When the weather was good, they sunbathed. In order to save electricity, they rose at sunrise and went to bed at sunset. When Halliwell's small inheritance ran out, they set about working for six months to save up enough money for half a year of uninterrupted writing. Under Halliwell's guidance, Orton read the classics. 'I admire Voltaire, Aristophanes. I read him in prose translations,' Orton said. 'I like Lucian and the classical writers, and I suppose that's what gives my writing a difference, an old-fashioned classical education! Which I never received, but I gave myself one, reading them all in English, for I have so little Latin and less Greek.'

With a few exceptions, Orton wrote independently of Halliwell after 1957. Neither had any success. 'I don't know if you have any convictions about the way life is run: its inexorable rules and so on,' Halliwell wrote to Charles Monteith after a refusal of his novel *Priapus in the Shrubbery* (1959). 'Personally, I am convinced that "what you lose on the swings, you gain on the roundabouts" and vice versa. So it wouldn't, quite frankly, be in the logic of things for John or I to have much success in any sphere. We live much too comfortably and pleasantly in our peculiar little way.'

Their Islington bedsitter was decorated from floor to ceiling with illustrations stolen from library art books. The decoration shrank an already small space. Everyone who visited their austere and tidy flat came away with a sense of its startling claustrophobia. Orton's fictional alter-ego, Gombold, imprisoned and lost in a behemoth body, expresses Orton's despair at his literary failure and the oppressive isolation of his life:

One day Gombold made a paper dart of another poem: it was the kind of writing he had never done before, indeed he was convinced it was of a type no one had ever attempted in any language. After a second or two the dart was returned unopened. His heart sank. There seemed no one here either to appreciate his writing and engineer his escape

In *Head To Toe*, Gombold prays: '. . . Cleanse my heart, give me the ability to rage correctly.' Orton's anger then was more articulate in his pranks than in his writing. Since 1959 Orton had been stealing books from libraries and taking humorous revenge on 'all the rubbish that was being published' by altering the bookjackets and blurbs and replacing the books on the shelves. 'The thing that put me in a rage about libraries was that when I went to quite a big library in Islington and asked for Gibbon's *Decline and Fall of the Roman Empire* they told me they hadn't got a copy of it. They could get it for me, but they hadn't one on their shelves. This didn't start it off, but it was symptomatic of the whole thing. I was enraged that there were so many rubbishy novels and rubbishy books.' Orton turned the library into his private theatre, planning his mischief and then watching surreptitiously while others perused the books he'd doctored:

I did things like pasting a picture of a female nude over a book of etiquette, over the picture of the author who, I think, was Lady Lewisham. I did other things, very strange things. There was the business when I got the biography of Sir Bernard Spilsbury and there was an illustration which said, 'The remains discovered in the cellar at number 23 Rosedown Road.' I pasted over the illustration, which was a very dreary one of a lot of earth, David's picture of Marat dead in his bath. It was in black and white. I left the original caption underneath so that it really did look like what it said, 'The remains discovered in the cellar at number 23 Rosedown Road.' The picture of the corpse in the bath had quite an effect on people who opened the book. I used to write false blurbs on the inside of Gollancz books because I discovered that Gollancz books had blank yellow flaps and I used to type false blurbs on the insides. My blurbs were mildly obscene. Even at the trial they said they were only mildly obscene. When I put the plastic covers back over the jackets you couldn't tell that the blurbs weren't printed. I used to stand in corners after I'd smuggled the doctored books back into the library and then watch people read them. It was very funny, very interesting. There was a biography of Sybil Thorndike in which there was a picture of her locked up in a cell as Nurse Edith Cavell. I cut the caption from another picture and pasted it under the picture, so that it read: 'During the war I received many strange requests'. One of the interesting things at the trial was that the greatest outrage, the one for which I think I was sent to prison, was that I had stuck a monkey's face in the middle of a rose, on the cover of something called *Collins Book of Roses*. It was a very beautiful yellow rose. What I had done was held as the depth of iniquity for which I should probably have been birched. They won't ever do that so they just sent me to prison for six months.

On 15 May 1962, Orton and Halliwell (who assisted him) were charged with malicious damage to 83 books and removing 1,653 plates from library books. Besides earning Orton and Halliwell a jail sentence, the prank also brought them public attention. The *Daily Mirror* headlined the story 'Gorilla In the Roses'. What the magistrate found objectionable was later picked up by *Reader's Digest* as good family fun. Orton was not contrite; but success allowed him to admit in retrospect that 'they said something about resentment at being a failed writer at the trial, and they were probably right'. Prison changed Orton. It was the first time he'd been separated from Halliwell for any extended time. 'Before, I had been vaguely conscious of something rotten somewhere; prison crystallized this,' Orton said. 'The old whore society lifted up her skirts, and the stench was pretty foul. Not that the actual prison treatment was bad; but it was a revelation of what really lies under the surface of our industrialized society.' Within a year of his release, the BBC accepted the radio version of *The*

Ruffian on tne Stair; and Orton, buoyed by his first acceptance in a decade, began a full-length play, *Entertaining Mr Sloane*. 'Being in the nick brought detachment to my writing. I wasn't involved any more and it suddenly worked.' His writing took on a playful antic quality of a man who, now a 'criminal', had nothing to lose from society.

When *Entertaining Mr Sloane* opened in May 1964, it was clear that Orton's voice was an exciting and unusual one. Sir Terence Rattigan, responding to the play's language and its careful construction, proclaimed it 'the best first play' he'd seen in 'thirty odd years'. It would be performed all over the world, made into a film and a television play. According to the *Times*, '*Entertaining Mr Sloane* made more blood boil than any other British play in the last ten years'. Orton had launched himself in the style of his laughter – with a vengeance.

Sloane was the first play to dramatize the psycopathic style of the Sixties – that ruthless, restless, single-minded pursuit of satisfaction – transformed by drugs and rock music into myth. 'In Germany,' Orton wrote to the director of the Broadway production, Alan Schneider, 'Eddie was the central pivot of the play. His stalking of the boy's arse was as funny and wildly alarming as Kath's stalking of his cock. Unless this is so – you're in trouble.' In following the rapaciousness of his characters' needs – their ignorance and their unwitting violence – Orton was not being heartless, merely accurate. Sloane has killed one man when he walks into Kath's house looking for a room to let. By the time the play is over, he will have dispatched a second – Kath's father – only to be blackmailed into bed by Kath and her brother, Ed. Sloane feels no guilt and his refusal to experience shame is what disturbs and amuses audiences. Sloane is a survivor whose egotism is rewarded, not punished. Orton wrote to Schneider:

I don't know what you mean about the Eddie–Sloane relationship. Quite clear. Sloane knows Eddie wants him. He has absolutely no qualms about surrendering his body. None. He's done it many, many times. Sloane is no virgin. He's been in bed with men and women in the past. But he isn't going to give in until he has to. And while he can get away with . . . riding around in cars, just fucking Kath a couple of times a week, getting paid a good salary, why should he give up the trump card. Eddie, naturally, doesn't know how amoral Sloane is. He imagines that he has a virgin on his hands. He thinks he can get Sloane. Sure he can. But it may take a bit of time – cause Sloane is such a nice kid. Where's the problem ?

When the play transferred to the West End, impresario Emile Littler and Peter Cadbury, chairman of London's biggest ticket bureau, joined forces in an attack hotly reported in the press, damning *Entertaining Mr Sloane* as a dirty highbrow play which should never have been allowed in the West End. Orton savoured the outcry and let Edna Welthorpe throw more fat in the fire with one of 'her' letters to the *Daily Telegraph* which sent up the violence beneath the calls for propriety.

NAUSEATED

As a playgoer of forty years may I sincerely agree with Peter Pinnell in his condemnation of *Entertaining Mr Sloane*.

I myself was nauseated by this endless parade of mental and physical perversion. And to be told that such a disgusting piece of filth now passes for humour.

Today's young playwrights take it upon themselves to flaunt their contempt for ordinary decent people. I hope that ordinary decent people will shortly strike *back*!

Yours sincerely,
Edna Welthorpe (Mrs)

The only brickbat that angered Orton was the grudging praise of his plays as 'commercial' from John Russell Taylor in his introduction to the play in Penguin's New English Dramatists 8. 'Living theatre needs good commercial dramatists as much as the original artist,' Taylor wrote. Orton was furious at such critical stupidity. 'Are they different, then ?' he asked, quoting John Russell Taylor's distinction between commercial success and art to his agent and asking to withdraw the play from the volume. '*Hamlet* was written by a commercial dramatist. So were *Volpone* and *The School for Scandal* and *The Importance of Being Earnest* and *The Cherry Orchard* and *Our Betters*. Two ex-commercial successes of the last thirty years are about to be revived by our non-commercial theatre: *A Cuckoo In the Nest* and *Hay Fever*, but if my plays go on in the West End, I don't expect this to be used as a sneer by people who judge artistic success by commercial failure. There is no intrinsic merit in a flop.'

The radio version of *Ruffian* had grafted Orton's obsessions on to a structure borrowed from Pinter who, along with Beckett, was the only contemporary playwright besides himself Orton respected. The opening of *Ruffian* was alibied from the opening of *The Birthday Party*, a steal which Orton eschewed two years later when, with success and in control of his talent, he rewrote the play for the stage. 'Everything the characters say is true . . . The play mustn't be presented as an example of the now out-dated "mystery" school – *vide* early Pinter,' Orton noted for the Royal Court production. 'Everything is as clear as the most reactionary *Telegraph* reader could wish. There is a beginning, a middle and an end . . . The play must be directed without long significant pauses. Any pauses must be natural pauses. Pace, pace, pace as well. Go for the strong and the natural climaxes. Everything else should be simple.' In Orton's theatre there was no need for obfuscation. 'The number of humiliating admissions I've made,' says Joyce in *Ruffian*. 'You'd think it would draw me closer to somebody. But it doesn't.' The line is more than a good joke; it contains a vision of desolation whose centripedal force only farce could evoke. In farce, people are victims of their momentum. Survival and identity are at stake. Characters state their needs; but in the panic of events, their words are abused or unheard. The body and mind are pulverized in their pursuit of order. Unheeding and frantic, characters rebound off one another groping for safety. Orton's plays aimed at evolving a form which celebrated the joy and terror of this disenchantment.

The cut and thrust dialogue in *Entertaining Mr Sloane*'s third act had a potential for mayhem that never got beyond the vaudeville of language to movement. Orton wanted to create visual as well as verbal anarchy; and he knew the limitation of his first full-length play. 'What I wanted to do in *Sloane* was to break down all the sexual compartments that people have. It didn't entirely succeed because it's very difficult to persuade directors and actors to do what you want. When *Sloane* had been running for a while, it had got into compartments, so that Madge (Ryan) was the nympho, Peter (Vaughan) was the queer and Dudley (Sutton) was the psycho. Which wasn't what I wanted and which wasn't what I intended at all, but people *will* put things into compartments. It's very bad in class, in sex, in anything.' Orton set about forging an unequivocal style, the theatrical equivalent of a shout to the hard of hearing. 'The new full-length play,' Orton told the BBC in 1964 speaking of *Loot*, 'is an advance. Of course you can't tell until you've written it. But I think it's an advance.'

The transition from *Sloane* to *Loot*, from the innuendo of a comedy of manners to outrageous farcical explicitness, was *The Good and Faithful Servant* (1964, televised 1967). In this poignant, angry TV play about a worker (Buchanan) retiring from his firm after fifty years of service, Orton's outrage at the violence of authority and the lifesleep of the credulous starts to take on a more aggressively macabre form. Buchanan has lost an arm on the job. His body, like the toaster and clock the firm give him, is on the verge of breaking down. When he visits a lady friend on the evening of his retirement, she's shocked at the sight of a whole man:

> EDITH. Your arms! Where has the extra one come from?
>
> BUCHANAN. It's false.
>
> EDITH. Thank God for that. I like to know where I stand in relation to the number of limbs a man has.

Orton's laughter begins to display its jugular instinct as it tilts directly against sources of oppression. Buchanan tries to talk his lay-about grandson, Ray, into the same work routine that has eroded his own life.

> RAY. I don't work.
>
> BUCHANAN. Not work!? (*He stares, open-mouthed.*) What do you do then?
>
> RAY. I enjoy myself.
>
> BUCHANAN. That's a terrible thing to do. I'm bowled over by this I

can tell you. It's my turn to be shocked now. You ought to have a steady job.

EDITH. Two perhaps.

Orton's scepticism about authority was as profound as his hatred of the slavish routines by which man gave up the responsibility for his own life. The grotesque would become his theatrical means of shocking the public into a renewed sense of its own life. In *The Good and Faithful Servant* Orton's withering irony concentrated on exploring how that life was wasted. 'An affirmation of anything is cheering nowadays,' says Mrs Vealfoy, the firm's public relations officer who, like her name, is the voice of faith. 'Say "Yes" as often as possible, Raymond. I always do. (*Laughs*). Always. (*Smiles*.) . . .'

The Good and Faithful Servant follows Buchanan from retirement to death, analyzing the emptiness of company allegiance as well as the social pressures which force the young into the same stifling work routine. For all the fervour of the play, the blast of its laughter is curiously muted by its naturalistic format. *Loot*, completed in October 1964, four months after *The Good and Faithful Servant*, breaks away from earnestness into manic frivolity as a barometer of disgust. The issues become larger than life and the method of attack more freewheeling and dangerous. *Loot*, whose original title was *Funeral Games*, sports with the culture's superstitions about death as well as life. 'It's a Freudian nightmare,' says the son, Hal, who is about to dump his mother's corpse into the wardrobe in order to hide money he's stolen in her coffin. And so it is. Comedy always acts out unconscious wishes suppressed in daily life; and Orton seized this liberation with gusto. 'You're at liberty to answer your own doorbell, miss,' says the notorious Detective Truscott. 'That is how we tell whether or not we live in a free country.' Orton's laughter was offensive, elegant, cruel, shocking, monstrous, hilarious, and smart. 'Your style is simple and direct,' says the oafish Detective Truscott of the nurse's confession of foul play. 'It's a theme which less skilfully handled could've given offence.' The joke lampoons the critical appraisal of Orton's style, disarming an audience while sticking the boot further in.

Loot was launched with an all-star cast (Geraldine McEwen, Kenneth Williams, Duncan Macrae and Ian McShane) and directed by Peter Wood. It was scheduled for a short provincial tour and a West End run. But the plans came a cropper. The combination of frivolity and ferociousness which Orton had discovered as his mature comic milieu was new to the English stage and it was difficult for any troupe to find the correct playing style. The confusion in Peter Wood's concept was immediately visible in the elegant but cartoonish black and white sets; Kenneth Williams' outrageous mugging as Detective Truscott; and the continual demand on Orton for rewrites which never allowed the performers the security of the same script from one day to the next. *Loot*, which opened in Cambridge in February 1965 and closed in Wimbledon in March, was a notorious flop. No West End Theatre would take it. 'The play is clearly not written naturalistically, but it must be directed and acted with absolute realism,' Orton wrote about the stage production of *Ruffian* with the experience of *Loot*'s failure still vividly in his mind. 'No "stylization", no "camp". No attempt in fact to match the author's extravagance of dialogue with extravagance of direction.' The first production of *Loot* suffered and sank because of these excesses. '*Loot* is a serious play', Orton wrote to his producers. 'Unless *Loot* is directed and acted perfectly seriously the play will fail. As it failed in its original touring version. A director who imagines that the only object is to get a laugh is not for me.'

Orton was angry and shattered by *Loot*'s failure. In the rest of 1965, he produced only one television play, his version of *The Bacchae*, a fun palace revolution set in a Butlin's holiday resort: *The Erpingham Camp*. The play was part of an ITV series on 'The Seven Deadly Sins'; and *The Erpingham Camp*, like all Orton's farces, satirized Pride. Orton had explored the notion as a film treatment for Lindsay Anderson and then developed it as a Brechtian epic complete (in early drafts) with illustrative banners such as SCENE 5: AN EXAMPLE OF THE ACTIVE LIFE OF THE CHURCH. ERPINGHAM PREPARES HIMSELF TO MEET THE PEOPLE. THEOLOGY DISCUSSED. THE PADRE PROVES THAT CHRISTIANITY IS ESSENTIAL TO GOOD HEALTH. The television play, which was aired in 1966, was a tepid version of the drastically rewritten and dazzlingly epigrammatic Royal Court production in 1967. '*Erpingham* is the best play of mine performed so far,' Orton noted in his diary after the ragged dress rehearsal. 'If only Arthur Lowe were playing Erpingham they'd all be raving.' Besides the television play, Orton made his first visit to Morocco where, in spite of boys and hash, he continued to brood about the fate of *Loot*. 'I think it's disgusting with so much utter shit put on in both the commercial and subsidized theatres that a play like *Loot* should have this difficulty. I'd understand it after Wimbledon, but not after a really pretty average Rep production which succeeded in attracting a glowing notice in the *Telegraph*,' Orton wrote to his agent, Peggy Ramsay, who was having difficulty finding another London production for the play. 'I'm sick, sick, sick of the theatre . . . I think you'd better warn Oscar [Lewenstein] that if the *Loot* option runs out in January with no signs of the play being put on I shan't renew the option. I shall throw the play on the fire. And I shan't write a third stage play. I shall earn my living on T.V. I'm really quite capable of carrying out this. I've always admired Congreve who, after the absolute failure of *The Way of the World*, just stopped writing. And Rimbaud who turned his back on the literary world after writing a few volumes of poems . . .'

However, Orton did see his play remounted in London by Charles Marowitz. On 27 September 1966 at the Jeanetta Cochrane Theatre,

Loot reopened; both the times and Orton's luck had changed. The play was an overwhelming hit.

Well, the sound and fury is over. And LOOT and JOE ORTON (as you can see from the reviews) are a great success. [Orton wrote to an American friend.] I feel exhausted. 18 months of struggling to vindicate the honour of my play (my own is beyond vindication) have left me weak at the knees.

There were other reviews which I haven't enclosed because I can't lay my hands on a spare copy. The *Express*, for instance, is a rave. Which pleases the management; it's supposed to sell a lot of tickets. The *Financial Times* was excellent. We had two bad ones. The *Mail* (not exactly bad, but sniffy) and the *Birmingham Post* (which doesn't sell a seat anyway, but was furious . . .). But who cares. We've scooped the pool with the rest.

Loot won the *Evening Standard* Award and *Plays and Players* Award for the best play of the year. Orton was, to his delighted surprise, a new star. 'I'm now engaged in writing a film [*Up Against It*, commissioned by the Beatles but unproduced] for which I'm being paid (the equivalent) of 30,000 dollars,' Orton wrote to a friend in 1967. 'I'm going up, up, up.' Despite *Loot*'s success, Orton was never thrilled with the production. 'In general the tone of the London production is OK. Of course a lot of lines are muffed. This is the fault of having inexperienced actors in the parts . . .', Orton wrote to his producers about *Loot*'s forthcoming Broadway production. 'The way it was done was on the right lines. Ideally, it should be nearer *The Homecoming* rather than *I Love Lucy*. Don't think I'm a snob about *I Love Lucy*. I've watched it often. I think it's very funny. But it's aimed purely at making an audience laugh. And that isn't the prime aim of *Loot* . . . I also think it might be wise to reconsider Marowitz as a director. God knows I'm not a fan of his. I think a lot of the direction in *Loot* is atrocious. But on the principle of better the Devil you know than the Devil you don't, I'd think about it. With a stronger cast his direction wouldn't stick out so much. And it is a success in London!! Remember that.'

In its capering with 'human remains' and its gleeful celebration of police corruption, *Loot* attacked the most deep-seated myths of English culture. 'I never understand why [people are offended],' Orton said mischievously. 'Because, if you're absolutely practical – and I hope I am – a coffin is a box. One calls it a coffin and once you've called it a coffin it immediately has all sorts of associations.' Orton's art, as his diary recounts, had a curious way of haunting his life. Reality was the ultimate outrage:

Monday 26th December. I began writing *What the Butler Saw* at eleven o'clock this morning. At twenty past the telephone rang. It was from a call-box and the caller had difficulty getting through.

When they did it was George [Barnet, Orton's brother-in-law]. He said, 'I've rung to tell you that your mum died this morning. It was very quick. She had a heart attack.' He didn't say anything else.

My father, who has just come out of hospital having been run over by a car, is staying with Leoni [Barnet, Orton's youngest sister]. The funeral is Friday. . . .

Tuesday 27th December. . . . . Leoni hasn't rung. I'll have to send a telegram to find out details of my mother's funeral. I can't go home if there's nowhere to sleep.

And I don't fancy spending the night in the house with the corpse. A little too near the Freudian bone for comfort. . . .

Wednesday 28th December. . . . Leoni rang at about six. I'd sent a telegram earlier today. She'd just got it from work. She said that Dad has gone back home. Sleeps in my mother's bed downstairs with the corpse. After his accident he can't piss straight and floods the lavatory with it whenever he goes. She said, 'Well, I'm shocked by our Marilyn, you know.' I said, 'Why, what's she done?' Leonie said, 'Oh, you know, she behaves very ignorantly all round. And when I told her Mum was dead all she said was – "I'm not surprised." Well, you know, what kind of a remark is that?' Dougie [Orton's younger brother] was upset. Remarkable how those without hearts when young suddenly develop them in later life.

I promised to go home tomorrow. Leoni and George will come round in the evening. As the corpse is downstairs in the main living room it means going out or watching television with death at one's elbow. My father, fumbling out of bed in the middle of the night, bumped into the coffin and almost had the corpse on the floor. Peggy Ramsay said how dreadfully reminiscent of *Loot* it all was.

Thursday 29th December. I arrived in Leicester at four thirty. I had a bit of quick sex in a derelict house with a labourer I picked up . . .

I got home at five-thirty. Nobody in the house. My father was across the road with friends. He can't see now. The accident has affected his walking. He trembles all the time. I said I'd take him to the doctor's tomorrow. He should be in a hospital. Later on George and Leoni came round. We went to see Mum's body. It isn't at home as I supposed. It's laid out in a Chapel of Rest. Betty [Orton, his sister-in-law] came round with Susan and Sharon [his nieces]. Both very giggly. Dougie also with them. He wasn't coming to see the body. He said he'd lifted Mum from the chair where she died and put her into the bed. He didn't want to see her again.

We all went to the Chapel of Rest. It's a room, bare white-washed. Muted organ music from a speaker in the corner. The coffin lid propped up against the wall. It said 'Elsie Mary Orton aged 62 years'. Betty said, 'They've got her age wrong, see. Your Mum was 63. You should tell them about that. Put in a complaint.' I said, 'Why? It doesn't matter now.' 'Well,' said Betty, 'You want it done right, don't you? It's what you pay for.'

Mum quite unrecognizable without her glasses. And they'd scraped her hair back from her forehead. She looked fat, old and dead. They'd made up her face. When I asked about this the mortician said, 'Would you say it wasn't discreet then, sir?' I said, 'No. It seems all right to me.' 'We try to give a lifelike impression,' he said. Which seems to be a contradiction in terms somehow. I've never seen a corpse before. How cold they are. I felt Mum's hand. Like marble. One hand was pink, the other white. I suppose that was the disease of which she died. The death certificate said, 'Coronary thrombosis, arteriosclerosis and hyper-tension'.

Great argument as we left. The undertaker gave Marilyn a small parcel containing the nightgown Mum was wearing when she died. Nobody wanted it. So the undertaker kept it. Not for himself. 'We pass it on to the old folks,' he said. 'Many are grateful, you know.'

Didn't sleep much. Awful bed. Damp. And cold. House without Mum seems to have died.

Friday 30th December. I got up at eight o'clock. I went downstairs to the kitchen. My father appeared in the doorway of the living room dressed only in a shirt. He looks thin and old. Hardly more than a skeleton. He weighs six stone four. I said, 'Hallo.' He peered blindly for a second and said, 'Hallo.' After a pause he said, 'Who are you?' 'Joe,' I said. He couldn't remember I'd come last night. Then he said, 'D'you know where my slippers are?' I said, 'What do you mean – where are my slippers?' He got down on his knees and began feeling around. 'I can't find my slippers,' he said. 'They're on your feet,' I said. And they were. He'd been wearing them all the time.

. . . At ten the undertaker arrived, 'What about the flowers?' he said. I said I'd no idea what to do with the flowers. 'Where's father's tribute?' he said. 'I think just father's tribute on the coffin.' He found my father's wreath and put it on the coffin. Then we all got into the cars. My aunt Lucy was upset because strict protocol wasn't observed. 'They're all walking wrong,' she said. 'They shouldn't be with husbands and wives. Just immediate circle should be in the first car.' Several women were at their garden gates as the cortege passed. I noticed two old women weeping on each other's shoulders.

At the chapel in the cemetery they held a brief burial service. They didn't carry the coffin into the chapel. They wheeled it in on a trolley. The vicar, very young and hearty, read the service in a droning voice. And then the coffin was wheeled out and to the graveside. It was a cold, bright morning. My mother's grave was a new one. Her last wish was to be buried with Tony my nephew who was drowned aged seven, eighteen months ago, but Pete and Marilyn refused to have the grave reopened and so my mother's last wish was ignored.

The coffin was lowered. The vicar said his piece. The earth was sprinkled over the coffin. My father began to cry. And we walked back to the waiting cars. Immediately the mourners left the grave-side a flock of old women descended on the grave, picking over the wreaths and shaking their heads.

We got back home at half-past ten. Sandwiches had been prepared by a neighbour. The party got rather jolly later . . . My father sat through the party looking very woebegone. The only person who seemed to be at a funeral, Mrs Riley, Mum's lifelong friend, was crying quietly in a corner and drinking endless cups of tea. 'I don't expect I'll see you again,' she said as she left. 'Your mother was very dear to me. I've known her all my life. I shan't come up here now she's gone. Goodbye,' she said, kissing my cheek. 'I hope you have a happier life than your Mum did.'

Leoni and I spent part of the afternoon throwing out cupboardsful of junk collected over the years: magazines, photographs, Christmas cards. We burnt eight pairs of shoes. I found a cup containing a pair of false teeth and threw it in the dustbin. Then I discovered that they belonged to my father. I had to rescue them. I found my mother's teeth in a drawer. I kept them. To amaze the cast of *Loot* . . .

Monday 2nd January. Spent the day working on *What the Butler Saw*. In the evening Peter Willes [Yorkshire Television producer] rang . . . I told him about the funeral. And the frenzied way my family behave. He seemed shocked. But then he thinks my plays are fantasies. He suddenly caught a glimpse of the fact that I write the truth. . . .

Wednesday 4th January. . . . I'd taken my mother's false teeth down to the theatre. I said to Kenneth Cranham [who played Hal], 'Here, I thought you'd like the originals.' He said 'What.' 'Teeth,' I said. 'Whose?' he said. 'My mum's,' I said. He looked very sick. 'You see,' I said, 'It's obvious that you're not thinking of the events of the play in terms of reality if a thing affects you like that.' Simon Ward [who played Dennis] shook like a jelly when I gave them to him . . .

Buoyed by *Loot*'s success, Orton's writing took on new verve and complexity. His idiom and stage effects became more brazen. It was an exciting, fecund period in his writing career fed also by the emotional tensions between himself and Halliwell who was oppressed by his own inadequacy and increasingly distressed at Orton's celebrity. Between October 1966 and August 1967, Orton wrote his ghoulish capriccio about the Church, *Funeral Games*, for television; a film script; the major revisions of *Ruffian* and *Erpingham*, published as they were produced under the title *Crimes of Passion*; and his farce masterpiece, *What the Butler Saw*. *Butler* consolidated all the verbal and visual experiments Orton had made haltingly in his one-act plays. Originally, he had subtitled *Loot* 'a farce' but edited out the phrase from the final script. *Butler* had the frenzy and arithmetic logic that finally achieved the kind of ferocious playfulness he'd always envisioned. 'Why are there so many doors?' asks the inspecting psychiatrist, Dr Rance, as he stalks through the garden into Dr Prentice's clinic. 'Was this house designed by a lunatic?' Orton parodied farce (and himself) in the play and made use of its conventions for his own serious and sublime comic ends. Orton made comedy out of the ideas behind the farce form. Violence was enacted; and the resulting psychic numbness became a statement about life. A bellboy caught up in the carnival chaos confronts Dr Rance and points to his bleeding shoulder:

NICK. . . . Look at this wound. That's real.
RANCE. It appears to be.
NICK. If the pain is real I must be real.
RANCE. I'd rather not get involved in metaphysical speculation.

'As I understand it, farce originally was very close to tragedy and differed only in the *treatment* of its themes – themes like rape, bastardy, prostitution.' *What the Butler Saw* put these subjects back on stage with a robust delight in human animality. 'Oh this is a madhouse,' shrieks Mrs Prentice. 'You must help me doctor. I keep seeing naked men.' Orton raised the stakes of farce's game. Farce had never had movement complemented by such crystalline wit. 'Reject any para-normal phenomena,' says Dr Rance. 'It's the only way to remain sane.' And where Orton's earlier plays had lacked the scenic surprise to match the jolt of his lines, Orton was now using the stage with an inventiveness that no modern comic playwright had dared. At one point in Act Two, the psychiatrists declare each other insane at gun-point. An alarm is pressed. Metal grilles fall over the doors and windows. They clang down with an impressive thud. The sound is terrifying and funny; the bars are a stunning image of spiritual stalemate. Orton's *coup de théâtre* elevates his farce onto an imaginative level unique in contemporary theatre. He had worked the same kind of magic into the rewrite of *Erpingham Camp*'s ending:

I had an inspiration on the end. In the original television play Erpingham falls from a high-diving board. I'd rather clumsily made this possible for the stage by making him fall out of the window. This isn't good. I'd been trying to think of some way to kill him swiftly, dramatically, not involving too many production difficulties and possible on the stage, also ludicrous. I had a vision of him shooting up into the air. This wasn't practical – how could someone do that? And then I got it – he must fall through the floor! . . .

'And when I beheld my devil, I found him serious, thorough, profound, solemn,' wrote Nietzsche in *Thus Spake Zarathustra*. 'It was the Spirit of Gravity, through him all things are ruined. One does not kill by anger, but by laughter. Come let us kill the Spirit of Gravity.'

Laughter's disdain for boundaries also contained a yearning for an impossible freedom. Orton's plays wanted to defy gravity (in both senses of the word). *What the Butler Saw*, better than any of his other plays, found the visual correlative for this antic spirit. In its send up of a Euripidean ending, Orton's final image in *What the Butler Saw* acted out the comic hope of transcendence. A rope ladder descends from the skylight with Sergeant Match still pursuing the missing parts of Sir Winston Churchill. 'They pick up their clothes,' Orton's stage directions read, 'and weary, bleeding, drugged and drunk, climb the rope ladder into the blazing light.'

Orton finished typing out the final copy of *What the Butler Saw* from the single space pages of his rough draft on 11 July 1967. Both he and Halliwell were pleased with it:

> Yesterday Kenneth read the script and was enthusiastic – he made several important suggestions which I'm carrying out. He was impressed by the way in which, using the context of a farce, I'd managed to produce a 'Golden Bough' subtext – even (he pointed out) the castration of Sir Winston Churchill (the father figure) and the descent of the god at the end – SERGEANT MATCH, drugged and dressed in a woman's gown. It was only to be expected that Kenneth would get these references to classical literature. Whether anyone else will spot them is another matter. 'You must get a director who, while making it funny, brings out the subtext,' Kenneth said. He suggests that the dress MATCH wears should be something suggestive of leopard-skin. This would make it funny when NICK wears it and get the right 'image' for the Euripidean ending when MATCH wears it.

Orton's final polishing of the farce was completed on 16 July. 'I added very little on this version (just incorporated Kenneth's suggestions which were excellent), except the description of the light from the garden when the lights in the room go out. And stressed the leopard spotted dress of MATCH,' he wrote in his diary. 'The Euripidean ending works, surprisingly, as "all is forgiven" – just as in the later Shakespeare plays.' The excited reaction to *What the Butler Saw* was immediate. Within a fortnight, Orton and Halliwell were visiting Orton's producer, Oscar Lewenstein, to discuss production plays for the play. Lewenstein was worried about the Lord Chamberlain's reaction to incest and the flourishing of the cock from the statue of Sir Winston Churchill. Orton agreed, if necessary, to change the figure of authority, but never the incest.

> 'What am I saying about Churchill, though ?' I said. 'You're saying he had a big prick,' Oscar said. 'That isn't libellous, surely ?' I said. 'I wouldn't sue anybody for saying I had a big prick. No man would. In fact I might pay them to do that.'

Lewenstein thought it might be fun to stage Orton's play with Binkie Beaumont at the Haymarket, the very bastion of bourgeois 'enchantment' Orton was satirizing. 'That would be wonderful,' I said. 'It'd be a sort of a joke even putting *What the Butler Saw* on at the Haymarket – Theatre of Perfection.' Lewenstein also suggested Ralph Richardson for Dr Rance. 'Although I admire Richardson,' Orton wrote. 'I'd say he was a good ten years too old for the part. And he isn't primarily noted for his comic acting ... Both Kenneth and I thought Oscar misguided in suggesting Richardson.' By the time *What the Butler Saw* opened in the West End on 5 March 1969, there was no Lord Chamberlain to censor the play. But Orton's phallic fun was edited out just the same and the missing part of Sir Winston Churchill was turned into a cigar. The change found its way into the script and was printed in the first published version. What was intended as an image of triumphant and mischievous stage anarchy (Rance: 'How much more inspiring, if in those dark days, we'd seen what we see now. Instead we had to be content with a cigar – the symbol falling far short, as we all realize, of the object itself.') turned into a giggle. Although launched with a star-studded cast (Richardson, Stanley Baxter, Coral Browne, Julia Foster), the production was a fiasco. On opening night, the gallery barracked the farce with cries of 'Filth'! Critics mistook the flaws in the production as limitations in the play and Orton's best work became the most underrated. Still, the play has become part of the repertoire of modern theatre. Not until Lindsay Anderson's brilliant revival at the Royal Court in 1975 was Orton's comic business and the reputation of his finest farce restored.

'We sat talking of how happy we felt,' Orton wrote in his diary from Tangiers in late May 1967. 'And how it couldn't, surely, last. We'd have to pay for it. Or we'd be struck down from afar by disaster because we were, perhaps, too happy. To be young, good-looking, healthy, famous, comparatively rich *and* happy is surely going against nature, and when to the list one adds that daily I have the company of beautiful fifteen year old boys who find (for a small fee) fucking with me a delightful sensation, no man can want for more. "*Crimes of Passion* will be a disaster," Kenneth said, "that will be the scapegoat. We must sacrifice *Crimes of Passion* in order to be spared disaster more intolerable".' But it was Orton himself, not Orton's play, who would be sacrificed for his glorious talent. On 10 August 1967, in the early morning, Halliwell beat Orton's brains out with a hammer and then swallowed twenty-two sleeping pills to kill himself. Halliwell achieved in murder the association with Joe Orton that he'd been denied in Orton's successful literary life. At the time, Orton's death was more famous than his plays. But the years and our farcical history have reversed this situation. Nobody came closer than Orton to reviving on the English stage the outrageous and violent prankster's spirit of comedy and creating the purest (and rarest) of drama's by-products: joy. In showing us how we destroy ourselves, Orton's plays are themselves a survival tactic. Orton expected to die young, but he built his plays to last.

                                                                John Lahr

The Ruffian on the Stair

'Madam Life's a piece in bloom,
Death goes dogging everywhere:
She's the tenant of the room,
He's the ruffian on the stair.'

W. E. HENLEY

The original version of *The Ruffian on the Stair* was broadcast
on BBC Radio in 1964 and subsequently published by the BBC
in a volume of *New Radio Drama*.

The Ruffian on the Stair was given its first stage performance
in a production without decor by the English Stage Society on
21 August 1966 with the following cast:

MIKE	Bernard Gallagher
JOYCE	Sheila Ballantine
WILSON	Kenneth Cranham

Directed by Peter Gill

The Ruffian on the Stair was later produced at the Royal Court
Theatre in the revised version printed here on 6 June 1967 in a
double-bill entitled *Crimes of Passion* with the following cast:

MIKE	Bernard Gallagher
JOYCE	Avril Elgar
WILSON	Michael Standing

Directed by Peter Gill
Designed by Deirdre Clancy

SCENE ONE

A kitchen/living-room with a bedroom alcove. MIKE *is shaving by the sink.* JOYCE *enters from the bedroom carrying a tray with cups, saucers, egg cup, etc. She puts the tray on to the table.*

JOYCE. Have you got an appointment today?

MIKE. Yes. I'm to be at King's Cross station at eleven. I'm meeting a man in the toilet.

He puts away his shaving materials.

JOYCE. You always go to such interesting places. Are you taking the van?

MIKE *puts on a made-up bow tie.*

MIKE. No. It's still under repair.

JOYCE *takes the tray to the sink and puts the dishes into a bowl. She pours water on them.*

JOYCE (*putting on a pair of rubber gloves*). Where did you go yesterday?

MIKE. I went to Mickey Pierce's. I'd a message to deliver. I had a chat with a man who travels in electrically operated massage machines. He bought me a ham roll. It turns out he's on the run. He didn't say as much in so many words. (*He winks.*) But I gathered.

JOYCE. A wanted man?

MIKE. I don't suppose his firm would pay the insurance if they realised his position.

JOYCE. No.

She begins to wash the dishes. MIKE *puts on his coat.*

JOYCE. You lead a more interesting life than I do.

MIKE. Hard, though.

JOYCE. Still, you've kept your looks.

MIKE. Yes. I'm a powerfully attractive figure. I can still cause a flutter in feminine hearts.

He puts a flower into his buttonhole, and brushes his coat down.

JOYCE. Have you seen the date?

MIKE. No.

JOYCE. It's our anniversary.

MIKE. As long as that, is it? How time flies.

JOYCE. Two years ago you came to my flat and persuaded me to give up the life I'd been leading.

MIKE. You're better off.

JOYCE. Nobody ever calls me Maddy now.

MIKE (*pause*). What?

JOYCE. Nobody calls me Madelein. I used that name for five years. Before that I was Sarah up North somewhere.

MIKE (*pause, he frowns*). Have you ever, since I met you, allowed another man to be intimate with you?

JOYCE. No!

MIKE. Good. I'd kill any man who messed with you. Oh, yes. I'd murder him.

Silence.

JOYCE (*taking off her rubber gloves*). The papers were on form this morning.

MIKE. Were they? I'm glad people are still reading them.

JOYCE. I see where a man has appeared in court charged with locking his wife in a wardrobe. She tells of her night of terror. (*Pause.*) What a way to celebrate your wedding anniversary.

MIKE picks up his raincoat and folds it across his arm.

MIKE. I'd do the same. I'd lock you up if you gave me cause for displeasure.

JOYCE. And, in the local paper, I saw there'd been an accident involving a tattooed man. He had a heart, a clenched fist and a rose all on one arm. And the name 'Ronny' was on his body in two different places.

MIKE. Was that his name?

JOYCE. No. His name was Frank. A van ran him down.
Silence.

MIKE. I'm going now.

JOYCE. Are your boots clean?

MIKE. Yes.

JOYCE. Keep them clean. You may meet important people.
You never know.

MIKE. Cheerio.

JOYCE. Give me a kiss. (*He kisses her cheek.*) Do I have to
remind you now? Two years ago you did it without thinking.

MIKE. I was young then. See you tonight.
He exits. JOYCE *goes into the bedroom, straightens the bed.
She pushes* MIKE'S *pyjamas under the pillow. The doorbell
rings. She answers it.* WILSON *is standing outside.*

WILSON (*smiling*). I've come about the room.

JOYCE. I'm afraid there's been a mistake. I've nothing to do
with allotting rooms. Make your enquiries elsewhere.

WILSON. I'm not coloured. I was brought up in the Home
Counties.

JOYCE. That doesn't ring a bell with me, I'm afraid.

WILSON. Is that the room?

JOYCE. That's my room.

WILSON. I couldn't share. What rent are you asking?

JOYCE. I'm not asking any.

WILSON. I don't want charity. I'd pay for my room.

JOYCE. You must've come to the wrong door. I'm sorry you've
been troubled.
She tries to close the door, but WILSON *blocks it with his
foot.*

WILSON. Can I come in? I've walked all the way here.
(*Pause. He smiles.*)

JOYCE. Just for a minute.
She lets him in and closes the door. He sits down.
I'm so busy. I'm run off my feet today.

WILSON. How about a cup of tea? You usually make one about now.

JOYCE *nods. She goes to the sink but is pulled up sharp.*

JOYCE. How do you know?

WILSON. Oh, I pick up all sorts of useful information in my job.

JOYCE. What's that?

She pours water from the kettle into the teapot.

WILSON. I'm a Gents hairdresser. Qualified. My dad has a business. Just a couple of chairs. I've clipped some notable heads in my time. Mostly professional men. Though we had an amateur street musician in a few weeks ago. We gave him satisfaction, I believe.

JOYCE *puts out two cups and pours his tea.*

WILSON. My brother was in the business too. Until he was involved in an accident.

He puts sugar into his tea and milk.

JOYCE. What happened?

WILSON. A van knocked him down.

JOYCE *pours her own tea.*

JOYCE. Was he tattooed?

WILSON. You've heard of him?

JOYCE. I've heard of his tattoos.

WILSON. They were unique. He had them done by a well-known artist. (*He takes a biscuit from the barrel.*) His funeral was attended by some interesting people. He was a sportsman before his decease. He wore white shorts better than any man I've ever come in contact with. As a matter of fact, strictly off the record, I'm wearing a pair of his white shorts at this moment. They're inconvenient ... because ... (*He blurts it out.*) – there's no fly. (*Pause.*) He wore them two days before he was killed.

JOYCE *looks away in a brief spasm of embarrassment which quickly passes.*

I wasn't mentioned in the press. They didn't realise the

important part I played in Frank's life. So I didn't get the coverage. I thought of revealing myself. But what's the good? (*Pause.*) My brother's fiancée had her photo taken. Bawling her head off. She insisted we bury the engagement ring with him. It was just an idle, theatrical gesture. It's too much trouble now to put a bunch of flowers on the grave.

JOYCE. Perhaps the accident unhinged her mind.

WILSON. It wasn't an accident. (*He drinks his tea.*) He was murdered.

JOYCE. You don't know that.

WILSON. Don't contradict me!

    JOYCE *stares in surprise.*

JOYCE (*angry*). This is a private house. What do you mean by raising your voice? I'm not having perfect strangers talking to me like that.

    WILSON *drinks his tea and eats a biscuit.*

Drink that tea and clear off. I don't want to see you here again. My husband will be back soon.

WILSON. He's not your husband.

JOYCE (*furious*). How dare you. You've gone too far. Leave my room at once.

WILSON. You're not married. You want to watch yourself.

JOYCE. I've a good mind to call a policeman.

WILSON. You aren't on the phone.

JOYCE. I can knock on the floor.

WILSON. There's nobody downstairs.

JOYCE. I'll report you.

    WILSON *stands to his feet.*

WILSON. Come here.

JOYCE (*alarmed*). Keep away!

    WILSON *looks at her, cup in hand. He takes a sip of tea.*

WILSON. Do you know I could murder you. Easy as that. (*He snaps his fingers.*) That's how these assaults on lonely women are all committed. I could make a very nasty attack on you at this moment. If I was so inclined.

JOYCE (*with a note of hysteria*). Don't come any nearer.

WILSON. Is your husband passionate with you?

   JOYCE *draws in a sharp breath.*

JOYCE. I'm reporting you. Using filthy language.

WILSON. If I were to assault you would he avenge it?

JOYCE. Yes.

WILSON. Where does he keep his gun?

JOYCE. He hasn't got a gun.

WILSON. I have it on good authority that he keeps it loaded.

   He takes a step towards her. She backs away.

   Where is it?

JOYCE. In the drawer. Over there.

   WILSON *goes to the drawer. He puts down his cup, opens the
   drawer and takes out a revolver. He checks that it is loaded,
   puts it back into the drawer and closes the drawer. Then he
   walks back to the table with the cup in his hand and drinks
   the last of his tea, placing the cup back on to the saucer.*

WILSON (*smiling*). Thanks for the tea.

   JOYCE *stares, puzzled.*

JOYCE. Are you going?

WILSON. The room's not available, is it? I expect you think
   I'm Jewish or something. (*Pause.*) Have you got a couple of
   bob to spare? I can't walk all the way back.

   JOYCE *opens her handbag.*

JOYCE (*giving him money*). Here's half-a-crown. Don't let me
   see you round here again.

   WILSON *goes off.* JOYCE *takes a bottle of pills from her
   handbag and swallows several.*

SCENE TWO

Later.
The remains of an evening meal are on the table. MIKE *is
smoking a small cigar.* JOYCE *is reading a book. She has a
pair of glasses on.*

MIKE. I went to the King's Cross toilet like I told you. I met my contact. He was a man with bad feet. He looked as though life had treated him rough. He hadn't much to live for. I gave him the message from the – er – (*Pause.*) The message was delivered. I went outside on to the platform. It was cold. I saw an old girl hardly able to breathe. Had something wrong with her. Hardly able to breathe. Her face was blue. (*Pause.*) Are you listening, Joycie?

JOYCE (*taking off her glasses, and putting her book down*). Yes. (*Pause.*) I've had a busy day.

MIKE. Are you tired?

JOYCE. A bit.

MIKE. Have a busy day, did you?

JOYCE (*sharply*). Yes. Why don't you listen? You never listen to anyone but yourself.

MIKE. I do.

JOYCE. You never listen to me.

MIKE. You never say anything interesting.

JOYCE. I might as well be dead. (*Pause.*) What if you came home and I was dead?

MIKE. Are you queer?

JOYCE. No.

MIKE (*pause*). Is your insides playing you up?

JOYCE. I'm all right.

MIKE. Is your liver upset then?

JOYCE. No.

MIKE. It's that fried food you eat. You wolf it down. Put something in the pan and have a fry. That's your motto.

JOYCE. You seem to thrive on it.

MIKE. I'm a man. A man has different glands. You can't go on what I eat.

JOYCE. Oh, well, if you must know, I think it's my nerves.

MIKE. You can't die of nerves.

JOYCE. Can't you?

MIKE. I'm going to the free library tomorrow. I'll look it up.

JOYCE (*pause*). What if I were done in?

MIKE. Who'd do you in?

JOYCE. Somebody might. You read of attacks every day on lonely defenceless women.

MIKE. You could call for help.

JOYCE. Who to?

MIKE. Mary.

JOYCE. She's not in. She's working again. I'm alone in the house.

MIKE. You could break a window. That would attract attention.

JOYCE (*pause*). Don't go out tomorrow.

MIKE. I can't mope around here. I'm active. It gets on my tits.

> JOYCE *closes her book, marking the place.* MIKE *begins to clear the supper things away and puts them into the sink.*

Mary used to be on her own. She was all right.

JOYCE. Mary can cope.

> MIKE *turns from the sink.*

MIKE. And why's that? Because she's a Catholic. She carries her Faith into her private life. That's what we're taught to do. We don't always succeed. But we try.

> *He takes off his coat.*

Why don't you have a chat with Mary? She'd put you right. Give you the address of a priest with an enquiring mind. He'd stop your maundering.

> *He takes off his shoes.*

You've a vivid imagination. A fertile mind. An asset in some people. But in your case it's not. (*Pause.*) It's in the mind. That's what the Father would say. You'd be better if you'd accept the Communion. That's what you need. I've said so for years.

JOYCE. I'd still be alone.

MIKE. You'd have the Sacrament inside you. That would be something. (*Pause.*) Anyway who'd assault you? Who? He'd

have to be out of his mind. Look at your face. When did
it last see water?

JOYCE. I've been crying.

MIKE. Crying? Are you pregnant?

JOYCE. No. I'm worried.

MIKE. No one would be interested in assaulting you. It's pride
to think they would. The idea is farcical. Please don't
burden me with it.

*He takes off his bow tie, goes into the bedroom, turns back
the sheets and picks up his pyjamas.*

JOYCE *comes to the bedroom entrance.*

JOYCE. Mike ... (*Pause.*) A kid came here today.

MIKE *takes off his waistcoat.*

MIKE. One of the Teds?

JOYCE. No. He tried to molest me.

MIKE. These kids see you coming. Why didn't you call for
Mary?

JOYCE. She's not in! She's not in! Do I talk for the sake of it?
(*Pause.*) Mike ... If he pays another visit – what shall I
do? Give me a word of advice?

MIKE *unbuttons his shirt.*

MIKE. Bring me my overcoat, will you? It's raw tonight.
We'll need extra on the bed.

SCENE THREE

Morning.

JOYCE *pauses in cleaning the room.*

JOYCE. I can't go to the park. I can't sit on cold stone. I might
get piles from the lowered temperature. I wouldn't want
them on top of everything else.

She puts down the duster, apathetically.

I'd try, maybe, a prayer. But the Virgin would turn a deaf
ear to a Protestant. (*Pause.*) I can't be as alone as all that.
Nobody ought to be. It's heartbreaking.

She listens. There is silence.

The number of humiliating admissions I've made. You'd think it would draw me closer to somebody. But it doesn't.

Three short rings are given on the doorbell.

Who's there?

No answer.

What do you want? (*Making up her mind.*) I'll answer the door to no one. They can hammer it down. (*Pause.*) Is it the milk? (*Calling.*) Are you deaf? No, it wouldn't be him. He only rings for his money.

She stands behind the door.

(*Loudly.*) Are you the insurance? (*Pause.*) But he comes on Friday. This is a Wednesday.

She backs away from the door, anxious.

Nobody comes of a Wednesday. (*She bends down and peeps through the letter-box.*) If it's my money you're after, there's not a thing in my purse.

She bites her lip, standing in thought.

(*Loudly.*) Are you from the Assistance? They come any time. I've had them on Monday. They come whenever they choose. It's their right. (*With a smile and growing confidence.*) You're the Assistance, aren't you? (*Her voice rises.*) Are you or aren't you?

Glass is heard breaking from the bedroom. She runs to the entrance of the bedroom and leaps back, startled; a piece of brick has been thrown through the window. JOYCE stares, her mouth trembling. Another piece of brick hurtles through the window, smashing another pane.

(*Screaming.*) It's him! He's breaking in. God Almighty, what shall I do? He'll murder me!

She stamps on the floor.

Mary! Mary!

She runs to the door, opens it and runs out into the passage. Her frantic tones can be heard crying:

Mrs O'Connor! Mrs O'Connor!

She runs back into the room; slams the door shut. The lock drops with a crash on to the floor. She picks it up and stares at it and then shrieks with fright.

It's come off! It's broke!

She tries to fit the lock back on to the door.

I've told him so often. I've – told him to – mend it!

She gives up, breathless. Then she tries to pull the settee out into the room, but gives up and picks up a chair which she pushes against the door and sits on.

He'll easily fling this aside. Oh, Michael, I'm to be murdered because you're too bone idle to fix a lock.

There is a prolonged ringing on the doorbell.

Let me alone! I'm going to report you. I've seen them at the station. They've set a trap. I'm safe in here. We have an extremely strong and reliable Chubb lock on the door. So you're trapped. Ha, ha! The detectives are watching the house.

The front door is kicked. The chair pushes away and JOYCE *is flung aside. She backs into the bedroom.*

If it's the gun you want, I don't know where he's put it. He's taken it. (*Pause.*) I may be able to find it. Is that what you want?

Outside the door a burst of music is heard from a transistor radio. There is knocking. The bell rings. A sudden silence. Laughter. Silence. A splintering of wood.

(JOYCE *calls shrilly.*) I've told my hubby. He's seeing some-one. You'll laugh on the other side of your face.

Suddenly, giving up all pretence, she bursts into tears.

Go away. There's a good boy. I don't know what you want. I've no money. Please go away. Please, please, please ... (*She sobs.*)

SCENE FOUR

Later.
MIKE *sits at the table reading a newspaper.* JOYCE *enters in outdoor clothes.*

MIKE. Where've you been? (*He folds up the paper.*)
JOYCE *takes off her hat and coat and puts them into the wardrobe.*

JOYCE. Out.

MIKE. Out? What about my tea? It wasn't ready.

JOYCE. I've been walking round. I didn't come back till I saw the light in the window.

MIKE. Where did you go?

JOYCE. Into Woolworths.

MIKE. What for?

JOYCE. The people. The lights. The crowds. (*Pause.*) That kid came again. He broke two windows today in the bedroom.

MIKE. I thought it was them next door.

JOYCE. Have you seen the banisters? Smashed to bits. Wantonness.. I couldn't stop him. (*Lowering her voice.*) He pissed on the floor in the passage. I had to clean it up. Been ringing the doorbell half the day. Running up and down the stairs. I'm nearly out of my mind. It didn't stop till four. (*Pause.*) I can hardly think with worry.

MIKE. Did you witness him?

JOYCE. I was in here.

MIKE. Did you see him?

JOYCE (*furiously*). I won't stand it. I want something done. Look at that lock. Why don't you mend it?

MIKE. I'll try and borrow a set of screws.

JOYCE. You can decide what you're doing. I can't keep pace with the excitement. I'll be in a home.

MIKE. Did he try to get into the room?

JOYCE. No.

MIKE. Could he have got in if he'd wanted?

JOYCE (*pause*). Yes.

MIKE. Did he speak?

JOYCE. No.

MIKE. Then how d'you know it was him from yesterday? If
you didn't see him and he didn't speak? How d'you know?
Silence.

JOYCE. It must be the same man.

MIKE. Why didn't you go outside and see?

JOYCE. He'd've killed me.

MIKE. How do you know that? You've no evidence to support
your theory.

JOYCE. But ... (*Wide-eyed.*) ... I'd be dead if I'd got evidence.

MIKE. I'd prosecute him on your behalf, Joycie.

JOYCE *blows her nose; she doesn't speak.*

JOYCE (*at last, wearily*). Will you mend the lock for me? I'll
feel safer then.

MIKE. I'll see to it when I get back.
*He goes into the bedroom and picks up his coat from the
end of the bed.*

JOYCE. Back? Back from where?

MIKE (*entering, putting on his coat*). I'm seeing a man who could
put me in touch with something.
He goes to the sink and puts the flower into his buttonhole.

JOYCE. I'll go down to Mary. (*Pause.*) Would you like a bikky
before you go?

MIKE. No. I'll have something on the way.

JOYCE. Is it important tonight?

MIKE. I may be employed to do another job in the van. We're
fixing the details.
The doorbell is rung violently. MIKE *puts the silver paper
from the flower into the waste bin.*

MIKE. Is that the bell?

JOYCE. Yes.

MIKE (*going into the bedroom*). Answer it then. I'm here with you.

> *The bell is rung again.* MIKE *takes the packet of cigarettes from the drawer and fills his cigarette case.* JOYCE *opens the door.* WILSON *is outside.*

WILSON (*smiling*). Are you the lady I saw yesterday?

JOYCE. It's you!

WILSON. You are the lady?

JOYCE. What do you mean by pestering me?

WILSON. There's no need to raise your voice.

JOYCE. My husband is in. Coming here, trying your tricks. Making a nuisance. I've only to call and he'll soon put a stop to you. Do you understand?

WILSON. I'm afraid I don't.

JOYCE. Coming here playing me up. What do you mean by it? It's disgusting. Anyone would think you were a kid. Behaving like that. You know what I mean, don't you? You know. Like an animal. (*Pause.*) Are you paying for those windows?

WILSON. I don't know what you're talking about.

JOYCE. You're a liar! A bloody little liar!

WILSON. Don't speak to me like that, lady. I'm not used to it.

JOYCE. I've had enough. I'm putting a stop to this. (*Calls.*) Michael!

> MIKE *enters from the bedroom. He slips his cigarette case into his pocket.*

JOYCE. Come here. (*To* WILSON.) Stay where you are! Stay here!

> *She attempts to grab his arm. He tries to shake her off. She hangs on. He shrugs her away, violently. She comes back. They struggle.* MIKE *goes to the mirror and runs a comb through his hair.*

JOYCE (*shouting excited*). Mike! Michael! (*To* WILSON.) I'll have my husband to you. (*Turning, excited.*) Where are you, Michael! For God's sake!

MIKE *puts the comb away and strolls to the door.*

MIKE (*coolly*). What's the matter?

JOYCE. This is him. The one that's been coming here.

MIKE (*to* WILSON). What's this, I hear? Have you been annoying my wife?

JOYCE. Yes. He has.

MIKE (*to* JOYCE). Let's hear his version of it. (*To* WILSON) Tell me the truth.

WILSON. I wanted a room.

MIKE. We haven't got a room.

WILSON. You're Irish! My mother was Irish. My father was Mediterranean. I have difficulty with rooms for that reason. (*Smiles.*) I've walked all the way from the bus station by Victoria. Do you know that district at all?

MIKE. I know King's Cross intimately.

WILSON. Victoria is a different place entirely. In the summer it has a character of its own. Are you a Londoner?

MIKE. No. I was born in the shadow of the hills of Donegal. We had a peat farm. It was the aftermath of the troubles drove us away. Otherwise there'd be people called Mike in Donegal to this day.

WILSON. I love Ireland. I'd go there tomorrow if it wasn't for my dad. He's a hard man to please. My feet are killing me. Could I have a drink of water?

MIKE. Certainly. Come on in.

JOYCE. You're not letting him in?

MIKE. Be quiet. You're making yourself look ridiculous. (*To* WILSON.) This way. And take no notice of her She can't help herself.

He leads the way into the room.

Get the lad a glass of water, Joycie.

JOYCE *goes to the sink and fills a glass with water.*

(*To* WILSON.) What part of Ireland is your mother from?

WILSON. Sligo.

MIKE. I once knew a lad from Sligo. Name of Murphy. I wonder if maybe your Ma would've come across him?

WILSON. I'll make enquiries.

MIKE. I'd be obliged if you would. He had dark curly hair and talked with a pronounced brogue. Not an easy man to miss in a crowd.

JOYCE *hands* WILSON *the glass of water.*

JOYCE (*to* MIKE). What did you let him in for?

MIKE. He isn't a leper.

JOYCE. Ask him.

MIKE. What?

JOYCE. Ask him about his conduct. He won't be able to face it out.

MIKE (*to* WILSON). About these things she tells me. Did you cheek her yesterday?

WILSON. It depends on which way you look at it. I thought my behaviour was exemplary.

MIKE. Did you molest her?

WILSON (*to* JOYCE). What've you been telling him? I never tried to interfere with you, did I?

JOYCE (*angry*). Stop using that kind of talk. (*To* MIKE.) You can see what I had to put up with.

MIKE. That's medical talk, Joycie. You should learn to control your temper. (*To* WILSON.) Why did you bring a suitcase with you?

WILSON. I wanted a room. (*Nods to* JOYCE.) I thought she might change her mind.

JOYCE. Who's she? The cat's mother.

MIKE (*to* WILSON). Bring it in. You don't want to leave it lying out there.

WILSON *exits.*

JOYCE. What are you playing at? After what he's done to me?

MIKE. Quiet!

JOYCE. What's his background? He could be anything.

MIKE. Give the lad a chance.

JOYCE. Chance? After what I've been through?

MIKE. Shut up!

JOYCE (*bewildered*). Shut up?

MIKE. You're heading for a belt around the ear. Go to Mary. Are you going?

> WILSON *enters with a suitcase.*

MIKE. Put it over there, lad. How about a cup of tea, Joycie?

> JOYCE *goes into the bedroom.*

MIKE. She's taken offence. (*Calls.*) Did you hear me? Why don't you show a few manners? (*To* WILSON.) What's your profession?

WILSON. I'm a Gents Hairdresser.

MIKE. You wouldn't have to be dabbling with birth-control devices? That's no way for a Catholic to carry on.

WILSON. I don't handle that part of the trade. My old man does it. He has the free-thinking frame of mind. I can't approve, of course. It's the Latin temperament which has been the curse of our religion all along.

MIKE. The Pope is Italian.

WILSON. You have something there. I'd like to see a Liffey man on the throne of St Peter myself. I'd be proud to hear the Lateran ring with the full-throated blasphemies of our native land.

MIKE. What are you thinking of? The Vicar of Christ doesn't blaspheme.

WILSON. He would if he was Irish and drank Guinness.

MIKE. You're a lad after my own heart. You'll not know me by name, I suppose?

WILSON. I didn't quite catch it.

MIKE. Michael O'Rourke. I was known as Mike or Mickey O'Rourke in the days when you were a nipper. I used to be respected in the boxing profession. I was thought to be heading for the top at one time. Then I had my trouble. (*He turns to the bedroom and calls.*) Isn't that right? Wasn't I handy with my fists then? In the days after the second German war? (*Turns back to* WILSON.) Ignorant cow. (*Into bedroom.*) Are you going to behave decent?

JOYCE *is sitting on the bed. She gives a toss of her head.*

WILSON. I'll go.

MIKE. Don't let her drive you away. You stay.

JOYCE *picks up a cardigan. She enters from the bedroom.*

JOYCE (*in a tight, angry voice*). I'm going downstairs!

She goes off into the hall, slamming the door behind her.

MIKE. Take no notice. She'll come round. She's nervous, you know. It's the life she led before I took up with her. I have to watch her. She'd get me into all sorts of trouble. She has no religious feelings. That's the worst of it. She never had the benefit of the upbringing.

WILSON. My mum was brought up by nuns.

MIKE. Is she still alive?

WILSON. She's in hospital with an infectious disease of the hip-joint. The nuns think the world of her.

MIKE. Is she in pain?

WILSON. She screams out. It's terrible to hear her.

MIKE. I wish I could do something. Would it be any use to burn a candle? I don't think I've the cash on me.

WILSON. Wouldn't the priest lend you the cash?

MIKE. I'd not like to ask. I'd pop across and burn a candle myself. But he might ask questions. It's his business, of course. He's a right to ask. But why should I subject myself to scrutiny? (*Pause.*) Is your mother expected to recover?

WILSON. It's touch and go.

MIKE. She's maybe doomed. She's likely to be a candle herself already. She's probably being stripped by the angels as we speak. I suppose we are roasted nude? I've never seen fit to ask. It's not a question you can put to the Father. Though he is a Jesuit. And that makes a difference. (*Pause.*) Is your da in good health?

WILSON. He's fine. (*Pause.*) I'm not keeping you, am I? ....

MIKE. No. (*Pause, looks at his watch.*) As a matter of fact you've kept me. I've missed my appointment. I shall have to drop them a line and apologise for my absence.

He takes off his coat, puts the flower from his buttonhole into a glass, and puts water into the glass.

(*Putting the glass on to the draining board*). If you're desperate for a room we could put you up. On the bed-settee. It's quite comfortable.

WILSON. Is it new?

MIKE. No.

WILSON. You surprise me.

MIKE. I bought it a long time ago. I couldn't afford such luxury today. Financially I'm in a bad way.

WILSON. Well, my money will help you out.

MIKE. It's the Assistance Board. I'm not a believer in charity. Unless I need it. With the cost of living being so high I'm greatly in need of a weekly donation from the Government. They say my circumstances have altered. I haven't any circumstances to alter. They should know that. I've filled in a form to the effect that I'm a derelict.

WILSON. Yes. My brother and me had the same trouble.

MIKE. They haven't the insight into the human heart that we have in Ireland.

WILSON. We lived in Shepherd's Bush. We had a little room. And our life was made quite comfortable by the N.A.B. for almost a year. We had a lot of friends. All creeds and colours. But no circumstances at all. We were happy, though. We were young. I was seventeen. He was twenty-three. You can't do better for yourself than that, can you? (*He shrugs.*) We were bosom friends. I've never told anyone that before. I hope I haven't shocked you.

MIKE. As close as that?

WILSON. We had separate beds – he was a stickler for convention, but that's as far as it went. We spent every night in each other's company. It was the reason we never got any work done.

MIKE: There's no word in the Irish language for what you were doing.

WILSON. In Lapland they have no word for snow.

MIKE. I'd rather not hear. I'm not a priest, you know.

WILSON. I wasn't with him when he died. I'm going round the twist with heartbreak.

MIKE. He's dead?

WILSON. Yes. I thought of topping myself. As a gesture. I would've done but for my strict upbringing. Suicide is difficult when you've got a pious mum.

MIKE. Kill yourself?

WILSON. I don't want to live, see. That's a crude way of putting it. I've lived among rough people.

MIKE. You won't do it, though?

WILSON. No. I've made a will, of course. In case anything should happen in the future.

MIKE. What might happen?

WILSON. I might get killed.

MIKE. How?

WILSON. I don't know. (*Pause.*) In my will I state that I want to be buried with Frank. It's my last request. They'll be bound to honour it. His fiancée won't mind. She's off already with another man. He's not cold and already it's too much trouble for her to put a bunch of flowers on his grave. She's a typical woman. You've met with it yourself?

MIKE. I have. Some of them are unholy bitches.

WILSON. He wouldn't have benefited from her. I was more intimate with him than she was. I used to base my life round him. You don't often get that, do you?

MIKE (*uneasily*). No.

WILSON. I heard he was a friend of yours. You were pointed out as a man that knew him.

He takes a snapshot from his pocket and hands it to MIKE.

Recognise him?

MIKE *looks at the snapshot.*

MIKE (*pause*). He was nice looking.

WILSON. He had personality. That indefinable something. That was taken two days before he was killed. (*Pause.*) What's the matter? The light hurting your eyes.

MIKE *hands the snapshot back.*

MIKE. Take it away. It upsets me. The thought of him being dead. He was so young.

WILSON. Do you recognise him?

MIKE. I may have seen him once or twice. I may have spoken to him.

WILSON. A van knocked him down.

MIKE (*pause*). Did he say anything? Was there a death-bed scene?

WILSON. He was killed instantaneous. (*Pause.*) You recently had a smash-up in your van, didn't you? I checked with the garage. You've had five major repair jobs in under two years. Why don't you learn to drive properly? You're a disgrace to your profession.

MIKE. I feel bad. I'll have to ask you to go now. It's embarrassing to be ill in a stranger's presence.

WILSON *smiles.*

WILSON. I was going to live here, I thought.

MIKE. I've just realised. We can't put you up.

WILSON. Why not?

MIKE. Her aunt may drop in. I'm sorry I raised your hopes.

WILSON. Does she usually come this late?

MIKE. She does.

WILSON. She must be an ignorant kind of woman, turning up in the middle of the night. No consideration for others. What's her name?

MIKE. Snell.

WILSON. What's her first name?

MIKE. Bridie Francine. She uses the second. Everyone knows Francine Snell.

WILSON. I haven't had the pleasure. What does she look like?

MIKE. She has a growth on the side of her neck. She walks with a limp.

WILSON. She sounds a dear old lady. Where does she normally live? When she's not up half the night careering about visiting?

MIKE. In the suburbs. She prefers it to the city centre.

WILSON. Well, I'm sorry I can't stay. I must be going then. Before I say goodbye would you mind telling me, as briefly as possible, why you killed my brother.

MIKE. I didn't!

WILSON. You did. You were paid two hundred and fifty quid. Exclusive of repairs to the van.

MIKE. No!

WILSON. It was on October the twenty-first he was killed. What were you doing that day?

MIKE. I was fishing.

WILSON. Where?

MIKE. In the canal.

WILSON. Did you catch much?

MIKE. I put it back. That's the rules. The rules of the club.

WILSON. My brother belonged to the club. He was the best angler you had. He gave out the cards. (*Pause.*) What did you catch on the day he died?

MIKE. I can't be expected to remember.

WILSON. Did you have the good fortune to find a salmon on the end of your line?

MIKE. No. Whoever heard of catching salmon in a canal?

WILSON. You killed my brother. Your denials fall on deaf ears. (*Pause.*) You're a liar. That's what it amounts to.

MIKE (*frightened*). What are you going to do?

WILSON. Nothing I can do, is there? (*He picks up his suitcase*

and goes to the door.) I'll be off. (*He smiles, deliberately*.)
Give my love to Maddy.

MIKE. Let me alone. I'm ill. (*Pause*.) What did you say?

WILSON. Maddy. Your old scrubber.

MIKE *goes over to* WILSON

MIKE. Are you asking for a back-hander? What is this about
Maddy? I don't know any Maddy.

WILSON. She lives here.

MIKE. Her name's Joyce.

WILSON *shrugs, smiling*.

Out you go, you young whore's get!

WILSON *smiles*.

Piss off! Coming here trying to make trouble. I was
handy with my fists once. I could make pulp of you.

WILSON. All this energy. Nearly blowing your top. You ought
to get it regular. You'd feel better then.

MIKE. Don't come to me with your gutter talk. I won't listen
to it.

WILSON. You won't have been capable of a jump since the
Festival. It's the usual story.

MIKE *grabs* WILSON'S *arm*

MIKE. Why did you call her Maddy?

WILSON. She asked me to. In private. It's her trade
name.

MIKE. She never saw you till two days ago.

WILSON. She told you that? Do you believe her?

MIKE. Yes.

WILSON. It's your affair. I never believe a woman. I've had
experience.

MIKE. The only experience you've had is with your fist.

WILSON. What a coarse remark. How typical. (*He glances to
the bedroom*.) I wish she'd change the sheets on the bed.
Have you noticed? It's a bad sign.

MIKE. If you've had her I'll swing for you.

WILSON. Would you kill me?

MIKE. I would. I'd throttle you with my bare hands. I'd choke the filth out of you.

WILSON. You've got a gun. Kill me with that. (*Pause.*) I'll be back tomorrow. Tell Maddy I'll see her.

MIKE. You can believe me. I never murdered your brother. Don't you believe me?

WILSON. No. (*Pause.*) I might decide to put Maddy in the pudding club. Just to show my contempt for your way of life. I never take precautions. We're skin to skin. Nature's method.

> MIKE *gives a groan of pain. He runs to the drawer, rummages and takes the gun from the drawer.*

MIKE (*waving the gun before* WILSON). See this? I'll use it if I catch you with her.

WILSON. How good a shot are you?

MIKE. I'm an expert.

WILSON. The heart is situated ... (*He points.*) ... just below this badge on my pullover. Don't miss, will you? I don't want to be injured. I want to be dead.

MIKE. You think I'm joking?

WILSON. I hope you're not.

MIKE. You're an ignorant young sod! Like your brother. It must run in the family.

WILSON. Have you noticed that mole she has?

MIKE. Where?

WILSON. In a private place. I don't expect you've looked lately. That's why she's gone for someone younger.

MIKE (*screaming*). Get out!

> WILSON *smiles and exits.*

(*Softly*). I feel bad. I'm sickening for something.

> *He puts the gun away in the drawer.*

They think because you're a criminal they can treat you like dirt. Coming here like that. Telling a man to his face. The morals of Nineveh were hardly so lax.

> *He sits at the table closing his eyes.*

Oh, but he's playing with fire. I'll shoot him. I'll geld him. I've a clear case. I'm the injured party. I'll have the stones off him if he's done her. (*Pause.*) He'll be putting her into a whorehouse next. These kids have only one idea.

He goes into the bedroom, picks up his pyjamas and slippers, pulls the clothing and a pillow from the bed and enters the main room.

I'll sleep out here. I can't have her next to me.

He sits on the settee and begins to undress.

Oh, oh! I'm cuckolded. What a spectacle. Yet you'd swear you were safe with her. She's not much of a looker. The sex is rotten. Perfidious. Treacherous. She's old enough to be his mother. (*Pause.*) I shouldn't say that. That's a terrible thing to say.

He puts on his pyjama jacket.

She's whored herself under two assumed names. Before I met her she was known to the Directory of Directors as Madelein Scott-Palmer. And before that she'd led a loose life as Sarah Fielding. She wasted her auntie's legacy on cards for tobacconists' windows. Oh, it's too much! I'll have to kill her.

He puts on his pyjama trousers.

If I kill her I'll have to say goodbye. I'll never see her again. I'd be alone. The pain of it. I never realise the pain. I'm too old to start again. Too old. I love her. My heart aches to admit it. She's all I've got. I want her if she's the biggest old tart since the mother of Solomon.

He puts on his slippers.

What a life it is living in a country full of whores and communists.

He puts his coat on as a dressing-gown. JOYCE *enters. She takes off her cardigan.*

JOYCE. Has he gone?

MIKE (*looking up, narrowing his eyes*). What d'you mean?

JOYCE. I thought he was staying here.

MIKE. Do you want him to?

JOYCE. Do I want him to?

MIKE (*nodding his head*). I see your plan. I see it. You've the cunning of Luther.

    JOYCE *walks past him into the bedroom.*

Where are you going?

JOYCE. To bed. I'm not listening to you.

MIKE. What's she up to? (*Pause.*) I'll maybe forgive her. Our Lord forgave the woman taken in adultery. But the circumstances were different. (*Pause.*) It's a ludicrous business. Ludicrous. The deceit. At her age. She wants somebody younger. At her age they get the itch. It's like a tale told by a commercial traveller. Just for a few minutes' thrill. I don't know what she'd be like if we had a television.

JOYCE (*undressing for bed*). Are you giving a recitation out there?

MIKE (*entering bedroom*). What?

JOYCE. I thought you were entertaining the troops.

MIKE. I leave that to you. That's more your line, isn't it?

JOYCE. What's the matter?

MIKE. You cow! Playing me up.

JOYCE. You shouldn't've invited him in. You upset me.

MIKE. I've heard about you. You'll be taking your clothes off in the street next.

JOYCE. What's got into you?

MIKE. Some men would kill you. You're lucky I'm not some. A fine family. Your mother was doing it in a doorway the night she was killed. If she hadn't been such a wicked old brass she'd've been in the shelter with the rest. Taking the A.R.P. from their duty. Your granny spent Mafeking night on her back. That makes three generations of whores.

    He smacks her face. JOYCE *shrieks with surprise and fright.*

I'll murder you!

    He leaps upon her. They fall across the bed.

JOYCE (*shouting*). Mind the fish! You'll upset my goldfish.

MIKE (*standing up, taking off his coat*). What d'you want to keep fish in a bedroom for? It's not hygienic.

> *He gets into bed.* JOYCE *fetches the pillow and blanket from the main room and puts them on the bed.*

JOYCE. What's he been telling you?

MIKE. Did you let him?

JOYCE (*indignantly*). He never touched me.

MIKE. You'd have to say that. I don't want to lose you. I don't want to be on my own again. I was so lonely before.

JOYCE. Shall I put your coat on your feet? It's freezing again.

SCENE FIVE

> *Next morning.*
> JOYCE *is washing dishes. The doorbell rings.* JOYCE *takes off her gloves and wipes her hands. The door is pushed open and* WILSON *enters.*

JOYCE. What are you doing in here? That door is supposed to be locked.

WILSON. There's no lock.

JOYCE. My husband is downstairs. It's true. This time it's true.

WILSON. I know. I saw him hanging about down there. I told him we were having an affair last night. It didn't inconvenience you in any way?

> *He takes off his coat and spreads it on the settee.*

You don't want to have an affair with me by any chance?

JOYCE. You're only a little boy.

> WILSON *picks up a chair and wedges it under the handle of the door.*

What are you doing that for?

WILSON. So as when he comes up and tries the handle he'll think we're knocking it off.

JOYCE (*with distaste*). Don't use expressions like that. I'm not used to it.

WILSON. When you were on the game you must've been.

JOYCE. I never allowed anyone to take liberties with me. My people were good class. (*Pause.*) Who told you about me?

WILSON. My brother. He had it off with you after seeing *The Sound of Music*. I waited downstairs. He was as pissed as a fart. He would never have had a prostitute and seen *The Sound of Music* otherwise. (*Loosens his tie.*) You're like most women. Here today and gone tomorrow. My brother's fiancée resembled you in many ways. Fickle in her emotions. She was trying on her wedding-gown when we got news of Frank's death. Now she's had it dyed ice-blue and wears it to dinner dances. My only consolation is that she looks hideous in it. But it shows what kind of woman she is, doesn't it? I knew the type by the way she moved her knees up against my thighs at the funeral. I felt like throttling her. A whole hour she was at it. We went the long way round to avoid the procession.

JOYCE. What procession?

WILSON. They were celebrating some victory or other. We heard the bands playing in the distance. The Royal Family were out in full force. Furs and garters flying. My old man was in it. He couldn't come to the funeral because he was on the British Legion float. He represented something.

He sits, his shoulders hunched, staring into space.

He thought more of tarting himself up than burying his son. All our family seem to be some kind of idiot. If anybody so much as mentions the British Legion to my dad he goes into a trance. On armistice day he takes part in all the rituals. He eats poppies for a week beforehand. I haven't seen him since the funeral. I expect he's in a home by now.

He stands.

He should be up here.

JOYCE. Who?

WILSON. Your old man. We should have some warmth. Haven't you got an electric fire? I hadn't anticipated being frozen to death.

He goes off into the bedroom.

WILSON (*calling from the bedroom*). Are these some kind of carp?

JOYCE. No. Just goldfish.

WILSON enters the main room.

WILSON. You can catch germs from them, you know.

He takes off his tie.

My brother would've been twenty-four in three days' time. He had plans for a business.

He kicks off his shoes.

I expect he would have made good sooner or later. He was the go-ahead type. His mentality was fully developed. He used to read a lot about expansion. His death put a stop to that. I don't take after him. Except in the physical sense.

He sighs and shakes his head.

I get a bit lost without him, I don't mind admitting. (*Pause.*) He might have made a lot of money in his own line. It was my ambition to become the brother of a millionaire. (*Pause.*) I expect you're bored. You didn't know him. I can't expect you to see my point of view.

He takes his pullover off, unbuttons his shirt, pins a badge on his shirt above the heart, and unzips his fly.

JOYCE. Here, what are you doing?

WILSON. It ought to look as if we're on the job when he comes up.

JOYCE. Stop it! Stop it! Whatever will Michael think? He'll think we're carrying on. I never thought of that.

WILSON. I banked on him being up here by now. Rattling the door. He's probably gone back on his word.

He goes into the bedroom and looks out of the window.

He's not out there now.

JOYCE picks up his pullover and goes into the bedroom.

JOYCE (*handing him his pullover*). Put your clothes on. Don't be so silly.

WILSON (*accepting the pullover*). He won't come up. He won't. I can see this is a failure like everything else.

MIKE is heard coming up the stairs.

MIKE. Joycie! Joycie . . .

WILSON. I'm sorry if I've caused trouble. I'm not usually like this. My heart is breaking. I wish I'd been with him when he died.

JOYCE. You poor boy. Oh, you poor boy.

She kisses his cheek tenderly. He holds her close. MIKE crashes into the room. He advances slowly. Pause. WILSON turns from JOYCE, smiles at MIKE, and zips up his fly. MIKE fires the gun.

The shot crashes into the goldfish bowl. JOYCE screams. A second shot hits WILSON in the chest.

WILSON. He's shot me.

He crashes to the floor on his knees.

My will is in my overcoat pocket. My address in my pocket diary. Remember will you?

JOYCE (*to MIKE*). What've you done?

WILSON. He took it serious. How charming. (*He coughs, blood spurts from his mouth.*) He's a bit of a nutter if you ask me. Am I dying? I think . . . Oh . . .

He falls forward. Silence.

JOYCE. He's fainted.

MIKE (*laying the gun aside*). He's dead.

JOYCE. But he can't be. You haven't killed him?

MIKE. Bring a sheet. Cover his body.

JOYCE. I've a bit of sacking somewhere.

MIKE. I said a sheet! Give him the best.

He goes into the bedroom and drags a sheet from the bed which he puts over WILSON's body.

JOYCE. What excuse was there to shoot him?

MIKE. He was misbehaving himself with my wife.

JOYCE. But I'm not your wife. And he wasn't.

MIKE. He called you Maddy.

JOYCE. Somebody must've told him about my past. You know what people are. (*Pause.*) Did you have anything to do with his brother's death?

MIKE. Yes.

JOYCE. This is what comes of having no regular job. (*Pause.*) Is the phone box working by the Nag's Head?

MIKE. Yes.

JOYCE. Go to the telephone box. Dial 999. I'll tell them I was assaulted.

MIKE (*horrified*). It'll be in the papers.

JOYCE. Well, perhaps not assaulted. Not completely. You came in just in time.

MIKE. You'll stick by me, Joycie?

JOYCE. Of course, dear. (*She kisses him.*) I love you.
  She sees the shattered goldfish bowl.
  Oh, look Michael! (*Bursting into tears.*) My goldfish!
  She picks up a fish.

MIKE. One of the bullets must've hit the bowl.

JOYCE. They're dead. Poor things. And I reared them so carefully. And while all this was going on they died.
  She sobs. MIKE *puts his arm round her and leads her to the settee. She sits.*

MIKE. Sit down. I'll fetch the police. This has been a crime of passion. They'll understand. They have wives and goldfish of their own.

  JOYCE *is too heartbroken to answer. She buries her face in* MIKE'S *shoulder. He holds her close.*

Curtain

Entertaining Mr Sloane

To Kenneth Halliwell

Entertaining Mr Sloane was first presented in London at the New Arts Theatre on 6 May 1964 by Michael Codron Ltd and at Wyndham's Theatre on 29 June 1964 by Michael Codron and Albery, with the following cast:

KATH	Madge Ryan
SLOANE	Dudley Sutton
KEMP	Charles Lamb
ED	Peter Vaughan

Directed by Patrick Dromgoole
Designed by Timothy O'Brien
Costumes supervised by Tazeena Firth

Entertaining Mr Sloane was revived as part of the 'Joe Orton Festival' at the Royal Court Theatre, London, on 17 April 1975, subsequently transferring to the Duke of York's Theatre. The cast was as follows:

KATH	Beryl Reid
SLOANE	Malcolm McDowell
KEMP	James Ottaway
ED	Ronald Fraser

Directed by Roger Croucher
Designed by John Gunter
Costumes by Deirdre Clancy

Act One

A room. Evening.

> KATH *enters followed by* SLOANE.

KATH. This is my lounge.

SLOANE. Would I be able to use this room? Is it included?

KATH. Oh, yes. (*Pause.*) You mustn't imagine it's always like this. You ought to have rung up or something. And then I'd've been prepared.

SLOANE. The bedroom was perfect.

KATH. I never showed you the toilet.

SLOANE. I'm sure it will be satisfactory. (*Walks around the room examining the furniture. Stops by the window.*)

KATH. I should change them curtains. Those are our winter ones. The summer ones are more of a chintz. (*Laughs.*) The walls need re-doing. The Dadda has trouble with his eyes. I can't ask him to do any work involving ladders. It stands to reason.

Pause.

SLOANE. I can't give you a decision right away.

KATH. I don't want to rush you. (*Pause.*) What do you think? I'd be happy to have you.

Silence.

SLOANE. Are you married?

KATH (*pause*). I was. I had a boy . . . killed in very sad circumstances. It broke my heart at the time. I got over it though. You do, don't you?

Pause.

SLOANE. A son?

KATH. Yes.

SLOANE. You don't look old enough.

Pause.

KATH. I don't let myself go like some of them you may have noticed. I'm just over . . . As a matter of fact I'm forty-one.

Pause.

SLOANE (*briskly*). I'll take the room.

KATH. Will you?

SLOANE. I'll bring my things over tonight. It'll be a change from my previous.

KATH. Was it bad?

SLOANE. Bad?

KATH. As bad as that?

SLOANE. You've no idea.

KATH. I don't suppose I have. I've led a sheltered life.

SLOANE. Have you been a widow long?

KATH. Yes a long time. My husband was a mere boy. (*With a half-laugh*).) That sounds awful doesn't it?

SLOANE. Not at all.

KATH. I married out of school. I surprised everyone by the suddenness of it. (*Pause.*) Does that sound as if I had to get married?

SLOANE. I'm broadminded.

KATH. I should've known better. You won't breathe a word?

SLOANE. You can trust me.

KATH. My brother would be upset if he knew I told you. (*Pause.*) Nobody knows around here. The people in the nursing home imagined I *was* somebody. I didn't disillusion them.

SLOANE. You were never married then?

KATH. No.

SLOANE. What about – I hope you don't think I'm prying?

KATH. I wouldn't for a minute. What about –?

SLOANE. . . . the father?

KATH (*pause*). We always planned to marry. But there were difficulties. I was very young and he was even younger. I don't believe we would have been allowed.

SLOANE. What happened to the baby?

KATH. Adopted.

SLOANE. By whom?

KATH. That I could not say. My brother arranged it.

SLOANE. What about the kid's father?

KATH. He couldn't do anything.

SLOANE. Why not?

KATH. His family objected. They were very nice but he had a duty you see. (*Pause.*) As I say, if it'd been left to him I'd be his widow today. (*Pause.*) I had a last letter. I'll show you some time. (*Silence.*) D'you like flock or foam rubber in your pillow?

SLOANE. Foam rubber.

KATH. You need a bit of luxury, don't you? I bought the Dadda one but he can't stand them.

SLOANE. I can.

KATH. You'll live with us then as one of the family?

SLOANE. I never had no family of my own.

KATH. Didn't you?

SLOANE. No. I was brought up in an orphanage.

KATH. You have the air of lost wealth.

SLOANE. That's remarkable. My parents, I believe, *were* extremely wealthy people.

KATH. Did Dr Barnardo give you a bad time?

SLOANE. No. It was the lack of privacy I found most trying.

Pause.

And the lack of real love.

KATH. Did you never know your mamma?

SLOANE. Yes.

KATH. When did they die?

SLOANE. I was eight. (*Pause.*) They passed away together.

KATH. How shocking.

SLOANE. I've an idea that they had a suicide pact. Couldn't prove it of course.

KATH. Of course not. (*Pause.*) With a nice lad like you to take care of you'd think they'd've postponed it. (*Pause.*) Criminals, were they?

SLOANE. From what I remember they was respected. You know H.P. debts. Bridge. A little light gardening. The usual activities of a cultured community. (*Silence.*) I respect their memory.

KATH. Do you? How nice.

SLOANE. Every year I pay a visit to their grave. I take sandwiches. Make a day of it. (*Pause.*) The graveyard is situated in pleasant surroundings so it's no hardship. (*Pause.*) Tomb an' all.

KATH. Marble? (*Pause.*) Is there an inscription?

SLOANE. Perhaps you'd come with me this trip?

KATH. We'll see.

SLOANE. I go in the autumn because I clean the leaves off the monument. As a tribute.

KATH. Yes.

SLOANE. That's the main task I set myself.

KATH. Any relations?

SLOANE. None.

KATH. Poor boy. Alone in the world. Like me.

SLOANE. You're not alone.

KATH. I am. (*Pause.*) Almost alone. (*Pause.*) If I'd been allowed to keep my boy I'd not be. (*Pause.*) You're almost the same age as he would be. You've got the same refinement.

SLOANE (*slowly*). I need . . . understanding.

KATH. You do, don't you? Here let me take your coat. (*Helps him off with his coat.*) You've got a delicate skin. (*Touches his neck. His cheek.*)

　　He shudders a little. Pause.

KATH (*kisses his cheek*). Just a motherly kiss. A real mother's kiss. (*Silence. Lifts his arms and folds them about her.*) You'll find me very sentimental. I upset easy. (*His arms are holding her.*) When

I hear of . . . tragedies happening to perfect strangers. There are so many ruined lives. (*Puts her head on his shoulder.*) You must treat me gently when I'm in one of my moods.

Silence.

SLOANE. (*clearing his throat*). How much are you charging? I mean – I've got to know.

He drops his arms. She moves away.

KATH. We'll come to some arrangement. A cup of tea?
SLOANE. Yes I don't mind.
KATH. I'll get you one.
SLOANE. Can I have a bath?
KATH. Now?
SLOANE. Later would do.
KATH. You must do as you think fit.

A door slams. KEMP's *voice is heard off.*

KEMP. You there?
KATH (*calls*). I'm in here. Don't stand about. Sit down. Go on. We don't charge.

SLOANE *sits on the settee.*

That's a lovely shade of blue on your woolly. I'll fetch you one down later that I knitted for my brother.

KEMP *enters.*

(*loudly*). We have a visitor, Dadda.
KEMP. Eh?
KATH. A visitor.
KEMP (*stares, lifts his glasses and stares again*). Oh . . . It's Eddie?
KATH. You are the limit. You show me up no end. It isn't Ed. (*Pause.*) You behave like a sick child. I'm just about tired of it. Afraid to have a guest or a friend in the house. You put them off, Dadda. Let him shake your hand. Go on.

KEMP *shakes* SLOANE's *hand.*

KEMP. What's he want, then?

KATH. Mr Sloane is going to stay with us.

KEMP. Stay with us?

KATH. That's what I said.

KEMP. He can't. We've no room.

KATH. Make an effort will you? What will the gentleman think? He'll think you're a rude old man. (*Exchanges looks with* SLOANE.) I'm going to have to apologize for your boorish attitude. Do you feel embarrassed, Mr Sloane?

SLOANE. It's all right.

KATH. No, it isn't. (*To* KEMP) Pull yourself together! (*Silence.*) Can I trust you to behave yourself while I get something to eat?

KEMP *does not answer.*

Entertain Mr Sloane now. Give him the benefit of your experience. (*Pause.*) You want to learn manners. That's what you want. (*Picks up a basket of provisions from the floor.*) I'm a good mind to give you no tea. (*To* SLOANE) I'd not care to wonder what you must think of us. (*Takes a packet of crumpets from the basket. Hands it to* KEMP.) Here, toast these. Give yourself something to do. (*Exits.*)

KEMP *goes to fire. Begins to toast crumpets.*

SLOANE. Haven't we met before?

KEMP. Not to my knowledge.

SLOANE. Your face is familiar. Have I seen your photo in the paper? In connexion with some event?

KEMP. No.

SLOANE. Do you pop into the pub at the end of the road?

KEMP. I don't drink.

SLOANE. Are you a churchgoer?

KEMP. Not at the moment. I used to be. In the old days I'd knock up the Vicar at all hours. But then I lost touch.

SLOANE. I've seen you somewhere. I very rarely forget a face.

KEMP. Y've got me confused with another person.

SLOANE. Perhaps.

KEMP. Forget it, son. I'm not seen about much.

SLOANE. (*Pause*). You don't resent my being in the house, do you?

KEMP. Not at all.

SLOANE. I thought you did. Just now.

KEMP. No.

SLOANE. This seems a nice place. Friendly atmosphere. (*Pause.*) How many children have you?

KEMP. Two.

SLOANE. Is your daughter married?

KEMP. She was. Had a terrible time. Kiddy died.

SLOANE. You have a son, don't you?

KEMP. Yes, but we're not on speaking terms.

SLOANE. How long is it?

KEMP. Twenty years.

SLOANE. 'Strewth!

KEMP. You perhaps find that hard to believe?

SLOANE. I do actually. Not speaking for twenty years? That's coming it a bit strong.

KEMP. I may have exchanged a few words.

SLOANE. I can believe that.

KEMP. He was a good boy. Played some amazing games as a youth. Won every goal at football one season. Sport mad, he was. (*Pause.*) Then one day, shortly after his seventeenth birthday, I had cause to return home unexpected and found him committing some kind of felony in the bedroom.

SLOANE. Is that straight?

KEMP. I could never forgive him.

SLOANE. A puritan, are you?

KEMP. Yes.

SLOANE. That kind of thing happens often, I believe. For myself, I usually lock the door.

KEMP. I'd removed the lock.

SLOANE. Anticipating some such tendencies on his part?

KEMP. I'd done it as a precautionary measure.

SLOANE. There are fascinating possibilities in this situation. I'd get it down on paper if I were you. (*Goes to the window.*)

KEMP. Admiring the view?

SLOANE. A perfect skyline you've got here. Lord Snowdon would give you something for a shot of that. Stunning it is. Stunning. Was this house a speculation?

KEMP. Not exactly.

SLOANE. Who built it then? Was he a mad financier? The bloke who conceived the idea of building a house in the midst of a rubbish dump?

KEMP. It was intended to be the first of a row.

SLOANE. Go on. What happened?

KEMP. They gave up.

SLOANE. Lost interest?

KEMP. There were financial restrictions.

SLOANE. What a way to carry on!

KEMP. We've tried putting in complaints, but it's no good. Look at it out there. An eyesore. You may admire it. I don't. A woman came all the way from Woolwich yesterday. A special trip she made in order to dump a bedstead. I told her, what do you want to saddle us with your filthy mess for? Came over in a shooting-brake. She was an old woman. Had her daughter with her. Fouling the countryside with their litter.

SLOANE. What you want is someone with pull on the council.

KEMP. If my boss were here I'd go to him.

SLOANE. Wealthy, was he?

KEMP. He had holdings in some trust. He didn't go into details with me.

SLOANE. How old was he?

KEMP. Forty.

SLOANE. Early middle-age?

KEMP. Yes.

SLOANE. Dead, is he?

KEMP. Yes.

SLOANE. Did he die for his country?

KEMP. No. He was murdered. On the unsolved crimes list, he is.

SLOANE. A murderer not brought to justice. That's a sobering thought. (*Pause.*) Why can't they find the murderer? Didn't they advertise?

KEMP. Yes. They took a piece in the local paper.

SLOANE. How long ago was all this?

KEMP. Two years.

SLOANE. Do they have any clue to the murderer's identity?

KEMP. He was a young man with very smooth skin.

SLOANE (*pause*). Was your boss a small man?

KEMP. Yes. Wavy hair. Wore a tweed tie.

SLOANE. What was his profession?

KEMP. He was a photographer. Specialized in views of the river.

SLOANE. You were employed in his service?

KEMP. Yes. As a general handyman. (*Pause.*) We gave the murderer a lift on the night of the crime.

SLOANE (*pause*). You saw him then?

KEMP. Yes.

SLOANE. Why didn't you go to the police?

KEMP. I can't get involved in that type of case. I might get my name in the papers.

SLOANE. I see your point of view. (*Pause.*) They won't find the killer now.

KEMP. I should very much doubt it.

SLOANE. No, the scent's gone cold.

He watches KEMP *in silence.*

Have you ever toasted a crumpet before?

KEMP. Yes.

SLOANE. I thought it was your first time from the way you're messing that about.

KEMP *does not reply.*

KEMP (*pause*). Come here.

SLOANE. Why?

KEMP. I want to look at you.

SLOANE. What for?

KEMP. I think we have met before.

SLOANE. No, Pop. I'm convinced we haven't. I must have been getting you mixed up with a man called Fergusson. He had the same kind of way with him. Trustworthy.

KEMP. You think that?

SLOANE. Yes (*Laughs.*)

KEMP (*pause*). Fetch me a plate, will you?

SLOANE. Where from?

KEMP. The dresser. Back there.

> SLOANE *goes to the dresser. Fetches a plate. Comes to* KEMP, *bends down to give him the plate.* KEMP *seizes* SLOANE'S *arm, pulls him towards him.*

SLOANE. What's this!

KEMP. We have met before! I knew we had.

SLOANE. I've never met you.

KEMP. On my life. I remember.

SLOANE. Your eyes aren't good.

KEMP. I could still identify you.

SLOANE (*pause*). Identify me?

KEMP. If it was necessary.

SLOANE. How could it be necessary?

KEMP. It might be.

SLOANE. Do lay off, Pop. You couldn't identify a herring on a plate!

KEMP. Don't speak to me like that, sonny. You'll find yourself in trouble.

SLOANE. Go on, you superannuated old prat!

KEMP. I'll have somebody to you. See if I don't.

> SLOANE *turns away.*

SLOANE. Why don't you shut your mouth and give your arse a chance?

KEMP *lunges at* SLOANE *with the toasting fork.* SLOANE *gives a squeal of pain.*

SLOANE. Oh, you bleeding maniac! My leg. My leg.

KEMP. You provoked me!

SLOANE (*sinks into an armchair*). I'll be in a wheelchair for life. (*Examines his leg.*) Oh, you cow. I'm covered in blood! Call somebody!

KEMP (*goes to the door, shouting*). Kathy! Kathy!

KATH. (*runs on, drying her hands on her apron, sees* SLOANE, *screams*). What've you done?

KEMP. It wasn't intentional. (*Comes forward.*)

KATH (*shoos him away*). Is there pain?

SLOANE. I can't move.

KATH. Are you hurt bad?

SLOANE. He's got an artery. I must be losing pints. Oh, Christ!

KATH. Come on. You'll be better on the settee. (*He allows her to guide him over. She settles him.*) What happened? Did he attack you? He's never shown signs before.

KEMP. I thought he was further off. I can't judge distances.

KATH. Let Mr Sloane speak for himself.

SLOANE. He ought to be in Colney Hatch. He's a slate off. Throwing things about.

KATH. Throw them, did he?

SLOANE. I don't know what he did.

KATH. I'm ashamed of you, Dadda. Really ashamed. I think you behave very badly. Lie down, Mr Sloane. (*To* KEMP.) Go and get the Dettol and some water. Make yourself useful.

    KEMP *shuffles off.*

I never realized he was antagonistic to you, Mr Sloane. Perhaps he's jealous. We were getting on so well. (*Pause.*) Is it hurting you?

SLOANE. Can you get a bandage?

KATH. I will. (*Goes to the sideboard and rummages in a drawer. Rummages again. Repeat. Second drawer. Takes out and places on top of the sideboard a Boots folder containing snapshots and negatives, a reel of cotton, a piece of unfinished knitting, a tattered knitting pattern, a broken china figure, a magazine, a doorknob and several pieces of silk.*)

SLOANE (*calling impatiently*). There's blood running on your settee. You'll have a stain, I can see it coming.

KATH (*runs back with a piece of silk. Lifts his leg. Spreads the silk under the bloody patch*). This'll do. It's a piece of material my brother brought back. It's good stuff. I was intending to make a blouse but there's not enough.

SLOANE. What's he doing with that Dettol? Is he gone to Swansea for it?

KATH (*shouting*). What are you doing, Dadda? He gets that thick. (*Goes to sideboard.*)

KEMP *enters with a bottle of Dettol.*

KATH (*takes it from him*). You done enough damage for one day. Make yourself scarce.

He shuffles off.

And don't be eating anything out there. (*Pushes past him. Returns with a saucepan full of water. After hunting in sideboard finds a torn towel. Comes to* SLOANE. *Kneels.*) What a lovely pair of shoes you got. (*Unlacing his shoes she takes them off and places them under the settee.*)

SLOANE. I think I'm going to spew.

KATH *hastily holds the saucepan under him.*

No. I'll be all right.

KATH. I wonder, Mr Sloane, if you'd take your trousers off? I hope you don't think there's anything behind the request. (*Looks at him.*)

He unloosens his belt.

I expect you guessed as much before I asked. If you'll lift up I'll pull them off. (*Tugs the trousers free.*)

SLOANE *tucks the tail of his shirt between his legs.*

KATH. That's right. (*Pause.*) Where is it then?

SLOANE. Here. (*Pointing and lifting his leg.*)

KATH. He attacked you from behind? If you ask me it's only a deep scratch. (*Pause.*) I don't think we'll require outside assistance. (*Pause.*) Don't be embarrassed, Mr Sloane. I'd the upbringing a nun would envy and that's the truth. Until I was fifteen I was more familiar with Africa than my own body. That's why I'm so pliable. (*Applies Dettol.*)

SLOANE. Ouch!

KATH. Just the thing for the germs. (*Pause.*) You've a skin on you like a princess. Better than on those tarts you see dancing about on the telly. I like a lad with a smooth body. (*Stops dabbing his leg. Takes up the bandage. Rises. Fetches a pair of scissors. Cuts bandage. Ties it round* SLOANE's *leg.*) Isn't it strange that the hairs on your legs should be dark?

SLOANE. Eh?

KATH. Attractive, though.

SLOANE. Dark?

KATH. Yes. You being a blond.

SLOANE. Oh, yes.

KATH. Nature's a funny thing.

Ring on the doorbell.

SLOANE. Who's that?

KATH. Keep your voice down. (*Pause.*) It's probably her from the shops. I'll not answer it. She's only got one subject for talk.

SLOANE. She'll hear.

KATH. Not if you keep your voice down.

Prolonged ringing.

SLOANE. What about Pop?

KATH. He won't answer. I don't want her in here. She tells everybody her business. And if she found me in this predicament she'd think all kinds of things. (*Pause.*) Her daughter's involved in a court case at the moment. Tells every detail. The details are endless. I suffer as she recounts. Oh, Mr Sloane, if only I'd been born without ears. (*Silence. Finishes tying the bandage and squats on her haunches looking up at him. Pause.*) Is that bandage too tight?

SLOANE. No.

KATH. I wouldn't want to restrict your circulation.

SLOANE. It's O.K.

She picks up his trousers.

KATH. I'll sponge these, and there's a nick in the material. I'll fix it. (*Puts Dettol, bandage, etc, into the sideboard.*) This drawer is my medicine cabinet, dear. If you wants an occasional aspirin help yourself. (*She comes back.*)

He lies full length; she smiles. Silence.

KATH (*confidentially*). I've been doing my washing today and I haven't a stitch on ... except my shoes ... I'm in the rude under this dress. I tell you because you're bound to have noticed ...

Silence. SLOANE *attempts to reach his trouser pocket.*

Don't move, dear. Not yet. Give the blood time to steady itself.

SLOANE *takes the nylon stocking from between cushions of settee.*

I wondered where I'd left it.

SLOANE. Is it yours?

KATH. Yes. You'll notice the length? I've got long legs. Long, elegant legs. (*Kicks out her leg.*) I could give one or two of them a surprise. (*Pause.*) My look is quite different when I'm in private. (*Leans over him.*) You can't see through this dress can you? I been worried for fear of embarrassing you.

SLOANE *lifts his hand and touches the point where he judges her nipple to be.*

KATH (*leaps back*). Mr Sloane – don't betray your trust.

SLOANE. I just thought –

KATH. I know what you thought. You wanted to see if my titties were all my own. You're all the same. (*Smirks.*) I must be careful of you. Have me naked on the floor if I give you a chance. If my brother was to know . . . (*Pause.*) . . . he's such a possessive man. (*Silence. Stands up.*) Would you like to go to bed?

SLOANE. It's early.

KATH. You need rest. You've had a shock. (*Pause.*) I'll bring your supper to your room.

SLOANE. What about my case?

KATH. The Dadda will fetch it. (*Pause.*) Can you get up the stairs on your own?

SLOANE. Mmmm.

KATH (*motions him back. Stands in front of him*). Just a minute. (*Calls.*) Dadda! (*Pause.*) Dadda!

> KEMP *appears in the doorway.*

KEMP. What?

KATH. Turn your face away. Mr Sloane is passing. He has no trousers on. (*Quietly to Sloane.*) You know the room?

SLOANE. Yes.

> *Silence.* SLOANE *exits.*

KATH (*calling after him*). Have a bath if you want to, dear. Treat the conveniences as if they were your own. (*Turns to* KEMP.) I want an explanation.

KEMP. Yes. Kathy . . .

KATH. Don't Kathy me.

KEMP. But he upset me.

KATH. Upset you? A grown man?

KEMP. I've seen him before.

KATH. You've seen the milkman before. That's no cause to throw the shears at him.

KEMP. I didn't throw them.

KATH. Oh? I heard different. (*Picks up her handbag and takes out money.*) Go and fetch his case. It'll be about five pence on the bus.
(*Presses the money into his hand.*) The address is 39 St Hilary's Crescent.

KEMP. Where's that?

KATH (*losing her temper*). By the Co-op! Behave yourself.

KEMP. A teetotal club on the corner is there?

KATH. That's the one. Only it is closed. (*Pause.*) Can you find it?

KEMP. I expect so.

> There is a noise of tapping.

KATH (*goes to the window. Over her shoulder*). It's Eddie.

KEMP. What's that?

KATH (*speaking to someone outside*). Why don't you come round the right way?

ED (*outside the window*). I rung the bell but you was out.

KATH. Are you coming in?

ED. I'll be round. (*Closes the window.*)

KATH. It's Eddie.

KEMP. I'm not going to talk to him!

KATH. I don't expect he wants you to.

KEMP. He knows I'm in always on Friday. (*Pause.*) I'm signing nothing you can tell him that.

KATH. Tell him what?

KEMP. That I'm not signing nothing.

ED (*entering*). Is he still on? What's the matter with you?

> KEMP *does not reply.*

Always on about something.

KEMP. I'm not speaking to him.

ED (*patiently*). Go on, get out of it afore I kicks you out. Make me bad you do. With your silly, childish ways.

> KEMP *does not reply.*

KATH. Do what I told you, Dadda. Try not to lose yourself. Follow the railings. Then ask somebody.

> KEMP *exits.*
> KATH *dips towel in saucepan, begins to sponge bloody patch on settee.*

ED (*watches her. Takes a drag of his cigarette*). What's this I heard about you?

KATH. What?

ED. Listening are you?

KATH. Yes, Eddie, I'm listening.

ED. You've got a kid staying here.

KATH. No . . .

ED. Don't lie to me.

KATH. He's a guest. He's not a lodger.

ED. Who told you to take in lodgers?

> *Pause.*

KATH. I needed a bit extra.

ED. I'll give you the money.

KATH. I'm taking Dadda away next year.

> *Pause.*

ED. I don't want men hanging around.

KATH. He's a nice young man.

ED. You know what these fellows are – young men with no fixed abode.

KATH. No.

ED. You know what they say about landladies?

KATH. No, Eddie.

ED. They say they'd sleep with a broom handle in trousers, that's what they say.

KATH (*uneasy*). I'm not like that.

ED. You're good-natured though. They mistake it.

KATH. This young man is quite respectable.

ED. You've got to realize my position. I can't have my sister keeping a common kip. Some of my associates are men of distinction. They think nothing of tipping a fiver. That sort of person. If they realized how my family carry on I'd be banned from the best places. (*Pause.*) And another thing . . . you don't want them talking about you. An' I can't guarantee my influence will keep them quiet. Nosy neighbours and scandal. Oh, my word, the looks you'll get. (*Pause.*) How old is he?

KATH. He's young.

ED. These fellows sleep with their landladies automatic. Has he made suggestions? Suggested you bring him supper in bed?

KATH. No.

ED. That's what they do. Then they take advantage.

KATH. Mr Sloane is superior to that.

ED. Where did you find him?

KATH. In the library.

ED. Picked him up, did you?

KATH. He was having trouble. With his rent. (*Pause.*) His landlady was unscrupulous.

ED. How long have you been going with him?

KATH. He's a good boy.

ED *sees trousers, picks them up.*

KATH. It was an accident.

ED. Had the trousers off him already I see. (*Balls his fist and punches her upper arm gently.*) Don't let me down, darlin'. (*Pause.*) Where is he?

KATH. Upstairs.

ED. You fetch him.

KATH. He hurt his leg.

ED. I want to see him.

KATH. He's resting. (*Pause.*) Ed, you won't tell him to go?

ED (*brushing her aside*). Go and fetch him.

KATH. I'm not misbehaving. Ed, if you send him away I shall cry.

ED (*raising his voice*). Let's have less of it. I'll decide.

She exits.

ED (*calls after her*). Tell him to put his trousers on. (*Picks up the trousers and flings them after her.*) Cantering around the house with a bare bum. Good job I come when I did. (*Pause.*) Can't leave you alone for five minutes.

KATH (*off*). Mr Sloane! Would you step down here for a minute? My brother would like to meet you. (*Re-enters.*) He's trustworthy. Visits his parents once a month. Asked me to go with him. You couldn't object to a visit to a graveyard? The sight of the tombs would deter any looseness. (*Sniffs. Shrugs. Picks through the junk on the sideboard, finds a sweet and puts it in her mouth.*) He hasn't any mamma of his own. I'm to be his mamma. He's an orphan. Eddie, he wouldn't do wrong. Please don't send him away.

ED. It'd crease me if you misbehaved again. I got responsibilities.

KATH. Let him stay.

ED. Kid like that. Know what they'll say, don't you?

Pause.

KATH. He's cultured, Ed. He's informed.

ED *turns and lights another cigarette from the butt of the one he is smoking. Opens the window. Throws the butt out.* SLOANE *enters.*

KATH. This is my brother, Mr Sloane. He expressed a desire to meet you.

ED (*turns, faces* SLOANE). I . . . my sister was telling me about you.

Pause.

My sister was telling me about you being an orphan, Mr Sloane.

SLOANE (*smiling*). Oh, yes?

ED. Must be a rotten life for a kid. You look well on it though.

SLOANE. Yes.

ED. I could never get used to sleeping in cubicles. Was it a mixed home?

SLOANE. Just boys.

ED. Ideal. How many to a room?

SLOANE. Eight.

ED. Really? Same age were they? Or older?

SLOANE. The ages varied by a year or two.

ED. Oh well, you had compensations then. Keep you out of mischief, eh? (*Laughs.*) Well your childhood wasn't unhappy?

SLOANE. No.

ED. Sounds as though it was a happy atmosphere. (*Pause.*) Got anything to do, Kath?

KATH. No.

ED. No beds to make?

KATH. I made them this morning.

ED. Maybe you forgot to change the pillowslips?

KATH (*going*). Eddie don't let me be upset will you? (*Exits.*)

ED. I must apologize for her behaviour. She's not in the best of health.

SLOANE. She seems all right.

ED. You can't always go on appearances. She's . . . well I wouldn't say unbalanced. No, that'd be going too far. She suffers from migraine. That's why it'd be best if you declined her offer of a room.

SLOANE. I see.

ED. When are you going?

SLOANE. But I like it here.

ED. I dare say you do. The fact is my sister's taking on too many responsibilities. She's a charming woman as a rule. Charming. I've no hesitation in saying that. Lost her husband. And her little kid. Tell you did she?

SLOANE. She mentioned it.

ED (*wary*). What did she say?

SLOANE. Said she married young.

ED. She married a mate of mine – a valiant man – we were together in Africa.

SLOANE. In the army?

ED. You're interested in the army, eh? Soldiers, garrison towns, etc. Does that interest you?

SLOANE. Yes.

ED. Good, excellent. How old are you?

SLOANE. Twenty.

ED. Married?

SLOANE. No.

ED (*laughs*). Wise man, eh? Wise man. (*Pause.*) Girl ends?

SLOANE. No.

ED. No. You're a librarian?

SLOANE. No.

ED. I thought she said –

SLOANE. I help out at Len's ... the tobacconist. Give him a hand. I'm not employed there.

ED. I was told you were.

SLOANE. I help out. On Saturdays.

ED. I see. I've been mistaken. (*Silence.*) Well, as I just said ... I don't think it'd suit you. What with one thing and another. (*Pause.*) To show there's no hard feelings I'll make it worth your while. Call it a gift.

SLOANE. That's decent of you.

ED. Not at all. (*Pause.*) I'd like to give you a little present. Anything you care to name. Within reason.

SLOANE. What's within reason?

ED (*laughs*). Well ... no ... Jags. (*Laughs.*) ... no sports cars. I'm not going as far as that.

SLOANE (*relaxing*). I was going to suggest an Aston Martin.

ED (*walks from the window looking for an ashtray. He does not find one*). I wish I could give you one, boy. I wish I could. (*Stubs out his cigarrette into a glass seashell on the sideboard.*) Are you a sports fan? Eh? Fond of sport? You look as though you might be. Look the ... outdoor type, I'd say.

SLOANE. I am.

ED. I'd say you were. That's what struck me when you walked in. That's what puzzled me. She gave me the impression you were ... well, don't be offended ... I had the notion you were a shop assistant.

SLOANE. Never worked in a shop in my life.

ED. No. (*Pause.*) I see you're not that type. You're more of a ... as you might say ... the fresh air type.

SLOANE. I help out on Saturdays for a mate of mine. Len. You might know him. Lifeguard at the baths one time. Nice chap.

ED. You're fond of swimming?

SLOANE. I like a plunge now and then.

ED. Bodybuilding?

SLOANE. We had a nice little gym at the orphanage. Put me in all the teams they did. Relays ...

> ED *looks interested.*

... soccer ...

> ED *nods.*

... pole vault, ... long distance ...

> ED *opens his mouth.*

... 100 yards, discus, putting the shot.

> ED *rubs his hands together.*

Yes. yes. I'm an all rounder. A great all rounder. In anything you care to mention. Even in life.

> ED *lifts up a warning finger.*

... yes I like a good work out now and then.

ED. I used to do a lot of that at one time. With my mate ... we used to do all what you've just said. (*Pause.*) We were young. Innocent too. (*Shrugs. Pats his pocket. Takes out a packet of cigarettes. Smokes.*) All over now. (*Pause.*) Developing your muscles, eh? And character. (*Pause.*) . . . Well, well, well. (*Breathless.*) A little bodybuilder are you? I bet you are . . . (*Slowly.*) . . . do you . . . (*Shy.*) exercise regular?

SLOANE. As clockwork.

ED. Good, good. Stripped?

SLOANE. Fully.

ED. Complete. (*Striding to the window.*) How invigorating.

SLOANE. And I box. I'm a bit of a boxer.

ED. Ever done any wrestling?

SLOANE. On occasions.

ED. So, so.

SLOANE. I've got a full chest. Narrow hips. My biceps are –

ED. Do you wear leather . . . next to the skin? Leather jeans, say? Without . . . aah . . .

SLOANE. Pants?

ED (*laughs*). Get away! (*Pause.*) The question is are you clean living? You may as well know I set great store by morals. Too much of this casual bunking up nowadays. Too many lads being ruined by birds. I don't want you messing about with my sister.

SLOANE. I wouldn't.

ED. Have you made overtures to her?

SLOANE. No.

ED. Would you?

SLOANE. No.

ED. Not if circumstances were ripe?

SLOANE. Never.

ED. Does she disgust you?

SLOANE. Should she?

ED. It would be better if she did.

SLOANE. I've no interest in her.

Pause.

ED. I've a certain amount of influence. Friends with money. I've two cars. Judge for yourself. I generally spend my holidays in places where the bints have got rings through their noses. (*Pause.*) Women are like banks, boy, breaking and entering is a serious business. Give me your word you're not vaginalatrous?

SLOANE. I'm not.

ED (*pause*). I'll believe you. Can you drive?

SLOANE. Yes.

ED. I might let you be my chauffeur.

SLOANE. Would you?

ED (*laughs*). We'll see . . . I could get you a uniform. Boots, pants, a guaranteed 100 per cent no imitation jacket . . . an . . . er . . . a white brushed nylon T-Shirt . . . with a little leather cap. (*Laughs.*) Like that?

SLOANE *nods. Silence.*

Kip here a bit. Till we get settled. Come and see me. We'll discuss salary arrangements and any other business. Here's my card. (*Gives* SLOANE *a card.*) Have you seen my old dad?

SLOANE. I spoke to him.

ED. Wonderful for his age. (*Pause.*) Call her in will you?

SLOANE *exits.*

SLOANE (*off*). I think you're wanted. (*Re-enters.*)

ED. You'll find me a nice employer. (*Pause.*) When you come to see me we must have a drink. A talk.

SLOANE. What about?

ED. Life. Sport. Love. Anything you care to name. Don't forget.

SLOANE. I'm looking forward to it.

ED. Do you drink?

SLOANE. When I'm not in training.

ED. You aren't in training at the moment, are you?

SLOANE. No.

ED. I wouldn't want you to break your training. Drinking I don't mind. Drugs I abhor. You'll get to know all my habits.

KATH *enters,*

KATH. What you want?

ED. A word with you afore I go.

KATH. Are you staying, Mr Sloane?

ED. 'Course he's staying.

KATH. All right is it?

ED. He's going to work for me.

KATH (*pause*). He isn't going away is he?

ED. Offered him a job I have. I want a word with my sister, Sloane. Would you excuse us?

SLOANE *nods, smiles, and turns to go.*

KATH (*as he exits*). Have a meal, Mr Sloane. You'll find a quarter of boiled ham. Help yourself. You better have what's left 'cause I see he's been wolfing it. An' you heard me ask him to wait, di'n't you? I told him.

Exit SLOANE. *Silence.*

ED. You picked a nice lad there. Very nice. Clean. No doubt upright. A sports enthusiast. All the proper requisites. Don't take any money from him. I'll pay.

KATH. Can I buy him a shirt?

ED. What do you want to do that for?

KATH. His own mamma can't.

ED. He can buy his own clothes. Making yourself look ridiculous.

Pause.

KATH. When it's Christmas can I buy him a little gift?

ED. No.

KATH. Send him a card?

ED. Why?

KATH. I'd like to. I'd show you beforehand. (*Pause.*) Can I go to his mamma's grave?

ED. If you want. (*Pause.*) He'll laugh at you.

KATH. He wouldn't, Eddie.

Silence.

ED. I must go. I'll have a light meal. Take a couple of nembutal and then bed. I shall be out of town tomorrow.

KATH. Where?

ED. In Aylesbury. I shall dress in a quiet suit. Drive up in the motor. The Commissionaire will spring forward. There in that miracle of glass and concrete my colleagues and me will have a quiet drink before the business of the day.

KATH. Are your friends nice?

ED. Mature men.

KATH. No ladies?

Pause.

ED. What are you talking about? I live in a world of top decisions. We've no time for ladies.

KATH. Ladies are nice at a gathering.

ED. We don't want a lot of half-witted tarts.

KATH. They add colour and gaiety.

ED. Frightening everyone with their clothes.

Pause.

KATH. I hope you have a nice time. Perhaps one day you'll invite me to your hotel.

ED. I might.

KATH. Show me round.

ED. Yes.

KATH. Is it exquisitely furnished? High up?

ED. Very high. I see the river often.

A door slams.

Persuade the old man to speak to me.

KEMP (*off*). Is he gone?

KATH. Speak to him Dadda. He's something to ask you.

Silence.

ED (*petulant*). Isn't it incredible? I'm his only son. He won't see me. (*Goes to the door. Speaks through.*) I want a word with you.

(*Pause.*) Is he without human feelings? (*Pause. Brokenly.*) He won't speak to me. Has he no heart?

KATH. Come again.

ED. I'll get my lawyer to send a letter. If it's done legal he'll prove amenable. Give us a kiss. (*Kisses her. Pats her bottom.*) Be a good girl now. (*Exit.*)

KATH. Cheerio. (*Pause.*) I said Cheerio.

Door slams.

KATH (*goes to door*). Why don't you speak to him?

KEMP *enters. He does not reply.*

He invited me to his suite. The luxury takes your breath away. Money is no object. A waitress comes with the tea. (*Pause.*) I'm going to see him there one day. Speak to him Dadda.

KEMP. No.

KATH. Please.

KEMP. Never

KATH. Let me phone saying you changed your mind.

KEMP. No

KATH. Let me phone.

KEMP. No.

KATH (*tearfully*). Oh, Dadda, you are unfair. If you don't speak to him he won't invite me to his suite. It's a condition. I won't be able to go. You found that address?

KEMP. I got lost, though.

KATH. Why didn't you ask? (*Pause.*) You had a tongue in your head. Oh, Dadda, you make me so angry with your silly ways. (*Pause.*) What was the house like?

KEMP. I didn't notice.

KATH. He said it was a hovel. A boy like him shouldn't be expected to live with the rougher elements. Do you know, Dadda, he has skin the like of which I never felt before. And he confesses to being an orphan. His story is so sad. I wept when I heard it. You know how soft-hearted I am.

Silence.

KEMP. I haven't been feeling well lately.

KATH. Have you seen the optician?

KEMP. My eyes are getting much worse.

KATH. Without a word of a lie you are like a little child.

KEMP. I'm all alone.

KATH. You have me.

KEMP. He may take you away.

KATH. Where to?

KEMP. Edinburgh.

KATH. Too cold.

KEMP. Or Bournemouth. You always said you'd go somewhere with palms.

KATH. I'd always consult you first.

KEMP. You'd put me in a home. (*Pause.*) Would you be tempted?

Silence.

KATH. You ought to consult an oculist. See your oculist at once. (*Pause.*) Go to bed. I'll bring you a drinkie. In the morning you'll feel different.

KEMP. You don't love me.

KATH. I've never stopped loving you.

KEMP. I'm going to die, Kath . . . I'm dying.

KATH (*angrily*). You've been at that ham haven't you? Half a jar of pickles you've put away. Don't moan to me if you're up half the night with the tummy ache. I've got no sympathy for you.

KEMP. Goodnight then.

KATH (*watches him out of the door. Looks through into the kitchen*). All right, Mr Sloane? Help yourself . . . all right? (*Comes back into the room. Takes lamp from sideboard and puts it on to table beside settee. Goes to record player, puts on record. Pulls curtains across alcove and disappears behind them. The stage is empty. The record plays for a few seconds and then the needle jumps a groove, slides across record. Automatic change switches record off.* KATH *pokes her head from behind curtain, looks at record player, disappears again. Re-appears wearing a transparent négligé. Picks up aerosol spray, sprays room. Calls through door).* Have you finished, Mr Sloane, dear?

SLOANE (*off*). Ugh?

KATH. You have? I'm so glad. I don't want to disturb you at your food. (*Sees knitting on sideboard, picks it up.*) Come into the lounge if you wish. I'm just at a quiet bit of knitting before I go to bed.

SLOANE *enters wiping his mouth.*

A lovely piece of ham, wasn't it?

SLOANE. Lovely.

KATH. I'll give you a splendid breakfast in the morning. (*Realizes that there is only one needle in the knitting. Searches in the junk and finds the other. Takes it to the settee.* SLOANE *sits on one end.*) (*Pause.*) Isn't this room gorgeous?

SLOANE. Yes.

KATH. That vase over there come from Bombay. Do you have any interest in that part of the world?

SLOANE. I like Dieppe.

KATH. Ah . . . it's all the same. I don't suppose they know the difference themselves. Are you comfortable? Let me plump your cushion. (*Plumps a cushion behind his head. Laughs lightly.*) I really by rights should ask you to change places. This light is showing me up. (*Pause.*) I blame it on the manufacturers. They make garments so thin nowadays you'd think they intended to provoke a rape.

Pause.

Sure you're comfy? (*Leans over him.*)

SLOANE *pulls her hand towards him. She laughs, half in panic.*

SLOANE. You're a teaser ent you?

KATH (*breaks away*). I hope I'm not. I was trying to find the letter from my little boy's father. I treasure it. But I seem to have mislaid it. I found a lot of photos though.

SLOANE. Yes.

KATH. Are you interested in looking through them? (*Brings the snapshots over.*)

SLOANE. Are they him?

KATH. My lover.

SLOANE. Bit blurred.

KATH. It brings back memories. He reminds me of you. (*Pause.*) He too was handsome and in the prime of manhood. Can you wonder I fell. (*Pause.*) I wish he were here now to love and protect me. (*Leans her arm on his shoulder. Shows him another snap.*) This is me. I was younger then.

SLOANE. Smart.

KATH. Yes my hair was nice.

SLOANE. Yes.

KATH. An' this . . . I don't know whether I ought to let you see it.

    SLOANE *attempts to seize it.*

Now then!

    He takes it from her.

SLOANE. A seat in a wood?

KATH. That seat is erected to the memory of Mrs Gwen Lewis. She was a lady who took a lot of trouble with invalids. (*Pause.*) It was near that seat that my baby was thought of.

SLOANE. On that seat?

KATH (*shyly*). Not on it exactly. Nearby . . .

SLOANE. In the bushes? . . .

    She giggles.

KATH. Yes. (*Pause.*) He was rough with me.

SLOANE. Uncomfortable, eh?

KATH. I couldn't describe my feelings. (*Pause.*) I don't think the fastening on this thing I'm wearing will last much longer. (*The snapshots slip from her hand.*) There! you've knocked the photos on the floor.

(*Pause: he attempts to move; she is almost on top of him.*) Mr Sloane . . . (*Rolls on to him.*) You should wear more clothes, Mr Sloane. I believe you're as naked as me. And there's no excuse for it. (*Silence.*) I'll be your mamma. I need to be loved. Gently. Oh! I shall be so ashamed in the morning. (*Switches off the light.*) What a big heavy baby you are. Such a big heavy baby.

CURTAIN

Act Two

Some months later. Morning.

> SLOANE *is lying on the settee wearing boots, leather trousers and a white T-shirt. A newspaper covers his face.* KATH *enters. Looks at the settee.*

SLOANE. Where you been?

KATH. Shopping, dear. Did you want me?

SLOANE. I couldn't find you.

KATH (*goes to the window. Takes off her headscarf*). What's Eddie doing?

SLOANE. A bit of serviceing.

KATH. But that's your job.

> SLOANE *removes the newspaper.*

He shouldn't do your work.

SLOANE. I was on the beer. My guts is playing up.

KATH. Poor boy. (*Pause.*) Go and help him. For mamma's sake.

SLOANE. I may go in a bit.

KATH. He's a good employer. Studies your interests. You want to think of his position. He's proud of it. Now you're working for him his position is your position. (*Pause.*) Go and give him a hand.

SLOANE. No.

KATH. Are you too tired?

SLOANE. Yes.

KATH. We must make allowances for you. You're young. (*Pause.*) You're not taking advantage are you?

SLOANE. No.

KATH: I know you aren't. When you've had a drinkie go and help him.

SLOANE. If you want.

Pause.

KATH. Did mamma hear you were on the razzle?

SLOANE. Yes.

KATH. Did you go up West? You were late coming home. (*Pause.*) Very late.

SLOANE. Three of my mates and me had a night out.

KATH. Are they nice boys?

SLOANE. We have interests in common.

KATH. They aren't roughs are they? Mamma doesn't like you associating with them.

SLOANE. Not on your life. They're gentle. Refined youths. Thorpe, Beck and Doolan. We toured the nighteries in the motor.

KATH. Was Ed with you?

SLOANE. No.

KATH. Did you ask him? He would have come.

SLOANE. He was tired. A hard day yesterday.

KATH. Ask him next time.

Pause.

SLOANE. We ended up at a fabulous place. Soft music, pink shades, lovely atmosphere.

KATH. I hope you behaved yourself.

SLOANE. One of the hostesses gave me her number. Told me to ring her.

KATH. Take no notice of her. She might not be nice.

SLOANE. Not nice?

KATH. She might be a party girl.

Pause.

SLOANE. What exactly do you mean?

KATH. Mamma worries for you.

SLOANE. You're attempting to run my life.

KATH. Is baby cross?

SLOANE. You're developing distinctly possessive tendencies.

KATH. You can get into trouble saying that.

SLOANE. A possessive woman.

KATH. A mamma can't be possessive.

SLOANE. Can't she?

KATH. You know she can't. You're being naughty.

SLOANE. Never heard of a possessive mum?

KATH. Stop it. It's rude. Did she teach you to say that?

SLOANE. What?

KATH. What you just said.

> SLOANE *makes no reply.*

You're spoiling yourself in my eyes, Mr Sloane. You won't ring this girl will you?

SLOANE. I haven't decided.

KATH. Decide now. To please me. I don't know what you see in these girls. You have your friends for company.

SLOANE. They're boys.

KATH. What's wrong with them? You can talk freely. Not like with a lady.

SLOANE. I don't want to talk.

> *Pause.*

KATH. She might be after your money.

SLOANE. I haven't got any.

KATH. But Eddie has. She might be after his.

SLOANE. Look, you're speaking of a very good class bird.

KATH. I have to protect you, baby, because you're easily led.

SLOANE. I like being led. (*Pause.*) I need to be let out occasionally. Off the lead.

> *Pause.*

KATH. She'll make you ill.

SLOANE. Shut it. (*Pause.*) Make me ill!

KATH. Girls do.

SLOANE. How dare you. Making filthy insinuations. I won't have it. You disgust me you do. Standing there without your teeth. Why don't you get smartened up? Get a new rig-out.

Pause.

KATH. Do I disgust you?

SLOANE. Yes.

KATH. Honest?

SLOANE. And truly. You horrify me. (*Pause.*) You think I'm kidding. I'll give up my room if you don't watch out.

KATH. Oh, no!

SLOANE. Clear out.

KATH. Don't think of such drastic action. I'd never forgive myself if I drove you away. (*Pause.*) I won't any more.

He attempts to rise.

KATH (*takes his hand*). Don't go, dear. Stay with me while I collect myself. I've been upset and I need comfort. (*Silence.*) Are you still disgusted?

SLOANE. A bit.

KATH (*takes his hand, presses it to her lips*). Sorry baby. Better?

SLOANE. Mmmm.

Silence.

KATH. How good you are to me.

KEMP *enters. He carries a stick. Taps his way to the sideboard.*

My teeth, since you mentioned the subject, Mr Sloane, are in the kitchen in Stergene. Usually I allow a good soak overnight. But what with one thing and another I forgot. Otherwise I would never be in such a state. (*Pause.*) I hate people who are careless with their dentures.

KEMP *opens a drawer.*

KEMP. Seen my tablets?

KATH. If you're bad go to bed.

KEMP. I need one o' my pills.

He picks his way through the junk.

SLOANE (*goes over to him*). What you want?

KEMP. Let me alone.

SLOANE. Tell me what you want.

KEMP. I don't want no help. (*Pause.*) I'm managing.

SLOANE. Let me know what you want and I'll look for it.

KEMP. I can manage.

SLOANE *goes back to the settee. Silence.*

KATH. What a lot of foreigners there are about lately. I see one today. Playing the accordion. They live in a world of their own these people.

KEMP. Coloured?

KATH. No.

KEMP. I expect he was. They do come over here. Raping people. It's a problem. Just come out o' jail had he?

KATH. I really didn't stop long enough to ask. I just commented on the tune he was playing.

KEMP. Oh, they're all for that.

KATH (*leans over* SLOANE). Mamma has something special to say to you.

KEMP. All for that.

SLOANE (*touches her hair*). What?

KATH (*to* KEMP, *louder*). I don't think he was dark enough to be coloured, Dadda. Honestly I don't.

KEMP. They should send them back.

SLOANE. What's your news?

KATH. Can't you guess.

SLOANE. No.

KATH. I know you can't.

KEMP. You should've put in a complaint.

KATH. Oh, no Dadda.

KEMP. Playing his bloody music in the street.

KATH. What language! You should be a splendid example to us. Instead of which you carry on like a common workman. Don't swear like that in my presence again.

   Silence. SLOANE *attempts to grab her shopping bag. She rises,* SLOANE *touches her up. She grunts. Smacks his hand.*

KEMP. What's up?

KATH. Nothing. Aren't the tulips glorious this year by the municipal offices. What a brave showing. They must spend a fortune.

SLOANE. What have you bought me?

KATH. Mamma is going to have a . . . (*Makes a rocking motion with her arms.*)

SLOANE. What? (*Pause.*) What?

KATH. A little – (*Looks over to* KEMP. *Makes the motion of rocking a baby in her arms. Purses her lips. Blows a kiss.*)

   SLOANE *sits up. Points to himself.*

KATH (*nods her head. Presses her mouth to his ear : whispers*). A baby brother.

KEMP. What are you having?

KATH. A . . . bath, Dadda. You know that woman from the shops? (*Pause.*) You wouldn't believe what a ridiculous spectacle she's making of herself.

KEMP. Oh.

KATH (*to* SLOANE). 'Course it's ever so dangerous at my age. But doctor thinks it'll be all right.

SLOANE. Sure.

KATH. I was worried in case you'd be cross.

SLOANE. We mustn't let anyone know.

KATH. It's our secret. (*Pause.*) I'm excited.

KEMP. Are you having it after tea, Kath?

KATH. Why?

KEMP. I thought of having one as well. Are you there?

KATH. Yes.

KEMP. Have you seen them pills?

KATH. Have I seen his pills. They're where you left them I expect. (*Goes to the sideboard. Finds bottle. Gives it to* KEMP.) How many you had today?

KEMP. Two.

KATH. They're not meant to be eaten like sweets you know.

He exits.

I been to the Register Office.

SLOANE. What for?

KATH. To inquire about the licence.

SLOANE. Who?

KATH. You

SLOANE. Who to?

KATH. Me. Don't you want to? You wouldn't abandon me? Leave me to face the music.

SLOANE. What music?

KATH. When Eddie hears.

SLOANE. He mustn't hear.

KATH. Baby, how can we stop him?

SLOANE. He'd kill me. I'd be out of a job.

KATH. I suppose we couldn't rely on him employing you any longer.

SLOANE. Don't say anything. I'll see a man I know.

KATH. What? But I'm looking forward to having a new little brother.

SLOANE. Out of the question.

KATH. Please . . .

SLOANE. No. In any case I couldn't marry you. I'm not the type. And all things being equal I may not be living here much longer.

KATH. Aren't you comfy in your bed?

SLOANE. Yes.

KATH (*folds her arms round him. Kisses his head*). We could marry in secret. Couldn't you give me something, baby? So's I feel in my mind we were married?

SLOANE. What like?

KATH. A ring. Or a bracelet? You got a nice locket. I noticed it. Make me a present of that.

SLOANE. I can't do that.

KATH. As a token of your esteem. So's I feel I belong to you.

SLOANE. It belonged to my mum.

KATH. I'm your mamma now.

SLOANE. No.

KATH. Go on.

SLOANE. But it was left to me.

KATH. You mustn't cling to old memories. I shall begin to think you don't love mamma.

SLOANE. I do.

KATH. Then give me that present. (*Unhooks the chain.*) Ta.

SLOANE. I hate parting with it.

KATH. I'll wear it for ever.

> ED *enters. Stands smoking a cigarette. Turns. Exits. Re-enters with a cardboard box.*

ED. This yours?

KATH (*goes over. Looks in the box*). It's my gnome.

ED. They just delivered it.

KATH. The bad weather damaged him. His little hat come off. I sent him to the Gnomes' Hospital to be repaired.

ED. Damaged, was he?

KATH. Yes.

ED. Well, well. (*Pause.*) It's monkey weather out there.

SLOANE. I wasn't cold.

ED. You're young. Healthy. Don't feel the cold, do you?

SLOANE. No.

ED. Not at all?

SLOANE. Sometimes.

ED. Not often. (*Pause.*) I expect it's all that orange juice.

KATH. Mr Sloane was coming out, Eddie. I assure you.

ED. I know that. I can trust him.

KATH. You've a lovely colour. Let me feel your hand. Why it's freezing. You feel his hand, Mr Sloane.

ED. He doesn't want to feel my hand. (*Pause.*) When you're ready, boy, we'll go.

SLOANE. Check the oil?

ED. Mmn.

SLOANE. Petrol?

ED. Mmn. (*Pause.*) Down, en it?

SLOANE. Down?

ED. From yesterday. We filled her up yesterday.

SLOANE. Did we? Was it yesterday?

ED. Mmn. (*Pause.*) We used a lot since then.

SLOANE. You ought to get yourself a new car. It eats petrol.

Pause.

ED. Maybe you're right. You didn't use it last night, did you?

SLOANE. Me?

ED. I thought you might have.

SLOANE. No.

ED. Funny.

Silence.

KATH. I see a woolly in Boyce's, Mr Sloane. I'm giving it you as a birthday present.

ED. What do you want to do that for?

KATH. Mr Sloane won't mind.

ED. Chucking money about.

KATH. Mr Sloane doesn't mind me. He's one of the family.

ED. Hark at it. Shove up, boy.

SLOANE (*moves*). Sit by me.

ED (*sits next to him*). You didn't use my motor last night then?

SLOANE. No.

ED. That's all I wanted. As long as you're telling the truth, boy.

He takes SLOANE's *hand.*

You've an honest hand. Square. What a grip you got.

SLOANE. I'm improving.

ED. Yes, I can tell that. You've grown bolder since we met. Bigger and bolder. Don't get too bold will you? Eh? (*Laughs.*) I'm going to buy you something for your birthday as well.

SLOANE. Can I rely on it?

ED. Aah.

SLOANE. Will it be expensive?

ED. Very. I might consider lashing out a bit and buying you a . . . um, er, aahhh . . .

SLOANE. Thank you. Thank you.

ED. Don't thank me. Thank yourself. You deserve it.

SLOANE. I think I do.

ED. I think you do. Go and put that box in the kitchen.

KATH. It's no trouble, Eddie.

ED. Let the boy show you politeness.

KATH. But he does. Often. He's often polite to me.

SLOANE *picks up the box and exits.*

KATH. I never complain.

Pause.

ED. Where was he last night?

KATH. He watched the telly. A programme where people guessed each other's names.

ED. What else?

KATH. Nothing else.

EL. He used the car last night.

KATH. No.

Pause.

ED. If he's not careful he can have his cards.

KATH. He's only young.

ED. Joy-riding in my motor.

KATH. He's a good boy.

ED. Act your age. (*Pause.*) Encouraging him. I've watched you. What you want to keep him in here for all morning?

KATH. I didn't want him here. I told him to go and help you.

ED. You did? And he wouldn't?

KATH. No. Yes.

ED. What do you mean?

KATH. I thought it was his rest period, Eddie. You do give him a rest sometimes. I know, 'cause you're a good employer. (*Sits beside him.*)

ED. What do I pay him for?

KATH. To keep him occupied, I suppose.

ED (*makes no reply. At last, irritated*). You're a pest, you are.

KATH. I'm sorry.

ED (*glances at her*). Keeping him in when he ought to be at work. How do you expect him to work well with you messing about?

KATH. He was just coming.

ED. Taking him from his duty. Wasting my money.

KATH. I won't any more.

ED. It's too late. I'll pay him off. Not satisfactory.

KATH. No.

ED. Not the type of person that I had expected.

KATH. He likes his work.

ED. He can go elsewhere.

KATH. He's a great help to me. I shall cry if he goes away. (*Pause.*) I shall have to take a sedative.

ED. I'll find someone else for you.

KATH. No.

ED. An older man. With more maturity.

KATH. I want my baby.

ED. Your what?

KATH. I'm his mamma and he appreciates me. (*Pause.*) He told me.

ED. When? When?

KATH. I can't remember.

ED. He loves you?

KATH. No, I didn't say that. But he calls me mamma. I love him 'cause I have no little boy of my own. And if you send him away I shall cry like the time you took my real baby.

ED. You were wicked then.

KATH. I know.

ED. Being rude. Ruining my little matie. Teaching him nasty things. That's why I sent it away. (*Pause.*) You're not doing rude things with this kiddy, are you, like you did with Tommy?

KATH. No.

ED. Sure?

KATH. I love him like a mamma.

ED. I can't trust you.

KATH. I'm a trustworthy lady.

ED. Allowing him to kip here was a mistake.

Silence.

KATH. I never wanted to do rude things. Tommy made me.

ED. Liar!

KATH. Insisted. Pestered me he did. All summer.

ED. You're a liar.

KATH. Am I?

ED. He didn't want anything to do with you. He told me that.

KATH. You're making it up.

ED. I'm not.

KATH. He loved me.

ED. He didn't.

KATH. He wanted to marry me.

ED. Marry you? You're a ridiculous figure and no mistake.

KATH. He'd have married me only his folks were against it.

ED. I always imagined you were an intelligent woman. I find you're not.

KATH. He said they was.

ED. Did he? When?

KATH. When the stork was coming.

ED (*laughs*). Well, well. Fancy you remembering. You must have a long memory.

KATH. I have.

ED. Let me disillusion you.

KATH. Don't hurt me, Eddie.

ED. You need hurting, you do. Mr and Mrs Albion Bolter were quite ready to have you marry Tommy.

KATH. No they wasn't.

ED. Allow me to know.

KATH (*pause*). He wouldn't have lied, Ed. You're telling stories.

ED. I'm not.

KATH. But he said it was 'cause I was poor. (*Pause.*) I couldn't fit into the social background demanded of him. His duty came between us.

ED. You could have been educated. Gone to beauty salons. Learned to speak well.

KATH. No.

ED. They wanted you to marry him. Tommy and me had our first set-to about it. You should have heard the language he used to me.

KATH. I was loved. How can you say that?

ED. Forget it.

KATH. He sent me the letter I treasure.

ED. I burned it.

> *Pause.*

KATH. It was his last words to me.

ED. And that kiddy out there. I'm not having him go the same way.

> KATH *goes to the window.*

KATH. Did you burn my letter?

ED. Yes. (*Pause.*) And that old photo as well. I thought you was taking an unhealthy interest in the past.

KATH. The photo as well?

ED. You forget it.

KATH. I promised to show it to someone. I wondered why I couldn't find it.

ED. You wicked girl.

KATH. I'm not wicked. I think you're wicked. (*Sniffs without dignity.*)

ED (*lights a cigarette. Looks at her*). While I'm at it I'll get the old man to look at those papers. (*Pause.*) Get my case in, will you?

She does not reply. He stands up. Exits. Returns with briefcase.

I made a mark where he's to sign. On the dotted line. (*Laughs.*) I'll be glad when it's over. To use an expression foreign to my nature – I'll be bloody glad. (*Stares at* KATH *as she continues to cry. Turns away. Pause.*) Quit bawling, will you?

KATH *blows her nose on the edge of her apron.*

You should be like me. You'd have something to cry over then, if you got responsibilities like me. (*Silence.*) Haven't you got a hankie? You don't want the boy to see you like that? (*Silence.*)

SLOANE *enters.*

Put it away, did you?

SLOANE. Yes.

ED. That's a good boy.

Pause.

KATH. Mr Sloane.

SLOANE. What?

KATH. Can *I* call you Boy?

SLOANE. I don't think you'd better.

KATH. Why not?

ED. I'm his employer, see. He knows that you're only his landlady.

SLOANE *smiles.*

KATH. I don't mean in front of strangers. (*Pause.*) I'd be sparing with the use of the name.

ED. No! (*Sharply.*) Haven't you got anything to do? Standing there all day.

KATH *exits.*

Getting fat as a pig, she is.

SLOANE. Is she?

ED. Not noticed?

SLOANE. No.

ED. I have.

SLOANE. How old is she?

ED. Forty-one. (*Shrugs.*) Forty-two. She ought to slim. I'd advise that.

SLOANE. She's . . .

ED. She's like a sow. Though she is my sister.

SLOANE. She's not bad.

ED. No?

SLOANE. I don't think so.

ED *goes to the window. Stands. Lost. Pause.*

ED. Where was you last night?

SLOANE. I told you –

ED. I know what you told me. A pack of lies. D'you think I'm an idiot or something?

SLOANE. No.

ED. I want the truth.

SLOANE. I went for a spin. I had a headache.

ED. Where did you go?

SLOANE. Along the A40.

ED. Who went with you?

SLOANE. Nobody.

ED. Are you being entirely honest?

Pause.

SLOANE. Three mates come with me.

ED. They had headaches too?

SLOANE. I never asked.

ED. Cheeky. (*Pause.*) Who are they? Would I want them in my motor?

SLOANE. You'd recognize Harry Thorpe. Small, clear complexioned, infectious good humour.

ED. I might.

SLOANE. Harry Beck I brought up one night. A Wednesday it was. But Dooloan no. You wouldn't know him.

ED. Riding round in my motor all night, eh?

SLOANE. I'd challenge that.

ED. What type of youth are they?

SLOANE. Impeccable taste. Buy their clothes up West.

ED. Any of them wear lipstick?

SLOANE. Certainly not.

ED. You'd notice, would you? (*Throws over a lipstick.*) What's this doing in the back of the motor?

> *Silence.*

SLOANE (*laughs*). Oh . . . you jogged my memory . . . yes . . . Dooloan's married . . . an' we took his wife along.

ED. Can't you do better than that?

SLOANE. Straight up.

ED (*emotionally*). Oh, boy . . . Taking birds out in my motor.

SLOANE. Would you accept an unconditional apology.

ED. Telling me lies.

SLOANE. It won't happen again.

ED. What are your feelings towards me?

SLOANE. I respect you.

ED. Is that the truth?

SLOANE. Honest.

ED. Then why tell me lies?

SLOANE. That's only your impression.

> *Pause.*

ED. Was this an isolated incident?

SLOANE. This is the first time.

ED. Really.

SLOANE. Yes. Can you believe me?

Pause.

ED. I believe you. I believe you're regretting the incident already.
But don't repeat it. (*Silence.*) Or next time I won't be so lenient.
(*Pause.*) I think the time has come for us to make a change.

SLOANE. In what way?

ED. I need you on tap.

SLOANE. Mmmn ...

Pause.

ED. At all hours. In case I have to make a journey to a distant
place at an unexpected and inconvenient hour of the night. In a
manner of speaking it's urgent.

SLOANE. Of course.

ED. I got work to do. (*Pause.*) I think it would be best if you leave
here today.

SLOANE. It might be.

ED. Give it a trial. (*Pause.*) You see my way of looking at it?

SLOANE. Sure.

ED. And you shouldn't be left with her. She's no good. No good
at all. A crafty tart she is. I could tell you things about – the
way these women carry on. (*Pause.*) Especially her. (*Opens
window. Throws cigarette out.*) These women do you no good. I
can tell you that. (*Feels in his coat pocket. Takes out a packet of
mints. Puts one in his mouth. Pause.*) One of sixteen come up to
me the other day – which is a thing I never expected, come up
to me and said she'd been given my address. I don't know
whether it was a joke or something. You see that sort of
thing ...

SLOANE. Well ...?

ED. You could check it.

SLOANE. I'd be pleased.

ED. Certainly. I got feelings.

SLOANE. You're sensitive. You can't be bothered.

ED. You got it wrong when you says that. I seen birds all shapes and sizes and I'm most certainly not . . . um . . . ah . . . sensitive.

SLOANE. No?

ED. I just don't give a monkey's fart.

SLOANE. It's a legitimate position.

ED. But I can deal with them same as you.

SLOANE. I'm glad to hear it.

ED. What's your opinion of the way these women carry on?

Pause.

SLOANE. I feel . . . how would you say?

ED. Don't you think they're crude?

SLOANE. Occasionally. In a way.

ED. You never know where you are with half of them.

SLOANE. All the same it's necessary.

ED. Ah well, you're talking of a different subject entirely. It's necessary. Occasionally. But it's got to be kept within bounds.

SLOANE. I'm with you there. All the way.

ED (*laughs*). I've seen funny things happen and no mistake. The way these birds treat decent fellows. I hope you never get serious with one. What a life. Backache, headache or her mum told her never to when there's an 'R' in the month. (*Pause. Stares from window.*) How do you feel then?

SLOANE. On the main points we agree.

ED. Pack your bags.

SLOANE. Now?

ED. Immediate.

SLOANE. Will I get a rise in pay?

ED. A rise?

SLOANE. My new situation calls for it.

ED. You already had two.

SLOANE. They were tokens. I'd like you to upgrade my salary.
  How about a little car?

ED. That's a bit (*laughs*) of an unusual request en it?

SLOANE. You could manage it.

ED. It all costs money. I tell you what – I'll promise you one for
  Christmas.

SLOANE. This year?

ED. Or next year.

SLOANE. It's a date.

ED. You and me. That's the life, boy. Without doubt I'm glad I
  met you.

SLOANE. Are you?

ED. I see you had possibilities from the start. You had an air.
  (*Pause.*) A way with you.

SLOANE. Something about me.

ED. That's it. The perfect phrase. Personality.

SLOANE. Really?

ED. That's why I don't want you living here. Wicked waste. I'm
  going to tell you something. Prepare to raise your eyebrows.

SLOANE. Yes.

ED. She had a kiddy once.

SLOANE. Go on.

ED. That's right. On the wrong side of the blanket.

SLOANE. Your sister?

ED. I had a matie. What times we had. Fished. Swam. Rolled home
  pissed at two in the morning. We were innocent I tell you.
  Until she came on the scene. (*Pause.*) Teaching him things he
  shouldn't 'a done. It was over . . . gone . . . finished. (*Clears his
  throat.*) She got him to put her in the family way that's what I
  always maintain. Nothing was the same after. Not ever. A
  typical story.

SLOANE. Sad, though.

ED. Yes it is. I should say. Of course in a way of looking at it it
  laid the foundation of my success. I put him to one side which
  was difficult because he was alluring. I managed it though. Got

a grip on myself. And finally become a success. (*Pause.*) That's
no mean achievement, is it?

SLOANE. No.

ED. I'm proud.

SLOANE. Why shouldn't you be?

ED. I'm the possessor of two bank accounts. Respected in my own
right. And all because I turned my back on him. Does that
impress you?

SLOANE. It impresses me.

ED. I have no hesitation in saying that it was worth it. None.

The door opens slowly, KEMP *stands waiting, staring in,
listening.*

SLOANE. What is it, Pop?

KEMP *enters the room, listens, backs to the door. Stops.*

KEMP. Is Ed there with you? (*Pause.*) Ed?

ED (*with emotion*). Dad . . . (*He goes to* KEMP, *puts an arm round
his shoulder.*) What's come over you?

KEMP *clutches* ED's *coat, almost falls to his knees.* ED *supports
him.*

Don't kneel to me. I forgive you. I'm the one to kneel.

KEMP. No, no.

ED. Pat me on the head. Pronounce a blessing. Forgive and forget,
eh? I'm sorry and so are you.

KEMP. I want a word with you. (*He squints in* SLOANE's *direction.*)
Something to tell you.

ED. Words, Dad. A string of words. We're together again.

Pause.

KEMP. Tell him to go.

ED. Dad, what manners you got. How rude you've become.

KEMP. I got business to discuss.

SLOANE. He can speak in front of me, can't he, Ed?

ED. I've no secrets from the boy.

KEMP. It's personal.

SLOANE. I'd like to stay Ed . . . in case . . .

KEMP. I'm not talking in front of him.

SLOANE. Pop . . . (*laughs*) . . . Ed will tell me afterwards. See if he doesn't.

Pause.

KEMP. I want to talk in private.

ED *nods at the door,* SLOANE *shrugs.*

SLOANE. Give in to him, eh, Ed? (*Laughs.*) You know, Pop . . . well . . . (*Pause.*) O.K., have it your own way. (*Exits.*)

KEMP. Is he gone?

ED. What's the matter with you?

KEMP. That kid – who is he?

ED. He's lived here six months. Where have you been?

KEMP. What's his background?

ED. He's had a hard life, dad. Struggles. I have his word for it. An orphan deserves our sympathy.

KEMP. You like him?

ED. One of the best.

Silence.

KEMP. He comes to my room at night.

ED. He's being friendly.

KEMP. I can't get to sleep. He talks all the time.

ED. Give an example of his conversation. What does he talk about?

KEMP. Goes on and on. (*Pause.*) An' he makes things up about
me. (*He rolls up his sleeve, shows a bruise.*) Give me a thumping, he did.

ED. When? (*Pause.*) Can't you remember?

KEMP. Before the weekend.

ED. Did you complain?

KEMP. I can't sleep for worry. He comes in and stands by my bed in the dark. In his pyjamas.

Pause.

ED. I'll have a word with him.

KEMP (*lifts his trouser leg, pulls down his sock, shows an Elastoplast*). He kicked me yesterday.

SLOANE (*appears in the doorway*). There's a man outside wants a word with you, Pop. (*Pause.*) Urgent he says.

KEMP. Tell him to wait.

SLOANE. How long?

KEMP. Tell him to wait will you?

SLOANE. It's urgent.

KEMP. What's his name?

SLOANE. Grove. Or Greeves, I don't know.

KEMP. I don't know nobody called that.

SLOANE. He's on about the . . . (*Pause*) . . . whether he can dump something. You'd better see him.

KEMP (*swings round, tries to bring* SLOANE *into focus*). Oh . . .

ED (*nods, winks*). In a minute, boy.

SLOANE *closes door, exits.*

Silence.

ED. Dad . . .

KEMP. He's in bed with her most nights. People talk. The woman from the shop spotted it first. Four months gone, she reckons.

Pause.

ED. That's interesting.

KEMP. She's like the side of a house lately. It's not what she eats. (*Silence.*) Shall I tell you something else?

ED. Don't.

Pause.

KEMP. He's got it in for me.

ED. . . . don't – tell me anything –

KEMP. It's because I'm a witness. To his crime.

ED. What crime.

SLOANE (*enters carrying a suitcase. Puts it on the table. Opens it*). Man en half creating, Pop. You ought to see to him. Jones or Greeves or whatever his name is. He's out the back.

ED. Go and see to him, Dad. (SLOANE *exits.*) See this man, Dad. Go on.

KEMP. There's no man there.

ED. How do you know? You haven't been and looked have you?

KEMP. It's a blind. (*Pause.*) Let me tell you about the boy.

ED. I don't want to hear. (*Pause.*) I'm surprised to find you spreading stories about the kiddy. Shocked. (SLOANE *returns with a pile of clothes.*) That's slander. You'll find yourself in queer street. (SLOANE *begins to pack the case.*) Apologize. (KEMP *shakes his head.*) The old man's got something to say to you, boy.

SLOANE (*smiling*). Oh, yes?

ED (*to* KEMP). Haven't you? (*Pause.*) Do you talk to him much? Is he talkative at night?

SLOANE. We have the odd confab sometimes. As I dawdle over my cocoa.

ED. You go and talk to that man, Dad. See if you can't get some sense into him. Dumping their old shit back of the house.

They watch KEMP *exit.*
Silence.

ED. He's just been putting in a complaint.

SLOANE. About me?

ED. I can't take it serious. He more or less said you . . . well, in so many words he said . . .

SLOANE. Really?

ED. Did you ever kick him?

SLOANE. Sometimes. He understands.

ED. An' he said . . . Is she pregnant?

Pause.

SLOANE. Who?

ED. Deny it, boy. Convince me it isn't true.

SLOANE. Why?

ED. So's I – (*Pause.*) Lie to me.

SLOANE. Why should I?

ED. It's true then? Have you been messing with her?

SLOANE. She threw herself at me.

Silence.

ED. What a little whoreson you are you little whoreson. You are
   a little whoreson and no mistake. I'm put out my boy. Choked.
   (*Pause.*) What attracted you? Did she give trading stamps?
   You're like all these layabouts. Kiddies with no fixed abode.

SLOANE. I put up a fight.

ED. She had your cherry?

SLOANE. No.

ED. Not the first time?

SLOANE. No.

ED. Or the second?

SLOANE. No.

ED. Dare I go on?

SLOANE. It's my upbringing. Lack of training. No proper
   parental control.

ED. I'm sorry for you.

SLOANE. I'm glad of that. I wouldn't want to upset you.

ED. That does you credit.

SLOANE. You've no idea what I've been through. (*Pause.*) I
   prayed for guidance.

ED. I'd imagine the prayer for your situation would be hard to
   come by. (*Pause.*) Did you never think of locking your bedroom
   door?

SLOANE. She'd think I'd gone mad.

ED. Why didn't you come to me?

SLOANE. It's not the kind of thing I could –

ED. I'd've been your confessor.

SLOANE. You don't understand. It gathered momentum.

ED. You make her sound like a washing machine. When did you stop?

SLOANE. I haven't stopped.

ED. Not stopped yet?

SLOANE. Here, lay off.

ED. What a ruffian.

SLOANE. I got my feelings.

ED. You were stronger than her. Why didn't you put up a struggle?

SLOANE. I was worn out. I was overwrought. Nervous. On edge.

Pause.

ED. You're a constant source of amazement, boy, a never ending tale of infamy. I'd hardly credit it. A kid of your age. Joy-riding in an expensive car, a woman pregnant. My word, you're unforgivable. (*Pause.*) I don't know whether I'm qualified to pronounce judgement.

Pause.

SLOANE. I'm easily led. I been dogged by bad luck.

ED. You've got to learn to live a decent life sometime, boy. I blame the way you are on emotional shock. So perhaps (*Pause*) we ought to give you another chance.

SLOANE. That's what I says.

ED. Are you confused?

SLOANE. I shouldn't be surprised.

ED. Never went to church? Correct me if I'm wrong.

SLOANE. You got it, Ed. Know me better than I know myself.

ED. Your youth pleads for leniency and, by God, I'm going to give it. You're pure as the Lamb. Purer.

SLOANE. Am I forgiven?

ED. Will you reform?

SLOANE. I swear it . . . Ed, look at me. Speak a few words of forgiveness. (*Pause.*) Pity me.

ED. I do.

SLOANE. Oh, Ed, you're a pal.

ED. Am I?

SLOANE. One of my mates.

ED. Is that a fact? How refreshing to hear you say it.

SLOANE. You've a generous nature.

ED. You could say that. I don't condemn out of hand like some. But do me a favour – avoid the birds in future. That's what's been your trouble.

SLOANE. It has.

ED. She's to blame.

SLOANE. I've no hesitation in saying that.

ED. Why conform to the standards of the cowshed? (*Pause.*) It's a thing you grow out of. With me behind you, boy, you'll grow out of it.

SLOANE. Thanks.

ED. Your hand on it. (SLOANE *holds out his hand.* ED *takes it, holds it for a long time, searches* SLOANE's *face.*) I think you're a good boy. (*Silence.*) I knew there must be some reasonable explanation for your otherwise inexplicable conduct. I'll have a word with the old man.

SLOANE. Gets on my nerves he does.

ED. Has he been tormenting you?

SLOANE. I seriously consider leaving as a result of the way he carries on.

ED. Insults?

SLOANE. Shocking. Took a dislike to me, he did, the first time he saw me.

ED. Take no notice.

SLOANE. I can't make him out.

ED. Stubborn.

SLOANE. That's why I lose my temper.

ED. I sympathize.

Pause.

SLOANE. He deserves a good belting.

ED. You may have something there.

SLOANE. I thought you might be against me for that.

ED. No.

SLOANE. I thought you might have an exaggerated respect for the elderly.

ED. Not me.

SLOANE. I've nothing against him. (*Pause.*) But he's lived so long, he's more like an old bird than a bloke. How is it such a father has such a son? A mystery. (*Pause.*) Certainly is. (ED *pats his pockets.*) Out of fags again, are you?

ED. Yes.

SLOANE. Give them up. Never be fully fit, Ed.

>   ED *smiles, shakes his head.*

SLOANE. Are you going to the shop?

ED. Yes.

SLOANE. Good. (*Silence.*) How long will you be?

ED. Five minutes. Maybe ten.

SLOANE. Mmmn. (*Pause.*) Well, while you're gone I'm going to have a word with Pop.

ED. Good idea.

SLOANE. See if we can't find an area of agreement. I'll hold out the hand of friendship an' all that. I'm willing to forget the past. If he is. (*Silence.*) I'd better have a word with him. Call him.

ED. Me?

SLOANE. No good me asking him anything is there?

ED. I don't know whether we're speaking.

SLOANE. Gone funny again has he?

ED (*goes to the window, opens it, looks out. Calls*). Dad! (*Pause.*) I want a word with you.

KEMP (*off*). What's that?

>   *Pause.*

ED. Me – me – I want to see you. (*He closes the window.*) He gets
worse. (*Silence.*) Appeal to his better nature. Say you're upset.
Wag your finger perhaps. I don't want you to be er, well . . . at
each other's throats, boy. Let's try . . . and . . . well be friends.
(*Pause.*) I've the fullest confidence in your ability. (*Pause.*)
Yes . . . well I'm going out now. (*Pause.*) . . . it's a funny business
en it? . . . I mean . . . well, it's a ticklish problem. (*Pause.*)
Yes . . . it is. (*Exit.*)

> SLOANE *sits, waits. Pause.* KEMP *enters.* SLOANE *rises, steps
> behind* KEMP, *bangs door.* KEMP *swings round, backs.*

KEMP. Ed? (*Pause.*) Where's Ed?
SLOANE (*takes hold of* KEMP's *stick, pulls it away from him.* KEMP
struggles. SLOANE *wrenches stick from his hand. Leads* KEMP *to
a chair*). Sit down, Pop. (KEMP *turns to go.* SLOANE *pushes him
into the chair.*) Ed's not here. Gone for a walk. What you been
saying about me?
KEMP. Nothing, sonnie.
SLOANE. What have you told him? What were you going to tell
him?
KEMP. I – (*Pause.*) Business.
SLOANE. What kind of business? (KEMP *does not reply.*) Told him
she's up the stick did you? (*No reply.*) Why did you tell him?
KEMP. He's her brother. He ought to know.
SLOANE. Fair enough.
KEMP. Got to know sometime.
SLOANE. Right. (*Silence.*) What else did you tell him? (KEMP
attempts to rise, SLOANE *pushes him back.*) Did you say anything
else? (KEMP *attempts to rise.*) Eh?
KEMP. No.
SLOANE. Were you going to?
KEMP. Yes.
SLOANE. Why?
KEMP. You're a criminal.
SLOANE. Who says I am?

KEMP. I know you are. You killed my old boss. I know it was you.

SLOANE. Your vision is faulty. You couldn't identify nobody now. So long after. You said so yourself.

KEMP. I got to go. (*Pause.*) I'm expecting delivery of a damson tree.

SLOANE. Sit still! (*Silence.*) How were you going to identify me?

KEMP. I don't have to. They got fingerprints.

SLOANE. Really?

KEMP. All over the shop.

SLOANE. It was an accident, Pop. I'm innocent. You don't know the circumstances . . .

KEMP. Oh . . . I know . . .

SLOANE. But you don't.

KEMP. You murdered him.

SLOANE. Accidental death.

Pause.

KEMP. No, sonnie . . . no.

SLOANE. You're pre-judging my case.

KEMP. You're bad.

SLOANE. I'm an orphan.

KEMP. Get away from me. Let me alone.

SLOANE (*puts the stick into* KEMP's *hand*). I trust you, Pop. Listen. Keep quiet.

Silence.

It's like this see. One day I leave the Home. Stroll along. Sky blue. Fresh air. They'd found me a likeable permanent situation. Canteen facilities. Fortnight's paid holiday. Overtime? Time and a half after midnight. A staff dance each year. What more could one wish to devote one's life to? I certainly loved that place. The air round Twickenham was like wine. Then one day I take a trip to the old man's grave. Hic Jacets in profusion. Ashes to Ashes. Alas the fleeting. The sun was declining. A few press-ups on a tomb belonging to a family name of Cavaneagh, and I left the graveyard. I thumbs a lift from a geyser who promises me a bed. Gives me a bath. And a meal. Very friendly. All you could wish he was, a photographer. He shows me one or two experimental studies. An experience for the retina and no mistake. He wanted to photo me. For certain interesting features I had that he wanted the exclusive right of preserving. You know how it is. I didn't like to refuse. No harm in it I suppose. But then I got to thinking . . . I knew a kid once called MacBride that happened to. Oh, yes . . . so when I gets to think of this I decide I got to do something about it. And I gets up in the middle of the night looking for the film see. He has a lot of expensive equipment about in his studio see. Well it appears that he gets the wrong idea. Runs in. Gives a shout. And the long and the short of it is I loses my head which is a thing I never ought to a done with the worry of them photos an all. And I hits him. I hits him.

Pause.

He must have had a weak heart. Something like that I should imagine. Definitely should have seen his doctor before that. I wasn't to know was I? I'm not to blame.

Silence.

KEMP. He was healthy. Sound as a bell.
SLOANE. How do you know?
KEMP. He won cups for it. Looked after himself.
SLOANE. A weak heart.
KEMP. Weak heart, my arse. You murdered him.
SLOANE. He fell.
KEMP. He was hit from behind.
SLOANE. I had no motive.
KEMP. The equipment.
SLOANE. I never touched it.
KEMP. You meant to.

SLOANE. Not me, Pop. (*Laughs.*) Oh, no.

KEMP. Liar . . . lying little bugger. I knew what you was from the start.

Pause.

SLOANE. What are you going to do? Are you going to tell Ed? (KEMP *makes no reply.*) He won't believe you. (KEMP *makes no reply.*) He'll think you're raving.

KEMP. No . . . you're finished. (*Attempts to rise.* SLOANE *pushes him back.* KEMP *raises his stick,* SLOANE *takes it from him.*)

SLOANE. You can't be trusted I see. I've lost faith in you. (*Throws the stick out of reach.*) Irresponsible. Can't give you offensive weapons.

KEMP. Ed will be back soon. (*Rises to go.*)

SLOANE. He will.

KEMP. I'm seeing him then.

SLOANE. Are you threatening me? Do you feel confident? Is that it? (*Stops. Clicks his tongue. Pause. Leans over and straightens* KEMP's *tie.*) Ed and me are going away. Let's have your word you'll forget it. (KEMP *does not reply.*) Pretend you never knew. Who was he? No relation. Hardly a friend. An employer. You won't bring him back by hanging me. (KEMP *does not reply.*) Where's your logic? Can I have a promise you'll keep your mouth shut?

KEMP. No.

SLOANE *twists* KEMP's *ear.*

KEMP. Ugh! aaah . . .

SLOANE. You make me desperate. I've nothing to lose, you see. One more chance, Pop. Are you going to give me away?

KEMP. I'll see the police.

SLOANE. You don't know what's good for you. (*He knocks* KEMP *behind the settee. Kicks him.*) You bring this on yourself. (*He kicks him again.*) All this could've been avoided. (KEMP *half-rises, collapses again. Pause.* SLOANE *kicks him gently with the toe of his boot.*) Eh, then. Wake up. (*Pause.*) Wakey, wakey. (*Silence. He goes to the door and calls.*) Ed! (*Pause.*) Ed!

KATH *comes to the door. He pushes her back.*

KATH (*off*). What's happened?
SLOANE. Where's Ed. Not you! I want Ed!

CURTAIN

Act Three

Door slams off.

ED (*entering*). What is it? (*Sees* KEMP *lying on the floor. Kneels.* SLOANE *enters, stands in the doorway.* KATH *tries to push past. Struggle.* SLOANE *gives up. She enters.*)

SLOANE. Some kind of attack.

ED. What did you do?

KATH. If only there were some spirits in the house. Unfortunately I don't drink myself. (*She loosens* KEMP's *collar.*) Somebody fetch his tablets.

Nobody moves.

ED. He's reviving.

KATH. Speak to me, Dadda. (*Pause.*) He's been off his food for some time. (*Pause.*) He's cut his lip.

ED (*lifts* KEMP). Can you walk?

KEMP (*muttering*). Go away . . .

ED. I'll carry you upstairs. (KATH *opens the door, stands in the passage.*) He'll be better in a bit. Is his bed made?

KATH. Yes. Let him lie still and he'll get his feelings back. (ED *exits with* KEMP. *Slowly.*) Mr Sloane, did you strike the Dadda?

SLOANE. Yes.

KATH. You admit it? Did he provoke you?

SLOANE. In a way.

KATH. What a thing to do. Hit an old man. It's not like you. You're usually so gentle.

SLOANE. He upset me.

KATH. He can be aggravating I know, but you shouldn't resort to violence, dear. (*Pause.*) Did he insult you? (*Pause.*) Was it a bad word? (*Pause.*) I don't expect you can tell me what it was. I'd blush.

SLOANE. I hit him several times.

KATH. You're exaggerating. You're not that type of young man. (*Pause.*) But don't do it again. Mamma wouldn't like it. (ED *enters.*) Is he all right?

ED. Yes.

KATH. I'll go up to him.

ED. He's asleep.

KATH. Sleeping off the excitement, is he? (*Exit.*)

ED (*taking* SLOANE *aside*). How hard did you hit him?

SLOANE. Not hard.

ED. You don't know your own strength, boy. Using him like a punchbag.

SLOANE. I've told you –

ED. He's dead.

SLOANE. Dead? His heart.

ED. Whatever it was it's murder, boy. You'll have some explaining to do. (*Lights a cigarette.* KATH *enters with a carpet sweeper, begins to sweep.*)

KATH. I'd take up a toffee, but he only gets them stuck round his teeth.

ED. You're not usually at a loss, surely? You can conjure up an idea or two.

KATH. Let Mr Sloane regain his composure, Ed. Let him collect his thoughts. Forget the incident. (*She goes upstage, begins to hum 'The Indian Love Call'.*)

SLOANE *looks at* ED. ED *smiles, shakes his head.*

ED. That isn't possible, I'm afraid.

KATH. He meant no harm.

ED. What are you doing?

KATH. My housework. I mustn't neglect my chores.

ED. Can't you find a better time than this?

KATH. It's my usual time. Guess what's for dinner, Mr Sloane.

SLOANE. I'm not hungry.

ED. He doesn't want any.

KATH. Guess what mamma's prepared?

ED. Let him alone! All you think of is food. He'll be out of condition before long. As gross as you are.

KATH. Is he upset?

ED. Tell her.

SLOANE. I'm really upset.

ED. Turned your stomach, has it?

KATH. Will you feel better by this afternoon?

SLOANE. I don't know.

ED. He's worried.

KATH. The Dadda won't say anything, dear, if that's what's on your mind. He'll keep quiet. (*Pause.*) That new stove cooks excellent, Eddie.

ED. Does it?

KATH. Yes. I cooked a lovely egg yesterday. Mr Sloane had it. I think they ought to have put the grill different, though. I burned my hand.

ED. You want to look what you're doing.

KATH. It's awkwardly placed.

ED. Cooking with your eyes shut.

KATH (*pause*). You haven't guessed yet what's for dinner. Three guesses. Go on.

SLOANE. I don't know!

KATH. Chips.

SLOANE. Really?

KATH. And peas. And two eggs.

SLOANE. I don't give a sod what's for dinner!

ED. Don't use those tones to my relations, Sloane. Behave yourself for a change. (*Lights a cigarette.*)

SLOANE. Can I see you outside?

ED. What do you want to see me outside for?

SLOANE. To explain.

ED. There's nothing to explain.

SLOANE. How I came to be involved in this situation.

KATH *puts the Ewbank away.*

ED. I don't think that would be advisable. Some things will have to be sorted out. A check on your excesses is needed.

SLOANE. Are you sure he's —

ED. As forty dodos. I tried the usual methods of ascertaining; no heartbeats, no misting on my cigarette case. The finest legal brains in the country can't save you now.

KATH *re-enters.*

SLOANE. I feel sick.

KATH. It's the weather.

SLOANE. No.

KATH. Take a pill or something. I had some recommended me the other day. (*Opens a drawer, searches. She finds the tablets, shakes out two into her hand. Offers them to* SLOANE.) Take them with a glass of water. Swallow them quick. They'll relieve the symptoms.

SLOANE. I don't want them! (*He knocks them from her hand.*) I don't want pills! (*Exits.*)

KATH. He's bad, isn't he?

ED. A very bad boy.

KATH (*picks up one tablet, searches for the others, gives up*). Somebody will tread on them. That's the reason for these stains. Things get into the pile. The Dadda dropped a pickled walnut and trod it into the rug yesterday. If only we had a dog we wouldn't have so much bother.

ED. You're not having a dog.

KATH. Eddie, is Mr Sloane ill?

ED. He may be.

KATH. He looks pale. I wonder if he isn't sickening for something.

ED. He might have to go away. Something has happened which makes his presence required elsewhere.

KATH. Where?

ED. I'm not sure. Not for certain.

KATH. Is he in trouble?

ED. Dead trouble.

KATH. It was an accident, surely?

ED. You know, then?

KATH. The Dadda told me about it. Mr Sloane was unfortunate. He was joking, I expect.

ED. He never jokes.

KATH. No, he's remarkably devoid of a sense of fun. Dadda was full of it.

ED. I don't understand you.

KATH. Oh, I said he had no proof. I didn't waste my energy listening to him. Sometimes I think he makes up these things to frighten me. He ought to curb his imagination. (*Exits.*)

ED. I should have asked for references. I can see that now. The usual credentials would have avoided this. An attractive kid, so disarming, to – to tell me lies and –

KATH (*enters carrying a china figure*). This shepherdess is a lovely piece of chinawork. She comes up like new when I give her a wash.

ED. Now?

KATH. The crack spoils it, though. I should have it mended professionally. (*Exit. Re-enters carrying large vase.*) Dadda gets up to some horrible pranks lately. Throwing things into my best vase now. The habits of the elderly are beyond the pale. (*She exits. ED sits on the settee.*)

ED. I must sort out my affairs and quick.

SLOANE (*enters, glances at ED. ED does not look up*). Accept my apology, Ed. Sorry I was rude, but my nerves won't stand much more, I can tell you. (*He opens the suitcase. Begins to pack.*) She's got two of my shirts in the wash. Good ones. (*Opens sideboard, takes out cardigan.*) Can't risk asking her for them. (*Looks under sideboard, finds canvas shoes.*) She's been using this razor again. (*Holding up razor.*) I can tell. That's not hygienic, is it?

ED. What are you doing?

SLOANE. Packing.

ED. Why?

SLOANE. I'm going away.

ED. Where?

SLOANE. With you.

ED. No boy. Not with me.

SLOANE. It was settled.

ED. I can't allow you to take up abode in Dulverton Mansions now.

SLOANE. Why not?

ED. What a fantastic person you are. You've committed a murder!

SLOANE. An accident.

ED. Murder.

SLOANE. Those pills were undermining his constitution. Ruining his health. He couldn't have lasted much longer.

ED. Attacking a defenceless old man!

SLOANE. He had his stick.

ED. He wasn't strong enough to use it.

SLOANE. I blame that on the pills. Who prescribed them?

ED. His doctor.

SLOANE. Reputable, is he?

ED. He's on the register. What more do you want?

SLOANE. You'll find medical evidence agrees with my theory.

ED. The pills had nothing to do with it. You've no excuse. None.

SLOANE. What kind of life is it at his age?

ED. You've abused my trust.

SLOANE. I did him a service in a manner of speaking.

ED. You'll have to face the authorities.

SLOANE. Look, I'm facing no one.

ED. You've no choice.

SLOANE. I'll decide what choice I have.

ED. Get on the blower and call the law. We're finished.

SLOANE. You wouldn't put me away, would you?

ED. Without a qualm.

SLOANE. You're my friend.

ED. No friend of thugs.

SLOANE. He died of heart failure. You can't ruin my life. I'm impressionable. Think what the nick would do to me. I'd pick up criminal connexions.

ED. You already got criminal connexions.

SLOANE. Not as many as I would have.

ED. That's a point in your favour.

SLOANE. Give me a chance.

ED. You've had several.

SLOANE. One more.

ED. I've given you chances. Expected you to behave like a civilized human being.

SLOANE. Say he fell downstairs.

ED. What kind of a person does that make me?

SLOANE. A loyal friend.

ED. You'll get me six months. More than that. Depends on the judge.

SLOANE. What a legal system. Say he fell.

ED. Aiding and abetting.

SLOANE. Fake the evidence.

ED. You're completely without morals, boy. I hadn't realized how depraved you were. You murder my father. Now you ask me to help you evade Justice. Is that where my liberal principles have brought me?

SLOANE. You've got no principles.

ED. No principles? Oh, you really have upset me now. Why am I interested in your welfare? Why did I give you a job? Why do thinking men everywhere show young boys the strait and narrow? Flash cheque-books when delinquency is mentioned? Support the Scout-movement? Principles, boy, bleeding principles. And don't you dare say otherwise or you'll land in serious trouble.

SLOANE. Are you going to help me?

ED. No.

SLOANE. We must find a basis for agreement.

ED. There can be no agreement. I'm a citizen of this country. My duty is clear. You must accept responsibility for your actions.

SLOANE (*sits beside* ED. *Lays a hand on his knee*). I accept responsibility.

ED. Do you?

SLOANE. Fully.

ED. Good. Remove that hand, will you?

SLOANE. Certainly.

ED. What you just said about no principles – That's really upset me. Straight. Really upset me.

SLOANE. Sorry, Eddie, sorry.

ED. One thing I wanted to give you – my principles. Oh, I'm disillusioned. I feel I'm doing no good at all.

SLOANE. I'm very bad. Only you can help me on the road to a useful life. (*Pause.*) A couple of years ago I met a man similar to yourself. Same outlook on life. A dead ringer for you as far as physique went. He was an expert on the adolescent male body. He's completed an exhaustive study of his subject before I met him. During the course of one magical night he talked to me of his principles – offered me a job if I would accept them. Like a fool I turned him down. What an opportunity I lost, Ed. If you were to make the same demands, I'd answer loudly in the affirmative.

Pause.

ED. You mean that?

SLOANE. In future you'd have nothing to complain of.

ED. You really mean what you say?

SLOANE. Let me live with you. I'd wear my jeans out in your service. Cook for you.

ED. I eat out.

SLOANE. Bring you your tea in bed.

ED. Only women drink tea in bed.

SLOANE. You bring me my tea in bed, then. Any arrangement you fancy.

KATH *screams loudly offstage. Pause. Screams again nearer. She enters.*

KATH. Ed!

ED. Come here.

KATH. Ed, I must – (ED *takes her arm, she pulls back*.) It's Dadda – he's dead. Come quick.

ED. Sit down. (*To* SLOANE.) Bring the car round. We'll fetch the doctor.

KATH. Eddie, he's dead.

ED. I know. We know. Didn't want to upset you.

SLOANE *exits.*

KATH. I can't believe he's dead. He was in perfect health.

ED. He was ill.

KATH. Was he?

ED. You told me he was.

KATH. I didn't believe it. I only took his word for it.

ED. Didn't he say he was ill?

KATH. Often. I took no notice. You know how he is. I thought he was having me on.

ED. He was telling the truth.

KATH (*begins to sniff*). Poor Dadda. How he must have suffered. I'm truly ashamed of myself. (*She wipes her eyes on her apron.*) It's all the health scheme's fault. Will I have to send his pension book in?

ED. Yes.

KATH. I thought I would.

ED. Now listen –

KATH. Eddie.

ED. – carefully to what I say. (*He passes a hand across his mouth.*) When the doctor comes what are you going to tell him?

KATH. Me?

ED. He'll want to know.

KATH. I'll say Dadda had an attack. He passed away sudden.

ED. What about the cuts on his face?

KATH. He was rude to Mr Sloane, Eddie. Provoked him.

ED. They won't wear that.

KATH. Won't they? (*Pause.*) I shall never get in my black. I've put on weight since we buried mamma.

ED. They'll get the boy for murder.

KATH. They'd never do that would they?

ED. They'll hang him.

Pause.

KATH. Hang him?

ED. They might. I'm not sure. I get confused by the changes in the law.

KATH. Is it bad?

ED. Awful. You wouldn't see him again. You understand?

KATH. The Dadda was rude. He said a rude word about me.

ED. That's no excuse in the eyes of the law. You must say he fell downstairs.

KATH. I couldn't.

ED. I would never suggest deceiving the authorities under normal circumstances. But we have ourselves to think of. I'm in a funny position. I pay his wages. That's a tricky situation.

KATH. Is it?

ED. I'm compromised. My hands are tied. If the situation was different I might say something. Depend on it.

KATH. Wouldn't they make an exception? If we gave him a good character?

ED. He hasn't got a good character.

KATH. We could say he had.

ED. That would be perjury.

KATH. He has nice manners when he wants. I've seen them.

ED. I feel bad doing this. You see the position? He went too far. But he did it out of respect for you. That's some consideration.

KATH. He did it out of love for me?

ED. You should be grateful. No doubt of that. (*Pause.*) Do you polish that lino?

KATH. Eh?

ED. On the stairs?

KATH. No, never. I have to think of the Dadda.

ED. Go and polish them.

KATH. Doctor will be cross.

ED. Let him be.

KATH. He'll think I'm silly. He'll think I caused Dadda's fall.

ED. It doesn't matter as long as he thinks it was an accident.

KATH (*bites her lip, considers*). Shall I put Dadda's new shoes on him?

ED. Now you're using your initiative. Slippy are they?

KATH. He only wore them once.

ED. Good girl.

SLOANE *enters.*

SLOANE. Ready? Come on, then.

ED *nods to* KATH, *waiting. She looks from one to the other. Notices the case.*

KATH. Why is he taking his case?

ED. He's coming with me. He can't stay here.

KATH. Why not?

ED. They'll suspect.

Pause.

KATH. When is he coming back?

ED. Day after next.

KATH. He doesn't need that big case. (*She exits.*)

ED. Get in the car, boy.

SLOANE. How about my shirts?

ED. I'll see about buying a couple.

KATH (*off*). Why is he taking his clothes?

ED. What are you on about?

KATH *returns.*

KATH. I've just checked. They aren't in the laundry basket.

ED. Snooping around. Don't you trust me?

KATH. You're taking him away.

SLOANE. We thought I ought to live in.

KATH. Do you want to leave?

SLOANE. I'll be back when this has blown over.

KATH. Why are you leaving your mamma? There's no need for him to go away, Eddie. Doctor knows he lives here.

ED. He'll instigate proceedings.

KATH. Doctors don't do that. He wants to stay.

ED. Ask him. (*To* SLOANE.) Do you want to stay?

SLOANE. No.

ED. The question is answered.

KATH. Ed –

ED. Send a wire –

KATH. I've something to tell you.

She lifts her apron. Shyly.

I've a bun in the oven.

ED. You've a whole bloody baker's shop in the oven from the look of that.

KATH. Mr Sloane was nice to me. Aren't you shocked?

ED. No, it's what I expect of you.

KATH. Aren't you angry with Mr Sloane?

ED. I'm angry with you.

KATH. Are you?

ED. Mr Sloane's already explained.

KATH. What did he explain?

ED. How you carried on.

KATH. I didn't carry on! What a wicked thing to say.

ED. Seducing him.

KATH. Did he say that?

ED. Told me the grisly details.

Silence.

KATH. Mr Sloane, dear, take back your locket.

ED. What locket?

KATH. He gave me a locket. (*She takes off the locket.* SLOANE *attempts to take it.*) I don't believe he'd take it if you weren't here, Ed. (*She puts the locket back. To* SLOANE.) How could you behave so bad. Accusing me of seducing you.

SLOANE. But you did!

KATH. That's neither here nor there. Using expressions like that. Making yourself cheap. (SLOANE *turns to the suitcase.*) I see the truth of the matter. He's been at you. Isn't that like him?

ED. He wants to come with me.

KATH. Let him decide for himself.

ED. He's got problems. Needs a man's hand on his shoulder.

KATH. I'm afraid you're unduly influencing him.

ED. You've been found out.

KATH. Found out?

ED. Exposed.

KATH. Rubbish!

ED. Making a spectacle of yourself. Corrupting a kid young enough to be your son.

KATH. He loves me.

ED. Prove it.

KATH. A woman knows when she's loved.

ED. I blame myself for letting him stay. Knowing your character.

KATH. My character will stand analysis.

ED. You're older than him.

KATH. I'm a benign influence. A source of good.

ED. You spoil him.

KATH. Who tucks him up at night? And he likes my cooking. He won't deny that.

ED. No.

KATH. See I'm right.

ED. I can't argue with you.

KATH. You can't.

ED. You don't make sense.

KATH. I do.

ED. You have no logical train of thought.

KATH. What is that?

ED. No power of argument.

KATH. I keep his trousers pressed nice. He's been smarter since I knew him.

ED. He's lost with you.

KATH. I gave him everything.

ED. No backbone. Spineless.

KATH. He's lovely with me. Charming little baby he is.

ED. No, he's soft. You softened him up.

KATH. I gave him three meals a day. Porridge for breakfast. Meat and two veg for dinner. A fry for tea. And cheese for supper. What more could he want?

ED. Freedom.

KATH. He's free with me.

ED. You're immoral.

KATH. It's natural.

ED. He's clean-living by nature; that's every man's right.

KATH. What are you going to give him?

ED. The world.

KATH (*comes round the case, looks in*). The state of this case. Mr Sloane, dear, you can't even pack. See how he needs me in the smallest things? Can't manage without a woman.

ED. Let him try.

KATH. Women are necessary.

ED. Granted.

KATH. Where's your argument?

ED. In limited doses.

KATH. You're silly, Eddie, silly . . .

ED. Let him choose. Let's have it in black and white, boy.

SLOANE. I'm going with Ed.

ED *nods, smacks* SLOANE's *shoulder, laughs.*

KATH. Is it the colour of the curtains in your room?

SLOANE. No.

KATH. Is it because I'm pregnant?

SLOANE. No. Better opportunities. A new life.

KATH. You vowed you loved me.

SLOANE. Never for a second.

KATH. I was kind to you.

SLOANE. Yes.

KATH. Are you grateful?

SLOANE. I paid.

KATH. I paid too. Baby on the way. Reputation ruined.

SLOANE. You had no reputation.

KATH. Is that what he's taught you?

ED. I taught him nothing. He was innocent until you got your
maulers on to him.

KATH. He'd packed the experience of a lifetime into a few short
years.

ED. Pure in heart, he was. He wouldn't know where to put it.

KATH. I attracted him instantly.

ED. You couldn't attract a blind man.

KATH. He wanted to marry me.

ED. What a bride!

KATH. We were to ask your consent.

ED. Look in the glass, lady. Let's enjoy a laugh. (*He takes her to
the mirror.*) What do you see?

KATH. Me.

ED. What are you?

KATH. My hair is nice. Natural. I'm mature, but still able to
command a certain appeal.

ED. You look like death!

She shakes him off. He drags her back to the mirror.

ED. Flabby mouth. Wrinkled neck. Puffy hands.

KATH. It's baby coming.

ED. Sagging tits. You cradle-snatcher.

KATH. He said I was a Venus. I held him in my arms.

ED. What a martyrdom!

KATH. He wanted for nothing. I loved him sincerely.

ED. You're appetite appalled him.

KATH. I loved him.

ED. Insatiable.

KATH (*to* SLOANE). Baby, my little boy . . .

ED. He aches at every organ.

KATH. . . . mamma forgives you.

ED. What have you to offer? You're fat and the crows-feet under your eyes would make you an object of terror. Pack it in, I tell you. Sawdust up to the navel? You've nothing to lure any man.

KATH. Is that the truth, Mr Sloane?

SLOANE. More or less.

KATH. Why didn't you tell me?

ED. How could he tell you? You showed him the gate of Hell every night. He abandoned Hope when he entered there.

KATH (*snaps the suitcase shut*). Mr Sloane, I believed you were a good boy. I find you've deceived me.

SLOANE. You deceived yourself.

KATH. Perhaps. (*She holds out her hand.*) Kiss my hand, dear, in the manner of the theatre. (*He kisses her hand.*) I shall cry. (*She feels for a handkerchief.*)

ED. On with the waterworks.

KATH. I'm losing you for ever.

SLOANE. I'll pop round.

KATH. I'll not be able to bear it.

SLOANE. You'll have the baby.

KATH. I shall die of it, I'm sure.

ED. What a cruel performance you're giving. Like an old tart grinding to her climax.

SLOANE *kisses* KATH's *cheek.*

KATH. Baby . . . (*She holds him close. Looks at* ED *over* SLOANE's *shoulder.*) Before you go, Mr Sloane, we must straighten things out. The Dadda's death was a blow to me.

SLOANE (*releases her*). Ed can vouch for me. You can support his story.

KATH. What story?

SLOANE. The old man fell downstairs.

KATH. I shall never under any circumstances allow anyone to perjure me. It was murder.

Pause. SLOANE *releases her. Pause.*

SLOANE. He was ill.

KATH. Ah, you know as well as I he was perfectly healthy this morning.

SLOANE. Ed will give me an alibi.

KATH. He wasn't there, dear. Respect the truth always. It's the least you can do under the circumstances.

SLOANE. He'll say he was a witness.

KATH. It's not in accordance with my ideas of morality.

SLOANE. Look – mamma . . . see –

KATH. When doctor comes he'll want to know things. Are you asking me to deceive our G.P.? He's an extremely able man. He'll notice discrepancies. And then where will we be? He'd make his report and mamma would be behind bars. I'm sure that isn't your idea. Is it?

SLOANE. Ed is supporting me.

KATH. He must decide for himself. I won't practise a falsehood.

SLOANE. You're not going back on your word?

KATH. You know how I go to pieces under cross-examination.

SLOANE. Make an effort.

KATH. Who for?

SLOANE. Me.

KATH. You won't be here.

SLOANE. I'll come and see you.

KATH. No. Call me names if you wish, but I won't tell stories. I'm a firm believer in truth.

ED. Look . . . Kathy – Say you were out when the accident occurred.

KATH. No.

ED. Down the shops.

KATH. But I wasn't.

ED. You didn't see him fall.

KATH. I would have heard him.

ED. Say you were out of range.

KATH. No.

ED. Forget the whole business.

KATH. No.

ED. Go to the police then. What will you achieve? Nothing. This boy was carried away by the exuberance of youth. He's under age.

KATH (*hands the suitcase to* ED). You struck the Dadda down in cold blood, Mr Sloane. In the course of conversations before his death he told me one or two things of interest.

SLOANE. Concerning whom?

KATH. We talked only of you. I could hardly give credence to the report of your crimes. I didn't believe the old man. I'm paid for it now.

ED. The last word, eh? Using your whore's prerogative?

KATH. Stay with me.

SLOANE. No.

KATH. Hold me tight again.

SLOANE. No.

KATH. There's no need to go away, dear. Don't make me unhappy.

SLOANE. I'm going with Ed.

KATH. I was never subtle, Mr Sloane . . . If you go with Eddie, I'll tell the police.

SLOANE. If I stay here he'll do the same.

ED. It's what is called a dilemma, boy. You are on the horns of it.

Silence.

KATH. You see how things are, Mr Sloane?

SLOANE *smacks her face, she screams.*

ED. What are you doing?

SLOANE. Leave her to me.

KATH. Don't attempt to threaten me.

ED. There's no suggestion of threats.

KATH. What's he doing then?

ED. Let her alone, boy.

SLOANE. Keep out of this! (ED *lays a hand on* SLOANE's *shoulder, tries to pull him away from* KATH. SLOANE *turns, shoves* ED *from him.*) Did you hear what I said? Keep out of it!

ED. Don't be violent. No violence at any cost. (SLOANE *gets* KATH *into a corner; struggles with her.*) What's this exhibition for? This is gratuitous violence. Give over, both of you!

SLOANE (*shakes* KATH). Support me, you mare! Support me!

KATH. Make him stop! I shall be sick. He's upsetting my insides.

ED (*runs round*). What did you want to provoke him for?

SLOANE *shakes* KATH *harder. She screams.*

KATH. My teeth! (*She claps a hand over her mouth.*) My teeth. (SLOANE *flings her from him. She crawls round the floor, searching.*) He's broke my teeth! Where are they?

ED. Expensive equipment gone west now see? I'm annoyed with you, boy. Seriously annoyed. Giving us the benefit of your pauperism. Is this what we listen to the Week's Good Cause for? A lot of vicars and actresses making appeals for cash gifts to raise hooligans who can't control themselves? I'd've given my cheque to the anti-Jewish League if I'd known.

KATH (*reaching under the settee*). I'll still forgive and forget.

ED. Coming in here as a lodger. Raised in a charity home. The lack of common courtesy in some people is appalling.

SLOANE. She's won! The bitch has won!

He grips ED's *arm.* ED *shrugs him away.*

ED. We'll discuss the matter.

SLOANE. We need action not discussion. Persuade her. Cut her throat, but persuade her!

ED. Don't use that tone of voice to me, boy. I won't be dictated to. (*Pause.*) Perhaps we can share you.

SLOANE. Deal with her.

ED. We'll think of something.

SLOANE. She must be primed. Get her evidence correct.

ED. Don't worry. I'm in perfect control of the situation.

SLOANE. You're in control of nothing! Where are your influential friends? Ring them, we need protection.

KATH. It's his nerves. He doesn't know what he's doing.

ED. Put your teeth in, will you? Sitting there with them in your hand.

KATH. He's broke them.

ED. They're only chipped. Go on, turn your back.

KATH (*puts her teeth in*). What are we going to do, Eddie?

ED. Stand up. We can't conduct a serious discussion from that position.

KATH. Help me up, Mr Sloane. Thank you, baby. See, Ed, he hasn't lost respect for me.

ED. An arrangement to suit all tastes. That is what's needed.

KATH. I don't want to lose my baby.

ED. You won't lose him.

KATH. But –

ED. (*holds up a hand*). What are your main requirements? I take it there's no question of making an honest woman of you? You don't demand the supreme sacrifice?

SLOANE. I'm not marrying her!

ED. Calm down will you?

SLOANE. Remember our agreement

ED. I'm keeping it in mind, boy.

SLOANE. Don't saddle me with her for life.

KATH. He's close to tears. Isn't he sweet?

ED. Yes, he's definitely attractive in adversity. Really, boy, what with one thing and another . . . I warned you against women, didn't I? They land you in impossible predicaments of this nature.

SLOANE. You can solve it, Ed.

ED. You believe that, do you? I hope so. Marriage is a non-starter, then?

KATH. He's led me on.

ED. Are you repentant now? Truly ashamed of yourself?

SLOANE. I am.

ED. You aren't going to press your claims are you? Even if he thee worshipped with his body, his mind would be elsewhere. And a wife cannot testify against her husband.

KATH. Can't she?

ED. No, a minor point.

KATH. I don't mind about marriage as long as he doesn't leave me.

ED. Fine. (*Pause.*) I think, boy, you'd better go and wait in the car. Keep the engine running. I won't be long. I want a private talk with my sister.

SLOANE. Is it going to be O.K.?

ED. Well . . . perhaps.

SLOANE. I'll be grateful.

ED. Will you?

SLOANE. Eternally.

ED. Not eternally, boy. Just a few years (*He pats* SLOANE *on the shoulder.* SLOANE *exits.*) What will the story be?

KATH. Like you said – he fell downstairs.

ED. That will explain the cuts and bruises. You'd better say you were out. Stick to that. You know nothing. I'll manage the doctor.

KATH. Yes, Ed.

ED. Can I trust you?

KATH. Yes.

ED. Then let's have no more threats. You'll support him?

KATH. As long as he stays here.

ED. You've had him six months; I'll have him the next six. I'm not robbing you of him permanently.

KATH. Aren't you?

ED. No question of it. (*Pause.*) As long as you're prepared to accept the idea of partnership.

KATH. For how long?

ED. As long as the agreement lasts.

KATH. How long is that?

ED. By the half-year.

KATH. That's too long, dear. I get so lonely.

ED. I've got no objections if he visits you from time to time. Briefly. We could put it in the contract. Fair enough?

KATH. Yes.

ED. I'd bring him over myself in the car. Now, you'll be more or less out of action for the next three months. So shall we say till next August? Agreed?

KATH. Perfect, Eddie. It's very clever of you to have thought of such a lovely idea!

ED. Put it down to my experience at the conference table.

Car sounds off.

KATH. Can he be present at the birth of his child?

ED. You're not turning him into a mid-wife.

KATH. It deepens the relationship if the father is there.

ED. It's all any reasonable child can expect if the dad is present at the conception. Let's hear no more of it. Give me that locket.

KATH. It was his present to me.

ED. You'll get it back in March. (*She hands him the locket. He puts it on.*) And behave yourself in future. I'm not having you pregnant every year. I'll have a word with him about it. (*He kisses her cheek, pats her bottom.*) Be a good girl.

KATH. Yes, Ed.

ED. Well, it's been a pleasant morning. See you later. (*He exits. The front door slams.* KATH *goes to the sideboard and rummages in drawer; takes out a sweet, unwraps it and puts it into her mouth. Sits on settee.*)

CURTAIN

The Good and Faithful Servant

'Well done, thou good and faithful servant.'
Matthew. 25: 21

'*Faith,* n. Reliance, trust, *in*; belief founded on authority.'
Concise Oxford Dictionary

The Good and Faithful Servant was first produced on television by Rediffusion on 6 April 1967 with the following cast:

BUCHANAN	Donald Pleasance
EDITH	Hermione Baddeley
MRS VEALFOY	Patricia Routledge
DEBBIE	Sheila White
RAY	Richard O'Callaghan
AN OLD MAN	Jack Bligh

Director: James Ormerod

Scene One

A long corridor.
Closed doors left and right line the corridor. From behind them come sounds of typing. A telephone is heard ringing, faintly.
At the end of the corridor, EDITH, *an old woman, is scrubbing the floor.*

BUCHANAN, *an old man, wearing a commissionaire's uniform, makes his way along the corridor towards* EDITH. *He stops beside her. Out of breath.*

BUCHANAN. Is this the Personnel section?

EDITH. Yes.

BUCHANAN. I've found it at last. I've had a long journey.

EDITH. Didn't they provide a map?

BUCHANAN. No. I was offered a guide, but I turned it down.

EDITH. Are you expected?

BUCHANAN. Yes. I'm retiring today. They're making a presentation. I'm the oldest living employee. My photograph will be in the firm's magazine. They've already arranged the particulars. I gave them every assistance, of course.

> EDITH *wrings water from a cloth into a bucket.*

I recall them building this block. My first day here coincided with the Foundation ceremony.

> EDITH *looks up.*

EDITH. So did mine. I was crushed up against a wall by a section of the crowd. My mother complained on my behalf. But nothing official ever came of it.

BUCHANAN. How long have you worked here?

EDITH. Fifty years. I have breaks, of course. For pregnancy and the occasional death of a near relative.

BUCHANAN. I've been here for fifty years, too. How strange we've never met.

EDITH. Which gate do you use?

BUCHANAN. Number eight.

EDITH. Ah, well, you see, that explains it. I've always entered by number fifteen.

She moves her bucket and cloth down the corridor.

BUCHANAN. I've a feeling we have met. In the distance, as I came along, there seemed something familiar. Something about your stance. Something that awaked memories.

EDITH begins to scrub the floor.

You've a look about you of the only woman I ever loved. I was a youngster when I met her. She was in difficulties by the roadside. I hesitated long enough to let her know I was a gentleman, and then I spoke. I attended to her problem and she was grateful. She let me see her home. And as luck would have it, our way lay through a meadow and the grass was high.

EDITH stops, looks up, gives a startled cry.

I'm sorry if I've offended you. These highly spiced tales aren't for the ears of the elderly. I apologize.

EDITH. No! Go on! What happened?

BUCHANAN. I couldn't tell you. I'm too ashamed. And she's been dead for years, I suppose. I can't bring disgrace upon her name.

EDITH. What was her name?

BUCHANAN. I can't recall. Though it was dear to me once.

EDITH. Was it Edith Anderson?

BUCHANAN. Yes. It was. How did you know?

EDITH stands. Tears glisten in her eyes.

EDITH. It was me!

BUCHANAN (*recoils*). You!

EDITH tugs off her plastic glove and shows him her hand.

EDITH. You gave me this ring.

BUCHANAN stares at the ring. Pause. Stares into EDITH's face.

BUCHANAN. But . . . (*He shakes his head.*) . . . you were so beautiful.

EDITH. I remained desirable until I was thirty.

BUCHANAN. You lasted so long?

EDITH. Then I had my first illness.

She puts on her glove, kneels, painfully, begins to scrub the floor.
You did me a great wrong.

BUCHANAN. No one knew.

EDITH. Not at the time. Later on it became only too obvious that I'd gone astray. I was turned out by my father. I wandered for a long time until I found somewhere to have the babies.

BUCHANAN. Two?

EDITH. Twins.

BUCHANAN. Promiscuity always leads to unwanted children, I should've known. Where are they now?

EDITH. In Heaven, I hope.

BUCHANAN. Dead?

EDITH. Killed in Italy.

BUCHANAN. What were they doing so far from home?

EDITH. They were wounded in a skirmish and taken to a peasant's hut for shelter. The peasant's son offered them water from a poisoned well – he meant no harm – it was an accident. The sanitary system of an alien country killed them. The authorities were good. They chose to believe that it was war wounds. I've the papers at home.

BUCHANAN takes out a handkerchief, blows his nose, bows his head.

BUCHANAN. Is there nothing left of them? No photographs?

EDITH. Before they died, they produced a son.

BUCHANAN. With whose help?

EDITH. A young girl of impeccable character who worked in a pub.

BUCHANAN. Was it legal?

EDITH. No.

BUCHANAN. Which one fathered the child?

EDITH. No one knows.

BUCHANAN. Their morals must surely have been below average?

EDITH. It was the conditions. You couldn't blame them. We were so frightened in those days. You lived through it same as I did. They panicked, I expect.

BUCHANAN. Is our grandson alive?

EDITH. Yes. I look after him. When he's settled I shall die.

BUCHANAN. What of?

EDITH. Does it matter?

> *She moves the bucket farther down the corridor, kneels again, painfully.*

BUCHANAN. You have philosophy then? (EDITH *nods, begins to scrub the floor.*) Are you resigned to anything in particular?

EDITH. No. Life in general. Isn't that enough?

> BUCHANAN *stands beside a door marked 'Mrs Vealfoy'.*

BUCHANAN. Shall I see you again?

EDITH. That would be pleasant.

BUCHANAN. Are you married?

EDITH. I was.

BUCHANAN. What became of your husband?

EDITH. He ran away during the depression.

BUCHANAN. I'll look you up. Expect me tonight.

> *He knocks on the door.*

MRS VEALFOY (*calls*). Come in.

> *He opens the door.*

Scene Two

MRS VEALFOY'*s office.*

MRS VEALFOY *sitting at her desk. She looks up, smiles.*

MRS VEALFOY. Do come in.

> BUCHANAN *enters.* MRS VEALFOY *indicates a seat in front of the desk.*
>
> BUCHANAN *sits.*

MRS VEALFOY. May we be completely informal and call you 'George'?

BUCHANAN. By all means.

MRS VEALFOY. Good, good. (*Laughs.*) My name is Mrs Vealfoy. I expect you know that, don't you?

BUCHANAN. I've seen you at functions organized by the firm. You're usually in the distance. I've never been close before.

MRS VEALFOY. That's right. I remember you well. (*Laughs.*) I have to ask you one or two questions.

She passes a printed form across the desk.

Fill that in, George.

BUCHANAN *begins to fill in the form.*

Are you excited?

BUCHANAN. Yes.

MRS VEALFOY. That's good, isn't it? (*Laughs.*) Your overalls, boots, gloves and any other equipment or clothing belonging to the firm must be given up by three-thirty. Ask your foreman or head of department for details.

BUCHANAN *hands back the form.* MRS VEALFOY *initials it and puts it into a wire tray.*

Have you your clock card with you?

BUCHANAN *hands her his clock card. She initials it and puts it into the tray.*

Are you a member of a union? Are your dues paid?

BUCHANAN. In full.

MRS VEALFOY. You leave the firm with no unpaid debts, no arrears of credit?

BUCHANAN. Yes.

MRS VEALFOY. Have you in your possession any object belonging to the firm? Any machine part, tools, plans of the premises? I'm sure you realize we can't be too careful.

BUCHANAN. I've nothing you'd want.

MRS VEALFOY. You're not free to divulge any information about the firm, the administration of the firm, or the firm's products. We should take proceedings, you see. (*Pause.*) You lost a limb in the service of the firm? (*She consults a file on her desk.*) You conceal your disabilities well.

BUCHANAN. I had therapy treatment in the medical wing of the firm's Benevolent Home.

MRS VEALFOY. And the pension paid to you by the firm for the loss of your arm plus the cash was legally binding. We are in no way responsible for your other limbs. If they deteriorate in any way the firm cannot be held responsible. You understand this?

BUCHANAN. Yes.

MRS VEALFOY hands him his National Insurance card.

MRS VEALFOY. Your 'cards', George.

They both laugh.

I think that's everything. Did we take your photograph?

BUCHANAN. Yes. (*Pause.*) Something was said about taking another – as I was leaving the firm. But I don't want any fuss made.

MRS VEALFOY. We have no intention of taking any more photographs. So you won't be bothered.

BUCHANAN (*with a laugh*). It's no bother to me.

MRS VEALFOY. It's no bother for you, I'm sure. (*Laughs.*) But we mustn't put upon you.

She takes her hat from the hatstand and puts it on.

BUCHANAN (*pause*). You aren't putting upon me. Whatever gave you that idea? Let them take as many photos as they like.

MRS VEALFOY (*at the mirror*). You hold the record for long service? Is that correct?

BUCHANAN. Quite correct. I'm hoping my grandson will come here. To carry on the tradition.

MRS VEALFOY turns from the mirror. She goes to the desk. She consults the file. She stares at BUCHANAN sharply.

MRS VEALFOY. Pay attention to me! What grandson? You've no descendants living. I have the information from our records.

BUCHANAN. I've just learned of a descendant of whom I had no knowledge.

MRS VEALFOY. Who told you?

BUCHANAN. A woman I met in the corridor.

MRS VEALFOY. Had she any right to inform you of an addition to your family?

BUCHANAN. She was the boy's grandmother.

MRS VEALFOY. Your wife is dead! Have you been feeding false information into our computers?

BUCHANAN. The woman wasn't my wife. I was young and foolish. It happened a long time ago.

MRS VEALFOY. I shall inform your section manager. He must straighten this out with Records.

BUCHANAN. It's a personal matter. My private life is involved.

MRS VEALFOY. Should your private life be involved, we shall be the first to inform you of the fact.

She opens the door.

Let my secretary have your grandson's address. I'll send him some of our literature.

Scene Three

The works canteen.
On a table at the end of the room are two parcels. Several MEN *and* WOMEN *are sitting in front of the table.*
BUCHANAN *and* MRS VEALFOY *enter. Applause.* MRS VEALFOY *holds up her hand for silence. She smiles.*

MRS VEALFOY. We all know why we are here. George Buchanan is retiring today after fifty years with the firm. Now, I want to tell you a little bit about him.

She smiles and looks at BUCHANAN. *Applause from the crowd.*
George left school at fourteen and joined the firm one year later, receiving the princely sum of seven shillings a week – which he will tell you went a long way in those far-off times. He quickly became known for his speed and intolerance of any work which was in the least 'slip-shod'.

She looks around her and at BUCHANAN.
At the outbreak of the Second World War, George was called upon to supervise his department, and to take on a lot of extra

responsibilities. He didn't complain, though. He shouldered his share of the burden which we all had in those days.

She pauses. She looks around the room. Her voice takes on a quieter, more meaningful note.

George has had his share of life's tragedies. We all remember reading that he was on the danger list some years ago. He soon returned to us, however, and his cheery laugh echoed once again through the canteen. He is now fit and still rides a bicycle. Nothing could quell George, I'm sure.

Friendly laughter.

I think, looking at him, we can hardly believe he will be sixty-five on Sunday. He is looking forward, I know, to an active retirement. And it is with retirement in mind that the men of your department, George, have pleasure in presenting you with this very lovely electric toaster. Which I believe, is what you wanted.

She unwraps the first parcel and hands the toaster to BUCHANAN. *Applause.*

And, as a parting present from the firm, I have great delight in giving you this electric clock.

She unwraps the second parcel and hands the clock to BUCHANAN. *Applause.*

When you look at it, you'll think of us, I'm sure.

Applause. BUCHANAN *clears his throat. Silence.*

BUCHANAN. As I stand on the eve of a well-earned rest I have no hesitation in saying that I've worked hard for it. (*Pause.*) Over the years I've witnessed changes both inside and outside the firm. The most remarkable is the complete overhaul of equipment which has taken place during the last year. I am truly sorry to leave without seeing much of it in operation. But – there it is – what will be, will be.

Pause.
He nods his head.

As I say, retirement is a big step. It's going to mean a break.

But I can say I've earned my rest. I hope to see you at the annual 'get together' in a month's time. So it isn't by any means 'Goodbye'.

MRS VEALFOY *looks at the clock. It is twelve-thirty.*

Well, I had better come to an end now, as I think the canteen ladies are impatient to begin serving dinner. So once again, thank you. God bless. And – thank you – thank you.

Cheers. The clatter of dishes. The clock says just after twelve-thirty. The AUDIENCE *push past* BUCHANAN *and* MRS VEALFOY. BUCHANAN *and* MRS VEALFOY *are alone beside the table.*

MRS VEALFOY. Make sure you hand in your uniform. After lunch you're free. We've no further need of you.

She smiles, and goes out. BUCHANAN *is alone. He picks up the parcels, joins the lunch queue. No one speaks to him, or is aware of his presence. The queue moves forward.*

Scene Four

MRS VEALFOY'*s office.*
MRS VEALFOY *at her desk. A knock on the door.* DEBBIE *enters.*

DEBBIE. Are you the lady that gives personal hints as well as for the firm?

MRS VEALFOY (*with a bright smile*). My advice covers all fields of endeavour. Won't you come in?

She indicates a seat. DEBBIE *closes the door and enters the room.*

MRS VEALFOY. What is your department?

She turns to the filing cabinet.

DEBBIE. I'm a typist. I've recently been transferred from the pool to the special services section. I'm highly recommended.

MRS VEALFOY *speaks from the filing cabinet.*

MRS VEALFOY. What is your name?

DEBBIE. Debbie Fieldman. (*Pause, with a nervous cough.*) I'm filed under Deborah.

    MRS VEALFOY *takes a file from the cabinet and sits at her desk.*
    She smiles at DEBBIE.

MRS VEALFOY. How can I help you?

DEBBIE. I was more or less bludgeoned into coming to you by a
friend of mine. You may recall helping her out of a sticky spot
when she was up before the council about the rateable value of
her flat?

MRS VEALFOY. Yes. I remember the girl well.

DEBBIE. She left the firm under a cloud, but she certainly profited
by your advice. (*Pause, she bites her lip.*) I don't know where to
begin. I'm nearly at my wit's end.

MRS VEALFOY. Take your time. Speak slowly and distinctly.
I'll be listening to every word.

    DEBBIE *twists her fingers together. Her lip trembles.*

DEBBIE. Well, you see, Mrs Vealfoy, I've become intimately
attached to a boy who means all the world to me. Against my
better judgement, I allowed him to persuade me to do something which I knew to be wrong. Oh, you'll never know what
I've been through these last few weeks . . . (*She blows her nose on
her handkerchief.*)

MRS VEALFOY (*quietly and with compassion*). Are you having a
baby, my dear?

DEBBIE. Yes.

MRS VEALFOY. Have you seen a doctor?

DEBBIE. Yes. I went to the hospital and said I was married. I had
to make up many of the details. I regret having to deceive the
Health Service in this way, but I daren't go to our doctor. My
secret wouldn't be safe for a second with him. We're on the
telephone at home, you see. And the doctor is always ringing us
up at inconvenient hours, and coming round . . . so I went to the
Out Patients. (*She bursts into tears.*)

    MRS VEALFOY *comes round the desk and puts an arm round*
    DEBBIE's *shoulder.*

MRS VEALFOY. Is the young man willing to marry you?

DEBBIE. I haven't asked.

MRS VEALFOY. You must.

DEBBIE. I can't.

MRS VEALFOY. Why not?

DEBBIE. I hardly know him.

MRS VEALFOY. Well, you must get to know him. Try to win his confidence. Has he any hobbies to which he is particularly attached?

DEBBIE. No.

MRS VEALFOY. Where does he work?

DEBBIE. He's unemployed.

MRS VEALFOY. Where did you meet him?

DEBBIE. He's never asked me to meet him. I usually do it by accident.

MRS VEALFOY *shakes her head: the unusualness of the case has her baffled for a moment.*

MRS VEALFOY. This is a shocking state of affairs. Do you know the young man's name?

DEBBIE. He asked me to call him Ray. What his motive was in asking me to do such a thing, I can't say. I was half asleep at the time. I'm not trying to excuse his behaviour. Or mine. I've always taken it for granted that he knew what he was up to.

MRS VEALFOY. He's got you into trouble, and he may have done it under an assumed name. That fact has to be faced. (*Pause.*) Have you told your parents yet?

DEBBIE. No.

MRS VEALFOY. Would they object to your having a baby?

DEBBIE. Mum would die. She couldn't put it in the paper, see. She'd feel she'd been cheated.

MRS VEALFOY. What about your father?

DEBBIE. He's always had a horror of anything unnatural. It'll come as a blow to him. He's only just got over the shock of my brother.

MRS VEALFOY. You'd better say nothing for the moment. You must arrange a definite time and place of meeting with the young man. Pin him down. Get him to come clean over the

matter of his name. That is most important. And then contact
me.

> *She scribbles a note and hands it to* DEBBIE.

That is my telephone number.

> DEBBIE *puts the note into her handbag.* MRS VEALFOY
> *glances at her watch. She opens the desk and takes out a
> brochure. She hands it to* DEBBIE.

MRS VEALFOY. Here is a plan of the firm's nurseries. You may
wish to book a place for the child now. I can do it for you.

DEBBIE. But I'm not married.

MRS VEALFOY. You will be, my dear. Leave everything to me.

> MRS VEALFOY *smiles.* DEBBIE *puts the brochure into her
> handbag.*

Scene Five

The firm's clothing store.
*A curtained cubicle, outside the cubicle, a tailor's dummy dressed in
the trousers, shirt, tie, shoes and hat belonging to* BUCHANAN's
uniform.
A MAN *in a brown overall takes the uniform coat which* BUCHANAN
*hands through the curtains. He puts it on to the dummy. Wheels it
slowly away.*
BUCHANAN *enters from behind the curtains, dressed in his own
clothes. He appears smaller, shrunken and insignificant.*
He watches the MAN *in the brown overall pull a dust sheet over the
tailor's dummy.*
BUCHANAN *shuffles from the store.*

Scene Six

EDITH's *living-room.*
She enters, followed by BUCHANAN. *He is carrying two parcels. He
places them on the table.* EDITH *stares in amazement.*

EDITH. Oh!

BUCHANAN. What is it?

EDITH. Your arms! Where has the extra one come from?

BUCHANAN. It's false.

EDITH. Thank God for that. I like to know where I stand in relation to the number of limbs a man has.

   She opens the first parcel.

An electric clock. (*She lifts it from the wrapping.*) They gave you the wire as well. Shows how much they think of you.

   She opens the second parcel.

A toaster. It's a good make too. We must have toast for tea to try it out.

   She puts the parcels to one side and looks at BUCHANAN *fondly.*

What a day. You'll re-live it many times in the future.

   BUCHANAN *takes the toaster, begins to strip the wires, attaches plug to flex.*

EDITH. I've several souvenirs of our children dotted about this room. I'll point them out later. When you've settled in. (*Pause.*) This tablecloth belonged to the mother of our grandson. She left it me in her will.

BUCHANAN. Is she dead?

EDITH. She took her own life, poor dear. When the boys were killed. She couldn't face the idea of living on, so she gassed herself. She was illegitimate as well. That was the bond between them.

BUCHANAN. Is there no respect for marriage in this district?

EDITH. Very little, you'll find.

   BUCHANAN *pauses in his work. Looks up.*

BUCHANAN. What are we going to tell Raymond?

EDITH. Do we have to say anything?

BUCHANAN. Oh, yes. It wouldn't be fair to keep it a secret.

EDITH. It will be a shock to him to learn that the older generation behaved in such a disgraceful way.

BUCHANAN. We must explain the circumstances. Ask him to be tolerant. We are going to get married after all.

EDITH (*pause*). Isn't it too late?

BUCHANAN. It's never too late for marriage. I'm surprised at you, I am. Talking like the worst elements in Society. We must put things to right. We'll do it quietly and without fuss.

Door slams.

EDITH. This is Ray. He always makes a noise when he enters. It's a tradition with him.

RAY *enters.* EDITH *smooths her dress and smiles.*

EDITH. Ray, I want you to meet someone. Mr George Buchanan.

RAY *shakes hands with* BUCHANAN.

RAY. Good evening.

BUCHANAN. I'm pleased to meet you, Raymond. Your grand-mother has said a lot in your favour.

He sits. EDITH *looks at* BUCHANAN. *Looks at* RAY, *a worried frown on her face.*

EDITH. Sit down, Ray. I've something to say to you which may come as a surprise.

RAY. Won't it wait?

EDITH. No. We must have it out now.

RAY *sits. Pause.* EDITH *and* BUCHANAN *exchange glances.*

EDITH. Mr Buchanan is your grandfather. The man who appears with me on my wedding photograph had nothing to do with you. Not even indirectly. I was very silly, and Mr Buchanan behaved badly. We would've got married, only we lost touch with one another. We were too young to know what we were doing. (*Pause.*) Don't blame us too much, Raymond. Try to imagine what it's like to be young.

BUCHANAN. I'm going to marry her. Do the right thing.

RAY *shrugs.*

RAY. Well, understandably I'm shocked by your revelations. The country's moral values far from changing, seem to remain unnaturally constant.

EDITH. I should've told you, I suppose. It would've been easier if your fathers were alive.

RAY *frowns. He turns to* EDITH, *puzzled.*

RAY. My fathers?

EDITH. Yes.

RAY. I had more than one?

    EDITH *clasps her hands in her lap and turns to* BUCHANAN.

EDITH. Just where to stop when telling the truth has always been a problem.

RAY. How could I have two fathers?

EDITH. Your mother was a generous woman. And your fathers – though one of them must surely have been your uncle – loved her dearly. You were the result.

RAY. And my mother?

EDITH. Her pedigree couldn't be subjected to scrutiny either. *Silence.* RAY *shakes his head.*

RAY. Bastardy for two generations and on both sides of the family!

BUCHANAN. Had you no idea? No suspicion?

RAY. How could I have?

BUCHANAN. Your birth certificate.

RAY. I've never seen it.

BUCHANAN. When you applied to join in the pension scheme.

RAY. What pension scheme?

BUCHANAN. At your firm. Where you work.

RAY. I don't work.

BUCHANAN. Not work!? (*He stares, open-mouthed.*) What do you do then?

RAY. I enjoy myself.

BUCHANAN. That's a terrible thing to do. I'm bowled over by this, I can tell you. It's my turn to be shocked now. You ought to have a steady job.

EDITH. Two perhaps.

BUCHANAN. In what direction do your talents lie?

RAY. I mended the bathroom tap once.

BUCHANAN. Technically minded, are you?

EDITH. He had nearly thirteen stamps on his card last year. He found himself a lovely situation.

RAY. Yes. Only they insisted that I curtail my freedom of speech. These firms make some impossible demands.

BUCHANAN. Is there any particular work you feel you're suited to?

RAY. I took a liftman's job once. For kicks.

BUCHANAN. Kicks? They're very much in the news at the moment, aren't they?

RAY. Yes.

BUCHANAN. Are they doing you any good?

RAY. They're not on prescription, you know.

BUCHANAN. You'll find a good steady job more rewarding in the long run, than purple hearts. I speak from experience. I'm going to talk to Mrs Vealfoy, our personnel lady. She'll advise you what to do with your life.

EDITH (*pause*). Is the toaster ready for trial?

BUCHANAN. Yes.

EDITH. That hand of yours is almost human. The things you contrive to do with it are miraculous.

BUCHANAN *plugs in the toaster. A loud bang and a flash.*

BUCHANAN. Oh!

He cowers away; covers his face with his hands. He begins to shake. Sniffs.

Pause.

I've never done a thing like that before. I'm quite capable of minor electrical jobs.

EDITH *leads him to the chair. He sits down. He hunches his shoulders; coughs a little.*

EDITH. You are in a state. We'll have to abandon my original plan of toast for tea.

RAY *pulls out the plug. He examines the toaster.*

RAY. Where did you get this load of old rubbish?

EDITH. Shhh! (*She nods to* BUCHANAN, *in a quiet voice to* RAY.) It was presented to Mr Buchanan by his firm. As a reward for fifty years' service.

Scene Seven

MRS VEALFOY's *office.*
DEBBIE *enters.* MRS VEALFOY *smiles.*

MRS VEALFOY. Have you any further news, Debbie?

DEBBIE. Yes, Mrs Vealfoy. I saw Raymond last night.

MRS VEALFOY. Did you speak to him?

DEBBIE. I waved, though.

MRS VEALFOY. Did he appear to resent your friendly action?

DEBBIE. No.

MRS VEALFOY. Good. Your relationship with the young man is progressing. Were you able to arrange a place of meeting?

DEBBIE. Yes. He sent a message by his friend. He wants to meet me at the Skating Rink.

MRS VEALFOY. A skating rink? That doesn't seem advisable in your condition, Debbie.

DEBBIE. I thought the same. I said I'd meet him after the Rink closed down. Outside.

MRS VEALFOY. And you'll broach the subject of your pregnancy whilst he's physically exhausted from an evening's skating?

DEBBIE. Yes.

MRS VEALFOY. Admirable. We're making real headway with the problem.

MRS VEALFOY *pushes several printed forms, typewritten sheets and carbon copies of documents across the desk to* DEBBIE.

Would you read these carefully? I've marked where you're to sign.

DEBBIE *begins to sign the forms.*

I've made a reservation for a cot at the firm's nurseries. There's a query beside the sex of the child. I hope it won't stay that way.

As DEBBIE *signs the forms she hands them across the desk to* MRS VEALFOY.

A telegram of congratulations will be sent to coincide with the baby's birth. My secretary has the details of the case. Have no fears. She's most discreet. (*Smiling.*) It won't be long now, my dear, before we place a definite order for your wedding bouquet. As, through no fault of your own, the ceremony looks like being delayed, we'd better make it of some large and showy bloom. Lilies won't be appropriate under the circumstances.

DEBBIE *pushes the last of the forms across the desk.*

Chrysanthemums would do. Or even peonies.

She puts the forms into a wire tray.

If we leave it much longer it will have to be sunflowers, I'm afraid.

Scene Eight

RAY's *bedroom.*
The room in darkness. The door opens. RAY *enters, guiding* DEBBIE *into the room.*

RAY (*in a whisper*). Don't make a sound.

He closes the door carefully and switches on the light.

(*In a whisper.*) You can open your eyes now.

DEBBIE *opens her eyes.*

DEBBIE (*looking around, horrified*). What's this?

RAY. Shhh! (*He locks the door.*)

DEBBIE (*in a panic-stricken whisper*). This is a man's bedroom! I can't stay here. It's two o'clock in the morning. What kind of a girl do you take me for?

She goes to the door and tries to open it.

(*Hissing.*) Give me the key!

A struggle, both trying not to make any sound. RAY *almost drags* DEBBIE *to the bed. They sit.*

RAY (*breathes*). You said you'd got something to say to me.

DEBBIE. In your study, you said. This isn't a study. It's a bedroom.

RAY. What's your news?

DEBBIE *stands, shrugs him away.*

DEBBIE (*coldly, after a pause*). I'm having a baby. You're the father. (*She stands by the door.*) Give me the key. I can't be found in a man's bedroom at two in the morning. It's not decent.

Scene Nine

BUCHANAN's *bedroom, morning.*
On a table, an artificial arm, a pair of glasses, a hearing aid. EDITH *enters.*

EDITH (*drawing the curtains*). Another day! What has it in store? Sunshine or showers?
> *She helps* BUCHANAN *to sit up and gives him his glasses.*
Now you can see the world.
> *She gives him his hearing-aid.*
Now you can hear. (*She places several leaflets on the table.*) The post brought some literature for you. I had a quick glance. Nice machines they have, don't they?
> BUCHANAN *picks up a leaflet, glances at it with interest.*
BUCHANAN. They were recently installed.
EDITH. I particularly liked the photos of the canteen. I swept it out once. When one of the kitchen staff was away they sent for me.
BUCHANAN. They recognized your worth?
EDITH. Yes.
BUCHANAN. They're good like that. (*Pause.*) I got these pamphlets for Ray. See if he can't find an interest in life. (*Pause.*) He made a lot of noise last night.
EDITH. These floors are very thin.
BUCHANAN. Sounded like he was dancing.
EDITH. Go and ask him when you've had your breakfast.

Scene Ten

Outside RAY'*s room.*
BUCHANAN *knocks on the door. Pause.*
RAY *opens the door. He is dressed in pyjamas.*

BUCHANAN. I'd like a few words with you, Raymond.
RAY. With me?
BUCHANAN. If it's convenient.
RAY. Just a minute.
  He closes the door. Pause. He re-opens it and allows BUCHANAN
  into the room.

Scene Eleven

RAY'*s bedroom.*
BUCHANAN *enters.*

RAY (*with a laugh*). I've just got up. Quite a surprise you gave me.
BUCHANAN. Did I inconvenience you?
RAY. No. I'd just finished.
BUCHANAN. Finished what?
RAY. Well – (*Laughs.*) getting up.
  BUCHANAN *sits.*
BUCHANAN. I want a serious talk with you. (*Pause.*) You can't go
  on like this, you know.
  RAY *doesn't answer.*
  Something's missing from your life. Do you know what it is?
  RAY *frowns, pause.*
RAY. Is it God?
BUCHANAN (*pause, suspicious*). Who told you about Him?
RAY. I read a bit in the paper once.
BUCHANAN. It's a deep subject, but in my own mind I'm certain
  God has nothing to do with you. It's work you want.

BUCHANAN *places several of the firm's pamphlets heavily on the table.*

(*With emphasis.*) My old firm would be delighted to employ you for a small remuneration.

RAY. What about my outside interests?

BUCHANAN. The firm has a Recreation Centre. They cater for most tastes. You'd have to do it after working hours naturally.

RAY. Do what?

BUCHANAN. Whatever you were inclined to. (*Pause.*) Give it a trial.

RAY. I'd like to. Only my plans are in the air at the moment. This bird I've been knocking about with is turning moody. I can't see my way clear to promising anything definite. Either to her or to you. I put something into operation a few months ago which looks like having far-reaching consequences.

Silence.

BUCHANAN. Raymond . . .

RAY. Yes?

BUCHANAN. Is your private life sound?

RAY. As a bell.

BUCHANAN. Good. What would really please your grandmother and me was if you'd find a decent girl and settle down. Do you know any women of the right calibre?

RAY. For what?

BUCHANAN. The altar. You'll have to think about getting married soon.

RAY. That is a distinct possibility.

BUCHANAN. Is she good? This girl you know?

RAY. Blonde with blue eyes. An angelic expression. She has strict views about . . . what we're talking about. I agree with her, of course. Because you should save it up, shouldn't you? Make it go further. Thrift, thrift.

BUCHANAN. Yes. You're not a bad lad at heart, Raymond. (*He indicates the pamphlets.*) Have a glance at these, won't you?

RAY. O.K.

> BUCHANAN *stands. As he does so a coin drops from his pocket and rolls under the bed.*

BUCHANAN. It's under the bed. Can you get it?

RAY. It's only a penny.

BUCHANAN. No, it's half a crown. Move the bed a bit.

RAY. I'll bring it down later.

BUCHANAN. It won't take a minute.

RAY. What's the matter? Think I'm robbing you or something?

> BUCHANAN *stares hard at* RAY. *He glances around the room. Sees* DEBBIE's *handbag on the windowsill. He suddenly bends to look under the bed.*
>
> *Shot of* DEBBIE *crouching under the bed, partly clothed.*
>
> BUCHANAN *straightens up.*

BUCHANAN. You wicked little devil!

> RAY *shrugs.*

This is striking out into new frontiers all right. Eleven o'clock of a Wednesday morning. Women under the bed!

RAY. You should've told me you were coming up.

BUCHANAN. I can hardly credit the degree to which our family has sunk.

RAY. D'you mind going? She's getting covered in dust under there.

> BUCHANAN *goes out.* RAY *lies on the bed.* DEBBIE *emerges.*

DEBBIE. Who was that old man?

RAY. My grandad.

DEBBIE (*opening the wardrobe and taking out her dress*). Why didn't you introduce me properly?

Scene Twelve

The living-room.
BUCHANAN *at the table.* EDITH *brings him a cup of tea and a slice of toast.*

EDITH. What an inconsiderate boy, though, keeping her under the bed. I don't know where he gets his ideas from?

BUCHANAN. I'm outraged by it, I am. Carrying on above our heads. I would never have slept easy if I'd known. Eleven o'clock on a weekday morning! How many of us did that kind of thing?

EDITH. Not many without a priest had sanctioned the act.

BUCHANAN. And not often then.

EDITH. It's something of a miracle we had a succeeding generation we were so unconscious of that side of things.

BUCHANAN. When I met you it was at least in the afternoon.

EDITH. And it was a hot afternoon. Almost evening.

BUCHANAN. I believe it's the lack of proper playing fields.

EDITH. And yet, I'd imagine more open spaces would increase the risk. Does the Duke of Edinburgh realize what he's letting us in for?

RAY *enters. Silence.* BUCHANAN *breaks the silence at last.*

BUCHANAN. Well, what have you to say for yourself?

RAY. Let's be fair about it, Grandad. You were upset and so was I. Draw a veil over the whole proceedings.

BUCHANAN. I can't do that.

RAY. Why not?

BUCHANAN. It might happen again.

RAY. Not if you give me warning.

BUCHANAN. We can have it stopped, you know. You're under age. Aren't you? (*Appealing to* EDITH.) Is it legal?

EDITH. He can't vote. I know that.

BUCHANAN. I'm trying to show you a different life from the one you're leading at present. A useful and constructive life such as I've led and –

He begins to cough. EDITH *pats his back.*

Oh, Christ! My lungs'll be on the rug in a minute.

They wait until he recovers.

Who is this girl?

RAY. She lives with her Mum and Dad.

BUCHANAN. What does she do for a living? She doesn't get paid for her activities this morning, does she?

RAY. I wouldn't pay for that.

BUCHANAN. I'm glad you've got a little decency.

RAY. I couldn't afford to.

BUCHANAN. Get a job. You'll have plenty of money then.

RAY. I'd have no time.

BUCHANAN. You'd have the week-ends.

RAY. I'd be too tired.

BUCHANAN. Not if you kept your health.

RAY. How much would I earn?

BUCHANAN. Fifteen pounds a week.

RAY. Where does fifteen quid go with a woman?

BUCHANAN. If you're determined to persevere with women I can see no future for you. There are other group activities, you know.

RAY. Yes, but the rules are in French.

BUCHANAN. Learn the language. Acquire a fluency in something else. Ludo would be less of a strain in the long run.

DEBBIE *enters. She stands uneasily at the door. Her lip trembles.*

DEBBIE. I'm sorry to barge in on you, but I'll have to be going. I'm late for work.

RAY (*pause, embarrassed*). This is Miss Fieldman. Debbie – my grandfather and grandmother.

Silence. DEBBIE *shuffles her feet, ill at ease.*

BUCHANAN. What explanation have you got for being under a man's bed at this time in the day?

DEBBIE. I'm sorry. It must seem awful to you. I had important news to communicate to Ray last night. And he persuaded me to stay.

EDITH. Were you under the bed all night?

DEBBIE. No. (*Pause, she becomes tearful.*) I'm not really like that at all. (*Crying.*) I'm having a baby! (*Defiant.*) I'm seeing someone this morning from the Welfare. (*To* RAY.) You'll have to settle it with them. They'll want details. I can't manage on my own.

BUCHANAN (*shocked, to* EDITH). He's put her in the family way. That is an act of indecency I will not tolerate. He must go.

EDITH. It's the sex-education. They think of nothing else.

RAY. We didn't receive any sex-education.

BUCHANAN. How did you learn?

RAY. From other boys.

BUCHANAN. What kind of boys are these that teach each other about the family way? Get away from me, Raymond. I'm disappointed in you.

RAY. But you did the same.

BUCHANAN. I had every excuse. Conditions were bad. You want for nothing today.

DEBBIE *dries her eyes.*

DEBBIE (*to* RAY). I can't stay any longer. I'm late as it is. (*She dabs at her nose.*) My Mum and Dad want to meet you. They don't know what's happened. Mum's arranging an outing next week and I thought that'd be a good opportunity of telling them.

She *takes his arm.*

See me to the door.

RAY *and* DEBBIE *go out.* BUCHANAN *picks up a piece of toast. He puts it down in disgust.*

BUCHANAN (*wearily*). Something's wrong with this toast.

EDITH. It's your toaster. It carries on in a most eccentric fashion. And the clock is about as useful. Tells whatever time it fancies.

BUCHANAN *goes to the shelf and picks up the clock.*

BUCHANAN. It's going backwards! Something's wrong with the works. (*He turns the clock over and drops it.*) Oh!

EDITH. What is it?

BUCHANAN. Gave me a shock it did. Right up my arm.

He *puts the clock beside the toaster on the table.*

EDITH (*with a shrug*). They seem more like murder weapons than gifts from a grateful employer.

Scene Thirteen

MRS VEALFOY's *office.*
MRS VEALFOY *speaking to a recording machine.*

MRS VEALFOY. Anyone found using the staff lifts without permission will be liable to instant dismissal. (*Pause.*) Circulate copies to all departments.

Silence.

Another notice. To all heads of departments. Capitals. LONELY PEOPLE. (*Pause.*) If you know of anyone who would be interested in joining the firm's recently formed 'Bright Hours' club would you kindly contact Mrs Vealfoy or any member of her staff. The person or persons of either sex must be old, lonely and ex-members of the firm. No other qualifications are needed.

She speaks on the intercom to her secretary.

Send Miss Fieldman in.

She turns to the mirror, and puts on her hat. DEBBIE *enters.*

MRS VEALFOY. Have you seen the young man?

DEBBIE. Yes, Mrs Vealfoy.

MRS VEALFOY. Have you told him the facts of the case?

DEBBIE. Yes.

MRS VEALFOY. Has he given you his address?

DEBBIE. Yes.

She takes a postcard from her handbag, and gives it to MRS VEALFOY.

MRS VEALFOY (*taking the postcard*). You may go. I'll contact your Supervisor immediately I've any news.

DEBBIE *goes out.* MRS VEALFOY *speaks to her secretary over the intercom.*

I'll be away for about an hour.

Scene Fourteen

EDITH's *living-room.*
EDITH *enters followed by* MRS VEALFOY.

MRS VEALFOY. Are you sure your grandson isn't at home?

EDITH. Yes. He's away for the day.

MRS VEALFOY. Is he seeking employment?

EDITH. I couldn't say. We've grown apart lately. We hardly exchange two words together.

MRS VEALFOY. Why?

EDITH. I didn't like to ask. They're so touchy these days.

MRS VEALFOY *takes out a card.*

MRS VEALFOY. See that he gets this. I want to see him. Tell him that. Tell him that Mrs Vealfoy is anxious to have a word with him.

EDITH *puts the card on the shelf.*

Is Mr Buchanan in?

EDITH. Well, he's in. Whether I consider he's in a fit state to receive visitors is a different matter.

MRS VEALFOY (*with a smile*). We must do something about that.

EDITH. He's been upset.

MRS VEALFOY. Has he had a check-up? Give me the name of his medical practitioner.

EDITH. He's depressed.

MRS VEALFOY. Is that the truth? I think I can clear things up.

EDITH. He broods, see.

MRS VEALFOY. Question him why he does that. Worm it out of him.

EDITH. Our grandson has misbehaved himself. The clock and the toaster have proved a disappointment. And to cap it all he's old. So what with one thing and another his attitude is of despair.

MRS VEALFOY (*sharply*). What did you say?

EDITH. He despairs.

MRS VEALFOY. Has he used that word in your presence?

EDITH. No.

MRS VEALFOY. He should forget about it. And to take his mind off things why not busy himself? A part-time job. Join a club. Make himself so busy he hasn't time to despair.

EDITH. He'll exhaust himself, poor darling.

MRS VEALFOY. What hobbies has he?

EDITH. None, if you can believe him. And personally I do. We have that sort of relationship, see?

MRS VEALFOY. Where is he now?

EDITH. In bed.

MRS VEALFOY (*laughing*). In bed? That isn't doing him any good, is it? He must take this matter seriously.

EDITH. We're going to be married on Saturday.

MRS VEALFOY. Are you? That's a good idea. Are you having a cake?

EDITH. No. We're not having anything. It's only for show. It's a waste getting married when you're my age. I'm only doing it for his sake. He's very much on his dignity about it. He's been like that all his life so he tells me. I can't vouch for it, of course, as I only met him briefly at the beginning and at the end.

MRS VEALFOY. Mr Buchanan must come to the 'Bright Hours' club. He'll meet old friends. I'll expect him. (*She opens her handbag, and takes out a circular.*) See that he's there. He'll forget his troubles, you'll see.

Scene Fifteen

MRS VEALFOY's *office.*

MRS VEALFOY *at her desk.* RAY *enters.* MRS VEALFOY *indicates a chair.*

MRS VEALFOY. Come along in, Raymond. Sit down.

RAY *sits,* MRS VEALFOY *smiles.*

MRS VEALFOY. I can't tell you how glad I am to meet you. I'm taking a great interest in you at the moment. (*Laughs.*) I hope that doesn't alarm you?

RAY. No.

MRS VEALFOY. Good. (*Laughs.*) Good. You know, Raymond, we're all pretty worried about you. How do you feel? Are you worried?

RAY. Yes.

MRS VEALFOY. I'm glad to hear it. There's nothing so impressive as disquiet in the young. It shows an awareness of the problems of life which is most encouraging.

She studies RAY *for a moment with a quizzical expression.*

One of the things that has caused me great concern is the apparent lack of any real direction to your life. And I think that this has caused your trouble. Don't you?

RAY (*not wishing to disagree*). Yes.

MRS VEALFOY. Ah, I'm glad you used that particular word. An affirmation of anything is cheering nowadays. Say 'Yes' as often as possible, Raymond. I always do. (*Laughs.*) Always. (*Smiles.*) Now, you must count me as a friend. A friend who will do all in her power to help you. Do you understand me?

RAY. Yes.

MRS VEALFOY. That's the spirit. (*Laughs.*) My goodness, we are getting on well, aren't we? (*She laughs and then, suddenly, serious.*) Do you love Debbie?

RAY. Yes.

MRS VEALFOY. And do you agree that what you have done is wrong?

RAY attempts to speak. MRS VEALFOY *holds up her hand, smiles.*

I'm not passing judgement. I merely want to ask if you agree with me. Do you think it wrong? (*Smiles.*) You don't have to say 'Yes' if you disagree with me. (*Pause.*) Do you think what you've done is wrong?

RAY. No.

MRS VEALFOY. I see. (*She smiles with no trace of disapproval.*) And why don't you think it is wrong?

RAY. If two people love each other why shouldn't they make love?

MRS VEALFOY (*simply and with candour*). Raymond, you mustn't imagine for one moment that I'm against two people expressing their love for each other. I'm most certainly not. Love-making is a beautiful thing. And we must treat it with the respect it deserves. Physical love is one of the finest ways a man can express his feelings for a woman. Therefore he must be very sure indeed that he really loves the woman to whom he gives his love. (*Pause.*) Do you really love Debbie?

RAY. Yes.

MRS VEALFOY. You want her to be happy?

RAY. I'm going to marry her.

MRS VEALFOY. That isn't quite the same thing. A baby on the way is no excuse for marriage nowadays. No one would suggest it was.

RAY. I want to marry her.

MRS VEALFOY. Good. (*Smiles.*) I always like the end achieved to coincide with established practice, though the means to the end may vary with custom. (*Pause.*) You see, Raymond, I think what you have done *is* wrong. Not for any religious reason (I'm an agnostic myself), but simply because love-making should be kept for one's marriage partner alone. Outside marriage the act may seem the same, but I have my doubts as to whether anyone derives any real and lasting satisfaction from it. There is no finer sight than two married people making love.

She looks at RAY *seriously.*

This thoughtless and selfish act may lead you to a much more worthwhile view of life. (*Pause.*) When you're married and have a wife and child you'll have to accept responsibility for them.

RAY. Yes.

MRS VEALFOY. You'll want a regular wage packet each week. (*With a smile, coup de grâce.*) And so, you see, you must have a steady job. It's high time you began to consider a career.

She takes a form from her desk and pushes it across to RAY.
Just fill that in, Raymond. (*Laughs.*) And afterwards I'll take
you down to our various departments. Show you round. See
what vacancies we have.

Scene Sixteen

A room in the firm's recreation centre.
*A number of old ex-employees are grouped around an upright piano
singing : 'We'll All Go Riding on a Rainbow to a New Land Far
Away'. Weary, apathetic voices.*
MRS VEALFOY *enters with* BUCHANAN. *She takes him to the group.*

MRS VEALFOY. Stop one moment everybody. (*The music dies
away.*) This is George. Do any of us remember him? (*Pause.*)
George retired recently after – how long, George?
BUCHANAN. Fifty years.
MRS VEALFOY. Fifty years. Yes, I believe I remember you. We
gave you an electric clock. Is that correct?
BUCHANAN. Yes.
MRS VEALFOY. And an electric shaver —
BUCHANAN. Toaster.
MRS VEALFOY. Toaster. Does anybody remember George?
Everybody stares at BUCHANAN. *No one says anything.*
Nobody? Are we sure? He has a distinctive face. Are we quite
sure we none of us are acquainted with our new member?
An OLD MAN *puts up his hand.*
OLD MAN. I remember him.
MRS VEALFOY *smiles.*
MRS VEALFOY. Isn't that nice. An old workmate of yours,
George. So you won't feel out of it.
The group around the piano drift away. MRS VEALFOY *takes*
BUCHANAN *around the room.*
Over here we have dominoes, cards and darts and all the pas-
times.

She points out a group of OLD MEN *and* WOMEN. *Two of them are in wheelchairs, one is blind, a couple are simple-minded. They stare at* BUCHANAN *without interest.* MRS VEALFOY *smiles and takes* BUCHANAN *across the room.*

And over here we have conversation.

Two or three VERY OLD WOMEN *are knitting.*

Would you like to talk over old times?

BUCHANAN. Yes.

MRS VEALFOY. Tea at three o'clock. Go and talk to your friend.

BUCHANAN goes over to the OLD MAN.

BUCHANAN. Hallo.

OLD MAN. Hallo, George.

BUCHANAN. I've never been in this room before.

OLD MAN. It's private.

BUCHANAN says nothing. A WOMAN *at the end of the room falls over. A flutter of excitement.* MRS VEALFOY *hurries to help her up. It is seen distantly.*

BUCHANAN. You remember me then?

OLD MAN. I retired a bit before you.

BUCHANAN. Did you see my photo in the magazine?

OLD MAN. No.

BUCHANAN. I was a long-service employee. A credit to canteen food they said I was. (*Pause.*) That's their words. I had dinner there since it opened. Can't be much wrong with the food, can there?

OLD MAN. I never used the canteen. I never liked that big woman as ran it.

BUCHANAN. She lost her husband recently.

OLD MAN. Is she left then?

Two OLD MEN *in wheelchairs pass across the room in the distance. A group has formed about the woman who fell over.* MRS VEALFOY *at the centre.*

Who was her husband? Did he work for us?

BUCHANAN. He was on the maintenance staff.

OLD MAN. I'm not up in that side of the firm. It never interested me.

MRS VEALFOY is seen shooing people away from the fallen woman. Two stretcher bearers have entered the room. The woman is put on the stretcher and hurried away. MRS VEALFOY's voice is heard faintly, from the distance.

MRS VEALFOY. Go back to what you were doing. It's quite all right. Off you go.

The group breaks up, wanders away.

OLD MAN. She's dead.

BUCHANAN. Who?

OLD MAN. The old girl as fell over. Didn't you see her?

BUCHANAN. No.

OLD MAN. Yes. She'll be dead.

Silence.

BUCHANAN. I looked forward to my retirement so's I could play skittles full time. I used to be a fan. I was in line for the cup. I just missed it. The mysterious thing was that I never came in line for it again.

OLD MAN. Bowls is my sport.

BUCHANAN. That's a nice game.

OLD MAN. I was almost mentioned in a well-known sporting periodical once.

BUCHANAN. I never got as far as that.

OLD MAN. I regard that as the high-spot of my life.

BUCHANAN. Yes. You would. (*Pause.*) The high-spot of my own career came when my photo appeared in the magazine. I didn't ask them to put it in. Some of them go round canvassing for support in their claims to be included. But I stood aside. And one day they came to my department and insisted I pose for them. I was unwilling at first. But I realized it was for my own good.

Silence.

MRS VEALFOY. Just one moment everybody. Listen to me please. Are you attending to what I say? (*Pause.*) Good.

She holds up a painting.

Isn't this delightful? Do you know who painted it?

OLD MAN (*calling*). You, miss!

Laughter.

MRS VEALFOY (*laughing*). What a flattering suggestion. No, I'm sure you didn't really think I could have done such a charming work of art. (*Pause.*) Well, since you pretend you can't tell me – Mrs Florence Thompson painted this splendid example of creative activity. Isn't she talented? Forty years on the shop floor hasn't dimmed her appreciation of the beautiful. Let's show our delight by a round of applause. Come along.

A patter of applause.

(*Putting the picture down.*) Everybody get on with what they were doing.

OLD MAN (*to* BUCHANAN). Where did you work?

BUCHANAN. I was almost Staff.

OLD MAN (*impressed*). Were you?

BUCHANAN. I was in charge of the Main Entrance. I saw the Chairman of the Board several times. I've even opened the door to him once. My immediate Superior was off with 'flu.

OLD MAN. You were on the doors?

BUCHANAN. It's a type of service I approve of.

Silence.

The local press sent somebody round last week.

OLD MAN. We don't take the local press.

BUCHANAN. You're like us then. Like us. I spoke a few words about my thoughts. I'm against the local paper because of the things they say about the Memorial to the Fallen. 'Isn't it a disgusting eyesore' and all that.

Silence. BUCHANAN *stares blankly ahead.*

(*At last.*) Who are these people who have no respect for the dead of two world wars? I'm bitter about it, I am. We fought for that Memorial. Men died for it.

OLD MAN. What edition were you in?

BUCHANAN. Ah, they didn't print it. Too controversial, I expect.

MRS VEALFOY *comes over.*

MRS VEALFOY. What are you saying? Is it interesting? Can I hear? Are you talking over old times as I told you?

BUCHANAN. No.

MRS VEALFOY. Why not? What were you talking about? Both of you have a lot to look back on. (*Pause, sharply.*) Answer my question! What were you talking about?

BUCHANAN. The war.

MRS VEALFOY. Were you in the war? (*Laughs.*)

BUCHANAN. I helped out as best I could. Three nights a week I was required to firewatch.

MRS VEALFOY. Who required you to do that?

BUCHANAN. Why – (*Puzzled.*) we all did it.

MRS VEALFOY. Good for you! Did you enjoy yourself? Were you on the roof?

BUCHANAN. Yes.

MRS VEALFOY. Splendid! I'm going to tell that to my friends. You see, I'll draw you out. You don't talk enough. (*Laughs.*) What happened before the war?

BUCHANAN. I can't recollect.

MRS VEALFOY. What a short memory you have. (*Laughs.*) Still, you've had a very full life without a long memory, haven't you? You must tell me sometime how you managed. (*Pause, she smiles at him, benevolently.*) And after the war? What did you do after the war?

BUCHANAN *is silent.*

Like that is it? You don't wish to talk? Keeping the fascinating details to yourself. (*Laughs.*) Well, you must tell me some day. Is that a promise?

BUCHANAN. Yes.

MRS VEALFOY. Good for you. Are you getting on well with your friend? Is he showing you the ropes? Are you having a good time?

BUCHANAN (*without conviction*). Yes.

MRS VEALFOY. That's the main thing. What about your depression? Have you forgotten about it?

BUCHANAN. No.

MRS VEALFOY. Why not?

BUCHANAN. I can't forget it. (*Pause.*) You wouldn't understand.

MRS VEALFOY (*laughs*). Don't say that to me. I understand everything. (*Laughs.*) Bring your problems to me. I'll unravel any difficulties. So don't let me catch you being depressed. (*Pause.*) Were you in the war? Is that why you're depressed? Did you have a terrible time? (*Pause.*) What did you do?

BUCHANAN. I was required to firewatch.

MRS VEALFOY. Who required you to do that? (*Pause.*) You don't like talking about it. Such a terrible time. (*Laughs brightly.*) We're going to sing in a minute. That will cure your depression, won't it? Will you join in? A jolly sing-song. All the old favourites. Don't be a spoil-sport. You'll join in, won't you?

BUCHANAN. Is it hymns?

MRS VEALFOY (*suddenly her face becomes set and serious*). We're strictly non-denominational. We can't have hymns. I'm sorry, but you know how it is.

She goes to the centre of the room.

Stop whatever you're doing! (*Pause.*) Now, before the sing-song, who is coming to the annual get-together? All of you, I'm sure. I want to make sure you all have tickets. Two tickets for each former employee. Only one visitor is allowed. (*Laughs.*) Come along now!

The ex-employees move towards MRS VEALFOY, *she hands out the tickets.*

OLD MAN (*to* BUCHANAN, *with curiosity*). Is your name Hyams?

BUCHANAN. No.

OLD MAN. Isn't it? (*Pause.*) Surely you're Georgie Hyams?

BUCHANAN. No, that's never been my name. My name is Buchanan.

OLD MAN (*getting up from his seat*). I'm afraid I don't know you then.

BUCHANAN. But – (*Shocked.*) you said you did.

OLD MAN (*moving towards the group around* MRS VEALFOY). I made a mistake. I thought you were an old mate of mine. His name was Hyams.

BUCHANAN (*catching hold of the* OLD MAN's *sleeve*). You don't know me then?

OLD MAN. No.

BUCHANAN. But I worked here. I was on the main entrance. Are you sure you don't remember me?

OLD MAN. I'm sorry.

He shrugs BUCHANAN *off and moves to the group around* MRS VEALFOY.

BUCHANAN. Nobody knows me. They've never seen me before.

MRS VEALFOY *claps her hands together.*

MRS VEALFOY. We're going to run through all the songs with 'Happy' in them. Let's bang out the words. Never mind the tune. We'll muddle through somehow.

The pianist strikes up 'Here We Are Again, Happy As Can Be'. The ex-employees crowd round the piano. MRS VEALFOY *in the centre.* BUCHANAN's *face is glimpsed. He begins to sing. Stops. Sings again. Several old, tired and depressed faces are seen.* MRS VEALFOY's *laughing face is seen as the music abruptly changes to 'Happy Days Are Here Again'.* BUCHANAN *stops singing and moves away from the group.* MRS VEALFOY *is beside him instantly.*

MRS VEALFOY (*raising her voice slightly above the singing*). Why aren't you joining in?

BUCHANAN. I don't know the words.

MRS VEALFOY. Follow me then. Repeat everything I say. Is that clear? What were you thinking just now?

BUCHANAN. Nothing.

MRS VEALFOY. I don't allow thoughts like that. So come on, cheer up, and if you don't know the words just hum the tune.

She leads him back to the centre of the group, between two old men in wheelchairs. BUCHANAN *joins in the singing.*

(*Her voice soaring above the rest as the music changes.*)
'I want to be Happy,
But I can't be Happy,
Till I've made you Happy too'.

Scene Seventeen

EDITH's *living-room.*
BUCHANAN *stands beside the table. On the table the clock and the toaster. He lifts a hammer and smashes them to pieces.*

Scene Eighteen

BUCHANAN's *bedroom.*
BUCHANAN *in bed.* EDITH *enters.*

EDITH. Another day has dawned. Bright and clear. Let's be thankful for it.

She plumps BUCHANAN's *pillow, hands him his glasses and hearing-aid.*

Look at the sun streaming through the window. A few weeks ago you'd have been at work. Now you can enjoy the good weather when it comes and you fall sick. That's no way to carry on.

She smiles at him.

The photos are here!

She shows him a series of wedding photographs. They show, in succession: DEBBIE *arriving at the church,* DEBBIE *and* RAY *at the altar,* DEBBIE *and* RAY *signing the register after the ceremony,* DEBBIE *and* RAY *walking down the aisle of the church,* DEBBIE *and* RAY *in front of the church doors.*

As the photographs are shown, the opening bars of Mendelssohn's wedding march are heard. This is abruptly cut off as the sixth photograph is shown – DEBBIE *fainting among a group of bridesmaids – and a wailing cry of a newborn child is heard.*

Her dress was quite ruined.

She puts the photographs to one side.

Aren't you interested, dear? (*Pause.*) The holiday season will soon be upon us. Everybody is talking of nothing else. There's a twitter in the air. A woman at work is taking her car abroad this year. She's on top of the world thinking about it. She's a dedicated holiday maker.

BUCHANAN *lies back, stares at the ceiling.*

Why, you're crying. (*She kisses him.*) Tears running down your cheeks. (*She hugs him.*) The tickets have arrived for the 'get-together'. It's to be held at the Bell Hotel. They've hired a name band. It's to be gayer than ever this year. So much laughter, so much joy in people's hearts, so many happy faces all around. Raymond will qualify for a ticket. So will Debbie. And Debbie's parents are going because they qualify. So we shall be a big party. I'm buying a new dress for the occasion. And I shall smile a lot, more than usual, because we have so much to be thankful for.

BUCHANAN *closes his eyes and dies.*

Raymond has quite reformed. Sees the error of his ways now. That's Debbie's influence. So you see even doing wrong as he did has its uses.

A clipping from a newspaper's 'Births, Marriages and Deaths' column is seen.

'DEATHS: At his home in Swinton Street, George Buchanan. Sadly missed by his wife, Edith, grandson, Raymond, and workmates. No flowers by request.'

EDITH (*continuing the previous speech over the newspaper clipping*). It got him married. Settled. With a future before him.

Scene Nineteen

The Bell Hotel.
Dance band playing. Dancers. Music comes to an end. MRS VEAL-FOY *steps on to the platform. Speaks into microphone.*

MRS VEALFOY. In the next dance the Gentlemen employees are at liberty to ask the Directors' wives for a dance. And I think we can invent a new little rule here – just a tiny new rule – the Lady Employees can ask the Directors for a dance. (*Laughter.*) Now, don't be shy. They're just the same as you are.

The band begins to play softly.

Before we carry on with our fun I have to announce a sad death. George Buchanan passed away last week. His wife wishes me to express thanks to all in the firm who sent beautiful floral tributes in her sad bereavement. And now, on with the dance and let us pray for good weather during the holiday season.

The band plays 'On the Sunny Side of the Street'. Dancers fill the floor. At the side of the dance-floor, EDITH *is seen with* DEBBIE's *family. The non-dancing employees begin to sing the words of the song. Everybody is singing,* MRS VEALFOY *is seen in company with the board of directors, they also are singing.*

Loot

LORD SUMMERHAYS. Anarchism is a game at which the Police can beat you. What have you to say to that?

GUNNER. What have I to say to it! Well I call it scandalous: that's what I have to say to it.

LORD SUMMERHAYS. Precisely: that's all anybody has to say to it, except the British Public, which pretends not to believe it.

Misalliance George Bernard Shaw

The first London production of *Loot* was given at the Jeanetta Cochrane Theatre by the London Traverse Theatre Company on 29 September 1966, with the following cast:

MCLEAVY	Gerry Duggan
FAY	Sheila Ballantine
HAL	Kenneth Cranham
DENNIS	Simon Ward
TRUSCOTT	Michael Bates
MEADOWS	David Redmond

Directed by Charles Marowitz
Designed by Tony Carruthers

Loot was revived as part of the 'Joe Orton Festival' at the Royal Court Theatre, London, on 3 June 1975, with the following cast:

MCLEAVY	Arthur O'Sullivan
FAY	Jill Bennett
HAL	David Troughton
DENNIS	James Aubrey
TRUSCOTT	Philip Stone
MEADOWS	Michael O'Hagan

Directed by Albert Finney
Designed by Douglas Heap
Costumes by Harriet Geddes

Act One

A room in MCLEAVY'S *house. Afternoon.*
Door left with glass panel. Door right. A coffin stands on trestles. MCLEAVY, *in mourning, sits beside an electric fan.*
FAY, *in a nurse's uniform, enters from the left.*

FAY. Wake up. Stop dreaming. The cars will be here soon. (*She sits.*) I've bought you a flower.
MCLEAVY. That's a nice thought. (*Taking the flower from her.*)
FAY. I'm a nice person. One in a million.

She removes her slippers, puts on a pair of shoes.

MCLEAVY. Are those Mrs McLeavy's slippers?
FAY. Yes. She wouldn't mind my having them.
MCLEAVY. Is the fur genuine?
FAY. It's fluff, not fur.
MCLEAVY. It looks like fur.
FAY. (*standing to her feet*). No. It's a form of fluff. They manufacture it in Leeds.

She picks up the slippers and takes them to the wardrobe. She tries to open the wardrobe. It is locked. She puts the slippers down.

You realize, of course, that the death of a patient terminates my contract?
MCLEAVY. Yes.
FAY. When do you wish me to leave?
MCLEAVY. Stay for a few hours. I've grown used to your company.

FAY. Impossible. I'm needed at other sickbeds. Complain to the Society if you disagree with the rules.

She picks up his coat, holds it out for him to put on.

You've been a widower for three days. Have you considered a second marriage yet?

MCLEAVY (*struggling into his coat*). No.

FAY. Why not?

MCLEAVY. I've been so busy with the funeral.

FAY. You must find someone to take Mrs McLeavy's place. She wasn't perfect.

MCLEAVY. A second wife would be a physical impossibility.

FAY. I'll hear none of that. My last husband at sixty came through with flying colours. Three days after our wedding he was performing extraordinary feats.

She takes the coathanger to the wardrobe. She tries to open the wardrobe door, frowns, puts the coathanger beside her slippers.

You must marry a girl with youth and vitality. Someone with a consistent attitude towards religion. That's most important. With her dying breath Mrs McLeavy cast doubt upon the authenticity of the Gospels. What kind of wife is that for you? The leading Catholic layman within a radius of forty miles. Where did you meet such a woman?

MCLEAVY. At an informal get-together run by a Benedictine monk.

FAY *takes the flower from his hand and pins it on to his coat.*

FAY. Was she posing as a Catholic?

MCLEAVY. Yes.

FAY. She had a deceitful nature. That much is clear. We mustn't let it happen again. I'll sort out some well-meaning young woman. Bring her here. Introduce you. I can visualize her – medium height, slim, fair hair. A regular visitor to

some place of worship. And an ex-member of the League of
Mary.

MCLEAVY. Someone like yourself?

FAY. Exactly. (*She takes a clothes brush and brushes him down.*)
Realize your potential. Marry at once.

MCLEAVY. St Kilda's would be in uproar.

FAY. The Fraternity of the Little Sisters is on my side.
Mother Agnes-Mary feels you're a challenge. She's treating
it as a specifically Catholic problem.

MCLEAVY. She treats washing her feet as a Catholic problem.

FAY. She has every right to do so.

MCLEAVY. Don't Protestants have feet then?

FAY. The Holy Father hasn't given a ruling on the subject and
so, as far as I'm concerned, they haven't. Really, I sometimes
wonder whether living with that woman hasn't made a free
thinker of you. You must marry again after a decent interval
of mourning.

MCLEAVY. What's a decent interval?

FAY. A fortnight would be long enough to indicate your grief.
We must keep abreast of the times.

She takes the brush to the wardrobe and tries to open it.

(*Turning, with a frown.*) Who has the key to this cupboard?

MCLEAVY. Harold.

FAY. Why is it locked?

MCLEAVY. He refused to give a reason.

MCLEAVY *shakes the wardrobe door.*

FAY. Your son is a thorn in my flesh. The contents of his
dressing-table are in indictment of his way of life. Not only
firearms, but family-planning equipment. A Papal dispensa-
tion is needed to dust his room.

She goes out left. MCLEAVY *follows her. She can be heard
calling:*

(Off.) Harold! *(Farther off.)* Harold!

> HAL *enters right. He goes to the wardrobe, unlocks it, looks
> in, and locks the wardrobe again. He stands beside the coffin
> and crosses himself.* FAY *and* MCLEAVY *re-enter left.*

FAY *(pause, with a smile).* Why is the wardrobe locked?

HAL. I've personal property in there.

MCLEAVY. Open the door. There's enough mystery in the
universe without adding to it.

HAL. I can't. You wouldn't wish to see. It's a present for your
anniversary.

MCLEAVY. What anniversary?

HAL. Your being made a knight of the Order of St Gregory.

MCLEAVY. I'm not convinced. Open the wardrobe.

HAL. No.

FAY *(to* MCLEAVY*).* You see how far things have progressed?
Your son won't obey you. *(To* HAL.*)* Are you still refusing
to attend your mother's funeral?

HAL. Yes.

FAY. What excuse do you give?

HAL. It would upset me.

FAY. That's exactly what a funeral is meant to do.

MCLEAVY. He prefers to mourn in private.

FAY. I'm not in favour of private grief. Show your emotions in
public or not at all.

HAL *(to* MCLEAVY*).* Another wreath has arrived.

MCLEAVY. Is it roses?

HAL. Roses and fern.

MCLEAVY. I must look.

> *He goes out left.*

FAY. I sometimes think your father has a sentimental attach-
ment to roses.

HAL. Do you know what his only comment was on my mother's
death?

FAY. Something suitable, I'm sure.

She takes the mattress cover from the mattress and folds it.

HAL. He said he was glad she'd died at the right season for roses. He's been up half the night cataloguing the varieties on the crosses. You should've seen him when that harp arrived. Sniffing the petals, checking, arguing with the man who brought it. They almost came to blows over the pronunciation.

FAY *hangs the folded mattress cover over the screen.*

If she'd played her cards right, my mother could've cited the Rose Growers' Annual as co-respondent.

FAY. The Vatican would never grant an annulment. Not unless he'd produced a hybrid.

HAL (*at the coffin, looking in*). Why was she embalmed?

FAY. She asked to be scientifically preserved after her last attack.

HAL *stares into the coffin, deep in thought.* FAY *joins him.*

You couldn't wish her life. She was in agony since Easter.

HAL. Yes, the egg I presented to her went untouched.

FAY. On doctor's orders, I can tell you in confidence.

Pause.

Sit down, Harold. I want a word with you. Your father can't be expected to help at the moment.

HAL *sits.* FAY *sits opposite him.*

(*Folding her hands in her lap.*) The priest at St Kilda's has asked me to speak to you. He's very worried. He says you spend your time thieving from slot machines and deflowering the daughters of better men than yourself. Is this a fact?

HAL. Yes.

FAY. And even the sex you were born into isn't safe from your marauding. Father Mac is popular for the remission of sins, as you know. But clearing up after you is a full-time job. He simply cannot be in the confessional twenty-four hours a day. That's reasonable, isn't it? You do see his point?

HAL. Yes.

FAY. What are you going to do about this dreadful state of affairs?

HAL. I'm going abroad.

FAY. That will please the Fathers. Who are you going with?

HAL. A mate of mine. Dennis. A very luxurious type of lad. At present employed by an undertaker. And doing well in the profession.

FAY. Have you known him long?

HAL. We shared the same cradle.

FAY. Was that economy or malpractice?

HAL. We were too young then to practise, and economics still defeat us.

FAY. You've confirmed my worst fears. You have no job. No prospects. And now you're about to elope to the Continent with a casual acquaintance and not even a baby as justification. Where will you end? Not respected by the world at large like your father. Most people of any influence will ignore you. You'll be forced to associate with young men like yourself. Does that prospect please you?

HAL. I'm not sure.

FAY. Well, hesitation is something to be going on with. We can build on that. What will you do when you're old?

HAL. I shall die.

FAY. I see you're determined to run the gamut of all experience. That can bring you nothing but unhappiness. You've had every chance to lead a decent life and rejected them. I've no further interest in your career. (*She rises to her feet.*) Call your father. He's surely had enough of the company of plants for the present

HAL *goes to the door left.*

HAL (*calling*). Eh, Dad!
FAY. Shhh! This is a house of mourning.

HAL *returns and sits.*

The priest that came to pay his condolences had such quiet
tones that at first I thought they'd sent along a mute.

MCLEAVY *enters carrying a large wreath marked off into
numbered squares.*

MCLEAVY. The Friends of Bingo have sent a wreath. The
blooms are breathtaking.

He puts the wreath down. Sits. Takes out a newspaper. FAY,
*standing beside the coffin, looking into it, silently moves her
lips in prayer, a rosary between her fingers.*

(*With a loud exclamation.*) Another catastrophe has hit the
district! Bank robbers have got away with a fortune.
FAY (*looking up*). Which bank?
MCLEAVY. Next door to the undertakers. They burrowed
through. Filled over twenty coffins with rubble.
FAY. Rubble?
MCLEAVY. From the wall. Demolished the wall, they did.
FAY. People are so unbalanced these days. The man sitting
next to you on the bus could be insane.
MCLEAVY. Where the money has gone is still occupying the
police. It's one of the big gangs, I expect.
HAL. What do you known of the big gangs? It's a small gang.
Minute.
FAY. Do you know the men concerned?
HAL. If I had that money, I wouldn't be here. I'd go away.
FAY. You're going away.
HAL. I'd go away quicker.
FAY. Where would you go?

HAL. Spain. The playground of international crime.

FAY. Where are you going?

HAL. Portugal.

Pause.

You'll have to get up early in the morning to catch me.

Door chimes. HAL goes to the window, draws back the curtains and looks out.

Dennis is here with the cars.

FAY. Is he driving?

HAL. Yes. He looks impressive. Close proximity to death obviously agrees with him.

He goes out left.

MCLEAVY (*putting away the newspaper*). What's the plan for the afternoon?

FAY. The funeral will occupy you for an hour or so. Afterwards a stroll to the house of a man of God, a few words of wisdom and a glance through the Catholic Truth Society's most recent publication should set your adrenalin flowing. Then a rest. I don't want you overstrained.

MCLEAVY. When did you say you were leaving? I don't wish to cause you any inconvenience.

FAY. I'll decide when you've inconvenienced me long enough.

MCLEAVY. You're very good to me.

FAY. As long as you appreciate my desire to help. My own life has been unhappy. I want yours to be different.

MCLEAVY. You've had an unhappy life?

FAY. Yes. My husbands died. I've had seven altogether. One a year on average since I was sixteen. I'm extravagant you see. And then I lived under stress near Penzance for some time. I've had trouble with institutions. Lack of funds. A court case with my hairdresser. I've been reduced to asking people for money before now.

MCLEAVY. Did they give it to you?

FAY. Not willingly. They had to be persuaded. (*With a bright smile.*) I shall accompany you to your lawyers. After the reading of your wife's will you may need skilled medical assistance.

MCLEAVY (*with a laugh*). I don't think there are any surprises in store. After a few minor bequests the bulk of Mrs McLeavy's fortune comes to me.

FAY. I've also arranged for your doctor to be at your side. You've a weak heart.

DENNIS enters left.

DENNIS. Good afternoon. I don't want to be too formal on this sad occasion, but would you like to view the deceased for the last time?

FAY takes out a handkerchief.
HAL enters.

(*To HAL.*) Give us a hand into the car with the floral tributes.

HAL takes out several wreaths, DENNIS picks up the rest.

(*To FAY.*) We'll need help with the coffin. (*Nods to MC-LEAVY.*) He's too near the grave himself to do much lifting.

FAY. Harold can carry his mother to the car.

DENNIS. A charming suggestion. (*To MCLEAVY.*) If you'll be making your last good-byes while I give them a hand?

Takes the wreaths to the door. HAL enters left.

(*Passing HAL in the doorway.*) I want a word with you.

DENNIS goes out left. HAL is about to follow him.

FAY (*calling*). Come and see your mother, Harold. You'll never see her again.

MCLEAVY, HAL *and* FAY *stand beside the coffin, looking in.*

She looks a treat in her W.V.S uniform. Though I'd not care to spend Eternity in it myself.

HAL. She's minus her vital organs, isn't she?

FAY. It's a necessary part of the process.

MCLEAVY. Where are they?

FAY. In the little casket in the hall. Such tranquillity she has. Looks as though she might speak.

MCLEAVY (*taking out a handkerchief, dabbing his nose*). God rest the poor soul. I shall miss her.

FAY. Death can be very tragic for those who are left.

They bow their heads in silence.

HAL. Here, her eyes are blue. Mum's eyes were brown. That's a bit silly, isn't it?

FAY. I expect they ran out of materials.

MCLEAVY. Are her eyes not natural, then?

FAY. No. (*With a smile, to* HAL.) He's such an innocent, isn't he? Not familiar with the ways of the world.

MCLEAVY. I thought they were her own. That surprises me. Not her own eyes.

DENNIS enters with a screwdriver.

DENNIS. The large harp we've placed on top of the motor. On the coffin we thought just the spray of heather from her homeland.

MCLEAVY. It's going to take me a long time to believe she's dead. She was such an active sort of person.

FAY (*to* DENNIS). You're going abroad, I hear?

DENNIS. Yes.

FAY. Where did you get the money?

DENNIS. My life insurance has matured.

MCLEAVY (*to* DENNIS). Tragic news about your premises. Was the damage extensive?

DENNIS. The repair bill will be steep. We're insured, of course.

MCLEAVY. Was your Chapel of Rest defiled?

DENNIS. No.

MCLEAVY. Human remains weren't outraged?

DENNIS. No.

MCLEAVY. Thank God for that. There are some things which deter even criminals.

DENNIS. I'm concerned with the actual furnishings damaged – I mean, the inside of the average casket is a work of art – time and labour, oh, it makes you weep.

MCLEAVY. The bodies laid out. Waiting for burial. It's terrible thoughts that come to me.

DENNIS. It broke my heart. Dust and rubble.

MCLEAVY. What a terrible thing to contemplate. The young men, thinking only of the money, burrowing from the undertakers to the bank. The smell of corruption and the instruments of death behind them, the riches before them. They'd do anything for money. They'd risk damnation in this world and the next for it. And me, a good man by any lights, moving among such people. They'll have it on their conscience. Even if they aren't caught, they'll suffer.

DENNIS. How?

MCLEAVY. I don't know. But such people never benefit from their crimes. It's people like myself who have the easy time. Asleep at nights. Despite appearances to the contrary, criminals are poor sleepers.

FAY. How do you sleep, Harold?

HAL. Alone.

DENNIS. We'll be leaving in a short time, Mr McLeavy. I'd like to satisfy myself that everything is as it should be. We pride ourselves on the service.

MCLEAVY. What clothes would they wear, d'you suppose? Dust is easily identified. They'd surely not work in the nude? God have mercy on them if they did. Even to avoid the hangman I'd not put up with precautions of that nature.

FAY. They'd wear old clothes. Burn them after.

MCLEAVY. If you could get a glance between their toes you'd find the evidence. But to order a man to remove his clothes isn't within the power of the police. More's the pity, I say. I'd like to see them given wider powers. They're hamstrung by red tape. They're a fine body of men. Doing their job under impossible conditions.

HAL. The police are a lot of idle buffoons, Dad. As you well know.

MCLEAVY. If you ever possess their kindness, courtesy and devotion to duty, I'll lift my hat to you.

DENNIS. I'm going to batten down the hatches now.

MCLEAVY (*glancing into the coffin*). Treat her gently. She was very precious to me.

He goes out left.

FAY (*following* MCLEAVY, *turning in the doorway*). I'll be consoling your father if I'm needed. Be careful what you talk about in front of the dead.

She goes out left.
DENNIS opens a packet of chewing-gum, puts a piece in his mouth, takes off his hat.

DENNIS. Lock the door.

HAL. It won't lock.

DENNIS. Put a chair under the handle. We're in trouble

HAL wedges a chair under the handle.

We've had the law round our house.

HAL. When?

DENNIS. This morning. Knocked us up they did. Turning over every bleeding thing.

HAL. Was my name mentioned?

DENNIS. They asked me who my associate was. I swore blind

I never knew what they were on about. 'Course, it's only a matter of time before they're round here.

HAL. How long?

DENNIS. Might be on their way now. (*He begins to screw down the lid of the coffin.*) Don't want a last squint, do you? No? Where's the money?

HAL taps the wardrobe.

In there? All of it? We've got to get it away. I'll lose faith in us if we get nicked again. What was it last time?

HAL. Ladies' overcoats.

DENNIS. See? Painful. Oh, painful. We were a laughing-stock in criminal circles. Banned from that club with the spade dancer.

HAL. Don't go on, baby. I remember the humiliating circumstances of failure.

DENNIS. We wouldn't have been nicked if you'd kept your mouth shut. Making us look ridiculous by telling the truth. Why can't you lie like a normal man?

HAL. I can't, baby. It's against my nature.

He stares at the coffin as DENNIS screws the lid down.

Has anybody ever hidden money in a coffin?

DENNIS looks up. Pause.

DENNIS. Not when it was in use.

HAL. Why not?

DENNIS. It's never crossed anybody's mind.

HAL. It's crossed mine.

He takes the screwdriver from DENNIS, and begins to unscrew the coffin lid.

It's the comics I read. Sure of it.

DENNIS (*wiping his forehead with the back of his hand*). Think of your mum. Your lovely old mum. She gave you birth.

HAL. I should thank anybody for that?

DENNIS. Cared for you. Washed your nappies. You'd be some kind of monster.

HAL takes the lid off the coffin.

HAL. Think what's at stake.

He goes to wardrobe and unlocks it.

Money.

He brings out the money. DENNIS *picks up a bundle of notes, looks into the coffin.*

DENNIS. Won't she rot it? The body juices? I can't believe it's possible.

HAL. She's embalmed. Good for centuries.

DENNIS puts a bundle of notes into the coffin. Pause. He looks at HAL.

DENNIS. There's no room.

HAL lifts the corpse's arm.

HAL (*pause, frowns*). Remove the corpse. Plenty of room then.

DENNIS. Seems a shame really. The embalmers have done a lovely job.

They lift the coffin from the trestles.

There's no name for this, is there?

HAL. We're creating a precedent. Into the cupboard. Come on.

They tip the coffin on end and shake the corpse into the wardrobe. They put the coffin on the floor, lock the wardrobe and begin to pack the money into the coffin.

DENNIS. What will we do with the body?

HAL. Bury it. In a mineshaft. Out in the country. Or in the marshes. Weigh the corpse with rock.

DENNIS. We'll have to get rid of that uniform.

HAL (*pause*). Take her clothes off?

DENNIS. In order to avoid detection should her remains be discovered.

HAL. Bury her naked? My own mum?

He goes to the mirror and combs his hair.

It's a Freudian nightmare.

DENNIS (*putting lid upon coffin*). I won't disagree.

HAL. Aren't we committing some kind of unforgivable sin?

DENNIS. Only if you're a Catholic.

HAL (*turning from the mirror*). I am a Catholic. (*Putting his comb away.*) I can't undress her. She's a relative. I can go to Hell for it.

DENNIS. I'll undress her then. I don't believe in Hell.

He begins to screw down the coffin lid.

HAL. That's typical of your upbringing, baby. Every luxury was lavished on you – atheism, breast-feeding, circumcision. I had to make my own way.

DENNIS. We'll do it after the funeral. Your dad'll be with the priest.

HAL. O.K. And afterwards we'll go to a smashing brothel I've just discovered. Run by a woman who was connected with the Royal Family one time. Very ugly bird. Part Polish. Her eyes look that way. Nice line in crumpet she has. (*He sits astride the coffin.*)

DENNIS. I can't go to a brothel.

HAL. Why not?

DENNIS. I'm on the wagon. I'm trying to get up sufficient head of steam to marry.

HAL. Have you anyone in mind?

DENNIS. Your mum's nurse.

HAL. She's older than you.

DENNIS. An experienced woman is the finest thing that can happen to a lad. My dad swears by them.

HAL. She's three parts Papal nuncio. She'd only do it at set times.

DENNIS. Oh, no. She does it at any time. A typical member of the medical profession she is.

HAL. You've had her? (DENNIS *grins*.) Knocked it off? Really?

DENNIS. Under that picture of the Sacred Heart. You've seen it?

HAL. In her room. Often.

DENNIS. On Wednesday nights while you're training at St Edmund's gymnasium.

They lift the coffin back on to the trestles.

I'd like to get married. It's the one thing I haven't tried.

HAL. I don't like your living for kicks, baby. Put these neurotic ideas out of your mind and concentrate on the problems of everyday life. We must get the corpse buried before tonight. Be in a tricky position else. And another stretch will be death to my ambitions. I put my not getting on in life down to them persistently sending me to Borstal. I might go permanently bent if this falls through. It's not a pleasant prospect, is it?

The coffin is back upon the trestles.
DENNIS *takes the chewing-gum from his mouth and sticks it under the coffin. He puts on his hat.* HAL *sits.*

Was it Truscott searched your house?

DENNIS. Yes. And he had me down the station for questioning. Gave me a rabbit punch. No, I'm a liar. A rabbit-type punch. Winded me. Took me by the cobblers. Oh, 'strewth, it made me bad.

HAL. Yes, he has a nice line in corporal punishment. Last time he was here he kicked my old lady's cat and he smiled while he did it. How did he get into your house?

DENNIS. He said he was from the sanitary people. My dad let him in. 'Course, I recognized him at once.

HAL. Did you tell him?

DENNIS. Yes.

HAL. What did he say?

DENNIS. Nothing. He kept on about testing the water supply. I asked him if he had a warrant. He said the water board didn't issue warrants.

HAL. You should've phoned the police. Asked for protection.

DENNIS. I did.

HAL. What did they say?

DENNIS. They said that one of their men called Truscott was at our house and why didn't we complain to him?

HAL. What did Truscott say?

DENNIS. He said he was from the water board. My nerves were in shreds by the end of it.

FAY approaches the door left. Her shadow is cast on the glass panel.

FAY (*off*). What are you doing, Harold?

HAL goes to the coffin and kneels in prayer.

HAL. That brothel I mentioned has swing doors. (*He bows his head.*) You don't often see that, do you?

DENNIS takes the chair from under the door handle and opens the door quietly.

DENNIS. We're ready now.

FAY enters in mourning with a veil over her hair. She carries an embroidered text. Her dress is unzipped at the back. She goes to the wardrobe and tries to open the door. She sees in the mirror that her dress is unzipped, comes to the coffin and bows her head over it. HAL, still kneeling, zips her dress up. MCLEAVY enters blowing his nose, a sorrowful expression upon his face.

MCLEAVY (*to* DENNIS). Forgive me being so overwrought, but it's my first bereavement.

DENNIS. The exit of a loved one is always a painful experience.

FAY, *the dress zipped, straightens up.*

FAY. Here – (*she puts the embroidered text on to the coffin.*) – the Ten Commandments. She was a great believer in some of them.

HAL *and* DENNIS *lift the coffin.*

MCLEAVY (*greatly moved, placing a hand on the coffin*). Good-bye, old girl. You've had a lot of suffering. I shall miss you.

HAL *and* DENNIS *go out with the coffin.* FAY *throws back her veil.*

FAY. She's gone. I could feel her presence leaving us. Funny how you know, isn't it?

MCLEAVY. That dress is attractive. Suits you. Black.

FAY. It's another piece of your late wife's finery. Some people would censure me for wearing it. (*She puts a hand on his arm, smiles.*) Are you feeling calmer now?

MCLEAVY. Yes. I've a resilient nature, but death upsets me. I'd rather witness a birth than a death any day. Though the risks involved are greater.

TRUSCOTT *enters left.*

TRUSCOTT. Good afternoon.

FAY. Good afternoon. Who are you?

TRUSCOTT. I am attached to the metropolitan water board. I'm on a fact-finding tour of the area. I'd like to inspect your mains supply.

MCLEAVY. It's outside.

TRUSCOTT. Is it?

Pause, ruminates.

I wonder how it came to be put out there. Most ingenious. You're sure there isn't a tap in this cupboard?

He tries the wardrobe door and smiles.

MCLEAVY. It's in the garden.

TRUSCOTT. Where?

MCLEAVY. I don't know.

TRUSCOTT. I suggest, then, that you find it, sir. Any property belonging to the council must be available on demand. The law is clear on that point.

MCLEAVY. I'll find it at once, sir. I wouldn't wish to place myself outside the law.

He goes off right.

TRUSCOTT (*turning to* FAY). Who has the key to this cup-board?

FAY. The son of the house.

TRUSCOTT. Would he be willing to open it? I'd make it worth his while.

FAY. I've already asked for it to be opened. He refused point-blank.

TRUSCOTT. I see. (*Chews his lip.*) Most significant. You'll be out of the house for some considerable time this afternoon?

FAY. Yes. I'm attending the funeral of my late employer.

TRUSCOTT. Thank you, miss. You've been a great help. (*He smiles, goes to window.*) Who sent the large wreath that has been chosen to decorate the motor?

FAY. The licensee of the King of Denmark. I don't think a publican's tribute should be given pride of place.

TRUSCOTT. You wouldn't, miss. You had a strict upbringing.

FAY. How do you know?

TRUSCOTT. You have a crucifix.

FAY'S *hand goes to the crucifix on her breast.*

It has a dent to one side and engraved on the back the

words: 'St Mary's Convent. Gentiles Only.' It's not difficult
to guess at your background from such tell-tale clues.

FAY. You're quite correct. It was a prize for good conduct. The
dent was an accident.

TRUSCOTT. Your first husband damaged it.

FAY. During a quarrel.

TRUSCOTT. At the end of which you shot him.

FAY (*taken aback*). You must have access to private information.

TRUSCOTT. Not at all. Guesswork mostly. I won't bore you
with the details. The incident happened at the Hermitage
Private Hotel. Right?

FAY (*a little alarmed*). This is uncanny.

TRUSCOTT. My methods of deduction can be learned by anyone with a keen eye and a quick brain. When I shook your
hand I felt a roughness on one of your wedding rings. A
roughness I associate with powder burns and salt. The two
together spell a gun and sea air. When found on a wedding
ring only one solution is possible.

FAY. How did you know it happened at the Hermitage Private
Hotel?

TRUSCOTT. That particular hotel is notorious for tragedies of
this kind. I took a chance which paid off.

He takes out his pipe and chews on it.

Has it never occurred to you to wonder why all your husbands met with violent deaths?

FAY. They didn't!

TRUSCOTT. Your first was shot. Your second collapsed whilst
celebrating the anniversary of the Battle of Mons. Your
third fell from a moving vehicle. Your fourth took an overdose on the eve of his retirement from Sadler's Wells. Your
fifth and sixth husbands disappeared. Presumed dead. Your
last partner suffered a seizure three nights after marrying
you. From what cause?

FAY (*coldly*). I refuse to discuss my private life with you.

TRUSCOTT. For ten years death has been persistently associated with your name.

FAY. You could say the same of an even moderately successful undertaker.

TRUSCOTT. Undertakers have to mix with the dead. It's their duty. You have not that excuse. Seven husbands in less than a decade. There's something seriously wrong with your approach to marriage. I find it frightening that, undeterred by past experience, you're contemplating an eighth engagement.

FAY. How do you know?

TRUSCOTT. You wear another woman's dress as though you were born to it.

FAY (*wide-eyed with wonder*). You amaze me. This dress did belong to Mrs McLeavy.

TRUSCOTT. Elementary detection. The zip is of a type worn by elderly women.

FAY. You should be a detective.

TRUSCOTT. I'm often mistaken for one. Most embarrassing. My wife is frequently pestered by people who are under the impression that she is a policeman's wife. She upbraids me for getting her into such scrapes. (*He laughs.*) You recognize the daily bread of married life, I'm sure. (*He chews on his pipe for a moment.*) When do you intend to propose to Mr McLeavy?

FAY. At once. Delay would be fatal.

TRUSCOTT. Anything taken in combination with yourself usually results in death.

FAY. How dare you speak to me like this! Who are you?

TRUSCOTT *takes out his notebook and pencil.*

TRUSCOTT (*pleasantly*). I'm a council employee who has let his imagination wander. Please forgive me if I've upset you.

He tears a page from the notebook and hands it to FAY.

Sign this chit.

FAY (*looking at it*). It's blank.

TRUSCOTT. That's quite in order. I want you to help me blindly without asking questions.

FAY. I can't sign a blank sheet of paper. Someone might forge my name on a cheque.

TRUSCOTT. Sign my name, then.

FAY. I don't know your name.

TRUSCOTT. Good gracious, what a suspicious mind you have. Sign yourself Queen Victoria. No one would tamper with her account.

FAY *signs the paper and gives it back to* TRUSCOTT.

I think that's all I want from you, miss.

FAY. Will you do one thing for me?

TRUSCOTT. What?

FAY. Let me see you without your hat.

TRUSCOTT (*alarmed*). No. I couldn't possibly. I never take my hat off in front of a lady. It would be discourteous.

MCLEAVY *enters right.*

Have you been successful in your search, sir?

MCLEAVY. Yes. Next to my greenhouse you'll find an iron plaque. Under it is a tap.

TRUSCOTT. Thank you, sir. I shall mention your co-operation in my next report. (*He touches his hat.*) Good afternoon.

He goes off right.

MCLEAVY. I hope he finds what he's looking for. I like to be of assistance to authority.

FAY. We must watch that he doesn't abuse his trust. He showed no credentials.

MCLEAVY. Oh, we can rely on public servants to behave themselves. We must give this man every opportunity to do his duty. As a good citizen I ignore the stories which bring officialdom into disrepute.

HAL enters left.

HAL. There's a delay in starting the car. A flat tyre. (*Taking off his coat.*) We're changing the wheel.

MCLEAVY. I hardly think it proper for a mourner to mend the puncture. Is your mother safe?

HAL. Dennis is guarding the coffin.

MCLEAVY. Be as quick as you can. Your mother hated to miss an appointment.

HAL. The contents of that coffin are very precious to me. I'm determined to see they get to the graveyard without mishap.

He goes off left.

MCLEAVY (*with a smile, shaking his head*). It's unusual for him to show affection. I'm touched by it.

FAY. Mrs McLeavy was a good mother. She has a right to respect.

MCLEAVY. Yes. I've ordered four hundred rose trees to help keep her memory green. On a site, only a stone's throw from the church, I intend to found the 'Mrs Mary McLeavy Memorial Rose Garden'. It will put Paradise to shame.

FAY. Have you ever seen Paradise?

MCLEAVY. Only in photographs.

FAY. Who took them?

MCLEAVY. Father Jellicoe. He's a widely travelled man.

FAY. You mustn't run yourself into debt.

MCLEAVY. Oh, Mrs McLeavy will pay for the memorial herself. The will is as good as proven.

FAY sits beside him, takes his hand.

FAY. I don't know whether you can be trusted with a secret, but it would be wrong of me to keep you in the dark a moment longer. Your wife changed her will shortly before she died. She left all her money to me.

MCLEAVY. What! (*Almost fainting.*) Is it legal?

FAY. Perfectly.

MCLEAVY. She must've been drunk. What about me and the boy?

FAY. I'm surprised at you taking this attitude. Have you no sense of decency?

MCLEAVY. Oh, it's God's judgement on me for marrying a Protestant. How much has she left you?

FAY. Nineteen thousand pounds including her bonds and her jewels.

MCLEAVY. Her jewels as well?

FAY. Except her diamond ring. It's too large and unfashionable for a woman to wear. She's left that to Harold.

MCLEAVY. Employing you has cost me a fortune. You must be the most expensive nurse in history.

FAY. You don't imagine that I want the money for myself, do you.

MCLEAVY. Yes.

FAY. That's unworthy of you. I'm most embarrassed by Mrs McLeavy's generosity.

MCLEAVY. You'll destroy the will?

FAY. I wish I could.

MCLEAVY. Why can't you?

FAY. It's a legal document. I could be sued.

MCLEAVY. By whom?

FAY. The beneficiary.

MCLEAVY. That's you. You'd never sue yourself.

FAY. I might. If I was pushed too far. We must find some way of conveying the money into your bank account.

MCLEAVY. Couldn't you just give it to me?

FAY. Think of the scandal.

MCLEAVY. What do you suggest then?

FAY. We must have a joint bank account.

MCLEAVY. Wouldn't that cause an even bigger scandal?

FAY. Not if we were married.

MCLEAVY. Married? But then you'd have my money as well as Mrs McLeavy's.

FAY. That is one way of looking at it.

MCLEAVY. No. I'm too old. My health wouldn't stand up to a young wife.

FAY. I'm a qualified nurse.

MCLEAVY. You'd have to give up your career.

FAY. I'd do it for you.

MCLEAVY. I can give you nothing in return.

FAY. I ask for nothing. I'm a woman. Only half the human race can say that without fear of contradiction. (*She kisses him.*) Go ahead. Ask me to marry you. I've no intention of refusing. On your knees. I'm a great believer in traditional positions.

MCLEAVY. The pains in my legs.

FAY. Exercise is good for them. (MCLEAVY *kneels.*) Use any form of proposal you like. Try to avoid abstract nouns.

HAL *enters left.*

HAL. We're ready. The leader of the Mother's Union has given the signal for tears. (*He picks up his coat.*) We must ride the tide of emotion while it lasts.

FAY. They'll have to wait. Your father is about to propose to me. I think you may stay.

MCLEAVY (*struggling to his feet*). I'm giving no exhibition. Not in front of my son.

HAL. I'm surprised he should wish to marry again. He couldn't do justice to his last wife.

Car horn. DENNIS *enters left.*

DENNIS. Would everybody like to get into the car? We'll have the priest effing and blinding if we're late.

MCLEAVY (*to* FAY). This is so undignified. My wife isn't in her grave.

FAY. And she never will be if you insist on prolonging the proceedings beyond their natural length.

MCLEAVY. I'll propose to you on the way to the cemetery, Nurse McMahon. Will that satisfy you?

DENNIS (*to* FAY). You can't marry him. You know the way I feel about you.

FAY. I couldn't marry you. You're not a Catholic.

DENNIS. You could convert me.

FAY. I'm not prepared to be both wife and missionary.

HAL (*putting an arm round* DENNIS). He's richer than my dad, you know.

FAY. Has he his bank statement on him?

DENNIS. I came out without it.

Car horn.

MCLEAVY. Mrs McLeavy is keeping her Maker waiting. I'll pay my addresses to you after the interment.

Prolonged car horn.

Come on! We'll have a damaged motor horn to pay for next!

FAY. I've decided not to attend. I shall wave. Show my respects from afar.

MCLEAVY. The number of people staying away from the poor woman's funeral is heartbreaking. And I hired a de luxe model car because they're roomier. I could've saved myself the expense.

He goes off left.

DENNIS (*to* FAY). I'd slave for you.

FAY (*pulling on her gloves*). I can't marry boys.

HAL. He'd grow a moustache.

FAY. It really doesn't concern me what he grows. Grow two if it pleases him.

HAL. Would it please you? That's the point.

FAY. The income from fairgrounds might interest me. Otherwise a man with two has no more fascination than a man with one.

DENNIS. A fully productive life isn't possible with a man of Mr McLeavy's age.

FAY. We shall prove you wrong. He'll start a second family under my guidance.

HAL. You're wasting your time. He couldn't propagate a row of tomatoes.

Car horn.

FAY (*to* DENNIS). Get in the car! I've no intention of marrying you.

DENNIS (*to* HAL, *in tears*). She's turned me down. She's broken my heart.

HAL. She doesn't know what she's missing, baby.

DENNIS. But she does! That's what's so humiliating. (*He wipes his eyes with the back of his hand.*) Well, the funeral is off as far as I'm concerned.

HAL. You're driving the car. People will notice your absence.

FAY *is at the wardrobe.*

FAY (*pause*). Where did you get your money?

DENNIS. My auntie left it to me.

FAY. Is that true, Harold?

HAL (*after an inner struggle*). No.

DENNIS. I mean my uncle.

FAY (*to* HAL). Is that true?

HAL (*desperate, looking at* DENNIS). No.

DENNIS. You make our life together impossible. Lie, can't you?

HAL. I can't, baby. It's my upbringing.

Car horn.

DENNIS. Try to control yourself. If I come back and find you've been telling the truth all afternoon – we're through!

He goes off left. FAY *takes two black-edged handkerchiefs from her handbag, shakes them out, gives one to* HAL.

FAY. Blow your nose. People expect it.

She lowers her veil. They both go to the window. They wave. Sound of a car receding. Pause. FAY *turns from the window. She goes to the wardrobe. She throws off her veil.*

Come here. Open this cupboard.

HAL *puts his handkerchief into his pocket.*

Don't hesitate to obey me. Open this cupboard.

HAL. Why are you so interested?

FAY. I've a coatee in there.

HAL. Really?

FAY. I bought it three days ago. I must change. Mourning gets so grubby if you hang around in it for long.

She looks at HAL *in silence.*

I've got a key. I could see in. Quite easy.

HAL. I've got something in there.

FAY. What?

HAL. A corpse.

FAY. You've added murder to the list of insults heaped upon your family?

HAL. One doesn't have to murder to acquire a corpse.

FAY. You're running a private mortuary, then?

Pause.

Where are you concealing the money?

HAL. In my mother's coffin.

FAY. That'd be an unusual hiding-place.

Pause.

Where is it now? Answer at once. I shan't repeat my question.

HAL. The money is putting on incorruption. The flesh is still waiting.

FAY. Where is it waiting?

HAL. In that cupboard.

FAY. Open it.

HAL. You have a key.

FAY. I haven't.

HAL. You were lying?

FAY. Yes.

HAL *gives her the key. She opens the wardrobe, looks in, closes the door and screams.*

This is unforgivable. I shall speak to your father.

Pause.

She's standing on her head.

HAL. I concealed nothing from you.

FAY. Your explanation had the ring of truth. Naturally I disbelieved every word.

HAL. I want her buried. Are you prepared to help me?

FAY. Oh, no! I couldn't. This is a case for the authorities.

HAL. You'll never make it to the altar without my help.

FAY. I need no help from you to get a man to bed.

HAL. My father holds it as a cherished belief that a whore is no fit companion for a man.

FAY. As a creed it has more to offer than most.

HAL. My mate Dennis has done you. He speaks of it with relish.

FAY. Young men pepper their conversation with tales of rape. It creates a good impression.

HAL. You never had the blessing of a rape. I was with him at his only ravishment. A bird called Pauline Ching. Broke a tooth in the struggle, she did. It was legal with you. While Jesus pointed to his Sacred Heart, you pointed to yours.

FAY. I never point. It's rude.

HAL. If I tell my father, he'll never marry you.

FAY. I haven't decided whether I wish to marry your father. Your friend is a more interesting proposition.

HAL. He won't be if you grass to the police.

FAY (*pause*). Blackmail? So early in the game.

HAL *takes out a comb and goes to the mirror. He combs his hair.*

HAL. I want the body stripped. All I ask is an hour or two of Burke and Hare. It isn't a thing someone of the opposite sex can do. And I'm a relative, which complicates the issue.

FAY. You intend a country burial?

HAL. Yes.

FAY. Suppose a dog were to discover her? When they were out hunting for foxes. Do you set no store by the average foxhound?

HAL. Perfectly preserved body of a woman. No sign of foul play. The uniform we'll burn. The underwear you can keep.

FAY. Your mother's underclothes?

HAL. All good stuff.

FAY. I couldn't. Our sizes vary.

HAL. For the bonfire then. Her teeth can go in the river.

FAY. We're nowhere near the river.

HAL. We can borrow your car.

FAY. Provided you pay for the petrol.

HAL. Right.

FAY. Where will she be?

HAL. In the back seat. (*He puts the comb away.*) She always was a back-seat driver.

He opens the wardrobe and wheels the bed to the wardrobe door.

FAY. What about payment?

HAL. Twenty per cent.

FAY. Thirty-three and a third.

HAL. You can keep her wedding ring.

FAY. Is it valuable?

HAL. Very.

FAY. I'll add it to my collection. I already have seven by right of conquest.

HAL pulls the screen round the bed.

Thirty-three and a third and the wedding ring.

HAL. Twenty per cent, the wedding ring and I pay for the petrol?

FAY. Thirty-three and a third, the wedding ring and you pay for the petrol.

HAL. You drive a hard bargain.

FAY. I never bargain.

HAL. Done.

He throws the mattress cover to her.

Put her in that.

FAY goes behind the screen.

FAY. I need help to get her out of the cupboard.

HAL goes behind the screen.

I'm not taking the head end.

HAL. She won't bite. You have your gloves on.

They lift the corpse from the wardrobe and lay it on the bed. Something drops from it and rolls away.

FAY. What's that?

HAL (*appearing from behind the screen, searching*). Nothing, nothing.

FAY (*poking her head over the screen*). A screw from the coffin, perhaps?

HAL. Was it the wedding ring?

FAY (*looking*). No. Nothing important.

HAL. I'm inclined to agree.

> FAY *goes behind the screen.* HAL *takes a sheet from off the screen and spreads it on the floor.*

FAY (*from behind the screen*). Lovely-shaped feet your mother had. For a woman of her age.

> *She hands a pair of shoes across the screen.* HAL *places them in the centre of the sheet.*

What will you do with the money?

> *She hands a pair of stockings over the screen.*

HAL. I'd like to run a brothel. (*He pushes the stockings into the shoes.*) I'd run a two-star brothel. And if I prospered I'd graduate to a three-star brothel. I'd advertise 'By Appointment'. Like jam.

> FAY *hands a* W.V.S. *uniform across the screen.* HAL *folds it up and puts it into the sheet.*

I'd have a spade bird. I don't agree with the colour bar. And a Finnish bird. I'd make them kip together. To bring out the contrast.

> FAY *hands a slip across the screen.* HAL *puts it into the pile.*

I'd have two Irish birds. A decent Catholic. And a Protestant. I'd make the Protestant take Catholics. And the Catholic take Protestants. Teach them how the other half lives. I'd have a blonde bird who'd dyed her hair dark. And a dark bird who'd dyed her hair blonde. I'd have a midget. And a tall bird with big tits.

FAY *hands across the screen in quick succession, a pair of corsets, a brassiere and a pair of knickers.* HAL *puts them into the pile.*

FAY. Are you committed to having her teeth removed?
HAL. Yes.

Pause.

I'd have a French bird, a Dutch bird, a Belgian bird, an Italian bird—

FAY *hands a pair of false teeth across the screen.*

—and a bird that spoke fluent Spanish and performed the dances of her native country to perfection. (*He clicks the teeth like castanets.*) I'd call it the Consummatum Est. And it'd be the most famous house of ill-fame in the whole of England.

FAY *appears from behind the screen.* HAL *holds up the teeth.*

These are good teeth. Are they the National Health?
FAY. No. She bought them out of her winnings. She had some good evenings at the table last year.

FAY *folds up the screen. The corpse is lying on the bed, wrapped in the mattress cover, tied with bandages.*

HAL (*approaching the bed, bowing his head*). She was a great lady. Nothing was too good for her. Which is why she had to go.
FAY (*taking a key from her handbag, gives it to* HAL). Fetch the car. Pay cash. It's not to be charged to my account.

TRUSCOTT *approaches the door left. His shadow is cast upon the glass panel. He knocks on the door.* HAL *picks up the sheet with the clothes in it. He looks for somewhere to put them.* FAY *opens the door.* TRUSCOTT *stands outside, smiling.*

TRUSCOTT (*touching his hat*). I'm back again, miss.

> FAY *slams the door.* HAL *stuffs the sheet and clothes into the bedpan attached to the invalid chair.* FAY *pulls the screen round the bed.*

(*Calling.*) Might I have a word with you.

> HAL *closes the lid of the bedpan, concealing the clothes.*

FAY (*calling, answering* TRUSCOTT). Yes.

TRUSCOTT. Let me in, then, I can't hold a conversation through a keyhole. I'm a council employee. I might lose my pension.

> HAL *sits in the invalid chair.* FAY *opens the door.* TRUSCOTT *enters.*

What's going on in this house?

HAL. Nothing.

TRUSCOTT. You admit it? You must be very sure of yourself. Why aren't you both at the funeral? I thought you were mourners.

FAY. We decided not to go. We were afraid we might break down.

TRUSCOTT. That's a selfish attitude to take. The dead can't bury themselves, you know.

> *He takes his pipe from his pocket and plugs it with tobacco.*

FAY. What are you doing here?

TRUSCOTT (*smiling*). I've been having a look round your charming house. Poking and prying.

HAL. Have you a search warrant?

TRUSCOTT. What for?

HAL. To search the house.

TRUSCOTT. But I've already searched the house. I don't want to do it again.

FAY. It's common knowledge what police procedure is. They must have a search warrant.

TRUSCOTT. I'm sure the police must, but as I've already informed you, I am from the water board. And our procedure
is different.

He puts the pipe into his mouth, lights it, draws on it.

(*Chewing on his pipe.*) Now, I was sent on a fool's errand a
few minutes ago. Unless I'm much mistaken, the object of
my search is in that cupboard.

Pause.

Open it for me.

HAL. It isn't locked.

TRUSCOTT. I can't take your word for it, lad.

*HAL opens the wardrobe door. TRUSCOTT puts on a pair of
spectacles, and stares in. He shakes his head. He takes off
his spectacles.*

This puts an entirely different complexion on the matter.

FAY. It's empty.

TRUSCOTT. Exactly. There's still a lot of routine work to be
done, I can see that. Would you mind waiting outside, miss ?
I'd like a word with this lad alone. I'll let you know when
you're wanted.

FAY and HAL exchange bewildered glances. FAY goes off left.

(*Laughing pleasantly.*) I always have difficulties with the
ladies. They can't accept a *fait accompli*.

*Pause. He takes the pipe from his mouth and stares specula-
tively at HAL.*

What do you know of a lad called Dennis ?

HAL. He's a mate of mine.

TRUSCOTT. You don't want to spend your time with a youth
like him. He's not your type. He's got five pregnancies to his
credit.

HAL. Anyone can make a mistake.

TRUSCOTT. Maybe. But he's obviously getting into the habit of making mistakes. Where does he engender these unwanted children? There are no open spaces. The police patrol regularly. It should be next to impossible to commit the smallest act of indecency, let alone beget a child. Where does he do it?

HAL. On crowded dance floors during the rhumba.

FAY *enters left.*

TRUSCOTT (*removing his pipe, patiently*). I'm a busy man, miss. Do as you're told and wait outside.

FAY. What's your name?

TRUSCOTT. I prefer to remain anonymous for the present.

FAY. Your Christian name.

TRUSCOTT. I'm not a practising Christian.

FAY. Is it Jim?

TRUSCOTT. No.

FAY. A man at the door says it is.

TRUSCOTT. I'd like to help him, but I'm not prepared to admit to any name other than my own.

FAY. He says his name is Meadows.

TRUSCOTT (*pause, nods his head sagely*). One of my names is Jim. Clearly this fellow is in possession of the fact and wishes to air his knowledge. I shall speak to him.

TRUSCOTT *goes off left.*

FAY (*closing the door, whispers*). There's a uniformed policeman at the door! They're on to us.

HAL. It's bluff.

FAY. No. God works for them. They have Him in their pockets like we've always been taught.

HAL. We've got to get rid of him. He'll find the body next.

He opens the wardrobe door and puts FAY'S *shoes and the coathanger inside. He closes the door quickly and turns to* FAY.

Remember when we were wrapping her up?

FAY. It's not something I care to reminisce about.

HAL. Something dropped out? We couldn't find it?

FAY. Yes.

HAL. I know what it was.

FAY. What?

HAL. One of her eyes!

They drop to their knees. They search. TRUSCOTT *enters. They stand*

TRUSCOTT (*smiling*). Just a bobby making a nuisance of himself.

He goes to the screen and glances behind it. Pause. He takes the pipe from his mouth.

The theft of a Pharaoh is something which hadn't crossed my mind.

He folds the screen revealing the corpse, swathed in the mattress cover and tied with bandages.

Whose mummy is this?

HAL. Mine.

TRUSCOTT. Whose was it before?

HAL. I'm an only child.

TRUSCOTT. A word of warning. Don't take the mickey. You'll make me angry. (*He smiles.*) O.K.?

FAY. It's not a mummy. It's a dummy. I used to sew my dresses on it.

TRUSCOTT. What sex is it?

FAY. I call it 'she' because of my sewing. The garments were female and because I'm literal-minded I chose to believe I was making them on a lady.

TRUSCOTT. Splendid. Excellently put.

HAL. No actual evidence of sex can be given. It's contrary to English law.

TRUSCOTT. Yes, a tailor's dummy provided with evidence of sex would fill the mind of the average magistrate with misgiving. Why is it wrapped?

HAL. We were taking it in the car.

FAY. To a carnival. She's part of a display.

TRUSCOTT. What part?

FAY. A sewing-class. Prewar. The difference in technique is to be demonstrated.

TRUSCOTT. Is this dummy a frequent visitor to exhibitions?

FAY. Yes.

TRUSCOTT. When is the object's outing to take place?

FAY. It isn't going now.

TRUSCOTT. The treat has been cancelled?

FAY. Yes.

TRUSCOTT. Why?

HAL. My mate Dennis was to have arranged transport. He let us down.

TRUSCOTT. I can believe that. From all I've heard of your friend I'd say he was quite capable of disappointing a tailor's dummy.

He puts his pipe into the corner of his mouth. He takes out his notebook and makes notes.

You claim this object is awaiting transport to a carnival where it will be used to demonstrate the continuity of British needlework?

FAY. Yes.

TRUSCOTT. Sounds a reasonable explanation. Quite reasonable.

He puts the notebook away and chews on his pipe. He observes HAL narrowly.

What were you doing on Saturday night?

Pause as HAL tries to avoid telling the truth. He stares at FAY in an agony.

HAL (*at last*). I was in bed.

FAY *breathes a sigh of relief.*

TRUSCOTT. Can you confirm that, miss?

FAY. Certainly not.

TRUSCOTT (*to* HAL). What were you doing in bed?

HAL. Sleeping.

TRUSCOTT. Do you seriously expect me to believe that? A man of your age behaving like a child? What was your mate doing on Saturday night?

HAL. He was in bed as well.

TRUSCOTT. You'll tell me next he was sleeping.

HAL. I expect he was.

TRUSCOTT (*to* FAY). What a coincidence, miss. Don't you agree? Two young men who know each other very well, spend their nights in separate beds. Asleep. It sounds highly unlikely to me. (*To* HAL.) What is your excuse for knowing him?

HAL. He's clever. I'm stupid, see.

TRUSCOTT. Why do you make such stupid remarks?

HAL. I'm a stupid person. That's what I'm trying to say.

TRUSCOTT. What proof have I that you're stupid. Give me an example of your stupidity.

HAL. I can't.

TRUSCOTT. Why not? I don't believe you're stupid at all.

HAL. I am. I had a hand in the bank job.

FAY *draws a sharp breath.* HAL *sits frozen.* TRUSCOTT *takes his pipe from his mouth.*

(*With a nervous laugh.*) There, that's stupid, isn't it? Telling you that.

TRUSCOTT (*also laughing*). You must be stupid if you expect me to believe you. Why, if you had a hand in the bank job, you wouldn't tell me.

FAY. Not unless he was stupid.

TRUSCOTT. But he is stupid. He's just admitted it. He must be
the stupidest criminal in England. Unless – (*He regards* HAL
with mounting suspicion.) – unless he's the cleverest. What
was your motive in confessing to the bank job?

HAL. To prove I'm stupid.

TRUSCOTT. But you've proved the opposite.

HAL. Yes.

TRUSCOTT (*baffled, gnawing his lip*). There's more to this than
meets the eye. I'm tempted to believe that you did have a
hand in the bank job. Yes. I shall inform my superior officer.
He will take whatever steps he thinks fit. I may be required
to make an arrest.

FAY. The water board can't arrest people.

TRUSCOTT. They can in certain circumstances.

FAY. What circumstances?

TRUSCOTT. I'm not prepared to reveal the inner secrets of the
water board to a member of the general public. (*To* HAL.)
Where's the money?

HAL (*closing his eyes, taking a deep breath*). It's being buried.

TRUSCOTT. Who's burying it?

HAL. Father Jellicoe, S.J.

TRUSCOTT. Come here! Come here!

HAL goes over, his hands trembling as they button up his coat.

I'm going to ask you a question or two. I want sensible
answers. None of your piss-taking. Is that understood? Do I
make myself plain? I'm talking English. Do you understand?

HAL. Yes.

TRUSCOTT. All right then. As long as we know.

A pause, in which he studies HAL.

Now, be sensible. Where's the money?

HAL looks at his watch.

HAL. By now I'd say it was half-way up the aisle of the Church of St Barnabas and St Jude.

He half turns away. TRUSCOTT *brings his fist down on the back of* HAL'S *neck.* HAL *cries out in pain and collapses on to the floor rubbing his shoulder.*

FAY (*indignant*). How dare you! He's only a boy.

TRUSCOTT. I'm not impressed by his sex, miss. (*To* HAL.) I asked for the truth.

HAL. I'm telling the truth.

TRUSCOTT. Understand this, lad. You can't get away with cheek. Kids nowadays treat any kind of authority as a challenge. We'll challenge you. If you oppose me in my duty, I'll kick those teeth through the back of your head. Is that clear?

HAL. Yes.

Door chimes.

FAY. Would you excuse me, Inspector?

TRUSCOTT (*wiping his brow*). You're at liberty to answer your own doorbell, miss. That is how we tell whether or not we live in a free country.

FAY *goes off left.*

(*Standing over* HAL.) Where's the money?

HAL. In church.

TRUSCOTT *kicks* HAL *violently.* HAL *cries out in terror and pain.*

TRUSCOTT. Don't lie to me!

HAL. I'm not lying! It's in church!

TRUSCOTT (*shouting, knocking* HAL *to the floor*). Under any other political system I'd have you on the floor in tears!

HAL (*crying*). You've got me on the floor in tears.

TRUSCOTT. Where's the money?

HAL. I've told you. In church. They're quoting St Paul over it.

TRUSCOTT. I don't care if they're quoting the Highway Code over it. One more chance. Where is it?

HAL (*desperate, trying to protect himself*). In church! In church. My dad's watching the last rites of a hundred and four thousand quid!

> TRUSCOTT *jerks* HAL *from the floor, beating and kicking and punching him.* HAL *screams with pain.*

TRUSCOTT. I'll hose you down! I'll chlorinate you!

> HAL *tries to defend himself, his nose is bleeding.*

You'll be laughing on the other side of your bloody face.

> FAY *enters left, supporting* MCLEAVY, *who is heavily bandaged.*

FAY. They've had an accident!

> TRUSCOTT *leaves* HAL, *pulls the bed from the wall and shoves it to* MCLEAVY, *who faints on to it, just missing the corpse.* HAL *drags the corpse from the bed and shoves it behind the screen.*

TRUSCOTT (*to* MCLEAVY). Have you reported the accident?

> MCLEAVY *opens his mouth. He is too overcome by emotion to speak.*

FAY. It's the shock. Taken away his power of speech, it has.

TRUSCOTT. Has this happened before?

FAY. Yes. Six or seven times.

TRUSCOTT. If he's going to make a habit of it he ought to learn a sign language. (*To* MCLEAVY.) Do you understand me, sir?

> MCLEAVY *closes his eyes, shudders.* TRUSCOTT *straightens up.*

I've known people communicate with the dead in half this time.

MCLEAVY (*moaning*). Oh . . . Oh . . .

TRUSCOTT. What has happened, sir?

MCLEAVY. I've had an accident.

TRUSCOTT. I shall have to make a full report.

He takes out his note-book.

MCLEAVY. Are you qualified?

TRUSCOTT. That needn't concern you at present, sir. I shall let you know later. Now give me a full statement.

MCLEAVY *passes a hand across his brow and clears his throat.*

MCLEAVY. We set off in high spirits. The weather was humid, a heat mist covered the sky. The road to the graveyard lay uphill. It was a sad occasion for me. In spite of this I kept a tight hold on my emotions, refusing to show the extent of my loss. Along the route perfect strangers had the courtesy to raise their hats. We got admiring glances for the flowers and sympathetic nods for me.

Pause.

The dignity of the event was unsurpassed.

He bows his head, everyone waits. TRUSCOTT *taps sharply on the bedrail with his pencil.*

Then, as the solemn procession was half-way up the hill, a lorry, clearly out of control, came hurtling down on top of us. It struck the first car, holding the remains, and killed the undertaker—

HAL. Not Dennis!

MCLEAVY. No. Mr Walter Tracey. The hearse was a wreck within seconds. Meanwhile the second part of the cortège crashed into the smoking wreckage. I was flung to one side, hitting my head on the bodywork of the vehicle. The next thing I knew I was being helped out by passers-by. The road looked like a battlefield. Strewn with the injured and dying. Blood, glass.

He chokes. Pause.

Several fires were started.

HAL. Was the actual fabric of the coffin damaged?

MCLEAVY. No. Your mother is quite safe.

HAL. No dents? No holes?

MCLEAVY. No. People remarked on the extreme durability of the lid. I was about to give the undertaker a recommendation. Then I remembered that he wasn't capable of receiving one.

TRUSCOTT. Surely he understood when he took on the job that he couldn't make capital out of his own death?

FAY. Where is the coffin?

MCLEAVY. Outside.

FAY (*to* TRUSCOTT). Can it be brought in?

TRUSCOTT. By all means. We mustn't keep a lady waiting.

HAL *goes off.* TRUSCOTT *turns to* MCLEAVY.

Why are you bandaged? Is that a result of the accident?

MCLEAVY. Indirectly. My wounds stem from a fear-crazed Afghan hound that was being exercised at the time. I was bitten about the face and hands. In my nervous state I was an easy target.

TRUSCOTT. Did you take the owner's name?

MCLEAVY. No.

TRUSCOTT. It all seems highly irregular. The dog will have to be destroyed.

MCLEAVY. I don't hold it responsible for its actions. It was frightened.

TRUSCOTT. I've been frightened myself on occasions. I've never bitten anyone. These people should learn to control their pets.

MCLEAVY. The woman who owned the dog had fainted.

TRUSCOTT. She sounds an unstable kind of person to me.

HAL and DENNIS enter with the coffin. It is charred, blackened and smoking.

FAY. Who'd think she'd be back so soon?

MCLEAVY. She could never make up her mind in life. Death hasn't changed her.

DENNIS. Your wreaths have been blown to buggery, Mr McLeavy. We might manage a repair job on that big harp.

HAL. What are we going to do for the replay?

MCLEAVY. Buy fresh ones, I suppose. Always some new expense.

The coffin is set down. The side falls away, revealing the banknotes inside. DENNIS stands in front of the coffin, shielding the contents from TRUSCOTT and MCLEAVY. MCLEAVY holds out a hand and tries to shake DENNIS'S hand.

(*To* TRUSCOTT.) You must congratulate this boy. He rescued the coffin from the blazing car at considerable personal risk.

TRUSCOTT (*dryly*). If he behaves with such consideration to a dead woman, what might we not expect with a live one?

HAL. We need a finishing touch. Know what it is? A holy image. Centre. Between candles.

FAY. I have a Madonna.

HAL. What could be better? Make a gesture. She knew what disappointment was, didn't she? Same as us. A little imagination. What wonders can't it accomplish.

DENNIS. Oh, yes. We've found in the trade that an impression can be created with quite humble materials: a candle, half a yard of velvet and a bunch of anemones and the effect is of a lying in state.

MCLEAVY. My photo of His Holiness would enhance the scene, only it's three Popes out of date.

FAY. Mrs McLeavy won't mind. She wasn't a woman who
followed the fashions. Go and get it.

MCLEAVY *stands, moves to the door.* TRUSCOTT *bars his
path.*

TRUSCOTT. I must ask you to remain where you are. No one
is to leave without my permission.
MCLEAVY. Why?
TRUSCOTT. When you disobey my orders, sir, you make my
job doubly difficult.
MCLEAVY. On what authority do you give orders?
TRUSCOTT. You'd be considerably happier if you allowed me
to do my duty without asking questions.
MCLEAVY. Who are you?
TRUSCOTT. I'm an official of the Metropolitan Water Board,
sir, as I've already told you.
MCLEAVY. But the water board has no power to keep law-
abiding citizens confined to their rooms.
TRUSCOTT. Not if the citizens are law abiding.
MCLEAVY. Whether they're law abiding or not the water
board has no power.
TRUSCOTT. I don't propose to argue hypothetical cases with
you, sir. Remain where you are till further notice.
MCLEAVY. I shall take legal advice.
TRUSCOTT. That is as may be. I've no power to prevent you.
MCLEAVY. I want to telephone my lawyer.
TRUSCOTT. I can't allow you to do that. It would be contrary
to regulations. We've no case against you.

TRUSCOTT *chews on his pipe.* MCLEAVY *stares in fury.*

FAY. Can't he fetch the Pope's photo?
TRUSCOTT. Only if some responsible person accompanies him.
HAL. You're a responsible person. You could accompany him.
TRUSCOTT. What proof have I that I'm a responsible person?

DENNIS. If you weren't responsible you wouldn't be given the power to behave as you do.

> TRUSCOTT *removes his pipe, considers.*

TRUSCOTT. That is perfectly correct. In which case I shall accompany you, sir. Come with me.

> TRUSCOTT *and* MCLEAVY *go off left.*

HAL (*closing the door*). We must return the remains to the coffin and the money to the cupboard.

DENNIS. Why?

FAY. Mr McLeavy may ask for the coffin to be opened. Formaldehyde and three morticians have increased his wife's allure.

DENNIS. But a corpse is only attractive to another corpse.

HAL. We can't rely on him having heard that.

> DENNIS *begins to unscrew the coffin lid.* FAY *and* HAL *drag the corpse from behind the screen.*

DENNIS (*looking up*). What's that!

FAY. Mrs McLeavy.

DENNIS (*to* HAL). How much have you told her?

HAL. Everything.

DENNIS. We've never involved a woman in anything unsavoury before.

> *He takes the lid off the coffin.* FAY *piles money into his arms.* HAL *does the same.*

(*To* FAY.) Half of this money is mine. Will you marry me?

HAL. We're splitting the money three ways now, baby. You'll have thirty-four thousand.

DENNIS (*to* FAY). Is that enough?

FAY. You've a slight lead on Mr McLeavy at the moment.

> *She kisses him.* DENNIS *trembles and drops the money back into the coffin.*

HAL (*angry*). Hurry up! What's the matter with you?

DENNIS. My hands are trembling. It's excitement at the prospect of becoming engaged.

HAL. You're too easily aroused. That's your trouble.

MCLEAVY'S *shadow appears on the glass panel.* DENNIS *tips the money into the coffin.*

MCLEAVY (*off*). I'll complain to my M.P. I'll have you reported.

HAL *shoves the lid on to the coffin.* MCLEAVY *enters.*

He's turned the water off. I've just been trying to use the toilet—

FAY (*standing in front of him, preventing him seeing the corpse*). Oh, please! You don't have to explain.

HAL *tries to drag the corpse away.* DENNIS *opens the wardrobe.*

MCLEAVY. I don't believe he's anything to do with the water board. I was handcuffed out there. D'you know that? Handcuffed.

He sees the corpse. He gives a shriek of horror.

What in Heaven's name is that!

FAY. It's my appliance.

MCLEAVY. I've never seen it before.

FAY. I kept it in my room. It was personal.

MCLEAVY. What is it doing down here?

FAY. I'm going to do some work. For charity.

MCLEAVY. What kind of work?

FAY. I'm making the vestments for Our Lady's festival. I was commissioned. My altar cloth at Easter brought me to the attention of the Committee.

MCLEAVY. My congratulations. You'll want plenty of room to work. (*To* DENNIS.) Take Nurse McMahon's applicance to my study.

FAY (*anxious, with a smile*). It's most kind of you, Mr McLeavy, but I'd prefer to work down here. Mrs McLeavy's presence will bring me inspiration.

MCLEAVY. Very well, you have my permission to work down here. I look forward to seeing the finished results.

TRUSCOTT *enters.*

TRUSCOTT (*To* MCLEAVY). Do you still want your padre's photograph, sir?

MCLEAVY. Yes.

TRUSCOTT. You'll find a policeman outside. He will accompany you. Off you go.

MCLEAVY. I resent your manner of speaking! I'm the householder. I can't be ordered about like this.

TRUSCOTT (*shoving him to the door*). Don't make my job any more tiring than it is, sir. Fetch the photograph in question and wait outside until I call.

MCLEAVY *goes off left.*

(*To* DENNIS.) I want a word with you. (*To* HAL *and* FAY.) The rest of you outside!

HAL. Can't I stay with him? He's the nervous type.

TRUSCOTT. I'm nervous as well. I'll be company for him—

FAY. It'd be better if I was present. He's more relaxed in the company of women.

TRUSCOTT. He'll have to come to terms with his psychological peculiarity. Out you go!

FAY *and* HAL *go off left.*

(TRUSCOTT *faces* DENNIS, *the corpse between them.*) Now then, I'm going to ask a few questions. I want sensible answers. I've had enough fooling about for one day. (*He observes* DENNIS *narrowly.*) Have you ever been in prison?

DENNIS. Yes.

TRUSCOTT. What for?

DENNIS. Stealing overcoats and biting a policeman.

TRUSCOTT. The theft of an article of clothing is excusable. But policemen, like red squirrels, must be protected. You were rightly convicted. What do you know of paternity orders?

DENNIS. Is that when birds say you've put them in the club?

TRUSCOTT. Don't try to evade the issue. How many women have you made pregnant?

DENNIS. Five.

TRUSCOTT. You scatter your seed along the pavements without regard to age or sex. (*He taps the corpse.*) What are you doing with this? Have you taken up sewing?

DENNIS. I was putting it in the cupboard.

TRUSCOTT. Why?

DENNIS. To keep it hidden.

TRUSCOTT. Don't try to pull the wool over my eyes. I've been told the whole pathetic story. You ought to be ashamed of yourself.

DENNIS (*pause, with resignation*). Am I under arrest, then?

TRUSCOTT. I wish you were. Unfortunately what you've done isn't illegal.

DENNIS (*pause, with surprise*). When did they change the law?

TRUSCOTT. There never was any law.

DENNIS. Has it all been a leg-pull? My uncle did two years.

TRUSCOTT. What for?

DENNIS. Armed robbery.

TRUSCOTT. That is against the law.

DENNIS. It used to be.

TRUSCOTT. It still is.

DENNIS. I thought the law had been changed.

TRUSCOTT. Who told you that?

DENNIS. You did.

TRUSCOTT. When?

DENNIS. Just now. I thought there'd been a reappraisal of society's responsibilities towards the criminal.

TRUSCOTT. You talk like a judge.

DENNIS. I've met so many.

TRUSCOTT. I'm not impressed by your fine friends.

He chews on his pipe and watches DENNIS *closely.*

Where's the money from the bank job?

DENNIS. What bank job?

TRUSCOTT. Where's it buried?

DENNIS. Buried?

TRUSCOTT. Your mate says it's been buried.

DENNIS (*indignant*). He's a liar!

TRUSCOTT. A very intelligent reply. You're an honest lad. (*He smiles and puts an arm around* DENNIS'S *shoulders.*) Are you prepared to co-operate with me? I'll see you're all right.

DENNIS *edges away.*

I'll put a good word in for you.

DENNIS (*nervous, laughing to hid his embarrassment*). Can't we stand away from the window? I don't want anybody to see me talking to a policeman.

TRUSCOTT. I'm not a policeman.

DENNIS. Aren't you?

TRUSCOTT. No. I'm from the Metropolitan Water Board.

DENNIS. You're the law! You gave me a kicking down the station.

TRUSCOTT. I don't remember doing so.

DENNIS. Well, it's all in the day's work to you, isn't it?

TRUSCOTT. What were you doing down the station?

DENNIS. I was on sus.

TRUSCOTT. What were you suspected of?

DENNIS. The bank job.

TRUSCOTT. And you complain you were beaten?

DENNIS. Yes.

TRUSCOTT. Did you tell anyone?

DENNIS. Yes.

TRUSCOTT. Who?

DENNIS. The officer in charge.

TRUSCOTT. What did he say?

DENNIS. Nothing.

TRUSCOTT. Why not?

DENNIS. He was out of breath with kicking.

TRUSCOTT. I hope you're prepared to substantiate these accusations, lad. What evidence have you?

DENNIS. My bruises.

TRUSCOTT. What is the official version of those?

DENNIS. Resisting arrest.

TRUSCOTT. I can see nothing unreasonable in that. You want to watch yourself. Making unfounded allegations. You'll find yourself in serious trouble.

He takes DENNIS *by the collar and shakes him.*

If I ever hear you accuse the police of using violence on a prisoner in custody again, I'll take you down to the station and beat the eyes out of your head.

He shoves DENNIS *away.*

Now, get out!

DENNIS *is about to leave the corpse.*

And take that thing with you. I don't want to see it in here again.

DENNIS *goes off left with the corpse.*
TRUSCOTT *closes the door and, as he does so, sees something on the floor. He puts his pipe into the corner of his mouth and picks up the glass eye. He holds it to the light in order to get a better view. Puzzled. He sniffs at it. He holds it close to his ear. He rattles it. He takes out a pocket magnifying-glass and stares hard at it. He gives a brief exclamation of horror and surprise.*

Curtain

Act Two

TRUSCOTT, *by the window, is examining the eye under a pocket magnifying-glass.*

MCLEAVY *enters carrying a photograph of Pope Pius XII. FAY follows him.*

MCLEAVY. Is it possible to use the toilet, sir?

TRUSCOTT (*putting the eye into his pocket*). The water is off.

FAY. Who turned it off?

TRUSCOTT. My men did.

MCLEAVY (*handing the photograph to* FAY). I'm getting on the phone. I'll have your particulars filed.

TRUSCOTT. I've disconnected the telephone.

MCLEAVY. Why?

TRUSCOTT. You always begin your sentences with 'Why?' Did they teach you to at school?

MCLEAVY. Now, look here – I've a right to know – are you from the sanitary people? I never knew they had power over the post office. Aren't they separate entities? (*To* FAY.) The water board and the post office? Or have they had a merger? (*To* TRUSCOTT.) They'd never connect up the water board and the post office, would they?

TRUSCOTT. I'm not in a position to say, sir.

MCLEAVY. Produce your warrant and you're justified. If not, get out of my house. Even a Government department should take account of death.

TRUSCOTT. Less of that. I must ask you to respect my cloth.

MCLEAVY (*to* FAY). Is he a priest?

FAY. If he is he's an unfrocked one.

MCLEAVY (*stares at* TRUSCOTT, *goes closer to him, wonderingly*). Who are you?

TRUSCOTT. My name is Truscott.

MCLEAVY. What in Hell kind of a name is that? Is it an anagram? You're not bloody human, that's for sure. We're being made the victims of some kind of interplanetary rag. (*To* FAY.) He's probably luminous in the dark. (*To* TRUSCOTT.) Come on, I don't care what infernal power you represent. I want a straight answer.

    TRUSCOTT *regards* MCLEAVY *calmly and in silence.*

I'll go next door – they're Dubliners. If you're the Angel of the Lord Himself, they'll mix it with you.

TRUSCOTT. I've warned you already about leaving this room. Do as you're told or take the consequences.

MCLEAVY. I'll take the consequences.

TRUSCOTT. I can't allow you to do that.

MCLEAVY. You've no power to stop me.

TRUSCOTT. I must disagree. I'm acting under orders.

MCLEAVY. Whose?

TRUSCOTT. My superior officer's.

MCLEAVY. I don't believe he exists!

TRUSCOTT. If you don't control yourself, I shall have to caution you.

MCLEAVY. I know we're living in a country whose respect for the law is proverbial: who'd give power of arrest to the traffic lights if three women magistrates and a Liberal M.P. would only suggest it; but I've never heard of an employee of the water board nicking a kid for stealing apples, let alone a grown man for doubting whether he had any right to be on the planet.

    Silence. TRUSCOTT *removes his pipe from his mouth slowly, weighing his words before he speaks.*

TRUSCOTT. If you'll give me your undivided attention for a few

moments, sir, I promise you we'll have this whole case
sorted out. It isn't a game we're playing. It's my duty, and
I must do it to the best of my ability.

The door right is flung open, DENNIS *and* HAL *burst in with
the corpse.* TRUSCOTT *looks steadily and searchingly at them.
He points to the corpse with his pipe.*

What are you doing with that thing?

DENNIS. We were taking it outside.

TRUSCOTT. Why? Did it need the air?

HAL. We were putting it in the garage.

TRUSCOTT. This isn't the garage. What do you mean by
bringing it back into this room?

HAL. A police sergeant was in the garage.

TRUSCOTT. I'm sure he has no particular aversion to sharing a
garage with a tailor's dummy.

HAL. He wanted to undress it.

TRUSCOTT. What possible objection could there be to an
officer undressing a dummy?

DENNIS. It isn't decent.

HAL. It's a Catholic.

TRUSCOTT (*with contempt*). The things you say are quite
ludicrous, lad. (*He laughs mirthlessly.*) Ho, ho ho. Take it to
the garage. The bobby won't interfere with it. He's a married
man with children.

No one moves. TRUSCOTT *chews on his pipe; he takes pipe
from his mouth.*

Go on! Do as I say.

FAY. No! I'd rather it didn't go. I want it here.

TRUSCOTT. Why?

FAY. It's valuable.

TRUSCOTT. Has its value increased during the last few minutes?

FAY. No.

TRUSCOTT. If it's your usual custom to encourage young men to run up and down garden paths with tailor's dummies, you must be stopped from exercising such arbitrary power.

FAY. I did want it in the garage, but after what has been said I feel I can't allow her out of my sight.

TRUSCOTT. Really, miss, your relationship with that object verges on the criminal. Has no one in this house any normal feelings? I've never come across such people. If there's any more of it, I shall arrest the lot of you.

MCLEAVY. How does the water board go about making an arrest?

TRUSCOTT. You must have realized by now, sir, that I am not from the water board?

MCLEAVY. I have. Your behaviour was causing me grave concern.

TRUSCOTT. Any deception I practised was never intended to deceive you, sir. You are – if I may say so – an intelligent man. (*He laughs to himself.*) You saw through my disguise at once. It was merely a ruse to give me time to review the situation. To get my bearings on a very tricky assignment. Or two tricky assignments. As you will shortly realize. (*He smiles and bows to* MCLEAVY.) You have before you a man who is quite a personage in his way – Truscott of the Yard. Have you never heard of Truscott? The man who tracked down the limbless girl killer? Or was that sensation before your time?

HAL. Who would kill a limbless girl?

TRUSCOTT. She was the killer.

HAL. How did she do it if she was limbless?

TRUSCOTT. I'm not prepared to answer that question to any-one outside the profession. We don't want a carbon-copy murder on our hands. (*To* MCLEAVY.) Do you realize what I'm doing here?

MCLEAVY. No. Your every action has been a mystery to me.

TRUSCOTT. That is as it should be. The process by which the

police arrive at the solution to a mystery is, in itself, a mystery. We've reason to believe that a number of crimes have been committed under your roof. There was no legal excuse for a warrant. We had no proof. However, the water board doesn't need a warrant to enter private houses. And so I availed myself of this loophole in the law. It's for your own good that Authority behaves in this seemingly alarming way. (*With a smile.*) Does my explanation satisfy you?

MCLEAVY. Oh, yes, Inspector. You've a duty to do. My personal freedom must be sacrificed. I have no further questions.

TRUSCOTT. Good. I shall proceed to bring the crimes to light. Beginning with the least important.

HAL. What is that?

TRUSCOTT. Murder.

FAY (*anxiously*). Murder?

TRUSCOTT. Yes, murder. (*To* MCLEAVY.) Your wife passed away three days ago? What did she die of?

FAY. The death certificate is perfectly legible.

TRUSCOTT. Reading isn't an occupation we encourage among police officers. We try to keep the paper work down to a minimum. (*To* MCLEAVY.) Have you no grumble at the way your wife died?

MCLEAVY. None.

TRUSCOTT. You're easily satisfied, I see. I am not.

FAY. Mrs McLeavy's doctor signed the death certificate.

TRUSCOTT. So I understand. But he'd just come from diagnosing a most unusual pregnancy. His mind was so occupied by the nature of the case that he omitted to take all factors into consideration and signed in a fuzz of scientific disbelief. Has anyone seen Mrs McLeavy since she died?

HAL. How could we?

TRUSCOTT. Can all of you swear you've had no commerce with the dead?

DENNIS. We're not mediums.

TRUSCOTT. That's a pity. It would have considerably simpli-
fied my task if you had been.

FAY. I wasn't going to mention it, but I had a psychic experience last night. Three parts of Mrs McLeavy materialized
to me as I was brushing my hair.

TRUSCOTT. Was her fate discussed?

FAY. Yes. In great detail.

MCLEAVY. I never knew you had visions.

TRUSCOTT (to FAY). Mrs McLeavy and I are perhaps the two
people most closely involved in her death. I'd be interested
to hear her on the subject.

FAY. She accused her husband of murder.

Sensation.

MCLEAVY. Me? Are you sure she accused me?

FAY. Yes.

MCLEAVY. Complete extinction has done nothing to silence her
slanderous tongue.

TRUSCOTT. Was anyone with her at the end? (*To* HAL.)
Were you?

HAL. Yes.

TRUSCOTT. Was she uneasy? Did she leave no last message?

HAL. No.

TRUSCOTT. Was this her usual custom?

HAL. She hadn't died before.

TRUSCOTT. Not to the best of your knowledge. Though I've no
doubt our information isn't as up to date as we supposed.
Did she whisper no last words? As you bent to kiss her
cheek before she expired?

HAL. She spoke of a book.

TRUSCOTT. Which?

HAL. A broken binding recurred.

TRUSCOTT. Was it a metaphor?

HAL. I took it to be so.

TRUSCOTT goes to the bookcase. He takes down a book.

TRUSCOTT. Apart from Bibles, which are notorious for broken bindings, there is this – The Trial of Phyllis McMahon. Nurse accused of murdering her patient.

He fixes FAY with a steely look; she turns pale.

One of my own cases.

He turns over pages, staring hard and with recognition at the photograph.

Look at this photograph.

HAL. It's you.

TRUSCOTT. Yes, most unflattering, isn't it? They always choose the worst. I cannot get them to print a decent picture.

He tears the photograph from the book, screws it into a ball and stuffs it into his pocket.

DENNIS. Is there a photo of the nurse?

TRUSCOTT. Unfortunately not. Someone has torn every picture of the nurse from the book.

Once again he turns his piercing gaze upon FAY; she looks uncomfortable.

However, we have something equally damning – the handwriting of the accused.

He opens the book at a page of handwriting.

And here – (*Triumphantly he takes a sheet of paper from his pocket.*) – the evidence on which I propose to convict: a recent specimen of the handwriting of your late wife's nurse. Identical in every respect.

MCLEAVY (*staring at the sheet of paper*). But this is signed Queen Victoria.

TRUSCOTT One of her many aliases.

MCLEAVY *stares in amazement at the evidence.*

HAL. If it was one of your own cases, how is it she didn't recognize you?

TRUSCOTT. Two very simple reasons. I conduct my cases under an assumed voice and I am a master of disguise. (*He takes off his hat.*) You see – a complete transformation. (*To* MCLEAVY.) You've had a lucky escape, sir. You'd've been the victim of a murder bid inside a month. We've had the tabs on her for years. Thirteen fatal accidents, two cases of suspected fish poisoning. One unexplained disappearance. She's practised her own form of genocide for a decade and called it nursing.

FAY (*staring at him, agitatedly*). I never killed anyone.

TRUSCOTT. At the George V hospital in Holyhead eighty-seven people died within a week. How do you explain that?

FAY. It was the geriatric ward. They were old.

TRUSCOTT. They had a right to live, same as anybody else.

FAY. I was in the children's ward.

TRUSCOTT. How many innocents did you massacre – Phyllis?

FAY. None.

TRUSCOTT. I fail to see why you choose to cloak the episode in mystery. You can't escape.

FAY. Mrs McLeavy accused her husband.

TRUSCOTT. We can't accept the evidence of a ghost. The problems posed would be insuperable.

FAY. You must prove me guilty. That is the law.

TRUSCOTT. You know nothing of the law. I know nothing of the law. That makes us equal in the sight of the law.

FAY. I'm innocent till I'm proved guilty. This is a free country. The law is impartial.

TRUSCOTT. Who's been filling your head with that rubbish?

FAY. I can't be had for anything. You've no proof.

TRUSCOTT. When I make out my report I shall say that you've

given me a confession. It could prejudice your case if I have
to forge one.

FAY. I shall deny that I've confessed.

TRUSCOTT. Perjury is a serious crime.

FAY. Have you no respect for the truth?

TRUSCOTT. We have a saying under the blue lamp 'Waste
time on the truth and you'll be pounding the beat until the
day you retire.'

FAY (*breaking down*). The British police force used to be run by
men of integrity.

TRUSCOTT. That is a mistake which has been rectified. Come
along now. I can't stand here all day.

FAY (*drying her eyes*). My name is Phyllis Jean McMahon alias
Fay Jean McMahon. I am twenty-eight years of age and a
nurse by profession. On the third of December last I
advertised in the trade papers for a situation. Mr McLeavy
answered my request. He wished me to nurse his wife back
to health: a task I found impossible to perform. Mrs McLeavy
was dying. Had euthanasia not been against my religion I
would have practised it. Instead I decided to murder her. I
administered poison during the night of June the twenty-
second. In the morning I found her dead and notified the
authorities. I have had nothing but heartache ever since. I
am sorry for my dreadful crime. (*She weeps.*)

TRUSCOTT (*looking up from his notebook*). Very good. Your style
is simple and direct. It's a theme which less skilfully handled
could've given offence. (*He puts away his notebook.*) One of
the most accomplished confessions I've heard in some time.

He gives MCLEAVY a police whistle.

I'll just arrange transport. Blow that if she should attempt
to escape. My men will come to your aid immediately. The
sooner we get a spoonful of Mrs McLeavy on a slide the
sooner McMahon faces that murder rap.

He goes off left.

MCLEAVY (*to* FAY). How could you rob me of my only support?

FAY. I intended to provide a replacement.

MCLEAVY. I never knew such wickedness was possible.

FAY. You were aware of my character when you employed me. My references were signed by people of repute.

MCLEAVY. You murdered most of them.

FAY. That doesn't invalidate their signatures.

MCLEAVY. Pack your bags! You're not being arrested from my house.

FAY *dabs at her eyes with a handkerchief.*

DENNIS. I've never seen you in adversity. It's an unforgettable experience. I love you. I'll wait for you for ever.

FAY. No, you'll tire of waiting and marry someone else.

HAL. He won't be able to. (*He runs his hand along the coffin lid.*) Not when the Inspector asks to see mum's remains. He'll have us by the short hairs, baby.

TRUSCOTT *re-enters left with* MEADOWS.

TRUSCOTT. We're ready when you are, McMahon.

FAY *holds out her hand to* HAL. HAL *shakes it and kisses her.*

HAL (*kissing* FAY'S *hand*). Good-bye. I count a mother well lost to have met you.

DENNIS *kisses* FAY'S *hand.*

DENNIS. I shall write to you. We're allowed one letter a week.

FAY. How sweet you are. I'd like to take you both to prison with me.

TRUSCOTT. They'd certainly do more good in Holloway than you will. Take her away, Meadows.

MEADOWS *approaches* FAY *with the handcuffs. She holds out her hands.* MEADOWS *hesitates, bends swiftly and kisses* FAY'S *hand.*

Meadows!

MEADOWS *handcuffs* FAY, *and leads her out.*

Nothing but a miracle can save her now.

MEADOWS *goes off with* FAY.

(*To* MCLEAVY). I understand your wife is embalmed, sir?
MCLEAVY. Yes.
TRUSCOTT. It's a delicate subject, sir, but for the post-mortem we shall want Mrs McLeavy's stomach. Where are you keeping it?
MCLEAVY. In the little casket.
TRUSCOTT. Where is it?
HAL. In the hall.
TRUSCOTT. Fetch it, will you?

HAL *goes off left.*

DENNIS. I have something to say which will be a shock to you, Inspector.
TRUSCOTT (*nodding, taking out his pipe*). What is it? Tell it to your uncle (*He smiles.*)
DENNIS. After I'd reached the coffin I went back for the little casket. As I reached it a violent explosion occurred. The lid of the casket was forced open and the contents dispersed.

HAL *enters left. He carries the casket. He turns it upside down. The hinged lid swings free.*

It's well known in the trade that the viscera, when heated, is an unstable element.
HAL. The contents of my mother's stomach have been destroyed.

TRUSCOTT *shakes his head, bowled over.*

TRUSCOTT. What an amazing woman McMahon is. She's got away with it again. She must have influence with Heaven.

HAL. God is a gentleman. He prefers blondes.

TRUSCOTT. Call her back! Look sharp! She'll sue us for wrongful arrest.

HAL *and* DENNIS *go off left.*

MCLEAVY (*to* TRUSCOTT). I'm sorry, sir, but I'm rather confused as to what has been said and in answer to whom.

TRUSCOTT. Briefly, sir, without your wife's stomach we have no evidence on which to convict.

MCLEAVY. Can't you do a reconstruction job on my wife's insides.

TRUSCOTT. Even God can't work miracles, sir.

MCLEAVY. Is the world mad? Tell me it's not.

TRUSCOTT. I'm not paid to quarrel with accepted facts.

FAY *enters with* HAL *and* DENNIS.

Well, McMahon, you've had another twelfth-hour escape?

FAY. Yes. I shall spend a quiet hour with my rosary after tea.

MCLEAVY (*to* FAY). I know one thing, you'll be black-listed. I'll see you never get another nursing job.

TRUSCOTT. There's no need to be vindictive. Show a little tolerance.

MCLEAVY. Is she going to get away with murder?

TRUSCOTT. I'm afraid so, sir. However, I've an ace up my sleeve. The situation for law and order, though difficult, is by no means hopeless. There's still a chance, albeit a slim one, that I can get McMahon as accessory to another crime. And one which the law regards as far more serious than the taking of human life.

MCLEAVY. What's more serious than mass murder?

TRUSCOTT. Stealing public money. And that is just what your son and his accomplices have done.

MCLEAVY. Harold would never do a thing like that. He belongs to the Sons of Divine Providence.

TRUSCOTT. That may make a difference to Divine Providence, but it cuts no ice with me.

He takes the eye from his pocket.

During the course of my investigations I came across this object. Could you explain to me what it is?

He hands the eye to MCLEAVY.

MCLEAVY (*examining it*). It's a marble.

TRUSCOTT. No. Not a marble. (*He regards* MCLEAVY *calmly.*) It looks suspiciously to me like an eye. The question I'd like answered is – to whom does it legally belong?

MCLEAVY. I'm not sure that it is an eye. I think it's a marble which has been trod on.

TRUSCOTT. It's an eye, sir. (*He takes the eye from* MCLEAVY.) The makers' name is clearly marked: J. & S. Frazer, Eye-makers to the Profession.

FAY. It's mine. My father left it to me in his will.

TRUSCOTT. That's a strange bequest for a father to make.

FAY. I always admired it. It's said to have belonged originally to a well-loved figure of the concert platform.

TRUSCOTT. You're a clever woman, McMahon. Unfortunately you're not quite clever enough. I'm no fool.

FAY. Your secret is safe with me.

TRUSCOTT. I've a shrewd suspicion where this eye came from. (*He smiles.*) You know too, don't you?

FAY. No.

TRUSCOTT. Don't lie to me! It's from your sewing dummy, isn't it?

FAY (*laughing*). It's no good, Inspector. You're too clever by half.

TRUSCOTT. I'm glad you've decided to tell the truth at last. We must return the eye to its rightful owner. Unwrap the dummy.

FAY. No, no! You can't undress her in front of four men. I must do it in private.

MCLEAVY. One moment. (*To* TRUSCOTT.) Let me see that eye.

TRUSCOTT *gives it to him.*

(*To* FAY.) Who gave you this?

FAY. It's from my dummy. Didn't you hear the Inspector?

MCLEAVY (*to* TRUSCOTT). Is it likely they'd fit eyes to a sewing machine? Does that convince you?

TRUSCOTT. Nothing ever convinces me. I choose the least unlikely explanation and file it in our records.

MCLEAVY (*to* FAY). Who gave you this? Come on now!

DENNIS. I gave it to her. A woman gave it to me as a souvenir.

MCLEAVY. Of what?

DENNIS. A special occasion.

MCLEAVY. It must've been a very special occasion if she gave you her eye to mark it. Come along, I'm not the police. I want a sensible answer. Who gave it to you?

HAL. I did.

MCLEAVY (*shrieks*). You! Oh, Sacred Heaven, no!

TRUSCOTT. We're open to serious discussion, sir, but not bad language.

MCLEAVY. This is stolen property. This eye belongs to my wife.

TRUSCOTT. On what do you base your assumption?

MCLEAVY. My wife had glass eyes.

TRUSCOTT. A remarkable woman, sir. How many were in her possession at the time of her death?

MCLEAVY. None.

TRUSCOTT. I see.

MCLEAVY. These were fitted after death. Her own were taken away.

TRUSCOTT. Where to?

MCLEAVY. I don't know.

TRUSCOTT. Did you never think to inquire?

MCLEAVY. No

TRUSCOTT. You act in a singularly heartless manner for someone who claims to have been happily married.

MCLEAVY. Oh, Inspector – (*Brokenly*) – my son, you heard
him confess it, has stolen the eyes from the dead; a practice
unknown outside of medical science. I have reared a ghoul at
my own expense.

Silence. TRUSCOTT *considers.*

TRUSCOTT. What do you wish me to do, sir?

MCLEAVY. Fetch a screwdriver. The coffin must be opened. I
want to know what else thievery stoops to. Her head may
have gone as well.

DENNIS. Might I advise caution, Mr McLeavy? From a professional point of view? The coffin took a pasting, you know.

FAY. She may be in pieces.

MCLEAVY. Fetch a screwdriver.

HAL. Couldn't we bury the eye separately?

MCLEAVY. I can't ask the priest to hold the burial service over
an eye. Fetch a screwdriver.

Nobody moves. TRUSCOTT *draws a deep breath.*

TRUSCOTT. What good will it do, sir?

MCLEAVY. I'm not interested in doing good. There are or-
ganizations devoted to that purpose. Fetch a screwdriver!
Do I have to repeat it like the muezzin?

DENNIS *gives* MCLEAVY *a screwdriver.* MCLEAVY *hands
the eye to* TRUSCOTT *and begins to unscrew the coffin lid.*

TRUSCOTT. This is unwarranted interference with the rights of
the dead. As a policeman I must ask you to consider your
actions most carefully.

MCLEAVY. She's my wife. I can do what I like with her. Anything is legal with a corpse.

TRUSCOTT. Indeed it is not. Conjugal rights should stop with the last heartbeat. I thought you knew that.

   MCLEAVY *begins to unscrew the second side of the coffin.*

I must say, sir, I'm aghast at this behaviour. Equivalent to tomb robbing it is. What do you hope to gain by it? An eyeless approach to Heaven is as likely to succeed as any. Your priest will confirm what I say.

   MCLEAVY *bows his head, continues his work.*

You strike me, sir – I have to say this – as a thoroughly irresponsible individual. Always creating unnecessary trouble.

HAL. We'll have the house full of the law. Half our fittings will be missing. That's why they have such big pockets on their uniforms.

TRUSCOTT. Your son seems to have a more balanced idea of the world in which we live than you do, sir.

MCLEAVY. My duty is clear.

TRUSCOTT. Only the authorities can decide when your duty is clear. Wild guesses by persons like yourself can only cause confusion.

   MCLEAVY *lifts the coffin lid.*

HAL. He's going to be shocked. See him preparing for it. His generation takes a delight in being outraged.

   MCLEAVY *looks into the coffin, gives a grunt of disbelief, staggers back, incredulous.*

DENNIS. Catch him! He's going to faint.

   He and FAY *support* MCLEAVY *and help him to the bed.* MCLEAVY *sinks beside the corpse in a state of shock.*

MCLEAVY. Where? (*Bewildered.*) Where? (*He follows* HAL's *glance to the corpse and recoils in horror.*) Oh, the end of the world is near when such crimes are committed.

TRUSCOTT. The opening of a coffin couldn't possibly herald Armageddon. Pull yourself together, sir.

FAY (*to* TRUSCOTT). The condition of the corpse has deteriorated due to the accident. Do you wish to verify the fact?

TRUSCOTT (*shuddering*). No, thank you, miss. I receive enough shocks in the line of duty without going about looking for them.

FAY (*to* DENNIS). Replace the lid on the coffin.

DENNIS *does so.*

MCLEAVY (*to* HAL). I shall disown you. I'll publish it abroad that I was cuckolded.

FAY (*to* TRUSCOTT). It's been a harrowing experience for him.

TRUSCOTT. He was warned in advance of the consequences of his action.

HAL (*kneeling to* MCLEAVY). I'm in a bit of a spot, Dad. I don't mind confessing. Don't get stroppy with me, eh?

MCLEAVY. I'm sorry I ever got you. I'd've withheld myself at the conception if I'd known.

TRUSCOTT. Such idle fantasies ill become you, sir.

MCLEAVY *chokes back his sobs.*

Fathers have discovered greater iniquities in their sons than the theft of an eye. The episode isn't without instruction.

MCLEAVY. Where did I go wrong? His upbringing was faultless. (*To* DENNIS.) Did you lead him astray?

DENNIS. I was innocent till I met him.

HAL. You met me when you were three days old.

MCLEAVY (*to* HAL). Where are your tears? She was your mother.

HAL. It's dust, Dad.

MCLEAVY *shakes his head in despair.*

A little dust.

MCLEAVY. I loved her.

HAL. You had her filleted without a qualm. Who could have affection for a half-empty woman?

MCLEAVY (*groaning*). Oh, Jesus, Mary, Joseph, guide me to the end of my wits and have done with it.

HAL. You've lost nothing. You began the day with a dead wife. You end it with a dead wife.

MCLEAVY. Oh, wicked, wicked. (*Wildly.*) These hairs – (*Points.*) – they're grey. You made them so. I'd be a redhead today had you been an accountant.

TRUSCOTT (*removing his pipe from his mouth*). We really can't accept such unlikely explanation for the colour of your hair, sir.

MCLEAVY *wails aloud in anguish.*

Your behaviour indicates a growing lack of control. It's disgraceful in a man of your age and background. I'm half inclined to book you for disturbing the peace.

FAY *hands* MCLEAVY *a handkerchief. He blows his nose. He draws himself up to his full height.*

MCLEAVY. I'm sorry, Inspector. My behaviour must seem strange to you. I'll endeavour to explain it. You can then do as you think fit.

FAY. Consider the consequences of telling the truth. It will kill Father Jellicoe.

DENNIS. My pigeons will die if I'm nicked. There'll be nobody to feed them.

Silence. TRUSCOTT *opens his notebook and looks at* MC-LEAVY.

MCLEAVY. I wish to prefer charges.

HAL (*desperate*). If my Aunt Bridie hears of this, she'll leave her money to an orphanage. You know how selfish she is.

TRUSCOTT. Whom do you wish to charge, sir?

MCLEAVY (*pause, struggles with his conscience, at last*). Myself.

TRUSCOTT (*looking up from his notebook*). What crime have you committed?

MCLEAVY. I— I— (*Sweating.*) I've given misleading information to the police.

TRUSCOTT. What information?

MCLEAVY. I told you that the eye belonged to my wife. It doesn't. (*Conscience stricken.*) Oh, God forgive me for what I'm doing.

TRUSCOTT. If the eye doesn't belong to your wife, to whom does it belong?

MCLEAVY *is unable to answer; he stares about him, perplexed.*

FAY (*with a smile*). It belongs to my sewing dummy, Inspector. Your original deduction was quite correct.

TRUSCOTT *slowly puts away his notebook and pencil.*

TRUSCOTT. I ought to have my head examined, getting mixed up in a case of this kind. (*To* MCLEAVY.) Your conduct is scandalous, sir. With you for a father this lad never stood a chance. No wonder he took to robbing banks.

MCLEAVY (*in shame*). What are you going to do?

TRUSCOTT. Do? I'm going to leave this house at once. I've never come across such people. You behave as though you're affiliated to Bedlam.

MCLEAVY. But – the bank robbery – is the case closed?

TRUSCOTT. No, sir, it's not closed. We don't give up as easily as that. I'm going to have this place turned upside down.

MCLEAVY. Oh, dear, what a nuisance. And in a house of mourning, too.

TRUSCOTT. Your wife won't be here, sir. I shall take possession of the remains.

FAY. Why do you need the remains? You can't prove Mrs McLeavy was murdered.

TRUSCOTT. There's no cause for alarm. It's a mere formality.

You're quite safe. (*He smiles. To* MCLEAVY.) There's no one more touchy than your hardened criminal. (*He puts his pipe away.*) I'll be back in ten minutes. And then, I'm afraid, a lot of damage will be done to your property. You'll be paying repair bills for months to come. One unfortunate suspect recently had the roof taken off his house.

MCLEAVY. Isn't there anything I can do to prevent this appalling assault upon my privacy?

TRUSCOTT. Well, sir, if you can suggest a possible hiding-place for the money?

MCLEAVY *hangs his head.*

MCLEAVY (*almost in a whisper*). I can't, Inspector

TRUSCOTT. Very well. You must take the consequences of ignorance. (*He tips his hat.*) I'll be back soon.

He goes off left.

MCLEAVY. Oh, what a terrible thing I've done. I've obstructed an officer in the course of his duty.

HAL (*hugging him*). I'm proud of you. I'll never feel ashamed of bringing my friends home now.

MCLEAVY I shan't be able to face my reflection in the mirror

FAY. Go to confession. Book an hour with Father Mac.

HAL. Oh, not him! Three brandies and he's away. The barmaid at the King of Denmark is blackmailing half the district.

MCLEAVY. I'll say nothing of what I've discovered if you return the money to the bank. You're not to keep a penny of it. Do you understand?

HAL. Yes, Dad. (*He winks at* DENNIS.)

MCLEAVY. I'll go and ring Father Jellicoe. My soul is in torment.

MCLEAVY *goes off left.*

HAL (*closing the door, to* FAY). Unwrap the body. Once we've got it back into the coffin we're home and dry.

FAY *pulls the screen round the bed. She goes behind the screen to unwrap the corpse.*

DENNIS What are we going to do with the money?
HAL. Put in into the casket.
DENNIS Won't he want that?
HAL. He knows it's empty.

DENNIS *takes the lid from the coffin.*

DENNIS. Why didn't we put it in there in the first place?
HAL. My mum's guts were in there. The damp would've got at the notes.

HAL *opens the casket.*

Got a hanky?

DENNIS *throws a handkerchief over.* HAL *wipes the inside of the casket.*

DENNIS. Oh, you've gone too far! Using my handkerchief for that. It was a birthday present.

HAL *throws him the handkerchief back.*

HAL. Relax, baby. You'll have other birthdays.

DENNIS *throws the bundles of notes to* HAL. HAL *packs them into the casket.*

I shall accompany my father to Confession this evening. In order to purge my soul of this afternoon's events.
DENNIS. It's at times like this that I regret not being a Catholic.
HAL. Afterwards I'll take you to a remarkable brothel I've found. Really remarkable. Run by three Pakistanis aged between ten and fifteen. They do it for sweets. Part of their religion. Meet me at seven. Stock up with Mars bars.

FAY *appears from behind the screen, folding the mattress cover.*

FAY. Don't look behind there, Harold.

HAL. Why not?

FAY. Your mother is naked.

She hangs the folded cover over the screen.
HAL packs the last bundle of notes into the casket.

HAL. We're safe.

He bangs down the lid.

Nobody will ever look in there.

TRUSCOTT enters left.

TRUSCOTT. I've fixed everything to my satisfaction. My men
will be here shortly. They're perfectly capable of causing
damage unsupervised, and so I shall take my leave of you.
(*He bows, smiles.*)

FAY (*shaking hands*). Good-bye, Inspector. It's been nice meeting you again.

TRUSCOTT. Good-bye. (*He nods to HAL and DENNIS.*) I'd
better take the little casket with me.

HAL. It's empty!

TRUSCOTT. I must have it certified empty before I close my
report.

FAY. We're having it de-sanctified. Mr McLeavy is on the
phone to the priest about it.

TRUSCOTT. Our lads in forensic aren't interested in sanctity.
Give me that casket!

MCLEAVY enters left. He sees TRUSCOTT and cowers back.

MCLEAVY. You're back already? Have you decided to arrest
me after all?

TRUSCOTT. I wouldn't arrest you if you were the last man on
earth. (*To HAL.*) Give me that casket! (*He takes the casket
from HAL. To MCLEAVY.*) I'll give you a receipt, sir.

He looks for somewhere to rest the casket, sees the empty coffin puts the casket down.

Where is Mrs McLeavy?

FAY. She's behind the screen.

TRUSCOTT *looks behind the screen and raises his eyebrows.*

TRUSCOTT. Did she ask to be buried like that?

MCLEAVY. Yes.

TRUSCOTT. She was a believer in that sort of thing?

MCLEAVY. Yes.

TRUSCOTT. Are you, sir?

MCLEAVY. Well no. I'm not a member myself.

TRUSCOTT. A member? She belonged to a group, then?

MCLEAVY. Oh, yes. They met a couple of times a week. They do a lot of good for the country. Raising money for charities, holding fetes. The old folk would be lost without them.

TRUSCOTT. I've heard many excuses for nudists, sir, but never that one.

MCLEAVY (*pause*). Nudists?

TRUSCOTT. Your wife was a nudist, you say?

MCLEAVY. My wife never took her clothes off in public in her life.

TRUSCOTT. Yet she asked to be buried in that condition?

MCLEAVY. What condition?

TRUSCOTT. In the nude.

MCLEAVY (*with dignity*). You'd better leave my house, Inspector. I can't allow you to insult the memory of my late wife.

TRUSCOTT (*tearing a sheet of paper from his notebook*). You give me a lot of aggravation, sir. Really you do. (*He hands the paper to* MCLEAVY.) You'll get your property back in due course.

He lifts casket, the lid swings away and the bundles of bank-notes fall to the floor. TRUSCOTT *stares at the notes scattered at his feet in silence.*

Who is responsible for this disgraceful state of affairs?

HAL. I am.

TRUSCOTT (*stoops and picks up a bundle of notes*). Would you have stood by and allowed this money to be buried in holy ground?

HAL. Yes.

TRUSCOTT. How dare you involve me in a situation for which no memo has been issued. (*He turns the notes over.*) In all my experience I've never come across a case like it. Every one of these fivers bears a portrait of the Queen. It's dreadful to contemplate the issues raised. Twenty thousand tiaras and twenty thousand smiles buried alive! She's a constitutional monarch, you know. She can't answer back.

DENNIS. Will she send us a telegram?

TRUSCOTT. I'm sure she will.

He picks up another bundle and stares at them.

MCLEAVY. Well, Inspector, you've found the money and unmasked the criminals. You must do your duty and arrest them. I shall do mine and appear as witness for the prosecution.

HAL. Are you married, Inspector?

TRUSCOTT. Yes.

HAL. Does your wife never yearn for excitement?

TRUSCOTT. She did once express a wish to see the windmills and tulip fields of Holland.

HAL. With such an intelligent wife you need a larger income.

TRUSCOTT. I never said my wife was intelligent.

HAL. Then she's unintelligent? Is that it?

TRUSCOTT. My wife is a woman. Intelligence doesn't really enter into the matter.

HAL. If, as you claim, your wife is a woman, you certainly need a larger income.

TRUSCOTT *takes his pipe from his pocket and sticks it into the corner of his mouth.*

TRUSCOTT. Where is this Jesuitical twittering leading us?

HAL. I'm about to suggest bribery.

TRUSCOTT *removes his pipe, no one speaks.*

TRUSCOTT. How much?

HAL. Twenty per cent.

TRUSCOTT. Twenty-five per cent. Or a full report of this case appears on my superior officer's desk in the morning.

HAL. Twenty-five it is.

TRUSCOTT (*shaking hands*). Done.

DENNIS (*to* TRUSCOTT). May I help you to replace the money in the casket?

TRUSCOTT. Thank you, lad. Most kind of you.

DENNIS *packs the money into the casket.* FAY *takes* MRS MCLEAVY'S *clothes from the bedpan on the invalid chair and goes behind the screen.* TRUSCOTT *chews on his pipe.* HAL *and* DENNIS *take the coffin behind the screen.*

MCLEAVY. Has no one considered my feelings in all this?

TRUSCOTT. What percentage do you want?

MCLEAVY. I don't want money. I'm an honest man.

TRUSCOTT. You'll have to mend your ways then.

MCLEAVY. I shall denounce the lot of you!

TRUSCOTT. Now then, sir, be reasonable. What has just taken place is perfectly scandalous and had better go no farther than these three walls. It's not expedient for the general public to have its confidence in the police force undermined. You'd be doing the community a grave disservice by revealing the full frighening facts of this case.

MCLEAVY. What kind of talk is that? You don't make sense.

TRUSCOTT. Who does?

MCLEAVY. I'll go to the priest. He makes sense. He makes sense to me.

TRUSCOTT. Does he make sense to himself? That is much more important.

MCLEAVY. If I can't trust the police, I can still rely on the Fathers. They'll advise me what to do!

He goes off left. HAL *appears from behind the screen.*

HAL. You'll be glad to know that my mother is back in her last resting-place.

TRUSCOTT. Good. You've carried out the operation with speed and efficiency. I congratulate you.

DENNIS *appears from behind the screen.*

DENNIS. We're ready for the eye now. If you'd like to assist us.

TRUSCOTT (*taking the eye from his pocket*). You do it, lad. You're more experienced in these matters than me.

He hands DENNIS *the eye.*

HAL. You'd better have these as well.

He hands DENNIS *the teeth.*
DENNIS *takes the eye and teeth behind the screen.*

TRUSCOTT. Your sense of detachment is terrifying, lad. Most people would at least flinch upon seeing their mother's eyes and teeth handed around like nuts at Christmas.

FAY *appears from behind the screen.*

FAY. Have you given a thought to the priest?

TRUSCOTT. We can't have him in on it, miss. Our percentage wouldn't be worth having.

FAY. Mr McLeavy has threatened to expose us.

TRUSCOTT. I've been exposed before.

FAY. What happened?

TRUSCOTT. I arrested the man. He's doing twelve years.

HAL. If you wish to arrest my dad, you'll find me an exemplary witness.

TRUSCOTT. What a bright idea. We've vacancies in the force for lads of your calibre. (*To* FAY.) Are you with us, McMahon?

FAY. Yes, it seems the best solution for all of us.

DENNIS folds up the screen. The coffin is lying on the bed.

TRUSCOTT (*to* DENNIS). And you?

DENNIS. I've never seen the view from the witness box. It'll be a new experience.

The door left bursts open. MCLEAVY *enters with* MEADOWS.

MCLEAVY (*pointing to* TRUSCOTT). This is the man. Arrest him.

TRUSCOTT. Good afternoon, Meadows. Why have you left your post?

MEADOWS. I was accosted by this man, sir. He insisted that I accompany him to the Catholic church.

TRUSCOTT. What did you say?

MEADOWS. I refused.

TRUSCOTT. Quite rightly. You're a Methodist. Proceed with the statement.

MEADOWS. The man became offensive, sir. He made a number of derogatory remarks about the force in general and yourself in particular. I called for assistance.

TRUSCOTT. Excellent, Meadows. I shall see H.Q. hear of this. You have apprehended, in full flight, a most dangerous criminal. As you know, we've had our eye upon this house for some time. I was about to unmask the chief offender when this man left the room on some excuse and disappeared.

MEADOWS. He was making a bolt for it, sir.

TRUSCOTT. You have the matter in a nutshell, Meadows. Put the cuffs on him.

MEADOWS handcuffs MCLEAVY.

You're fucking nicked, my old beauty. You've found to your cost that the standards of the British police force are as high as ever.

MCLEAVY. What am I charged with?

TRUSCOTT. That needn't concern you for the moment. We'll fill in the details later.

MCLEAVY. You can't do this. I've always been a law-abiding citizen. The police are for the protection of ordinary people.

TRUSCOTT. I don't know where you pick up these slogans, sir. You must read them on hoardings.

MCLEAVY. I want to see someone in authority.

TRUSCOTT. I am in authority. You can see me.

MCLEAVY. Someone higher.

TRUSCOTT. You can see whoever you like, providing you convince me first that you're justified in seeing them.

MCLEAVY. You're mad!

TRUSCOTT. Nonsense. I had a check-up only yesterday. Our medical officer assured me that I was quite sane.

MCLEAVY. I'm innocent. (*A little unsure of himself, the beginnings of panic.*) Doesn't that mean anything to you?

TRUSCOTT. You know the drill, Meadows. Empty his pockets and book him.

MCLEAVY *is dragged away by* MEADOWS.

MCLEAVY. I'm innocent! I'm innocent! (*At the door, pause, a last wail.*) Oh, what a terrible thing to happen to a man who's been kissed by the Pope.

MEADOWS *goes off with* MCLEAVY.

DENNIS. What will you charge him with, Inspector?

TRUSCOTT. Oh, anything will do.

FAY. Can an accidental death be arranged?

TRUSCOTT. Anything can be arranged in prison.

HAL. Except pregnancy.

TRUSCOTT. Well, of course, the chaperon system defeats us there.

He picks up the casket.

The safest place for this is in my locker at the station. It's a maxim of the force: 'Never search your own backyard – you may find what you're looking for.' (*He turns in the doorway, the casket under his arm.*) Give me a ring this evening. I should have news for you of McLeavy by then. (*He hands a card to* FAY.) This is my home address. I'm well known there.

He nods, smiles, and goes off left. Sound of front door slamming. Pause.

HAL (*with a sigh*). He's a nice man. Self-effacing in his way.

DENNIS. He has an open mind. In direct contrast to the usual run of civil servant.

HAL and DENNIS lift the coffin from the bed and place it on the trestles.

HAL. It's comforting to know that the police can still be relied upon when we're in trouble.

They stand beside the coffin, FAY in the middle.

FAY. We'll bury your father with your mother. That will be nice for him, won't it?

She lifts her rosary and bows her head in prayer.

HAL (*pause, to* DENNIS). You can kip here, baby. Plenty of room now. Bring your bags over tonight.

FAY *looks up.*

FAY (*sharply*). When Dennis and I are married we'd have to move out.

HAL. Why?

FAY. People would talk. We must keep up appearances.

She returns to her prayers, her lips move silently. DENNIS *and* HAL *at either side of the coffin.*

Curtain

The Erpingham Camp

The original version of *The Erpingham Camp* was produced on television by Rediffusion on 27 June 1966 with the following cast:

ERPINGHAM	Reginald Marsh
RILEY	Peter Reeves
LOU	Faith Kent
TED	Charles Rea
KENNY	John Forgeham
EILEEN	Angela Pleasence
W. E. HARRISON	Peter Honri
JESSIE MASON	Avril Fane
PADRE	Peter Evans

Directed by James Ormerod
Designed by Frank Nerini

The Erpingham Camp was first staged at the Royal Court Theatre in the revised version printed here on 6 June 1967 in a double-bill entitled *Crimes of Passion* with the following cast:

ERPINGHAM	Bernard Gallagher
RILEY	Roddy Maude-Roxby
LOU	Pauline Collins
TED	Johnny Wade
EILEEN	Yvonne Antrobus
KENNY	Michael Standing
PADRE	Roger Booth
W. E. HARRISON	Ken Wynne
JESSIE MASON	Josie Bradley
REDCOATS and CAMPERS	Andree Evans
	Rosemary McHale
	Peter John
	Malcolm Reid

Directed by **Peter Gill**
Designed by **Deirdre Clancy**

No attempt must be made to reproduce the various locales in a naturalistic manner. A small, permanent set of Erpingham's office is set on a high level. The rest of the stage is an un-localised area. Changes of scene are suggested by lighting and banners after the manner of the Royal Shakespeare Company's productions of Shakespeare's histories.

The lyric of the song 'My Irish Song of Songs'
is reproduced by permission of
B. Feldman & Co. Ltd.

© 1917 M. Whitmark & Sons, New York

SCENE ONE

ERPINGHAM's office. It is evening. ERPINGHAM is seated at his desk. RILEY enters and ERPINGHAM looks up.

ERPINGHAM. Where's your badge of office?

RILEY. An oversight, sir. I'm sorry.

ERPINGHAM. You should be wearing your decorations. You know the rules. Any member of the staff found improperly dressed on Saturday night is subject to instant dismissal. Only I am excused.

RILEY. I'll put them on at once.

ERPINGHAM. I didn't make the rules, Chief Redcoat Riley. I only carry them out. Is number four latrine unblocked?

RILEY. Yes.

ERPINGHAM. And the toddlers' paddling pool? Have you removed whatever was causing the disturbance?

RILEY. Yes.

ERPINGHAM. Good. What was it?

RILEY. Two ducks. Made of plastic. They were stuck together.

ERPINGHAM. Beak to beak? (*Pause.*) Was the joinery smutty?

RILEY. Well, sir – the Engineer in charge had to perform surgery.

ERPINGHAM. Did the kiddies see?

RILEY. No. They were having a quick run round with Matron.

ERPINGHAM. I want those ducks destroyed. We've no time for hedonists here. My camp is a pure camp. Give me the report for the day.

RILEY hands him the report. ERPINGHAM glances at it.

Touching the subject of purity, ask Miss Mason to watch

her language. She's not the only one with heat rash. We all suffer. I suffer myself. Considerably. Hand me that file, will you?

RILEY *gives him the file.* ERPINGHAM *puts the report into it.*

Has the Padre been released from custody yet?

RILEY. Yes. He's having a lie down. It's been a shattering experience for him.

ERPINGHAM. It'll be nice to have him back with us again. I'd like to see him when he's rested.

RILEY. Yes, sir. (*He twists his hands together nervously: swallowing hard.*) Sir . . .

ERPINGHAM. What?

RILEY. Who will organise the Entertainments tonight?

ERPINGHAM. That's been taken care of. Don't worry. Let me do the worrying. My shoulders are broad.

RILEY. Should the Organiser not arrive, sir, would you consider giving me a chance?

ERPINGHAM (*without a second thought*). No.

RILEY. I've the personality. Before I came to you I was Ringmaster for Flanegan's Travelling Circus. We did every port in Eire. When we played before the Brothers of St Vincent of Paul a Papal Medal was struck. (*Pause.*) You'll not find a harder audience than monks.

ERPINGHAM *sighs. He puts the file away, opens the desk, takes out a bottle and pours himself a drink.*

ERPINGHAM. You couldn't organise your own backside, Chief Redcoat Riley. Chances I've given you. Look at the Mother and Child competition. Disastrous. (*He sips his drink.*) Ugliest woman competition. You nearly won that yourself. Causing scandal. Oh, no. You can't possibly be considered for the job. I'm sorry to cause you disappointment. But there it is.

He sips his drink. Pause.

Pick up that flag I've dropped, will you.

RILEY *picks a paper flag from the floor.*

Put it where you'd like a new camp founded.

He turns to a map of the world hanging behind the desk.

Go on. Anywhere on the map. I might even name the new camp after you.

RILEY *sticks the flag into the map.*

(ERPINGHAM, *staring hard, shakes his head.*) You're not cut out to be a pioneer, Riley. Dagenham is already over-developed.

He takes the flag and pins it into the map.

There. That's the place for a new Holiday Centre.

RILEY *looks hard at the map.*

RILEY. It's National Trust territory, sir. There's a bird sanctuary nearby.

ERPINGHAM. Human beings need sanctuaries, Riley, as well as birds. The world is in danger of forgetting the fact. Open my drawer. Take out my personal file.

RILEY *opens the drawer and takes out a heavy folder.*

(ERPINGHAM *flicks open the file.*) I shall be a millionaire by the 'seventies.

RILEY. I'll take you up on it.

ERPINGHAM. Make a note if you like.

He lights a cigar, blows a cloud of smoke into the air, smiles, and gives an expansive wave of his hand.

Rows of Entertainment Centres down lovely, unspoiled bits of the coast, across deserted moorland and barren mountainside. The Earthly Paradise. Ah . . .

He stares raptly into the distance.

I can hear it. I can touch it. And the sight of it is hauntingly beautiful, Riley.

Music: 'The Holy City'.

There'll be dancing. And music. Colourful scenes. Official pageantry. Trained drum Majorettes will march hourly across the greensward. The shapeliest girls in Britain – picked from thousands of disappointed applicants. There'll be no shortage of horses. And heated pools. The accommodation will be lavish. Slot-machines will be employed for all tasks. They'll come from far and wide to stay at my entertainment centres. The great ones of this world and, if Fame's trumpet blows long and hard enough, of the next.

The music fades. ERPINGHAM *sinks back, shaking his head.* The Vision that delighted has gone. But – in a short time – I'll have it here. (*He bangs the folder.*) In black and white.

He puts the folder away. RILEY *shakes his head.*

RILEY. Oh, take care, sir. One flick of Fortune's wheel and you'll be brought low. I was taught by a nun once who itched like the Devil to become Superior. One day the message came from the Eternal City. Sister Mary had made it. Promoted to Higher Office. She was overjoyed. But – God's anger light upon me if I'm not telling the truth – as they sang the Te Deum she was seized in a sudden fit and fell to the ground mouthing something that nobody understood – save an old lay sister who'd once been an usherette at the Roxy and was more worldly than the rest. Sister Mary had got to be Superior, but she had to be put away for her foolish pride in believing she had it all worked out. So, take care, sir. I know too well what the punishment is for your kind of sin. It's written over and over again in the books of the Ancient East. And in the Bible too.

ERPINGHAM *swallows the last of his whisky.*

ERPINGHAM. We live in a rational world, Riley. I've no use for your Hibernian cant.

The telephone rings. ERPINGHAM *answers it.*

Good. I'll send someone down. (*He puts the phone down.*) The Entertainments Organiser has arrived. Go and welcome him.

RILEY *goes off.*

SCENE TWO

A chalet. LOU *and* TED *are dressing.*

LOU. I've invited a young couple over. I gave her some help
in the salad queue. We don't have to see them again if we
don't get on.

The loudspeaker crackles and ERPINGHAM'S *voice is heard.*

ERPINGHAM. Good evening, Ladies and Gentlemen. I've
one or two announcements to make.

TED puts on his coat. LOU brushes him down.

The Glamorous Granny competition was won by Mrs
Anthea Wong of Gresham Road, London, E.17.

LOU. That Chinese woman. See, I told you she'd win.

TED. They marry so young. Seems hardly fair on ordinary
people.

ERPINGHAM. The Mother and Child competition resulted in
a dead heat. Mrs J. M. Nash of Palmers Green and Mrs
Susanne Mitchel of Southampton both win cash prizes.

TED. That fair woman who entered with the dog got nowhere
then?

LOU puts the brush away.

ERPINGHAM. Our disability bonus was won by Mr Laurie
Russel of Market Harborough. Both Laurie's legs were
certified 'absolutely useless' by our Resident Medical
Officer. Yet he performed the Twist and the Bossa Nova
to the tune specified on the entrance form.

TED. He fell over, though. Twice.

LOU. They help them a lot, don't they? That blind woman
would've never found the diving-board if the audience
hadn't shouted out.

ERPINGHAM. There are a number of lost children awaiting collection. Would you check your family? A Jewish

ex-serviceman is at this moment telling of his experiences both during and after the Nazis' rise to power. In the Number Two dining hall. Admission free.

There is knocking at the chalet door.

All holidaymakers intending taking part in our evening routine should report in person with your numbered card to the Grand Ballroom at eight sharp. Thank you, Ladies and Gentlemen.

LOU *opens the chalet door, and cries loudly.*

LOU. It's Kenny and Eileen! Come in!

KENNY *and* EILEEN *enter, smiling.*

EILEEN. Hope we're not too early?

LOU. No. We're just finishing. This is my husband, Ted. Ted, this is Kenny and Eileen.

There are smiles and handshakes. EILEEN *gives a cry of surprise.*

EILEEN. Oh, Louie! What lovely glasses. I've always wanted a pair like that.

LOU. Why don't you get a pair?

EILEEN. My eyes aren't bad enough. (*She sits beside* KENNY.) And I can't take risks. I'm pregnant, you see.

KENNY. It's our first. (*He smiles, taking* EILEEN *by the hand.*) Not our last, though, eh? (*He kisses her cheek.*) We've only been married a year. We had trouble.

EILEEN. We were banned. I had a breakdown over it. We were so much in love, see.

She snuggles up against KENNY.

KENNY. Her parents caused trouble. We met at a club. We knew we were made for each other from the first moment. It was persuading her parents to see our point of view. That was the most urgent problem. Her father was stubborn, very much of his own frame of mind. Her mother sided with him, naturally. I was at my wits end to find a solution. In the end I bashed them both about the ear. And after that we had no trouble.

EILEEN. We're content now. We're expecting our first child. We have to give up luxuries. Chief among them not going abroad for the sun.

TED *puts his hand over* LOU'S.

TED. Lou and I don't have to bother with that sort of thing.

LOU (*smiling*). We've our sun-lamp, you see.

Pause. Awkward smiles. Pause.

TED. It's interesting you meeting your wife at a club, Ken. I met my wife outside the Young Conservatives.

LOU. I've always found them polite and sympathetic people. I used to spend an hour or two there every Thursday and Saturday. I met the daughter of a brain-specialist on one occasion. She was playing table-tennis and she asked me if I'd act as scorer. Of course, you get your snobs there, same as anywhere else. But on the whole, I enjoyed myself.

TED. Yes. It was outside the Young Conservative Club that I met my fate.

Laughter. Pause.

KENNY. I never liked the Tories 'cause I suspected they weren't decent.

TED *frowns.*

TED. What d'you mean?

KENNY. Well – look how they carry on. (*Laughing it off.*) They are the 'blue' party, aren't they?

Silence.

TED. It's clear, if you don't mind me saying so, Kenneth, that you've no real knowledge of the English political scene. Your Labour party scandals have increased considerably of latter years.

KENNY. I'm not a Labour man!

LOU *and* TED *smile.*

TED. I thought you were.

KENNY. I keep away from all that. I owe it to Eileen.

EILEEN. I'm expecting.

TED (*laughing lightly*). Our Socialist friends would stop you doing that. They'd ban it.

EILEEN. Our love was banned.

KENNY. I knocked her dad's teeth in. I can't stand intolerance.

EILEEN. We're saving up to buy a house.

LOU *smiles*.

LOU. We were left our house. There was never any question of paying for it.

EILEEN *colours pink*.

EILEEN. We've no use for that sort of thing. We don't agree with it.

LOU. You can't go all the way with that kind of philosophy, Eileen. You've got to face facts.

EILEEN. I was brought up to think different. (*Her voice rising.*) My mum was on a lecture once. She could tell you a thing or two. They exhibited her as a reference. My dad was with her. And although they got our love forbidden and made life not worth living, I'm pregnant now and they've been good parents. I can't accept what you say, Louie. It seems wrong to me.

She bursts into tears. KENNY *comforts her.* LOU *and* TED *stand.*

LOU (*at last, brightly*). I think it's time we joined the festivities.

EILEEN *dries her tears.*

SCENE THREE

ERPINGHAM'S *office.* RILEY *enters.*

RILEY. Oh, sir! Disaster has struck.

ERPINGHAM. Has the Padre been up to his tricks again?

RILEY. The Entertainments Organiser has been taken bad.

ERPINGHAM. Is he drunk?

RILEY. We don't know. It's a mysterious affliction that's come upon him.

ERPINGHAM. Where is he?

RILEY. In the Hospital Tent, sir. The Resident Medical Officer has given him up for lost.

W. E. HARRISON *enters.*

W. E. HARRISON. Sir! The Entertainments Organiser has been shown the four last things. The Padre is with him.

The PADRE *enters.*

PADRE. Sir! The Entertainments Organiser is dead.

ERPINGHAM (*to* RILEY). Remind me to send one of our Class A (Highest Employee) wreaths to his next of kin.

RILEY. Yes, sir.

ERPINGHAM *turns sharply to* W. E. HARRISON.

ERPINGHAM. Why aren't you in the Music Room, W. E. Harrison?

W. E. HARRISON. My partner, Miss Mason, is doing her solo number, sir.

ERPINGHAM. She can't manage on her own. Go and help her.

W. E. HARRISON *goes off.*

ERPINGHAM. Did you see this thing happen, Riley?

RILEY. Yes, sir. He was a grand chap, it seems. He'd many original ideas on mass entertainment. I was lapping it up – seeing as I'm ambitious. I made a few notes and was about to question him further when, without a word of warning, he slumps forward in his chair. God help us all, I thought to myself, though I didn't breathe the worst of it out loud, he's been done in.

ERPINGHAM (*to the* PADRE). Had he any enemies?

PADRE. We'd no time to ascertain, sir, before he lost consciousness.

ERPINGHAM *gives* RILEY *a shrewd, hard look.*

ERPINGHAM. Did you murder him, Chief Redcoat Riley?

RILEY. No.

ERPINGHAM. We can't have members of the staff taking

human life. We're not equipped to deal with such a situation. Consult the manual. You'll find funerals are frowned upon.

RILEY. He was struck down by something unknown to medical science.

ERPINGHAM. I shall have to take your word for it, Chief Redcoat Riley. Though you're a notorious liar.

RILEY *twists his fingers together in great excitement.*

RILEY. Sir – who will organise the entertainments tonight? We must make a quick decision. The campers are gathering under the bunting.

ERPINGHAM *chews his lip.* RILEY *holds his breath.*

ERPINGHAM. I'll be magnanimous, Riley, and give you the chance of a lifetime. Seize it with both hands.

ERPINGHAM *takes a box from the desk and hands it to the* PADRE. *The* PADRE *takes a sash from the box which he hands to* ERPINGHAM. RILEY *bows his head.* ERPINGHAM *puts the sash upon him.* ERPINGHAM *lifts another box and hands it to the* PADRE. *The* PADRE *opens it, removes a badge and pins it upon* RILEY's *blazer.* RILEY *is bathed in an unearthly radiance.*

Music: 'Zadok the Priest and Nathan the Prophet Anointed Solomon King'.

ERPINGHAM *embraces* RILEY.

ERPINGHAM. Serve us well, Chief Redcoat Riley. And my best wishes for the task ahead.

Music: 'Land of Hope and Glory'.

Your reward will be the heartfelt thanks of the whole of our community. Tonight is your testing time. Let the spirit of Enterprise and Achievement go with you. Remember our Glorious Dead. How many soldiers have had tasks like yours? And carried them through – though their lives were forfeit. The courage and grit that founded Empires still stands. And when, Riley, we plant our first flag upon the white, untouched plains of Asia – you will be in our thoughts that day. The Camps of India, the Eternal Tents of the East will echo to your name as we remember the deed with which you won your spurs. And in those times we shall rejoice that, of your own free will, you were born an Englishman.

The music fades.

RILEY. I was born in County Mayo, sir.

ERPINGHAM. Ireland counts as England.

RILEY. Not with the Irish, sir.

ERPINGHAM. It's England you're representing in the Great Fight. Ireland has empty roads, Galway Bay and the remains of Sir Roger Casement. Isn't that enough?

RILEY. More than enough, sir. We'd be a nation of poets and talkers still with only two of them.

ERPINGHAM *shakes him by the hand.*

ERPINGHAM. Good luck then. Away with you.

PADRE. Take God's blessing with you, my son. And remember always to keep the little text I gave you. The words are obscure but the picture will keep you from harm.

RILEY. Thank you, Father. And thank you, sir. I shall prove myself worthy. Goodbye.

He turns and goes off. ERPINGHAM *takes off his coat.*

ERPINGHAM. I'm going to undress, Padre. Cover up the portrait of Her Majesty.

The PADRE *covers over the large framed portrait of the Queen on the desk.* ERPINGHAM *strips down to his underwear.*

ERPINGHAM. Have you prepared your sermon for tomorrow?

PADRE. Yes, sir.

ERPINGHAM. Is it fit to be preached?

PADRE. I hope you'll give me any cuts that may be necessary, sir.

ERPINGHAM. What is the subject?

PADRE. The Miracles of Jesus.

ERPINGHAM. I hope we're not in for some far-fetched tale set among the Bedouin?

He hands his clothes to the PADRE *who goes off.*

ERPINGHAM *takes a pair of corsets from a drawer in the desk. The* PADRE *returns with a dress suit and shirt on a hanger. He lays them on the desk.* EPPINGHAM *puts on the corset.*

PADRE. I intend to deal with the meaning of the Gadarene demoniac. I shall draw one or two conclusions that may surprise you, sir.

ERPINGHAM. I don't go to Church on Sunday morning to be surprised, Padre. Lace me up, will you?

The PADRE *laces up* ERPINGHAM's *corset.* ERPINGHAM *lifts his leg. The* PADRE *fastens* ERPINGHAM's *suspenders and laces* ERPINGHAM's *shoes.*

PADRE. I wonder, sir, whether you've ever stopped to consider the meaning of the Gadarene swine?

ERPINGHAM. I haven't, Padre. Hand me my shirt.

The PADRE *hands* ERPINGHAM *his shirt and* ERPINGHAM *puts it on.*

PADRE. You recall, sir, how a madman was cured of his delusions. How the devils within him took up abode in a herd of swine? How the swine ran mad causing great destruction?

He hands ERPINGHAM *his trousers and* ERPINGHAM *puts them on.*

ERPINGHAM. It's a most instructive tale. What meaning do you attach to it?

PADRE. We are meant to understand, sir, that with madness, as with vomit, it's the passer-by who receives the inconvenience.

ERPINGHAM. If Christianity had been as powerful as your similes, Padre, it would've conquered the world. Pass my tie.

The PADRE *passes him the tie.*

SCENE FOUR

RILEY *and* JESSIE MASON.

MASON. I'll make the announcement, Chief Redcoat Riley. And then, to follow, I suggest my juggling act. You may remember it proved extremely popular at Catlin's Arcadia last summer?

RILEY. Just make the announcement. Leave the rest to me.

MASON. The public appreciate a highly skilled performer. Nobody remains unimpressed by the sheer professionalism I bring to my act.

RILEY. Just cue me in. That's all I require.

JESSIE MASON *tosses her head.*

MASON. You're making a big mistake in not taking advantage of my wide experience with the average holiday-maker.

W. E. HARRISON *enters.*

W. E. HARRISON. Everything is ready Chief Redcoat Riley. They're waiting for you in the Grand Ballroom.

RILEY. I'll require you and Mason to assist me with the distribution of prizes. And bring your squeeze-box, Mason. Music is most important in creating a relaxed, informal atmosphere.

He strides off. JESSIE MASON *and* W. E. HARRISON *follow.*

SCENE FIVE

ERPINGHAM'S *office.* ERPINGHAM *has finished dressing.*

ERPINGHAM. You're interested in religion then, Padre?

PADRE. From a purely Christian point of view, sir.

He helps ERPINGHAM *on with his tail-coat and brushes him down.*

I find great solace in the life of the Spirit.

ERPINGHAM. I'm sure you do. (*He turns to allow the* PADRE *to brush his back.*) What happened to you in court this morning?

PADRE. I was acquitted, sir. The young woman withdrew her charge.

ERPINGHAM. I'm pleased to hear it. You must give up your evangelical forays into teenage chalets. They're liable to misinterpretation. Take the blindfold from Her Majesty. I can give her an audience now.

The PADRE *uncovers the Queen's portrait.*

And you'd better find another subject for your sermon tomorrow. I don't feel that the story of the Gadarene swine has any real meaning for us today.

SCENE SIX

RILEY *is in the spotlight onstage in the Grand Ballroom. On either side of him stand* JESSIE MASON *and* W. E. HARRISON. MASON *smiles, archly.* HARRISON, MASON *and the assembled Redcoats sing and dance a medley of songs which includes 'Put on your Ta-Ta Little Girlie', 'Linger a Little Longer', 'In a Little Gypsy Tearoom', 'If I had my Way, Dear, You'd Never Grow Old', and 'Let the Great Big World go Turning'.* JESSIE MASON *accompanies on her concertina.*

MASON. And now, that likeable lad from across the Irish Sea, Chief Redcoat Kevin Riley!

RILEY *steps forward, modestly, yet with a cool, relaxed manner.*

RILEY. I'm in charge of entertainments tonight, Ladies and Gentlemen. And I'm going to see we all have a whale of a time. Tonight is fun night. And, as many of our old campers knows anything can happen on fun night at Camp Erpingham!

JESSIE MASON *plays a chord on her squeeze-box.* W. E. HARRISON *produces two flags and waves them with a gay flourish.* RILEY *beams.*

Who's going to be our 'Tarzan of the Apes' this week?
Who'll volunteer? Come along now. Don't hold back. Don't
spoil the fun. Our friend here (*Nods to* W.E.HARRISON.) has
a prize for the gent who'll volunteer. Now who'll be
'Tarzan'?

KENNY steps on to the stage, a little sheepishly.

KENNY. I'll have a go.

RILEY. Good lad. First a kiss from Jessie Mason, our glamorous songstress! (*Leads* KENNY *to* MASON.) Mind her
squeeze-box now! A fellow from Belfast got his hand caught
in it last week. (*Laughs, beerily.*) They all want to get their
fingers on Miss Mason's squeeze-box!

*MASON kisses KENNY. W. E. HARRISON produces a leopard
skin with a gay flourish. MASON plays a chord.*

(*To* KENNY). I want you to put this on. It's our resident
'Tarzan' gear.

*KENNY takes the skin and is about to put it on. RILEY
stops him.*

You'll have to drop your slacks, my lad.

*KENNY looks dubious. MASON gives a giggle and a pro-
fessionally coy smile.*

MASON. He doesn't want to take them off in front of a lady.

RILEY. Where's the lady? You're not trying to tell us that
you're a lady, Miss Mason?

MASON. I am.

RILEY. We'll have to check your credentials later. (*To* KENNY.)
Go with Miss Mason. She plays to the house. You'll have
a whale of a time, but remember to keep your cheques and
your legs crossed!

KENNY, with a blush, attempts a joke.

KENNY. I don't know whether I should do this. I'm a married
man.

RILEY. And Mason is a married woman. She's married to the
Chef. That's how she got on the game!

MASON leads KENNY off. W. E. HARRISON beams.

RILEY. And while we're waiting I'll sing you a little song I
was taught when I lived near Fermanagh as a youth.

W. E. HARRISON *accompanies* RILEY *on* MASON'S *squeeze-box.* RILEY *sings in a nasal Irish tenor.*

'Sure of all the Irish songs I know,
There's one I love the best,
'Tis a symphony of love to me—
'Tis sweeter than the rest.
My melody, my rosary, my tender lullaby
'Tis you I mean,
My sweet Colleen,
And here's the reason why.

Sure you have all the charms of my Mother Machree.
You're my wild Irish rose.
You remind me of a valley,
Where the River Shannon flows.
When your Irish eyes are smiling,
I know where my heart belongs.
You're a little piece of Heaven,
You're my Irish song of songs.

Sure there's music in your pretty smile,
There's music in your eyes.
There's a rhythm too,
In all you do,
That you don't realise.
There seems to be,
A melody,
In everything you say.
When you are near,
I seem to hear
The songs of yesterday.

He gathers himself up and finishes with a fine flourish.

When your Irish eyes are smiling,

I know where my heart belongs,
You're a little piece of Heaven,
You're my Irish song of songs!

As he acknowledges the end of the song, MASON *returns with*
KENNY. *He is dressed in the leopard skin. He looks sheepishly
around.* W. E. HARRISON *plays a frenzied cadenza on the
squeeze-box.* JESSIE MASON *produces two flags and waves
them with a gay flourish.* RILEY *approaches* KENNY.

Magnificent! Really wonderful!

KENNY *flexes his muscles. Everyone looks benevolent.*

You'll have a wonderful week as our resident 'Tarzan
of the Apes'. You'll be called upon to perform many
interesting acts. I'll give you the details later. And now I'd
like two ladies please! Who'll oblige? Come along now,
don't be shy.

EILEEN *and* LOU *step on to the stage.*

Ladies! Have you ever seen a finer specimen of young
manhood? (*He points to* KENNY.) Wouldn't you like to
find that in your 'in tray'?

EILEEN. I often do. (*With a quick giggle.*) He's my husband!

Everyone looks surprised. Laughter.

RILEY. Your husband, eh? Well, you almost lost him to
Jessie Mason our resident nymphomaniac!

EILEEN *pouts and pretends, rather archly, to be indifferent.*

EILEEN. She can have him if she fancies him. He's no good to
me!

RILEY. No good to you, eh? (*With a look at* EILEEN's *pregnant
belly.*) It looks as though you've been good to him, though?
Eh?

Everybody laughs. EILEEN *blushes.* W. E. HARRISON *hands
the squeeze-box to* MASON.

(*To* EILEEN *and* LOU). Who's going to scream the loudest?
Loudest scream wins a cash prize. Just scream. As loud
as you like! The winner will be given a voucher for

the Erpingham Stores. A voucher that will enable you to buy a week's groceries or, if you prefer, three days' luxuries, free of charge. Who's going to scream?

JESSIE MASON plays a few chords and a flourish on the squeeze-box. W. E. HARRISON produces two flags and waves them with a gay smile.

(*To* LOU). All you've got to do is scream!

LOU *begins to scream, but stops suddenly.*

(*To* EILEEN). All you've got to do is scream!

EILEEN screams and stops, then screams again. She gives a giggle. LOU screams, louder this time. KENNY, losing his shyness, flexes his muscles and walks around MASON like an ape. MASON smiles. LOU and EILEEN are now screaming loudly.

One more gentleman? Who else is game?

TED *runs on to the stage.*

Take your clothes off, sir. I'd like you to do the can-can.

Needing no more persuading TED takes off his trousers and coat and, to the tune of the can-can from 'Orpheus in the Underworld' played on MASON's squeeze-box, he dances a can-can with his shirt tails flying.

Oh, wonderful, wonderful! We're going to have a lovely time, Ladies and Gentlemen! A gorgeous time!

LOU *and* EILEEN *are screaming,* KENNY *is grunting and grinning like an ape, and flexing his muscles at an indifferent* MASON. TED *is dancing the can-can, whilst* MASON *plays the squeeze-box.* W. E. HARRISON *produces flags and waves them with a gay flourish.*

(*To* LOU *and* EILEEN). All right now! O.K.! That's enough of it. I'll judge the loudest scream now.

The two women continue to scream loudly and hysterically. He puts his hand on EILEEN's *shoulder, and drags her away from* LOU.

O.K.! (EILEEN *screams and weeps.*) Oh, God! She's hysterical. (*To* EILEEN.) Stop it, will you?

EILEEN *clings to him. He pushes her away and slaps her face.* EILEEN *collapses into hysterical sobbing. There is a loud shout from* KENNY *and* LOU *abruptly stops screaming.* KENNY *hurries over to* EILEEN.

KENNY. What did you do to her?

RILEY (*backing away from him*). I smacked her face. She was becoming hysterical.

KENNY. Is that your idea of a joke? Ask a woman to scream and then smack her in the mouth?

RILEY *draws himself up to his full height.*

RILEY. Get back to your place. There's been a misunderstanding.

KENNY. Hit a pregnant woman? You pig!

EILEEN *weeps.*

EILEEN. He hit me! I'm an expectant mother!

KENNY *knocks* RILEY *to the floor with a blow to the mouth. He falls upon him, and* EILEEN *dances over them screaming.* Hit him! Hit him!

Seeing what is happening, LOU *screams with fright and attempts to part the two men.* TED *is still dancing. Oblivious to the scene in front of them,* JESSIE MASON *is playing the squeeze-box and* W. E. HARRISON, *with a beaming smile, produces flags at intervals and waves them with a gay flourish. At last* MASON *becomes aware that something has gone wrong. She stops playing and stares, open-mouthed.*

MASON. Here! You weren't asked to do that. (*To* EILEEN.) Make him stop!

TED, *who has been dancing involuntarily without* MASON's *music, stops and ambles over with a cheeky expression.*

TED. When do we collect our prizes?

RILEY *staggers to his feet and wipes his nose with the back of his hand.*

RILEY. Get off the stage! You've forfeited your prizes.

TED, *upset, turns away and stares about him, puzzled.* KENNY *seizes* RILEY *by the lapels.*

KENNY. I'm having an apology out of you! Call yourself a man? Hitting a pregnant woman!

EILEEN *weeps, occasionally she says* 'Why don't you thump him one?' *or* 'He hit me, Ken'.

TED (*to* LOU). My trousers! Somebody's nicked my trousers!

LOU *gives a cry of distress. She goes to* RILEY.

LOU. My husband's trousers have been stolen! We shall hold you responsible for their loss.

W. E. HARRISON *looks on with a beaming smile and waves his flags with a gay flourish. He winks at* MASON.

W. E. HARRISON. Chief Redcoat Riley has earned his money tonight, Jes. Why, he's got them eating out of his hand.

There is a sudden cry of pain from RILEY, *accompanied by shouts of rage from* KENNY, *hysterical sobbing from* EILEEN *and indignant bellows of* 'My husband has had his trousers stolen!' *from* LOU. TED *is wandering about the stage searching.*

MASON (*frigidly to* W. E. HARRISON). This is what you can expect when you're not an experienced all-round family entertainer. Go and tell Mr Erpingham what's happened.

W. E. HARRISON *gives her a look of pained surprise and hurries away.* MASON *comes downstage and, with the screaming and arguing campers behind her, smiles brightly and begins to play and sing* 'Fold Your Wings of Love Around Me'.

SCENE SEVEN

ERPINGHAM's *office.* ERPINGHAM *is now fully dressed in white tie and tails. A noise of screaming is heard in the distance mingled with music and excited shouts.*

ERPINGHAM (*smoothing his hair with a brush*). I'd like your presence at the bathing beauty contest tomorrow, Padre.

A clerical face always inspires confidence at a gathering of semi-nude women. (*He puts the brush down.*) And, in the evening, perhaps you'd mingle with the older men and tell a few of your 'off-colour' stories?

PADRE. I'll make a note in my diary, sir.

He does so.

ERPINGHAM. Bearing in mind the large number of Roman Catholic guests we have this week it might be wise not to include the one about the Pope's mother-in-law.

The distant noise rises sharply.

Can you hear anything?

PADRE. I was aware of a growing tumult, sir. It's coming from the Grand Ballroom.

ERPINGHAM. It sounds like the Devil's Mass.

W. E. HARRISON *enters. He is dishevelled and out of breath.*

W. E. HARRISON. Would you come and cast your eye over the Grand Ballroom, sir?

ERPINGHAM. Why? What's going on?

W. E. HARRISON. Nothing, sir. Riley's got them a bit over-excited that's all. (*He laughs a little breathlessly.*)

ERPINGHAM. Pass me that gardenia.

The PADRE *hands him the gardenia.* ERPINGHAM *puts it into his buttonhole.*

Encouraging them to make that racket. He's exceeding his brief. (*He pins the gardenia on.*) Pass the spray.

W. E. HARRISON *passes a scent spray.*

What was the row about? Do you know?

W. E. HARRISON. Riley was trying to pacify some young chap's wife, sir. The husband got hold of the wrong end of the stick.

ERPINGHAM *sprays the gardenia with scent.*

ERPINGHAM. If we have complaints from women I'll see Riley is prosecuted. (*He puts the spray aside.*) Give me a cigar.

W. E. HARRISON *hands him a cigar.*

Every one of us must behave like Caesar's wife. (*He cuts the cigar.*)

    MASON *runs in. She looks pale and shaken. Her dress is torn and her hair is awry. She carries her squeeze-box.*

MASON (*to* ERPINGHAM). Oh, sir! Would you go to the Grand Ballroom? Chief Redcoat Riley is in considerable difficulties. Certain elements in the camp have taken advantage of his inexperience to behave badly. They've broken the mirror at the back of 'non-alcoholic' drinks bar.

    ERPINGHAM *turns to the* PADRE *with a frown.*

ERPINGHAM. You see, Padre, I act like a Christian and what happens? Property is damaged, women insulted and the representatives of lawful government frightened out of their wits.

    He turns crisply to W. E. HARRISON *and* JESSIE MASON.

I shan't need your help. Run over the menu for dinner. Come with me, Padre. I've made Riley and I'll break him. He'll be reduced to hanging around Irish Labour Rallies. Entertaining the Bishop of Armagh and that crowd.

    He sticks the cigar into the corner of his mouth and exits followed by the PADRE. W. E. HARRISON *and* MASON *stand at ease.*

W. E. HARRISON. My nerves will be on the twitch for weeks after this. A grown woman came up and spat in my face.

MASON. Would you recognise her again?

W. E. HARRISON. I wouldn't want to. Gob all over my carnation. Disgusting. I had to flush it down the teenagers toilet. (*He takes a notebook from his pocket.*) Chief Redcoat bloody Riley showed his incompetence tonight all right.

MASON. It went from bad to worse after you left. Some great lout climbed on the stage and tried to take my clothes off! (*With a smile.*) You see, Wally, he'd got a totally false impression of my character. When Riley said I was the resident nympho they took it as gospel. He had his hand up my skirt and my briefs round my ankles before I knew what had happened. Kept shrieking 'Give us a feel of your squeeze-box'. (*With a shrug.*) There should be a distance between the artist and her public. I don't like rowdy behaviour from my fans.

W. E. HARRISON *opens his note-book.*

W. E. HARRISON. We'll begin the inspection with the cold meats.

MASON *claps her hands.*

Music: 'Dead March' from 'Saul'.

WAITERS *enter slowly pushing a trolley upon which is a variety of cold meats:·hams, cold chickens, sausages, a pig's head and trotters. The cortège passes in front of* MASON *and* W. E. HARRISON *who bow their heads. The music fades as the* WAITERS *go off.*

SCENE EIGHT

ERPINGHAM *and the* PADRE *are walking swiftly to the Grand Ballroom.*

ERPINGHAM. You realise, of course, that Riley's behaviour is a legacy of the potato famine?

PADRE. I'm reminded of Moses on Sinai discovering the excesses of the Children of Israel. Once again the literal truth of the Bible has been demonstrated!

ERPINGHAM. I'd rather you didn't mention these Jewish myths, Padre. I don't know about you, but I'm a Christian.

RILEY *is seen between two men.* LOU, EILEEN *and several* CAMPERS *stand round him. Many have bleeding faces.* TED *is still without his trousers.* LOU *has wound bunting round herself. She has a distracted air.* KENNY, *still in the leopard skin, holds* RILEY *under the chin. Blood pours from* RILEY's *mouth and nose.*

KENNY. Apologise, you cowson! Give me an apology!

RILEY *shakes his head; he is hardly conscious.*

EILEEN (*with a shriek*). Hit him again! Give him a good hiding!

LOU *passes a hand across her brow, dazed. She laughs weakly.*

KENNY. Pregnant women, eh? I'll teach you to hit pregnant women!

ERPINGHAM *and the* PADRE *advance upon the group in horror.*

ERPINGHAM. Leave that man alone! He's a member of the staff.

KENNY *smacks* RILEY'*s face, first with the flat of his hand, then with the back.*

KENNY. I won't have pregnant women insulted.

ERPINGHAM. Any disciplinary action will be taken by me. You've no right to strike an official of the Camp.

He tries to thrust KENNY *out of the way. He struggles with* KENNY. LOU *tries to intervene.*

LOU. His wife was insulted.

TED. Carrying she is. She's four months.

ERPINGHAM (*staring at* TED, *outraged*). What has become of your trousers? (*To the* PADRE.) This is no place for a priest. (*Back to* TED.) I don't allow indecent exposure in my camp. Consult the manual. You'll find it in the drawer beside your bed.

KENNY, *emotionally, appeals to* ERPINGHAM.

KENNY. It's our first child. We've only been married a year. We were refused permission to wed.

EILEEN (*weeping*). We defied the ban on our love! (*She cries hysterically.*) I'm pregnant. I've a right to protection, haven't I?

LOU *bangs* RILEY *in the groin with her handbag.* RILEY *screams in pain and would collapse if* TED *didn't drag him to his feet.* ERPINGHAM, *extremely angry at the turn of events, tries to push* KENNY *aside and bring* RILEY *to safety.*

KENNY. Hanging's too good for the bleeder!

> ERPINGHAM *gives* KENNY *a shove which sends him spinning. He grabs* RILEY *by the arm.* KENNY *comes back;* EILEEN *hits* ERPINGHAM *on the back of the head with a bottle.* ERPINGHAM *sinks to his knees.*

PADRE (*lifting his hands in horror*). That's Mr Erpingham!

> *He supports* ERPINGHAM *and helps him to rise.*

(*White-faced*). You've struck a figure of authority!

> ERPINGHAM *shakes his head, dizzily. He stands upright, frees himself from the* PADRE *and turns coldly upon* EILEEN.

ERPINGHAM. You are banned from the Erpingham Camp for life!

> EILEEN *makes a farting noise. The rest of the* CAMPERS *jeer. The* PADRE *wrings his hands.*

(*Rounding upon the campers*). All of you return to your chalets! Quick now! I shall make an announcement!

> *There is angry jeering laughter and mocking whistles from* KENNY.

Let's get out of this, Padre. (*He turns to go.*)

PADRE. What about Chief Redcoat Riley, sir?

> TED *releases* RILEY *who drops to the ground in a faint.*

ERPINGHAM. Send the doctor over. The evening has been a complete disaster.

> ERPINGHAM *makes a speedy exit followed by the* PADRE.

SCENE NINE

> W. E. HARRISON *and* JESSIE MASON *are inspecting the food.* MASON *holds a menu.* W. E. HARRISON *has his notebook open.*

W. E. HARRISON. Trifles and assorted savouries.

> MASON *claps her hands.*

Music: 'Chinese Dance' from 'The Nutcracker Suite'.
WAITERS *enter quickly pushing a trolley upon which is a variety of jellies, pastries, trifles and sweets.*

W. E. HARRISON. Taste that trifle, Mason.

MASON *takes a cardboard spoon from the trolley and tastes the trifle.*

MASON. Very good, I'd say.

W. E. HARRISON. Destroy the spoon.

MASON *screws up the spoon and gives it to a waiter.*
WAITERS *push the trolley out of sight. The music fades.*
MASON *looks at the menu.* W. E. HARRISON *writes in his book.*

W. E. HARRISON. Drinks of choice with meal. We'll do them and sign the Chef's report.

ERPINGHAM'S *voice is heard.*

ERPINGHAM. Harrison! Harrison!

ERPINGHAM *enters with the* PADRE. *Both are distressed.*

MASON. Shall we inspect the doilies now or later?

ERPINGHAM. See the Main Gate is locked, Harrison. Bring the keys to me!

HARRISON *goes off.*

MASON (*with a charming smile, in a soothing voice*). We've checked the menu for tonight, sir. It's quite in order. Would you care to sign the Chef's report?

ERPINGHAM. No. (*He tears the menu apart.*) Lock the food away! I'm not feeding that Hellish squadron out there.

MASON *gives a squeak of surprise and alarm.*

MASON. Whatever has happened, sir?

PADRE. It was dreadful. Quite dreadful, Miss Mason. The bunting has been torn down from the Beauty Queen's Parade.

ERPINGHAM. They were running about half-naked spewing up their pork 'n beans. I counted eight pairs of women's briefs on the stairs. There'll be some unexpected visits to the Pre-natal clinic after tonight. (*He mops his brow.*) It

would take the pen of our National poet to describe the
scene that met my eyes upon entering the Grand Ballroom.
My Chief Redcoat was being savagely beaten about the
face by a man dressed as a leopard.

PADRE. It was like an allegorical painting by one of the lesser
Masters. I was forcibly reminded of a 'Christ Mocked'
which was, until recently, hanging in the cellar of the Walker
Art Gallery, Liverpool.

ERPINGHAM. When I remonstrated with them I was subjected to abuse. I was struck upon the head by a bottle. They
were completely out of control.

MASON (*with wonder*). Hit an official of the Camp? That's
never been done before.

> RILEY *enters; his uniform is torn; his face bleeding. He is
> dispirited and ashamed.* ERPINGHAM *rounds on him at once.*

ERPINGHAM. Another disaster to add to your ever-growing
list of failures, Riley!

> RILEY, *overcome by emotion, hangs his head.*

Your technique might have been admirable at Nuremberg,
but it's still in advance of the Home Counties. Give me
your sash and medal. You've proved yourself unworthy
of them.

> *He strips* RILEY'S *honours from him.*
> *Music: A single trumpet.*
> W. E. HARRISON *enters.*

W. E. HARRISON. They've sent a deputation, sir. They want
a word with you.

ERPINGHAM. Show them in.

> ERPINGHAM *stands to one side surrounded by his staff.*
> W. E. HARRISON *ushers in* KENNY *and* TED. TED *is fully
> dressed.* KENNY *still wears the leopard skin. He has put a
> woolly cardigan over it.*

What can I do for you, gentlemen?

TED. Mr Erpingham we won't waste time on coming to the
point. You know why we're here. The chalet area has

been locked. And, on your orders we're told, no meal will be served tonight. Is this true?

ERPINGHAM. Perfectly true. I intend to exact reparations for the damage done tonight.

TED. Certain elements on both sides are to blame for what has happened. We all of us regret it. Will you be reasonable and forget the whole sorry business?

ERPINGHAM (*with a charming smile*). I can't promise that, I'm afraid.

TED. Why not?

ERPINGHAM. You must realise that property has been damaged.

TED. The majority can't be held responsible for the exploits of an irresponsible minority.

ERPINGHAM. If majorities allow themselves to be swayed by minorities, irresponsible or not, they must take the consequences.

    KENNY, *who has been listening with mounting impatience, explodes with rage.*

KENNY. You can't repair the damage to your property by denying us food. Where's your logic?

    ERPINGHAM *gives* KENNY *a look of quiet contempt.*

ERPINGHAM. You stand dressed in a leopard skin and woolly cardigan calling on logic? You're like an atheist praying to his God.

    The staff laugh. KENNY *flushes angrily.*

KENNY. We want food and shelter and something to eat. Are you going to give it to us?

ERPINGHAM. Can't you even arrive on a Peace mission properly dressed?

KENNY. My clothes have been nicked. I can't get into my chalet.

ERPINGHAM. Why were you using violence on a member of my staff?

KENNY. He'd abused my wife. She's pregnant. He hit her.

ERPINGHAM. Why?

RILEY. She was screaming, sir.

ERPINGHAM. What was she screaming for?

KENNY. He asked her to. And then he hit her. I've never hit her. I agreed to waive my rights till she had the baby. I'd've killed him if I'd been left alone. It's every man's right to protect his wife.

> ERPINGHAM *smiles. There is contempt in his smile. He faces* KENNY *coolly.*

ERPINGHAM. You're talking nonsense. You have no rights. You have certain privileges which can be withdrawn. I am withdrawing them.

KENNY. You'll pay for this, you ignorant fucker!

> *There are cries of horror from the staff.*

ERPINGHAM. I think you're forgetting to whom you're speaking. Calm down before I have you thrown out.

KENNY. We want food. We demand bread. We expect shelter!

> ERPINGHAM *is made angry by the tone of* KENNY's *voice.*

ERPINGHAM. You have damaged my property, poured scorn upon my staff and insulted me. You've cast my hospitality in my face. And yet, the bitter taste of ingratitude not dry upon my lips, you come to me with your arrogant demands. No. You must be taught a lesson. There will be no food tonight. I shall not give way. You can sleep in the open. The chalet area is closed until further notice.

TED. We'll go to the village.

KENNY. Open the gates!

ERPINGHAM. No!

TED. You can't keep us here against our will.

RILEY. Let them go, sir. Cast them into the wilderness.

ERPINGHAM. No.

W. E. HARRISON. Your stiff-necked attitude will bring untold harm. Be warned before it's too late.

MASON. Let discretion play the better part, sir.

ERPINGHAM. Never! This is my kingdom. I make the laws.

We've our traditions. And they're not to be lightly cast aside at the whim of a handful of troublemakers. I'll never agree to their demands.

KENNY. Is that the message you want us to take back to the people?

ERPINGHAM. Yes. And now get your leopard-skin legs out of here!

TED. Very well then. We'll make the best of it tonight. In the morning I intend to lodge a formal protest with the Camps and Caravans Association. Holidaymakers must be protected from people like you!

TED *and* KENNY *go off.*

RILEY. Oh, sir, (*Pleadingly.*) call them back. Let's thrash it out over a cup of instant.

PADRE. Had Pharaoh done as Chief Redcoat Riley suggests, sir, the ten plagues would not have been inflicted on the fair land of Egypt.

MASON. All avenues haven't been explored.

HARRISON. Chief Redcoat Riley has the true liberal spirit, sir. Let's give his idea a try.

ERPINGHAM (*to* RILEY). I won't have your rubbishy ideas brought into my camp. If it's your ambition to be Secretary General of the United Nations, you're at liberty to apply for the post. Personally I think you're better employed blowing up balloons for the under-fives. (*He draws himself up with dignity.*) This whole episode has been fermented by a handful of intellectuals. If we stand firm by the principles on which the camp was founded the clouds will pass. To give in now would be madness.

He takes a deep breath. He has recovered his composure.

Behave as though nothing had happened. It's my intention to defy the forces of Anarchy with all that is best in twentieth century civilisation. I shall put a record of Russ Conway on the gram and browse through a James Bond.

He turns and goes off. The STAFF *follow him.*

SCENE TEN

KENNY *and* TED *are silhouetted against the sky.* LOU *and* EILEEN *are with them.* KENNY *addresses a crowd.*

KENNY. They have denied our children bread, insulted our womenfolk and ignored our every plea. There is nothing left but direct action. I say we should break open the Stores. Take the means of supply into our own hands!

TED. No! We'd be placing ourselves outside the law.

LOU. I have complete faith in my husband. He's had a lot of experience with disputes. He's in cakes.

KENNY. Trained locksmiths could open the food depot. It's not difficult.

TED. We've no authority to force the locks.

KENNY. We'll take the authority then.

KENNY *flings out his arms, embracing the crowd.*

I'm an ordinary man – I've no wish to be a leader – my only ambition is to rest in peace by my own fireside. But, in the life of every one of us, there comes a time when he must choose – whether to be treated in the manner of the bad old days. Or whether to take by force those common human rights which should be denied no man. (*He raises his voice.*) A place to sleep, food for our kids, and respect. That's all we ask. Is it too much?

TED. We must behave in a reasonable manner. Our hands are clean so far. We've acted entirely in accordance with the law. What Ken here proposes is illegal.

KENNY. So is insulting pregnant women.

EILEEN (*weeping*). Yes. I'm pregnant. I was insulted. Made to feel awful.

She weeps. TED *holds up his hands and speaks to the crowd in a calm, rational manner.*

TED. Ladies and Gentlemen. Listen to what I've got to say. Don't interrupt me. Form your own opinions and bring your intelligence to bear on the facts so that you can make an accurate decision. What are we losing? One night's sleep. One meal. I've arranged that our wives and children will have a roof over their heads. A makeshift one, it's true. Nevertheless somewhere to rest. In the morning we can make our complaints to the proper authorities. Nobody has been harmed. Let's keep it that way. We've the law on our side.

LOU *applauds. She smiles.*

LOU. My husband and I are civil defence workers. This is an emergency. We're taking over.

KENNY *addresses the crowd. His face flushed.*

KENNY. What Ted says is true. He's a good fella. We all know that. He's a reasonable man. We shouldn't forget it. But neither let us forget those pregnant women that've been insulted. And little kiddies crying for something to eat. (*Emotionally.*) Man does not live by bread alone! It's the small things in life that matter. And I'm prepared to risk a lot for those!

EILEEN *rests her head against* KENNY.

My missus and me – we've only been married a year. We're expecting our first baby. I'm terrified of anything happening to her. We're doing this thing not for ourselves, but for our wives and loved ones – pregnant now and in the times to come, that they may be safe from never knowing where the next meal is coming from. Have a bash, I say. Have a bash for the pregnant woman next door!

EILEEN *waves her hands. She jumps up and down.*

EILEEN (*screaming*). I'm in the family way!

KENNY. It's our first!

LOU *turns to the crowd.*

LOU. We're proceeding from page twenty of the Civil Defence Booklet. Will you all take up your respective positions?

EILEEN *runs across and smacks her across the face and pulls
her hair. They fall screaming to the floor.*

LOU. What'y'r doing?

EILEEN. Get out of here, you silly bitch! Go on before I kick
your dental plate to pieces.

TED *runs across and parts* EILEEN *and* LOU. *He lifts* LOU
up.

TED. This is most unpleasant. (*He protects* LOU *from* EILEEN.)
Stop playing the goat Eileen and behave like a grown-up.

EILEEN (*to* TED). Piss off you dirty middle-class prat! And
take your poxy wife with you.

KENNY (*coming over, to* EILEEN). Did he insult you?

TED (*to* LOU). We'd better leave them to it, dear. You don't
want to listen to a lot of foul language, do you?

LOU. I certainly don't. It won't make my holiday any more
enjoyable.

TED *and* LOU *go off.* KENNY *and* EILEEN *stand upon the
chairs.*

KENNY. To the Stores!

EILEEN. To the Stores!

Music: 'La Marseillaise'.

SCENE ELEVEN

ERPINGHAM'S *office.* ERPINGHAM *is sitting reading, with
a cigar in his hand and a glass of brandy beside him. There
are distant sounds of cheering, breaking glass and music.*
ERPINGHAM *turns a page in his book.* W. E. HARRISON
runs in.

W. E. HARRISON. Sir! (ERPINGHAM *looks up.*) There's been a
meeting in the Old Folks Wheelchair Court. A subversive
element in the camp has taken the law into its own hands.

They're using deckchair loungettes to break the windows of the food store!

ERPINGHAM *puts his book down.* JESSIE MASON *hurries in.*

MASON. Oh, Mr Erpingham, they've elected a leader! There are unconfirmed reports of looting. The food store has been ransacked. And some of the younger men have started raping.

ERPINGHAM *rises. The* PADRE *enters, quickly, his face a mask of horror.*

PADRE. Oh, sir! Let us pray for guidance. Your car has been pushed into the Experienced Swimmers Only.

There is a distant noise. Rockets are heard and a sudden roar. The room is lit by a sheet of flame. RILEY *enters.*

RILEY. They've set fire to the Grand Ballroom, sir. They're marching this way.

ERPINGHAM. Who gave them permission to do these things? Switch on the public address system. I shall broadcast an appeal for calm.

RILEY *switches on the address system.* EILEEN's *voice is heard singing.*

EILEEN. Eee-eye, Eee-eye, Eeee-eye-O!
Under the table you must go.
If I catch you bending,
I'll have your knickers down.
Knees-up, Knees-up,
Don't get the breeze-up.
Knees-up, Mother Brown-O!!

There are loud cheers and she begins again. ERPINGHAM *switches off the address system.*

ERPINGHAM (*outraged*). Who is that woman? Sack her at once!

RILEY. She's the wife of their leader, sir. She's dancing on Mason's baby grand.

MASON *gives a squeak of horror.*

ERPINGHAM. Call a staff meeting. The situation must be thoroughly looked into.

RILEY. You haven't got a staff, sir. The Resident Medical Officer went an hour ago. The Chief Engineer and the Security Officer have gone within the last few minutes.

ERPINGHAM. We've lost Medicine, Science and Defence. Any more?

RILEY. The Liberal Arts, sir. Represented by the woman at the postcard stand.

ERPINGHAM. What am I left with? (*He looks at the* PADRE, HARRISON, MASON *and* RILEY.) Music, Religion and the Spirit of Independent Ireland. The cause is lost.

RILEY. Let me make a suggestion.

ERPINGHAM. No!

W. E. HARRISON. We must do something, sir. And quick.

RILEY. I was brought up, as I expect you know, in the Ancient Faith. The Faith that nurtured Raphael, gentle artist of the Renaissance. As a child I was profoundly impressed by his picture – gem of the Vatican collection – 'Pope Leo turning back the Hordes of Attila'. You recall, sir, the calm, unwavering glance of the saint, at which the barbarian chieftain quails and gives up his avowed design of sacking the City of the Seven Hills, burial place of the Holy Martyrs?

ERPINGHAM. I know the picture well.

RILEY. Why can't we use the padre, as God used St Leo?
    ERPINGHAM *considers*.

ERPINGHAM. Yes. It's not a bad idea. We'll give it a try. Have you got a crucifix, Padre?

PADRE. No, sir. I've come out without it.

ERPINGHAM. Lend him yours, Chief Redcoat Riley.
    RILEY *takes off his crucifix and gives it to the* PADRE.

ERPINGHAM. Accompanied by a simple virgin – do your best, Mason – you will parley with these people. We shall await the result of your mission with interest. Off you go.
    The PADRE *and* JESSIE MASON *go off.*

ERPINGHAM. My field-glasses, Riley. In the drawer.

> RILEY *takes the field-glasses from the drawer. He hands them to* ERPINGHAM. ERPINGHAM *stares through them.*

The rabble, led by their leader, approaches the very doors of Government.

> *There are faintly heard cries and the crash of falling timbers. The red glare of fire fills the room. Distant strains of 'La Marseillaise' are heard.*

With revolutionary banners flying they stream through the mists of a bloody dawn!

> *There is a sound of wood and glass being smashed.*

RILEY (*beside* ERPINGHAM). They're tearing down the Pavilion of the Judges!

W. E. HARRISON. Where will the Lady Mayoress stand for tomorrow's march past of lovelies?

> *The air is filled with smoke and flame.*

ERPINGHAM. Clothed in the glory of God the Church approaches!

> *The* PADRE, *followed by* JESSIE MASON, *cross, slowly, with great dignity. A lambent light, not of this world, accompanies them.*
>
> *Music: Gounod 'Ave Maria'.*
>
> *They go off. A sudden silence falls.* ERPINGHAM, *staring through the field-glasses, gives an exclamation of wonder.*

ERPINGHAM. Blessed are the Meek! (*He lowers the glasses and turns to* RILEY *in joy.*) A simple parish priest has quelled the anger of the politically unawakened. As the dove alighted on the Ark after the Flood, bringing hope to those within, so too he settles our fears and calms our troubled thoughts.

> *There is a sudden howl from the mob and cheers.* ERPINGHAM *looks through the field-glasses.*

Oh! Oh!

> *He turns aghast to* W. E. HARRISON *and* RILEY.

RILEY. What is it?

ERPINGHAM. The Man of God is down! Twenty Christian centuries in the dust. The Devil's Congress has belted the Lord's Annointed.

    W. E. HARRISON takes up the glasses and stares. There is a squeal from MASON and cries of fright.

W. E. HARRISON. They're molesting Mason.

ERPINGHAM. She's no stranger to it. Virgin was an honorary title.

    There is an explosion, and dust and plaster fall from the ceiling. They drop to their knees.

RILEY. The power plant.

    The lights go out. The room is lit only by the fire outside. Smoke drifts across the room. ERPINGHAM stands and dusts himself down.

ERPINGHAM. What do you advise now, Chief Redcoat Riley?

RILEY. Flight, sir.

ERPINGHAM. I'm inclined to agree.

    ERPINGHAM clears his desk of papers. He puts them into a brief-case.

W. E. HARRISON. If we can get to the Transport Section, sir, we might find the Night Porter's bicycle.

ERPINGHAM. Oh, what a dreadful experience. Remind me to ring the insurance people first thing.

    The PADRE and JESSIE MASON stagger in, bruised, and bleeding, their clothes torn.

PADRE. Oh, sir, Miss Mason and I have had a dreadful experience.

ERPINGHAM. Not the same experience, I hope, Padre.

MASON. Everything is in a terrible state downstairs, sir. They've torn your Canvatex Van Gogh to shreds.

    ERPINGHAM flushes with anger.

ERPINGHAM. We'll have a couple of verses of 'Love Divine, All Loves Excelling', Padre. It's fire-hoses, tear-gas and the boot from then on.

They kneel. JESSIE MASON *accompanies the hymn on her squeeze-box.*

Love Divine, all loves excelling,
Joy of Heaven to earth come down,
Fix in us Thy humble dwelling,
All Thy faithful mercies crown.

Jesu, Thou art all compassion,
Pure unbounded Love Thou art:
Visit us with Thy salvation,
Enter every trembling heart.

Come Almighty to deliver,
Let us all Thy grace receive;
Suddenly return and never,
Never more Thy temples leave.

Aaaaamen.'

They bow their heads. KENNY *and* EILEEN *and several* CAMPERS *burst into the room.*

KENNY. The time of reckoning has come.

He advances. ERPINGHAM *and his* STAFF *rise.*

What've you got to say about pregnancy now?

ERPINGHAM. Pregnancy has nothing to do with me.

EILEEN (*hysterically*). Hit him! Go on, hit him! He insulted me.

KENNY *flings aside his woolly cardigan.*

KENNY. I'm going to give you a good hiding, Erpingham. I'm going to smash your face in for the gratification of those in the family way everywhere.

ERPINGHAM. I shall confiscate your luggage. What is your chalet number?

KENNY *butts* ERPINGHAM *in the stomach.* ERPINGHAM *crumples up in agony.* JESSIE MASON *seizes* KENNY *by the arm.*

MASON. You can't do this. Mr Erpingham is a gentleman.

EILEEN *drags* MASON *away.*

EILEEN (*screaming*). We were refused permission to wed. We defied the ban on our love. I was insulted. I'm an expectant mother.

> KENNY *punches* ERPINGHAM *in the mouth.* MASON *screams.* EILEEN *struggles with her. The* PADRE *tries to separate them.*

PADRE. Leave Miss Mason alone. She's a sensitive artiste.

> RILEY *and* W. E. HARRISON *are fighting off the attacks of the other* CAMPERS. KENNY *is viciously beating up* ERPINGHAM. EILEEN *is screaming and hitting* JESSIE MASON. *The* PADRE *kneels amid the carnage. His hands folded in prayer.*

PADRE. Oh, Merciful Father, in Thee we trust when dangers threaten.

> *He is hit by an egg. The* CAMPERS *and* STAFF *struggle and scream around the figures of* KENNY *and* ERPINGHAM. *Disaster strikes when* ERPINGHAM *abruptly disappears through a hole which opens up in the floor. A silence falls. They look down the hole. The* PADRE *rises and joins them. He looks down and shakes his head.*

PADRE. As the little foxes gnaw at the roots of the vine, so anarchy weakens the fibres of society.

EILEEN (*weeping*). I'm a mother-to-be. I should be protected from this kind of thing.

> TED *and* LOU *enter quietly. They are awed and amazed.*

LOU. Mr Erpingham has fallen through the ceiling on to a dancing couple! There's blood all over the place.

TED. They're in pretty bad shape. Erpingham is dead.

> *Everybody is distressed.* JESSIE MASON *weeps, dabbing her eyes with a handkerchief.* RILEY *turns to the* PADRE.

RILEY. I'll take charge downstairs, sir. Will you be able to manage up here?

> *The* PADRE *beams.*

PADRE. Have no worries, Chief Redcoat Riley. It's Life that

defeats the Christian Church. She's always been well-equipped to deal with Death.

> RILEY *and* W. E. HARRISON *go off. The* PADRE *turns to the sorrowing* STAFF *and* CAMPERS.

As witnesses to the surprising disappearance of Mr Erpingham you will all no doubt be called upon to give evidence before the authorities. Let us remember that in the days after Christ's glorious ascension into Heaven the apostles too must've appeared before some kind of Magistrates court to account for the no-less surprising disappearance of Jesus. The gospels are silent on that memorable encounter with a Jerusalem J.P. And if, in answer to your interrogator's question, 'What happened?' you reply, 'He fell through the floor', and are rewarded with incredulity; how much nearer the hairline the eyebrows of the Magistrate to whom Simon Peter made answer, 'He went up into the air'? In small things, as in great things, the disciples were remarkable men.

> *Music: A roll of drums.*

> RILEY *and* W. E. HARRISON *enter slowly with* ERPING-HAM'*s body on a bier. They lay it across the desk.*

KENNY (*emotionally*). It was that bastard insulting Eileen. It need never have happened. (*He shakes his head.*)

TED. No matter what happens, Louie and me will back you up, Ken. You'll find the Police sympathetic. They know how it feels. Most of them have had their own wives insulted at some time or another.

LOU. If there's any question of bail Ted and me will stand as surety. We can afford the money more than you.

> EILEEN *sniffs.*

EILEEN. I'm terrified all this will affect my baby. I'd hate it to grow up warped.

> KENNY *comforts her. The assembled* STAFF *and* CAMPERS *stand round the bier. A great cross of coloured light, as from distant stained glass, falls across* ERPINGHAM'S *body. Everyone bows their heads in silence.*

Music: Bach 'Toccata and Fugue'.

RILEY. He was a great man. One of the very greatest of our time. Poet, philosopher and friend of rich and poor alike. Distinctions were foreign to his nature. He was at all times a simple man. Little children loved him.

MASON breaks down and weeps uncontrollably.

He gave up a career as a missionary to come to us. Our need is greater than theirs. It was in the Erpingham Holiday Centre that he found the spiritual peace he had long been seeking. His death, when it came, found him quite prepared. He went quietly and with great dignity.

Music fades. The PADRE speaks in a low voice at the head of the bier.

PADRE. Day by day the Voice saith, "Come,
Enter thine eternal home";
Asking not if we can spare
This dear soul it summons there.

But the Lord doth nought amiss,
And since he hath ordered this,
We have nought to do but still
Rest in silence on his will.

Music The Last Post.

Four dozen red balloons – one for each year of ERPING- HAM's *life – fall slowly upon the bier. As the last balloon descends the trumpet fades.* RILEY *lifts his head.*

RILEY. We will now file past our beloved friend and leader for the last time.

Organ music.

The mourners file past the body and go off. RILEY *is left alone.*

Your tie is crooked. I'll straighten it before I go. (*He straightens* ERPINGHAM'S *tie.*) I'll have this as a relic. (*He takes the gardenia from* ERPINGHAM'S *buttonhole.*) I'll arrange a Class A (Higher Employee) wreath, sir. I hope that will be all right?

Turns to go. Looks back.

Goodbye, sir. Be seeing you.

He goes off. The body of ERPINGHAM *is left alone in the moonlight with the red balloons and dying flames in a blaze from the distant stained glass. A great choir is heard singing* 'The Holy City'.

Curtain

Funeral Games

Funeral Games was first presented by Yorkshire Television on 25 August 1968 with the following cast:

PRINGLE — Michael Denison

TESSA — Vivien Merchant

CAULFIELD — Ian McShane

MCCORQUODALE — Bill Fraser

FIRST MAN — Richard McNeff

Director: James Ormerod
Executive Producer: Peter Willes

PART ONE

Scene One

Pringle's study.
CAULFIELD *enters.*

CAULFIELD. My name is Caulfield. We spoke over the telephone.
PRINGLE. I remember you distinctly. Do come in.
  CAULFIELD *closes the door.*
PRINGLE. Sit down. Or kneel if you'd prefer. I want you to behave naturally.
  Pause.
  Shall I ring for a hassock?
CAULFIELD. These chairs look comfortable.
  He sits.
PRINGLE. They're unsuitable for trances. Are you a praying man?
CAULFIELD. I'm lost in thought occasionally.
PRINGLE. We've a house of contemplation, in the Arcade. Pay us a visit. (*Pause.*) Have you heard of my group? The Brotherhood. We hang about on street corners.
CAULFIELD. I've read of your activities in the Press. Weren't you had up for causing an affray?
PRINGLE. We were waylaid after conducting a 'God and You' meeting. Several of our members were arrested due to Jesuit intrigue. (*He takes a cigarette box from the desk.*) Have a herbal?
CAULFIELD. I'd rather smoke my own.
  He takes a packet of cigarettes from his pocket.
PRINGLE. Would you like to chew a bit of root I dug up in the garden of Gethsemane?
CAULFIELD. No. If it's all the same to you. (*He lights a cigarette.*)
PRINGLE. I never have to worry about dental decay since my Holy Land trip. (*Pause.*) Are you in need of refreshment?
CAULFIELD. I'm parched.

PRINGLE *takes a key from his pocket. He unlocks a desk drawer.*

PRINGLE. I've a bottle of water here from the Well at Bethsaida. (*He takes a stoppered flask from the cupboard.*) I have to keep it under lock and key. I can't trust the charwoman. (*He brings the flask to his desk.*) Will you have a nip?

CAULFIELD (*pause*). Is it pure?

PRINGLE. It's reputed to have miraculous powers. (*He pours some water into a glass.*) I use it as a laxative myself.

He puts the glass on the table beside CAULFIELD.

PRINGLE. What about food? Are you hungry?

CAULFIELD. Yes.

PRINGLE. Open the drawer at your elbow. You'll find a box of caraway seeds.

CAULFIELD *opens the drawer.*

PRINGLE. They represent many things to our sect. 'Food' being high on the list.

CAULFIELD *shakes a few seeds into the palm of his hand.*

PRINGLE. I'd like to ask you a question or two. Are you free from sin?

CAULFIELD. I'm as free as the next man.

PRINGLE. That's me. You're in good company. I could get into Heaven any time I chose. (*Pause.*) Have you ever had occasion to control yourself?

CAULFIELD. Yes.

PRINGLE. And succeeded?

CAULFIELD. Not since Christmas.

PRINGLE. Christmas. We call that the Festival of the Renewal of the Spirit. It's a time of rejoicing. We have a cot with a baby in it outside the church. I dare say you're surprised by the unusualness of the conception?

CAULFIELD. It sounds as though you have ideas of your own.

PRINGLE. We borrow from no one. Copies of my brochure *Blessings Abound* are still available. It'd be as well to purchase one. It gives the background to my teaching. (*Pause, he considers.*) What shape is your hot water bottle?

CAULFIELD. I haven't got one.

PRINGLE. Too proud. Mine takes the form of a cross. There's piety for you.

He stares hard at CAULFIELD.

CAULFIELD. Is there an ash-tray?

PRINGLE *picks one up. He brings it to* CAULFIELD.

PRINGLE. I stole this from under the very nose of a Doctor of Divinity. (*He puts it carefully beside* CAULFIELD.) I hope you never have occasion to do the same.

CAULFIELD *flicks ash into the tray.*

Are you available for hire? I've a job of work that wants doing.

CAULFIELD (*pause*). I won't be choirboy. I'm too old.

PRINGLE. We've no time for choristers in the Brotherhood. We've taken to handmaidens like ducks to water. We frown upon anything else.

He takes up a letter and hands it to CAULFIELD.

PRINGLE. Look at that.

CAULFIELD. What is it?

PRINGLE. An anonymous letter.

CAULFIELD. Who from?

PRINGLE. It's hard to say.

CAULFIELD. What does it accuse you of?

PRINGLE. Apart from a postscript suggesting that my lawn needs cutting, the writer is tolerant of my shortcomings. He brands my wife as an adulteress.

Long pause.

CAULFIELD *picks up the letter.*

CAULFIELD. It's a menu-type of hand. Have you insulted a café proprietor?

PRINGLE. I'm on bad terms with our tea-lady.

CAULFIELD. Have you seen her handwriting?

PRINGLE. I've never even seen her hands.

CAULFIELD. Get a glance at them. Maybe she isn't capable of committing the offence. (*He stubs out his cigarette.*) It gives the address where she misconducts herself.

PRINGLE. Hmm.

CAULFIELD. Where the intimacy takes place. Next door to a blue bookshop. I know the place well. It's run by a couple of ex-policemen.

PRINGLE. A love-nest adjacent to a bookshop. I do hope she hasn't betrayed me with a seedy intellectual.

CAULFIELD (*turning the letter over*). The watermark is in the form of a frog.

PRINGLE. A French intellectual would be even worse.

CAULFIELD. Is divorce against your code?

PRINGLE. We grant an annulment only in a case of possession by the Devil. If my wife is committing adultery my position would be intolerable. Being completely without sin myself I'd have to cast the first stone. And I'm dead against violence. I make no secret of my views.

   CAULFIELD *puts the letter away.*

CAULFIELD. I'll investigate this matter for you. Will I be paid?

PRINGLE. You'll receive a personal invitation to my exhibition of biblical documents. It's preceded by a buffet tea.

   They shake hands.

Make your report tomorrow. My candle burns until the third cock crow. (*He picks up some leaflets from his desk.*) Take these devotional reflections for your 'quiet time'. (*He opens the door.*) And should you wish to contribute to our Leprosy Mission you'll find a box in the hall.

   CAULFIELD *goes out.* PRINGLE *opens the door.*

Scene Two

MCCORQUODALE'*s room.*

TESSA. It's four o'clock. I've ordered my taxi. (*She places her hand on* MCCORQUODALE'*s brow.*) Has the attack passed?

MCCORQUODALE. Yes. I still feel fluttery. But I'll be all right.

TESSA. You were out for nearly an hour.

   She wipes his mouth with her handkerchief.

MCCORQUODALE. I heard you singing. I was miles away.

TESSA. It was a song in praise of sleep. The author took drugs and died of an overdose in Vienna at the turn of the century. (*She folds up the shawl.*) It's a pretty tune.

She puts the shawl aside and takes a cardigan from a drawer.

TESSA. I washed your face.

MCCORQUODALE. Whilst I was unconscious? You think of everything. (*He pinches her cheek.*) Did I wet myself?

TESSA. No.

MCCORQUODALE. That's because I'm wearing a device. I had it tailored by a young lady.

TESSA helps him to put on the cardigan.

TESSA. Did she see the wound in your thigh?

MCCORQUODALE. She máde the sign of the cross.

TESSA. Was that helpful?

MCCORQUODALE. Another blister appeared shortly afterwards.

TESSA helps him.

TESSA. Why are you wearing a dog-collar?

MCCORQUODALE. Force of habit.

TESSA. It's illegal. You'll get into trouble.

MCCORQUODALE. It keeps me warm. Since I received my marching orders I've had stiff necks galore. (*He hobbles to the table, opens a drawer, searches.*) I had bad legs for years after I was forced to give up the Roman skirt.

TESSA. You were a Catholic priest?

MCCORQUODALE. I saw a vision of the Virgin once. She wore a floppy hat and had a sweet smile.

TESSA. You've mixed with the mighty, then? Did you ever meet the Pope?

MCCORQUODALE. Yes. I haven't seen him for years, though. He must be getting on now.

TESSA puts on her coat.

TESSA. How did you disgrace yourself?

MCCORQUODALE. I was outside the basilica of St Peter arm in arm with a couple of nuns. A mendicant monk objected to something I'd said. Made a terrible mess of my face with his crucifix. Oh, they're perfect fiends some of them.

TESSAbuttons up the coat. She picks up her hat, goes to the mirror.

TESSA (*pause*). Who slashed the oil painting in the hall?

MCCORQUODALE. Someone from the public health.

TESSA takes a lipstick from her handbag.

MCCORQUODALE. Stay awhile. Another hour won't hurt.

TESSA. No. I must be off. I've business.

Pause.

MCCORQUODALE. You're still searching for your little friend?

TESSA. I found a man who saw her on a country road carrying a banner proclaiming the end of the world. But I don't think it has any significance.

MCCORQUODALE. I'll come with you tomorrow. We'll look in the park. She may be sleeping rough.

TESSA. There was nothing rough about Valerie.

MCCORQUODALE. We'll walk among the roses.

TESSA. Our names mustn't be linked. It would arouse comment.

MCCORQUODALE. You're hard, aren't you? I can't break down your resistance.

A taxi hoots from outside.

TESSA looks from the window. She puts her lipstick into her handbag, closes the handbag, picks up a pair of gloves.

TESSA (*pulling on her gloves*). I've laid out the needles. And the sterile wadding.

She kisses his forehead.

Tomorrow is library day.

MCCORQUODALE. Get me something with racy conversations.

TESSA. I'll phone you before lunch.

MCCORQUODALE. You're so exciting across the wires. You could be a terrible flirt if you'd only relax.

Taxi hoots again.

TESSA picks up her handbag, goes to the door.

TESSA. Nurse will be over in an hour to give you colonic irrigation. Hum to yourself if you're sad.

She goes out. Door slams. Silence.

MCCORQUODALE *reaches for his stick. He hobbles to the trolley.*

MCCORQUODALE. Oh, these contemporary young women. No romantic feelings. Brief and to the point. (*He picks up a hypodermic syringe.*) I must sort out my volumes of photographs. She might be interested in the visual arts. (*He rolls back his sleeve.*) My pictures of dizzy youth in pre-war Berlin. (*He fills the syringe from an ampoule.*) Those off-colour snaps of Frau Goebbels. (*He plunges the needle into his arm, gives a sigh.*) They'd make any man glad he wasn't a Semite.

He puts the hypodermic aside, picks up his stick, hobbles to the sofa. He turns.

CAULFIELD *is outside.*

CAULFIELD (*taking off his hat*). My name is Caulfield. I've broken into your house.

MCCORQUODALE. Did you force a window?

CAULFIELD. The wood was rotten. It gave way.

MCCORQUODALE. It's the worms. I sympathize with the timbers, having harboured the creatures myself.

CAULFIELD *twists his hat between his fingers.*

Come in. (*He returns from the door.*) Switch on the heater. My blood has ice in it. I'm like a penguin about the lumbar regions.

CAULFIELD *enters.*

MCCORQUODALE *sinks on to the sofa.*

CAULFIELD (*switching on the fire*). You shouldn't offer hospitality to rough young men. They might terrorize you.

MCCORQUODALE. It'd be something, wouldn't it? A step in the right direction. A bang on the nose is human contact. I've no money. My valuables amount to one slashed picture and an oleograph of an eighteenth-century lady. It was once spat upon by a maid of my mother's.

CAULFIELD *goes to the table. He picks up the hypodermic, examines boxes of pills, bottles of medicine.*

MCCORQUODALE (*pause, watching*). I've a dicky heart. So the possibility of murder mustn't be ruled out.

CAULFIELD. *puts the poker fireside companion set beside the boarded-up fireplace.*

CAULFIELD. I'm a sleuth. Employed by an irate husband. My cards are on the table.

MCCORQUODALE. I'm not a gambling man. I've seen the sorrow it brings.

CAULFIELD (*pause*). I'd like information about your companion. The little lady with the smile.

MCCORQUODALE. She's a health visitor.

CAULFIELD. Her husband is suspicious. He's a preacher of note. They sell the Bible on the strength of his name.

MCCORQUODALE. She never mentioned a husband. How remiss of her.

CAULFIELD. Adultery is a subject dear to his heart. He knows his onions.

MCCORQUODALE (*staring, aghast*). I haven't committed adultery. I wish to God I could.

CAULFIELD (*pause*). Are you past caring?

MCCORQUODALE. I'm past everything.

CAULFIELD. Have you tried nuts?

MCCORQUODALE. For a time. Indigestion was the only result.

CAULFIELD. Have you ever been birched?

MCCORQUODALE. By experts. I was being flogged for medicinal purposes before you were born. A Swedish gym instructress assured me that, with the correct treatment, I'd be glad to be alive at eighty.

CAULFIELD. What was the treatment?

MCCORQUODALE. Lettuce and sauna baths. Most disappointing.

CAULFIELD *chews his lip.*

CAULFIELD (*pause*). You swear no misconduct has occurred?

MCCORQUODALE. She's given me an enema once or twice. She did it with a sour face, though.

CAULFIELD *puts a cigarette into his mouth. He rolls it between his lips for a few seconds.*

CAULFIELD. How do you earn a living?

MCCORQUODALE. I'm a defrocked priest.

CAULFIELD. A holy man? Is there money in it?

He lights his cigarette with a taper from the pilot light on the electric fire.

MCCORQUODALE. Not any more. I bless a few babes in public parks to keep my hand in.

CAULFIELD *stubs out the taper into the sink. He turns to* MCCORQUODALE.

CAULFIELD. Speak to this woman again at your peril.

MCCORQUODALE. Is her husband up in arms?

CAULFIELD *nods.*

MCCORQUODALE. A jealous husband is no laughing matter.

CAULFIELD. You must give up seeing her.

MCCORQUODALE. That's hard. She's all I have. I'd hate to rely on nursie for company.

CAULFIELD. Isn't she no kind of fun?

MCCORQUODALE. She's a Welshwoman. Addicted to gambling. I go in fear of my life whenever she backs the wrong horse. Between the Derby and the Oaks I lost the skin from both buttocks. She was so careless. Woes nestle on my aged head like gathering swallows. I'm alone. Without faith. Staggering through a cruel and heartless world. (*He shakes with grief.*)

CAULFIELD (*pause*). Have you no family?

MCCORQUODALE. My wife is dead. A relief in many ways. I dreaded going first and having her leering round my death bed.

CAULFIELD. If you're lonely why not visit your wife's grave? You might meet people with similar interests.

MCCORQUODALE. My cellar is a God-forsaken spot.

CAULFIELD (*pause*). Is that where she's buried?

MCCORQUODALE. The actual burial was done by the National Coalboard. (*He faces* CAULFIELD, *earnest.*) She's under a ton of smokeless. I got it at the reduced summer rate.

CAULFIELD *stares. A sudden dawning. He gives a cry of horror and leaps away from* MCCORQUODALE.

CAULFIELD. You're a murderer?

MCCORQUODALE. These 'with it' expressions aren't familiar to me.

CAULFIELD. Wasn't it a happy marriage?

MCCORQUODALE. We bickered occasionally over the nature of God. Nothing more serious.

He takes a box of pills from his pocket.

CAULFIELD. Why did you kill her?

MCCORQUODALE (*swallowing some pills*). We belonged to a salvationist assembly: celebrating the Lord's Supper weekly and baptizing infants at the hinder end. One night I was watching and praying apart from the Brethren when I heard words which are not usual when saints meet. Upon investigation, I found our leader – a man known by the name of Bishop Goodheart – calling to order a number of female penitents on a straw mattress.

CAULFIELD. Was your wife with him?

MCCORQUODALE. She was. Standing in her true colours. And very little else. (*He gives a groan.*) Up to the Devil's tricks. And he was up to hers. Oh, the bacchic hound! And I'd given her my heart. (*He shakes, stricken by grief.*) My fury knew no bounds. I dragged her screaming into our caravanette which was parked in a lay-by. (*Pause.*) She was remarkably quiet on the way home. Later I discovered a broken neck, not a contrite heart, was responsible for her silence. (*Pause.*) I put her under the stairs until a heatwave – disastrous to the nation's water supply – almost undid me.

CAULFIELD (*pause*). What became of the Bishop?

MCCORQUODALE. He banished me for ever. Hurling curses as he ran.

CAULFIELD. Was 'Goodheart' his name in religion?

MCCORQUODALE. Yes.

CAULFIELD. What was his real name?

MCCORQUODALE. He didn't say.

CAULFIELD. Did that surprise you?

MCCORQUODALE. I've learned to accept the irrational in everyday life.

CAULFIELD considers. He shrugs his shoulders.

CAULFIELD. I'd get rid of the body. Take a tip from a member of the criminal classes.

MCCORQUODALE. All classes are criminal today. We live in an age of equality.

CAULFIELD. What are you doing to put yourself in the clear?

MCCORQUODALE. I go on my knees nightly.

CAULFIELD. Prayers won't keep the wolf from the door. (*Pause.*) Had your wife any relatives?

MCCORQUODALE. A father. He's blind.

CAULFIELD. Has he tried to contact you since your wife died?

MCCORQUODALE. No. He sent her a part share in a donkey for Christmas. So I'm in high hopes that he's going mad into the bargain.

CAULFIELD. Was she wealthy?

MCCORQUODALE. I can't touch her cheque book.

CAULFIELD. Why not?

MCCORQUODALE. My hand trembles so.

CAULFIELD (*pause*). Give me an example of her handwriting.
He takes off his coat.
MCCORQUODALE *opens a drawer in the table. He takes out a letter.*

MCCORQUODALE. This is an abusive letter she wrote to a Master of Foxhounds. It was returned wrapped around part of a dog-fox.
He hands the letter to CAULFIELD *by the corner of the page.*
We neither of us finished our haddock that morning.
CAULFIELD *puts the letter on the table. He shines a lamp on to the letter.*

CAULFIELD. Give me her cheque book.
MCCORQUODALE *takes a cheque book from the drawer and gives it to* CAULFIELD.

MCCORQUODALE. Are you a forger?

CAULFIELD. I slept with one once.
He writes a cheque with a flourish and hands it to MCCORQUO-DALE.

MCCORQUODALE (*after glancing at the cheque*). How refreshing to meet a genuine artist in today's world of highly praised fakes.

CAULFIELD *puts on his coat.*

CAULFIELD. I've made it two hundred, to begin with. Can you manage the paying in?

MCCORQUODALE. Oh, yes. It's taking money out that causes the unpleasantness.

CAULFIELD *picks up his hat.*

Don't go yet. I'm like a thing possessed at this time of the evening.

CAULFIELD. I've an appointment at the nude calendar shop. I've been commissioned to do February.

MCCORQUODALE. The *Church Gazette* put out a nice calendar. They might be able to use you. (*He hobbles to the sofa.*) Pass my shawl. I'm quite exhausted. I shan't sleep-walk tonight.

CAULFIELD *wraps him in the shawl.*

MCCORQUODALE. How comfy I am. (*He pinches* CAULFIELD'S *cheek.*) You're a good boy.

CAULFIELD. No. I'm bad.

MCCORQUODALE. As a bad boy you're a complete failure. Goodnight, lovey. Switch off the light.

CAULFIELD *switches off the light.*

See me tomorrow. I welcome intelligent conversation at any hour of the day.

CAULFIELD *goes out. Light falls from the window on to* MCCORQUODALE. *He breathes deeply, content.*

Scene Three

PRINGLE's *study.*

PRINGLE *at his desk. He is opening letters with a paper knife. He reads several. He puts them aside.*

CAULFIELD *enters.*

PRINGLE *wipes his mouth with a nervous gesture.*

PRINGLE. Is the prayer niche vacant?

CAULFIELD. Yes.

PRINGLE. I'll go down there in a bit. Knock up a few for the winning side. Did you speak to my wife?

CAULFIELD. No.

PRINGLE. Why not?

CAULFIELD. She refused to open the door. I heard bathwater running. She'd be naked, I expect.

PRINGLE (*sharply*). Did you imagine her without her clothes?

CAULFIELD. Yes.

PRINGLE (*pause*). I'd rather you didn't. It's no part of the bargain, is it? You were exceeding your duties. (*He returns to reading the letters.*) Make your report.

CAULFIELD. Your wife is engaged on a type of voluntary work. No more compromising than giving a blanket bath.

PRINGLE. Blanket baths are extremely compromising. Did you see her lover?

CAULFIELD. Yes.

PRINGLE. I've heard he lives like an animal. Is that true?

CAULFIELD. He's a defrocked priest. He made no secret of the fact that your wife was his only source of pleasure.

PRINGLE. What a disgraceful admission. He ought to be put in prison and visited by myself.

CAULFIELD. He hasn't infringed your marital rights. Your wife has done no wrong.

PRINGLE. It's too late now to say she's chaste. The fat is in the fire. (*He picks up a sheaf of letters.*) I had a remarkable experience last night. (*He puts the letters into a folder.*) The Lord came to me. I made a Covenant under the memorial arbour in the garden of the Lady of the Wand.

CAULFIELD. One of the Sisterhood?

PRINGLE. A woman of great humility and private fortune.

CAULFIELD. She's wealthy?

PRINGLE. She's a lost sheep with a golden fleece. We speak of her riches in hushed whispers. It means nothing to us.

CAULFIELD. Is she a philanthropist?

PRINGLE. She's a diamond. Lately she demonstrated her belief in Christian charity by building a synagogue on the banks of the Nile.

CAULFIELD. Is she Jewish?

PRINGLE. She's welcome anywhere. In Camden Town they call her Macushla. A very real honour. They accept that woman as a mother without question. In the garden of her detached ranch-type dwelling the vision of the Lord came upon me. I was swept up and the springs of my heart were opened. I made a vow. Taking my cue from Holy Writ. 'My wife must be punished.' The words I spoke weren't rejected or pooh-poohed. I was hoisted high on the shoulders of two priestly personalities. (*Tears roll down his cheeks.*) The Lady of the Wand shook out the glorious strands of her golden hair. There were loud hosannas. Palm branches. I was girt in white. The grounds of that Surrey mansion were ablaze with the ecumenical spirit until the small hours. My commandment was repeated like a catechism: 'Thou shalt not suffer an adultress to live.'

CAULFIELD (*pause*). You can't kill your wife. What about the sixth commandment?

PRINGLE. If she can break the seventh, I can break the sixth. Open that drawer. You'll find a gun.

CAULFIELD. What about the police?

PRINGLE. Christ didn't invite Pilate to the Last Supper. It would be as well to remember that.

He holds out his hand.

CAULFIELD. You can't shoot her. You're a member of the anti-blood-sports.

PRINGLE. That only applies to animals.

Pause.

CAULFIELD *opens the drawer. He takes out a gun.*

CAULFIELD (*handing* PRINGLE *the gun*). The civil arm will grasp the wrong end of the stick.

PRINGLE. No more argument. The humble and the meek are thirsting for blood.

He fires the gun and goes off.

Scene Four

MCCORQUODALE's *room.*

MCCORQUODALE *sitting in the armchair, a blanket over him.*

TESSA *enters with a large handbag. Pause. She puts the handbag down.*

TESSA (*pulling off her gloves*). Do you have anything to do with the old blind man who looks after the donkeys?

MCCORQUODALE. Is he a celibate?

TESSA. His donkeys are. It's part of their charter.

She takes off her coat and hangs it up.

Somebody put me on to him. He's supposed to be little Valerie's father. I found him in the yard. He was sending one of his charges away to be trained. Val was married he claims. (*Pause.*) Was your wife an amateur singer/accordionist?

MCCORQUODALE. She used to kick up a racket in her bath.

TESSA. This man says you married his only daughter.

MCCORQUODALE (*pause*). He's losing his wits. Donkey-minders are a byword for lunacy.

TESSA. What was your wife's name.

MCCORQUODALE. I called her Buzz.

TESSA. That was her pet name. You'd no right to be so familiar.

Silence. They face one another.

MCCORQUODALE *shivers. He stands abruptly to his feet.*

MCCORQUODALE. I must have a jab. My nerves are shot to pieces by your questions.

He hobbles to the table and rolls back his sleeve.

TESSA (*taking off her hat*). Where is she?

MCCORQUODALE *picks up the hypodermic syringe.*

What has happened to her?

MCCORQUODALE (*filling the syringe*). She packed her bags. Vanished into the night.

TESSA. Where to?

MCCORQUODALE. A nunnery. (*He injects the drug into his vein.*)

TESSA. I can find a list of recent vows taken in the trade paper of the monastic orders.

MCCORQUODALE. It's sold only to the pure in heart, and so, I'm afraid, has a limited circulation. You may have difficulty in obtaining a copy.

    He hobbles back to the sofa.

TESSA. I shall place an order with my bookseller. Why did she leave? Had you made life impossible?

MCCORQUODALE. Yes.

TESSA. You're a terrible tease. Have you always been like this?

MCCORQUODALE. I was even naughtier when I was young. The Unter Den Linden used to buzz with gossip as I passed by.

TESSA. The albums of photographs are most unsavoury. I'll say that to your face.

    She opens her handbag and takes out a parcel.

I've repaired the rent in your elastic bandage. (*She hands him the parcel.*) Go and get into the bath. I've brought my plastic apron.

    CAULFIELD *enters.*

CAULFIELD (*to* TESSA). May I speak to you? It's very urgent.

TESSA (*to* MCCORQUODALE). I shall give you post-sponge attention if we have time. Ring when you're ready.

    MCCORQUODALE *hobbles to the door.*

    TESSA *turns to her handbag.*

    MCCORQUODALE *exits.*

    TESSA *takes a plastic apron from her handbag.*

Who are you? And what do you want? I'm frightfully busy.

    She shakes out the apron.

CAULFIELD. Your husband is outside. He's going to murder you.

    TESSA *ties on the apron.*

TESSA. You must be mistaken. We celebrate our wooden wedding in a fortnight.

PRINGLE enters. He carries a gun. His face is pale.

PRINGLE (*to* TESSA). You've strayed from the paths of righteousness. I'm going to kill you.

TESSA. You'll be prosecuted. You haven't got a licence.

PRINGLE. Make your peace with God. On your knees. Pray, you sinner.

He advances, lifts the gun.

You'll soon be burning in some low, hot nook of Satan!

PRINGLE points the gun at TESSA's heart. She backs away. Screams, suddenly afraid.

CAULFIELD picks up a bottle and crashes it over PRINGLE's head.

PRINGLE drops the gun and falls to the ground.

TESSA (*pause, to* CAULFIELD). You want to be careful. You might hurt somebody.

CAULFIELD. Get a cold compress. Sponge his face.

TESSA goes out above table.

TESSA. Who put him up to this?

CAULFIELD. The Fathers of Love.

TESSA goes to the sink. She wets a towel.

Half his postbag this morning was from 'A Well-Wisher'.

TESSA. I know the name, but the face escapes me.

She returns with a towel. Kneels. Wipes PRINGLE's forehead.

PRINGLE revives.

He stares at TESSA.

PRINGLE. You're still alive? I've broken my vow. I'm unworthy of the name of Christian.

TESSA. What vow?

PRINGLE takes a newspaper from his pocket.

PRINGLE. The official organ has printed the text of my sermon with pictures and hostile comment. (*He opens the paper and shows it to* TESSA.) See the headline – (*Points.*) 'Pastor speaks his mind.' (*He lowers his finger.*) And underneath in heavy type: 'Sinners, stay away from Jesus.'

TESSA. Your words make powerful reading. (*She puts the paper aside.*)

PRINGLE. How shall I face the Lady of the Wand?

> PRINGLE *wrings his hands.*

PRINGLE. What shall I do now? To whom shall I turn?

> *A bell rings.*

CAULFIELD (*pause*). Perhaps we could pray.

PRINGLE. I'd be obliged if you'd treat this matter with due seriousness.

> *The bell rings again.*

CAULFIELD (*pause*). Why not forgive her?

PRINGLE. I won't tolerate forgiveness. It's a thing of the past.

CAULFIELD. Love thy neighbour.

PRINGLE. The man who said that was crucified by his.

> *The bell rings.*
>
> TESSA *goes to her handbag. She takes out a pair of rubber gloves.*

TESSA. Couldn't you just pretend to have murdered me? To save face?

PRINGLE. What an immoral suggestion.

TESSA. I could stay here with my elderly gentleman.

> *She goes to the cupboard and takes out a tin of talcum powder.*

CAULFIELD (*to* PRINGLE). You could say she'd gone to Australia. That's a synonym for death in the popular mind.

PRINGLE (*to* TESSA). She's shown no preference for the Colonies. Not even under hypnosis.

> TESSA *shakes powder into the rubber gloves.*

TESSA. During a mental disturbance at the age of fifteen I begged to be taken to Adelaide. My condition worsened after making the request.

> *She puts the powder back into the cupboard.*

CAULFIELD (*to* PRINGLE). Say she's on a surf-riding holiday. The quiet culture of the outback fascinates her. She takes up residence. And, after a decent interval, is swept out to sea on a rubber raft.

PRINGLE (*pause, to* TESSA). Would that suit you?

TESSA takes a scarf from her handbag and ties back her hair.

TESSA. It isn't the kind of death I'd hoped for. However, as long as I was fully dressed and had recently attended some place of worship I won't withhold my consent.

She rolls back her sleeves.

PRINGLE. The announcement can be made at my Blessing of the Spotless. I'll say you've made a journey to a far country. They'll think I've done you in and pray for your soul.

TESSA. Can I rely on that?

PRINGLE. Certainly. The Brethren are men of goodwill.

TESSA pulls on the rubber gloves.

TESSA. You'll find the manuscript of my history of our movement in the top drawer of my bureau. I'd like you to arrange publication to coincide with the news of my death. The photographs, taken by flashlight at our secret meetings, could be omitted if the publisher so desired.

PRINGLE. I'll see to it. Anything else?

TESSA. Remember never to smile again. It might arouse suspicion if you did.

PRINGLE. That'll be difficult. I've a naturally cheerful disposition. (*He kisses her cheek.*) You'll be sadly missed.

He picks up his hat and newspaper.

This'll be worth a million in publicity. Make a bit of a splash in the weekend Press. 'Vengeance is Mine', says 'No Nonsense Parson.' These human interest stories can increase a congregation a thousandfold.

He puts on his hat, opens the door, turns.

Trust in the Lord. We shall meet in the glory of the Infinite Morning. (*He nods and goes out.*)

The bell rings.

TESSA. I shall pretend to be Mr McCorquodale's wife. Valerie wouldn't mind. We've won prizes together.

CAULFIELD. Was she a personal friend?

TESSA. She kept her marriage dark. We'd lost touch to that extent. Her father is a blind animal lover.

CAULFIELD. Is he mad?

TESSA. Yes, I think he is. It makes talking to him very difficult.

    MCCORQUODALE enters wearing a ragged bathrobe.

MCCORQUODALE. I've been ringing and ringing. I'm out of my rubbers.

TESSA. Where are your keys? I'm going to pose as your wife.

MCCORQUODALE. Oh, you dreadful up-to-the-minute people with your unhealthy pranks.

    *TESSA takes a bunch of keys from the pocket of MCCORQUO-
DALE's bathrobe.*

TESSA. Do these keys speak for themselves?

MCCORQUODALE. You're not to open doors without my permission.

    TESSA puts the keys into the pocket of her apron.

TESSA. I'm going to make a tour of inspection. Follow me.

    She goes out.

CAULFIELD (*to* MCCORQUODALE). You should've got rid of the corpse. (*Pause.*) Did you cash the cheque?

    MCCORQUODALE hobbles to the sofa and lifts a cushion. He hands several notes to CAULFIELD.

CAULFIELD (*putting the money away*). I'll board up the cellar.

    He takes off his jacket and goes out.

    MCCORQUODALE hobbles to the table.

    He picks up a pill box.

    A bell rings.

MCCORQUODALE. Oh, my poor heart and kidneys are fluttering like love-birds.

    He shakes pills into the palm of his hand and swallows them. A bell rings.

            (*End of Part One.*)

PART TWO

Scene Five

PRINGLE's *study. Morning.*
PRINGLE *shaving with an electric razor.*
CAULFIELD *enters carrying a small parcel.*

PRINGLE (*over his shoulder*). Is that for me?
CAULFIELD. Delivered by hand.
PRINGLE. Open it. Was it a woman who brought it?
  He switches off the razor and blows the hair from the blades.
CAULFIELD. She drove up in a Rolls. Gave the Commissionaire a quid. (*He unties the string on the parcel.*) You've had several mysterious women visitors lately.
PRINGLE. It's my unsavoury reputation. Attracts them like flies.
  He puts the razor away and takes off his dressing-gown.
When rumour got around that I'd murdered my wife, my phone never stopped ringing. I had calls at every hour of the day and night. All from women making outrageous proposals.
  He opens a leather case and takes out a brush and comb.
I've a different set of handmaidens for each of our ceremonies. (*He combs his hair.*) I'm ex-directory now.
CAULFIELD. I've read your book.
PRINGLE. *Hard Looks At God?*
CAULFIELD. It pulled no punches.
PRINGLE. They're filming *Tales of an Urban Hermit.* The proceeds will help to maintain and extend the ministry. (*He puts the brush aside.*) At the moment I'm caught up in politics. The wife of a top-ranking Russian diplomat came to me at the prayer centre and begged to be allowed to betray the Marxist cause.
CAULFIELD. You admitted her to your flock?

PRINGLE. I had no choice. She's heavy-breasted and sensuous. I didn't want to trigger off a third world war.

CAULFIELD *has opened the parcel. He takes out a jewel box; opens it and removes a ring.*

Ah! Is there a card?

CAULFIELD *picks up a card.*

CAULFIELD (*reading the card*). 'From a fervent admirer of Western Civilization.' (*He puts the card aside.*) Lenin would turn in his grave.

PRINGLE *puts on the ring.*

PRINGLE. I'm proud of the way she's accepted the life of the spirit. It hasn't been easy for her. She did two years in a forced labour camp for throwing caution to the winds at a swimming gala. You don't have to explain to her the advantages of living in a free society. Pass my jacket.

CAULFIELD *hands him his coat and helps him into it.*

Fifty guineas it cost the Russian people. New members are asked to indicate, by an immediate sacrificial gift, their partnership with the Brotherhood.

He opens a leather case and takes out a silver-backed clothes-brush. This was a present from a woman journalist. She wanted the privilege of kissing hands that'd taken human life. It's so rare in her circle.

CAULFIELD *takes the brush and takes a letter from his pocket.*

CAULFIELD. This is for you. It was handed in early this morning.

PRINGLE. Open it.

CAULFIELD. It's confidential.

PRINGLE *takes the letter. He opens it. He reads in silence.*

PRINGLE (*putting the letter aside*). It's the product of a diseased mind. Public figures are subject to this kind of thing.

CAULFIELD *picks up the letter.*

CAULFIELD. Does it accuse you of murdering your wife?

PRINGLE. No. It says I didn't murder her. There's no end to the malice of people.

PRINGLE *throws down the letter and* CAULFIELD *picks it up.*

CAULFIELD (*reading the letter*). It claims your trendy success is a fraud. He's called Paterson. He's a crime reporter. He's calling on you for proof. (*He puts the letter down.*) Perhaps he's jealous of your success with women.

PRINGLE. The solution lies in his hands. He must murder his own wife.

CAULFIELD. Maybe he isn't married.

PRINGLE. Anyone can afford a licence.

> *He picks a Cologne bottle up from the desk, and pours Cologne on to his hands.*

I shall seek professional advice.

CAULFIELD. Who from?

PRINGLE. My lawyers. It's a clear case of a private citizen being persecuted by the Press. It's defamation of character. I'll take them to court. (*He puts the stopper into the Cologne bottle.*)

CAULFIELD. For saying you're innocent? You'd never get away with it. There must be hundreds of innocent people in the country.

> PRINGLE *picks up his watch and winds it.*
> *Pause.*

You'll have to knuckle under. Provide him with evidence of your guilt.

PRINGLE (*putting on his watch*). A bloodstained sheet?

CAULFIELD. Where would you get the blood?

PRINGLE. One of our altar servers works in a blood bank. She'd know how to lay hands on a couple of pints.

CAULFIELD. You'd need a body.

PRINGLE. Are mortuaries in the Classified Trades Directory?

> *He turns to the telephone book.*

CAULFIELD. A disappearing corpse would hit the headlines. They'd put two and two together.

PRINGLE (*pause*). What's to be done? Think of the scandal. I'd never live it down if I were found innocent.

CAULFIELD (*pause*). You don't need a complete body. An arm would do. (*Pause.*) Or a head.

PRINGLE. Where could I get a human head? Even Harrods wouldn't accept the order.

CAULFIELD. Is there anywhere I could get a meat cleaver?

Long pause.

PRINGLE. I'm part owner of the Pixies' Den. Try the kitchen after two o'clock. (*Pause.*) You won't strike down any member of the staff, will you? They're impossible to replace.

CAULFIELD. I'll respect private property.

He picks up his hat.

I shall take a stroll in London's country. Commune with nature.

PRINGLE. You're not going head-hunting in Epping Forest?

CAULFIELD. I shall look in on your late wife and her saintly lover. You can arrange a meeting with the gentlemen of the Press.

PRINGLE. You'll provide evidence of murder?

CAULFIELD. Where can I contact you this afternoon?

PRINGLE. At the Russian Embassy. I'm cementing East-West relations till four.

CAULFIELD. I'll give you a ring.

He turns at the door.

Be seeing you.

He goes out.

PRINGLE *picks up the letter. He glances at it and goes to the telephone.*

Scene Six

MCCORQUODALE's *room.*
Neater. A flowered cloth on the table. A bowl of fruit centre.
MCCORQUODALE *reading a newspaper, a rug over his knees.*
TESSA *enters with a shopping bag, carrying a sheaf of circulars. She puts down the shopping and glances through the circulars.*

TESSA. They're having a sale of damaged carpets. (*She throws the circulars into the wastebin.*) The fires do get at these firms, don't they?

She takes the shopping from the bag.

I heard noises from the cellar. Is it open?

MCCORQUODALE (*without looking up*). Young Caulfield is down there. (*He folds his newspaper.*) Your husband is in the news again.

TESSA. Is he?

MCCORQUODALE. Questions are being asked about your murder.

TESSA. I never think about it now.

MCCORQUODALE. You were upset at first though, weren't you?

TESSA. Well, nobody likes to be done in. It stands to reason.

MCCORQUODALE. He's made a lot of enemies. The Convocation of Canterbury are in a huff. They'll come for him one of these days.

TESSA puts the shopping away. She folds up the shopping bag and puts it into a drawer.

TESSA. They came for little Valerie's father last night.

MCCORQUODALE takes off his reading glasses and puts them into a case.

MCCORQUODALE. Recent figures show that the mad will outnumber the sane by the turn of the century.

TESSA. They never publish any comforting statistics, do they? These computers are always out to frighten people.

CAULFIELD enters wearing jeans and a singlet vest. His hands and face are smeared with coaldust. He carries a meat cleaver and a human hand, severed above the wrist, wrapped in sacking.

TESSA (*to MCCORQUODALE*). I've bought a cake.

MCCORQUODALE. Is it an anniversary?

TESSA. No. It's a Dundee.

She takes a cakestand from the cupboard and puts a doily upon it.

CAULFIELD puts the meat cleaver aside.

CAULFIELD (*to MCCORQUODALE*). I couldn't get her head off. It must be glued on.

MCCORQUODALE. She was always a headstrong woman.

CAULFIELD. I had to take a hand instead.

TESSA (*to* CAULFIELD, *over her shoulder*). Do you want to wash your hands before tea?

CAULFIELD. Yes.

TESSA picks up a teapot and goes out.

CAULFIELD goes to the sink. He washes the hand and his own.

MCCORQUODALE. How was she looking?

CAULFIELD. Black. And very uncomely.

MCCORQUODALE. She'll be mistaken for coloured in Heaven.

CAULFIELD. Do they let them in there?

MCCORQUODALE. One hears conflicting reports.

CAULFIELD dries his hands.

CAULFIELD. Is there a box to carry it away in?

MCCORQUODALE rises and searches. He picks up the cake tin and hands it to CAULFIELD.

MCCORQUODALE. Use that. Give it back when you've finished.

CAULFIELD puts the hand into the cake tin and puts the lid on the tin.

TESSA enters with the teapot. The kettle boils.

CAULFIELD goes to the table. He puts the cake tin beside his chair.

TESSA pours water into the teapot.

CAULFIELD (*to* MCCORQUODALE). D'you want this?

MCCORQUODALE. Her watch?

CAULFIELD. It came off once the wrist was severed. No proper support, see.

TESSA brings the teapot to the table and cuts the cake.

TESSA (*to* CAULFIELD). They're looking for a bright youngster to represent Britain. You ought to go in for it.

She puts a piece of cake on to a plate and hands it to MCCOR-QUODALE. *She does the same to* CAULFIELD.

The young woman by the bridge has left her husband.

CAULFIELD puts the watch on.

Rows over a snake. (*She pours tea.*) She was looking forward to a rabbit or a guinea-pig. Something for baby to play with. (*She hands a cup of tea to* MCCORQUODALE.) Then he tells her he's put a deposit on a five-feet-long python. (*She hands tea to* CAULFIELD.) She was horrified.

She sits, picks up her own tea.

Isn't it wicked, though, allowing a snake to jeopardize your marriage?

CAULFIELD *reaches for the sugar bowl.*

TESSA *hands it to him.*

Is that a new watch?

CAULFIELD. Yes. (*He puts sugar into his tea.*)

TESSA. It's a lady's. (*She drinks.*)

CAULFIELD. Yes.

TESSA. You want to be careful. People are funny about that sort of thing.

CAULFIELD *puts the sugar bowl aside. Pause.*

Let me see.

CAULFIELD *hesitates. He holds out his arm.*

TESSA (*pause*). Take it off. Give me a look.

CAULFIELD *takes off the watch. He hands it to her. She examines it.*

TESSA (*pause*). This is little Val's watch!

MCCORQUODALE. It's a well-known make. Could be anybody's. (*He dips his cake into his tea.*)

TESSA. No. She had everything individually styled. See! (*She shows* MCCORQUODALE *the back of the watch.*) Her personal emblem – a ballet girl blowing a kiss. She had it on all her belongings. (*To* CAULFIELD.) Where did you get this?

CAULFIELD. I found it. In the street.

TESSA. This has decided me. Something terrible has happened. (*She opens her handbag, and puts the watch into it.*) I shall take my troubles to the Police.

CAULFIELD. Haven't they got enough of their own?

TESSA. Val had a lot of friends in the Police. She used to sing songs in praise of Authority at her concerts.

She puts the cake on to a tray and clears the table. She puts the cups and saucers on to the tray.

She may be a prisoner. I was once touched on a tube train. Women aren't safe today. They should bring back the harem. We've got to be protected.

She puts the tray on the sideboard and looks about her, puzzled. She comes back to the table. Pause. She sees the cake tin and stoops to pick it up.

CAULFIELD. No! I want that tin!

TESSA (*indignant*). So do I. The cake will go stale. (*She takes the tin to the kitchen.*)

    MCCORQUODALE *and* CAULFIELD *exchange glances.*

    MCCORQUODALE *takes a box of pills from his pocket, shakes two into the palm of his hand and swallows them.*

    TESSA *wraps the cake in a piece of foil.*

    CAULFIELD *approaches the sink.*

CAULFIELD. Don't open that tin.

TESSA. Why not?

CAULFIELD. I bought a plastic hand from a Novelty shop. I put it into your cake tin.

    TESSA *turns from wrapping up the cake.*

TESSA. That was very silly of you. Neville down the road is in trouble of that sort. His little playmate had a convulsion. Her mother is putting it into the papers. (*She lifts the tin.*) I'm glad you had the sense to tell me.

    She takes off the lid and looks in. She gives a shriek of horror.

(*Gasping with fright.*) It's real.

MCCORQUODALE. Plastic.

TESSA. It's real. (*Trembling.*) I can spot plastic fingers a mile off.

    She turns to the sink and pours glass of water. She drinks.

A human hand in a Dundee cake tin. Whose is it? Do we know?

MCCORQUODALE. He found it in the long grass.

CAULFIELD. It'd been left by a courting couple.

MCCORQUODALE. It answers to the name of 'Billy'.

TESSA *puts the glass down.*

TESSA. Was the watch with it? (*Pause.*) I'm seeing the Sergeant at Val's station.

She reaches for her coat.

MCCORQUODALE. I won't have you going to the Police. I've criminal tendencies.

CAULFIELD. He's been using the alias Leonard Field to obtain preferential treatment at a West End store.

MCCORQUODALE. I've a roomful of stolen footwear downstairs.

TESSA. Is that why I'm never allowed into the cellar?

MCCORQUODALE *turns. He picks up a bottle of smelling salts and holds them under his nose.*

What has happened to your wife?

MCCORQUODALE. She was taken up to Heaven. In a fiery chariot. Driven by an angel.

TESSA. What nonsense. Valerie would never accept a lift from a stranger. (*She turns to the door.*) I'm going down to gauge the full extent of your crimes.

She goes out.

MCCORQUODALE (*pause, weary*). In the closet you'll find a rope.

CAULFIELD *opens the cupboard.*

I bought it a month ago. I intended hanging myself.

CAULFIELD. What stopped you?

MCCORQUODALE. The weather turned nice.

CAULFIELD *takes the rope from the cupboard.*

MCCORQUODALE. Tess is a member of the Book of the Month club. Sound in wind and limb. You'll have to manage on your own. (*He hobbles round the chair.*) I'm much too frail.

Screams from below.

CAULFIELD *runs the rope through his fingers.*

The door bursts open. TESSA *enters. Tears in her eyes.*

TESSA. Oh, poor little Valerie. Who did that to her? (*She sobs.*)

CAULFIELD *loops the rope into a noose and slips it around* TESSA's *throat from behind. He drags her choking to the floor.*

Scene Seven

PRINGLE's *study. Night.*

PRINGLE *chanting.*

CAULFIELD. Did you have your interview, with the Press?

PRINGLE. With the Press?

CAULFIELD. You established your guilt?

    PRINGLE *closes the bible.*

PRINGLE. He was an atheist. He took one look into that cake tin and fainted. These people without religion are broken reeds.

    He stands, walks to the mirror, straightens his tie.

When he came to, he kept asking how I could face God with a murder on my conscience. Which is ridiculous coming from a man who doesn't believe in God.

CAULFIELD. And anyway you haven't done a murder.

PRINGLE. Precisely. It takes no effort at all to face someone who doesn't exist with a murder that hasn't happened.

CAULFIELD. Did he go quietly?

PRINGLE. I got one of the Fathers of Love to throw him out. (*He puts on his coat.*)

CAULFIELD (*pause*). I'm having trouble with your wife. You ought to know how things are.

PRINGLE. I'll send a bunch of flowers by special courier.

CAULFIELD. I don't know how we're going to keep her quiet.

    PRINGLE *swings round, faces* CAULFIELD, *startled.*

PRINGLE. It wasn't her hand?

CAULFIELD. No. (*Pause.*) McCorquodale murdered his wife. It was her hand.

PRINGLE. She can have it back. It's not on permanent loan.

CAULFIELD. She was Valerie Fenton before her decease.

PRINGLE. Has my wife seen the body?

CAULFIELD. Yes.

PRINGLE. What happened?

CAULFIELD. She seemed genuinely upset.

PRINGLE. Well, Valerie was an old school-friend. They were very attached. She used to attend our meetings. Her salvation was assured.

>CAULFIELD *opens a drawer in the desk and takes out the gun. He holds it out to* PRINGLE. PRINGLE *shrinks away.*

What are you asking me to do?

CAULFIELD. Kill your wife.

PRINGLE. I've already killed her once. I couldn't do it again. I'd be a murderer.

CAULFIELD. You are a murderer. In the eyes of the world. I'm only asking you to live up to your public image.

PRINGLE. That's a terrible thing to ask a man to do.

CAULFIELD (*pause*). Unless you kill your wife she'll accuse you of not being her murderer.

>*He takes* PRINGLE *by the arm and shoves the gun into his pocket.*

You're a clergyman. It's time you practised what you preach.

>*He leads* PRINGLE *to the door.* PRINGLE *stops. He turns round.*

PRINGLE. We mustn't forget the hand.

>CAULFIELD *goes back to the desk. Picks up the cake tin. He returns to* PRINGLE.

We've a short-sighted tea lady. I don't want her handing that around in the mid-afternoon break.

>*They go out.*

Scene Eight

MCCORQUODALE's *room.*
TESSA *bound hand and foot, strapped to a chair.*
MCCORQUODALE *enters, dragging a large cabin trunk.*

TESSA. Untie me.

MCCORQUODALE. You'd escape.

TESSA. I'll forget what I've seen.

MCCORQUODALE. A mutilated corpse isn't something that'd slip my memory. But you young people are heartless. The whole post-war generation.

TESSA. Set me free.

MCCORQUODALE. I'm your gaoler. I can't possibly aid your escape. This isn't a State prison, you know.

He drags the trunk to the centre of the room and sits, exhausted by the effort.

Oh, I'll never survive a second murder. There's so much work involved.

He picks up his inhaler and inhales deeply. He tries to force back the catch on the trunk.

I'll ring nursie tomorrow. I need one of her medical romps.

He tugs at the catch unsuccessfully.

TESSA (*pause*). Let me help you. My feet are bound. I shan't run away.

MCCORQUODALE (*stands, picks up a pair of scissors*). It's most irregular. This is to be your coffin. It's tantamount to the undertaker employing the corpse.

He cuts the bonds on TESSA'S *wrists.*

TESSA (*kneeling*). What a lovely old trunk. Is it antique?

MCCORQUODALE *puts the scissors out of reach.*

MCCORQUODALE. It was purchased from a man who sailed to the Far East in search of adventure. He died of a skin complaint in Rangoon.

TESSA *forces back the clasp.*

It's full of souvenirs of happier days. My childhood was idyllic. I had the run of a Convent until I was eight. And then the Reverend Mother decided, quite wisely, that I was a threat to the chastity of her flock.

TESSA *pushes back the lid.*

So I was turfed out. The first of life's many bitter disappointments. I'd already decided, you see, to take the veil.

He kneels beside TESSA. *He lifts a book from the trunk.*

A history of the Ursulines written by an ex-member of the

Order. This was smuggled into the Convent and read against Mother's wishes. It contains many errors of doctrine.

He wipes dust from the book and puts it aside.

TESSA takes several objects from the trunk, dolls, a stuffed bird, a bundle of letters, a Cardinal's biretta. She lifts out a small framed painting and holds it up.

TESSA. A watercolour.

MCCORQUODALE. It was my intention to represent – in a symbolic fashion – the Christian Church.

TESSA. A bird of prey carrying an olive branch. You've put the matter in a nutshell.

MCCORQUODALE wipes a tear from his eye.

MCCORQUODALE. These mementoes of a blameless life contrast sadly with my present predicament. (*He weeps.*)

TESSA. Why did you kill poor Val?

MCCORQUODALE. All my misfortunes stem from a self-styled bishop. That wretched lackey in the Almighty's house has brought my grey hairs in sorrow to the grave.

He sobs, uncontrollably.

TESSA picks up a dagger from the bottom of the trunk and cuts through her bonds. She stands to her feet.

Pause.

You're free?

TESSA. I found a dagger at the bottom of the trunk.

MCCORQUODALE (*standing, reaching out*). My knife for circumcising the Faithful.

TESSA. You've been a Muslim, too?

MCCORQUODALE. Well, in Algiers during the depression. I had to live. Don't betray me.

He staggers towards her, a hand to his heart.

TESSA. Truth must win. Otherwise life is impossible.

She turns to the door and opens it.

PRINGLE and CAULFIELD are outside.

They enter, pushing TESSA aside.

CAULFIELD stands by the door.

PRINGLE (*to* CAULFIELD). Who is that man?

CAULFIELD. Your wife's lover.

MCCORQUODALE (*to* TESSA). Who is this man?

TESSA. My husband.

PRINGLE (*to* CAULFIELD). His name in God is Brother Sinceri-
tas. He badly injured me whilst I was engaged in a holy act.

MCCORQUODALE (*to* TESSA). This is my arch-enemy. I endured
humiliation at his hands in the greenwood. This is Bishop
Goodheart. Take my dying curse. You diabolic crumb from the
table of the damned!

He slaps PRINGLE *across the face.*

PRINGLE. I'll teach you to strike a man of admitted charity.

He seizes MCCORQUODALE *by the throat and shakes him.*

MCCORQUODALE *gasps with fury. He attempts to escape. They
fall about, buffeting one another.*

CAULFIELD (*pause*). What an amazing sight – two men of God
trying to throttle one another.

MCCORQUODALE *breaks free. He staggers to the table,
wheezing and spluttering.*

MCCORQUODALE. You ecclesiastical poltroon. You won't escape
your just deserts. I'll see every soul in Christendom knows that
the blood on your hands is a fraud.

He holds his inhaler to his mouth and takes deep gulps.

PRINGLE. You have no proof.

MCCORQUODALE *puts the inhaler aside. He pulls* TESSA *to him.*

MCCORQUODALE. Here's my proof. I'll produce your wife like a
rabbit from a Shakespearian hat.

Pause. PRINGLE *picks up the knife from the floor.*

PRINGLE. I'll have you yet. You anti-Christian pimp and witches'
comfort.

MCCORQUODALE. Being a man of goodwill I'm well prepared for
violence.

He transforms his stick into a dagger and prods PRINGLE *to a
distance.*

TESSA. You mustn't cause trouble. I shall deny that I'm alive.

MCCORQUODALE. I'll kill you, then.

He grabs her, and holds the sword to her breast.

TESSA. You can't destroy me. I'm the evidence.

PRINGLE. You can't expose his guilt without establishing my innocence.

> CAULFIELD *takes the gun from* PRINGLE's *coat and fires*
>
> TESSA, PRINGLE *and* MCCORQUODALE *scatter. Pause.*

TESSA *(running behind sofa).* Who's he after?

PRINGLE. You.

> CAULFIELD *fires again.* PRINGLE *disappears.*
>
> TESSA *throws the meat cleaver at* CAULFIELD. *It crashes among the medicine bottles, and drops down beside* MCCORQUO-DALE.

MCCORQUODALE. Oh, be careful. My pills.

> *Pills rain down upon him from the upset boxes. He crouches under the table.*
>
> CAULFIELD *approaches the screen and pulls it away.*
>
> TESSA *is trapped. She shrinks away.*

TESSA. No. Don't touch me. Please, let me alone.

> CAULFIELD *pushes the gun into her face. He pulls the trigger. Click of barrel turning. He pulls the trigger again. Click of barrel turning.* CAULFIELD *examines the gun.*

CAULFIELD. It's empty.

> TESSA *gives a cry of relief and bursts into tears.*

TESSA. Somebody is going to pay for Val's death.

MCCORQUODALE *(crawling from under the table).* Oh, my Lord Bishop, you should never have taken on that extra female penitent.

PRINGLE. You should've kept your evil temper under control.

MCCORQUODALE. You were teaching her tricks not even a grandmother should know.

TESSA. Was he misbehaving with Val?

MCCORQUODALE. He was making a breach in the seventh commandment and my wife. *(To* PRINGLE.) That's foul churching, Bishop.

TESSA (*to* PRINGLE). How long had it been going on?

PRINGLE. The spirit of the Brotherhood entered Valerie about a year prior to her death.

TESSA. How could she sink so low?

CAULFIELD. He got in under her guard. It's a familiar technique of dance-hall seducers.

TESSA. She was so well brought up.

CAULFIELD. It's the well brought up ones that go first. As every small-time Romeo knows.

TESSA. Stealing my husband and concealing the fact that she had one of her own. It's scandalous behaviour.

PRINGLE *picks up* TESSA's *coat. He holds it out for her.*

PRINGLE. This will have to come out at the trial?

TESSA. What trial? She tempted the Lord. It would be blasphemous to raise a hand in her defence. (*She buttons her coat.*)

The three MEN *exchange looks.*

TESSA *goes to the mirror. She puts on her hat.*

PRINGLE. None of this must leak out. You realize that, don't you? The Brethren would be ruined.

MCCORQUODALE. What about the corpse?

CAULFIELD. I'll take it to a deserted warehouse. (*To* PRINGLE.) You can identify her as your wife. Recognize her from some familiar article of jewellery.

TESSA (*turning from the mirror*). Take my badge from the Legion of Believers.

She unpins the badge from her coat and hands it to CAULFIELD. (*To* PRINGLE.) What will happen to me?

PRINGLE. You'll remain as the wife of Bishop Bonnyface. (*To* MCCORQUODALE.) I'll confirm the appointment later.

TESSA (*to* MCCORQUODALE). Shall I be your wife in name only?

MCCORQUODALE. Unless a miracle occurs.

CAULFIELD. I must have transport for the body.

PRINGLE. You can't use my van. It has 'God' printed on it.

TESSA. Use our portable chapel. It has a detachable altar.

CAULFIELD. I'll have to be compensated.

PRINGLE. In what way?

CAULFIELD. Taken on to God's payroll.

PRINGLE. We use volunteer labour in the vineyard of the Lord.

CAULFIELD. Have you ever been blackmailed?

PRINGLE. You'd be well advised not to try your tricks here. We're Children of Light. Not criminals. Tangle with the Prince of Peace and you'll find a knife in your back.

MCCORQUODALE. That's quite true. I myself once threw holy water in a woman's face. Marred her for life.

CAULFIELD. I was merely demonstrating the vulnerability of your position.

PRINGLE. I'll arrange for you to be shown the priestly path. You're a photographer's model?

CAULFIELD. Yes.

PRINGLE. I'm publishing my life story in picture form. I might use you to illustrate 'Glad Tidings'. (*To* MCCORQUODALE.) Was your wife given a Christian burial?

MCCORQUODALE. No.

PRINGLE. We must repair the omission.

    CAULFIELD *picks up the cake tin.*

CAULFIELD. We've the hand here. Can't we take the rest of her as read?

PRINGLE. Yes. That would be in order. (*He takes the tin.*) Pass me a book – and a bell.

    TESSA *goes to the bookcase.*

    CAULFIELD *opens the cake tin. He looks in. He takes out a human hand.*

    TESSA *draws a horrified breath.*

    MCCORQUODALE *flinches.*

    CAULFIELD *lifts out the hand. He breaks off a finger with a sharp crack.*

CAULFIELD. This isn't a real hand. It's a fake.

    PRINGLE *hurries across. He examines the hand.*

PRINGLE. Paterson. He's deceived me. Oh, the malice of the heathen is terrifying.

MCCORQUODALE. What would he want with a human hand?

TESSA. He might use it as a paperweight.

CAULFIELD (*to* PRINGLE). He's got evidence. We're sunk.

Knocking on the door.

The door opens. Two MEN *enter.*

FIRST MAN. We are plain-clothed Police Officers. We've a warrant to search these premises. (*Shows warrant.*) Who can identify the remains of the woman in the cellar?

PRINGLE. She was my wife.

FIRST MAN. Did you kill her?

PRINGLE. She was an adulteress.

FIRST MAN. You'd better come along with us. (*To his* COMPANION.) Book the others as accessories.

MCCORQUODALE. Shame. Shame. It'll be banner headlines. The daughters of the Philistines will rejoice.

PRINGLE. Let us go to prison. Some angel will release us from our place of confinement.

The door is opened.

Do not weep. Everything works out in accordance with the divine Will.

The POLICE *lead them out.*

What the Butler Saw

'Surely we're all mad people, and they
Whom we think are, are not.'

– *The Revenger's Tragedy*

The first London performance of *What the Butler Saw* was given at the Queen's Theatre by Lewenstein-Delfont Productions Ltd and H. M. Tennent Ltd on 5 March 1969, with the following cast in order of appearance:

DR PRENTICE	Stanley Baxter
GERALDINE BARCLAY	Julia Foster
MRS PRENTICE	Coral Browne
NICHOLAS BECKETT	Hayward Morse
DR RANCE	Ralph Richardson
SERGEANT MATCH	Peter Bayliss

Directed by Robert Chetwyn
Designed by Hutchinson Scott

What the Butler Saw was revived as part of the 'Joe Orton Festival' at the Royal Court Theatre, London, on 16 July 1975, subsequently transferring to the Whitehall Theatre. The cast was as follows:

DR PRENTICE	Michael Medwin
GERALDINE BARCLAY	Jane Carr
MRS PRENTICE	Betty Marsden
NICHOLAS BECKETT	Kevin Lloyd
DR RANCE	Valentine Dyall
SERGEANT MATCH	Brian Glover

Directed by Lindsay Anderson
Designed by Jocelyn Herbert

Act One

A room in a private clinic. Morning.
Doors lead to the wards, the dispensary and the hall. French
windows open on to pleasant gardens and shrubberies.
Sink. Desk. Consulting couch with curtains.

DR PRENTICE *enters briskly.* GERALDINE BARCLAY *follows*
him. She carries a small cardboard box.

PRENTICE (*turning at the desk*). Take a seat. Is this your first
job?

GERALDINE (*sitting*). Yes, doctor.

DR PRENTICE *puts on a pair of spectacles, stares at her. He*
opens a drawer in the desk, takes out a notebook.

PRENTICE (*picking up a pencil*). I'm going to ask you a few
questions. (*He hands her a notebook and pencil.*) Write
them down. In English, please. (*He returns to his desk, sits,*
smiles.) Who was your father? Put that at the head of the
page.

GERALDINE *puts the cardboard box she is carrying to one side,*
crosses her legs, rests the notebook upon her knee and makes a
note.

And now the reply immediately underneath for quick
reference.

GERALDINE. I've no idea who my father was.

DR PRENTICE *is perturbed by her reply although he gives no*
evidence of this. He gives her a kindly smile.

PRENTICE. I'd better be frank, Miss Barclay. I can't employ
you if you're in any way miraculous. It would be contrary
to established practice. You did have a father?

GERALDINE. Oh, I'm sure I did. My mother was frugal in her habits, but she'd never economize unwisely.

PRENTICE. If you had a father why can't you produce him?

GERALDINE. He deserted my mother. Many years ago. She was the victim of an unpleasant attack.

PRENTICE (*shrewdly*). Was she a nun?

GERALDINE. No. She was a chambermaid at the Station Hotel.

DR PRENTICE *frowns, takes off his spectacles and pinches the bridge of his nose.*

PRENTICE. Pass that large, leather-bound volume, will you? I must check your story. To safeguard my interests, you understand?

GERALDINE *lifts the book from the bookcase and takes it to* DR PRENTICE.

(*Consulting the index.*) The Station Hotel?

GERALDINE. Yes.

PRENTICE (*opening the book, running his finger down the page*). Ah, here we are! It's a building of small architectural merit built for some unknown purpose at the turn of the century. It was converted into a hotel by public subscription. (*He nods, wisely.*) I stayed there once myself as a young man. It has a reputation for luxury which baffles the most un-demanding guest. (*He closes the book with a bang and pushes it to one side.*) Your story appears, in the main, to be correct. This admirable volume, of course, omits most of the details. But that is only to be expected in a publication of wide general usage. (*He puts on his spectacles.*) Make a note to the effect that your father is missing. Say nothing of the circum-stances. It might influence my final decision.

GERALDINE *makes a jotting in her notebook.* DR PRENTICE *takes the leather-bound volume to the bookcase.*

PRENTICE. Is your mother alive? Or has she too unaccount-ably vanished? That is a trick question. Be careful – you could lose marks on your final scoring.

He returns to his desk and pours himself a whisky.

GERALDINE. I haven't seen my mother for many years. I was brought up by a Mrs Barclay. She died recently.

PRENTICE. From what cause?

GERALDINE. An explosion, due to a faulty gas-main, killed her outright and took the roof off the house.

PRENTICE. Have you applied for compensation?

GERALDINE. Just for the roof.

PRENTICE. Were there no other victims of the disaster?

GERALDINE. Yes. A recently erected statue of Sir Winston Churchill was so badly injured that the George medal has been talked of. Parts of the great man were actually found embedded in my step-mother.

PRENTICE. Which parts?

GERALDINE. I'm afraid I can't help you there. I was too upset to supervise the funeral arrangements. Or, indeed, to identify the body.

PRENTICE. Surely the Churchill family did that?

GERALDINE. Yes. They were most kind.

PRENTICE. You've had a unique experience. It's not everyone has their step-mother assassinated by the North Thames Gas Board.

He shakes his head, sharing the poor girl's sorrow.

Can I get you an aspirin?

GERALDINE. No, thank you, sir. I don't want to start taking drugs.

PRENTICE. Your caution does you credit, my dear. (*He smiles in a kindly fashion.*) Now, I have to ask a question which may cause you embarrassment. Please remember that I'm a doctor. (*Pause.*) What is your shorthand speed?

GERALDINE. I can manage twenty words a minute with ease, sir.

PRENTICE. And your typing speed?

GERALDINE. I haven't mastered the keyboard. My money ran out, you see.

DR PRENTICE *takes the notebook from her and puts it aside.*

PRENTICE. Perhaps you have other qualities which aren't immediately apparent. Lie on that couch.

GERALDINE. Why, doctor?

PRENTICE. Never ask questions. That is the first lesson a secretary must learn. (*He pulls aside the curtains on the couch.*) And kindly remove your stockings. I wish to see what effect your step-mother's death had upon your legs.

GERALDINE. Isn't this rather unusual, doctor?

PRENTICE. Have no fear, Miss Barclay. What I see upon the couch isn't a lovely and desirable girl. It's a sick mind in need of psychiatric treatment. The body is of no interest to a man of my stamp. A woman once threw herself at me. I needn't tell you that this is spoken in confidence. She was stark naked. She wished me to misbehave myself. And, d'you know, all I was conscious of was that she had a malformed navel? That's how much notice I take of women's bodies.

GERALDINE. Please forgive me, doctor. I wasn't meaning to suggest that your attentions were in any way improper.

She takes off her shoes and stockings and lies on the couch. DR PRENTICE *runs a hand along her legs and nods, sagely.*

PRENTICE. As I thought. You've a febrile condition of the calves. You're quite wise to have a check-up. (*He straightens and takes off his spectacles.*) Undress.

He turns to the desk and takes off his coat. GERALDINE *sits up alarmed.*

GERALDINE. I've never undressed in front of a man before.

PRENTICE. I shall take account of your inexperience in these matters.

He puts his spectacles on the desk and rolls back his cuffs.

GERALDINE. I couldn't allow a man to touch me while I was unclothed.

PRENTICE. I shall wear rubber gloves.

GERALDINE is worried and makes no attempt to conceal her growing doubts.

GERALDINE. How long would I have to remain undressed?

PRENTICE. If your reactions are normal you'll be back on your feet in next to no time.

GERALDINE. My headmistress made no mention of this in her booklet 'Hints to the School-leaver'.

PRENTICE. The chapter dealing with medical examinations may have been omitted from the text.

GERALDINE. But that would be ridiculous in a work intended only for use in schools!

PRENTICE. Your concern is well-founded, Miss Barclay. Our educational system needs thoroughly looking into. Speak to your headmistress at her next 'old girls' get-together'.

He turns to the sink and rinses his hands.

GERALDINE. I'd like another woman present. Is your wife available?

PRENTICE. Mrs Prentice is attending a more than usually lengthy meeting of her coven. She won't be back until this evening.

GERALDINE. I could wait until then.

PRENTICE. I haven't the patience, my dear. I've a natural tendency to rush things. I won't trouble you with the details of my private life till you're dressed.

He picks up a towel and dries his hands.

PRENTICE. Put your clothes on the chair provided.

GERALDINE unzips and removes her dress. DR PRENTICE watches her. Pause. He puts the towel aside and puts on his spectacles.

I must ask you not to mention this examination to my wife. I'm not doing it under the Health Scheme, you see. She'd

be sure to send in a bill. And that would be open to misunderstanding.

GERALDINE. What is Mrs Prentice like, doctor? I've heard so
many stories about her.

She puts her dress aside and stands in her panties and bra.

PRENTICE. My wife is a nymphomaniac. Consequently, like
the Holy Grail, she's ardently sought after by young men.
I married her for her money and, upon discovering her to be
penniless, I attempted to throttle her. She escaped my
murderous fury and I've had to live with her malice ever
since.

GERALDINE (*with a sigh*). Poor Dr Prentice. How trying it
must be for you. (*Climbing on to the couch.*) I wish there were
something I could do to cheer you up.

She pulls close the curtains. DR PRENTICE *puts on a white
surgical coat.*

PRENTICE. Well, my dear, if it'll give you any pleasure you
can test my new contraceptive device.

GERALDINE *looks over the curtain and smiles sweetly.*

GERALDINE (*throwing her panties and bra into a chair*). I'll be
delighted to help you in any way I can, doctor.

PRENTICE (*with an indulgent, superior smile*). Lie on the couch
with your hands behind your head and think of the closing
chapters of your favourite work of fiction. The rest may be
left to me.

GERALDINE *disappears behind the curtain.* DR PRENTICE
goes to the drawer in his desk. MRS PRENTICE *enters from the
hall. She is wearing a costly fur coat.*

MRS PRENTICE. Who are you talking to?

DR PRENTICE *is surprised and angry at his wife's unexpected
appearance.*

PRENTICE (*flushing, guilty*). I must ask you not to enter my consulting-room without warning. You're interrupting my studies.

MRS PRENTICE *stares about the room.*

MRS PRENTICE. There's no one here. Were you talking to yourself?

PRENTICE. I was dictating a message to Matron. She's worried by her inability to control her bladder.

MRS PRENTICE. Can urine be controlled by thinking of *Tess of the D'Urbevilles*?

PRENTICE. My theory is still in the planning stage. I'd rather not discuss it.

MRS PRENTICE *goes to the desk and pours herself a drink.*

PRENTICE. Why have you returned? You know I can't endure the torment of being in your company.

MRS PRENTICE. I arrived at my meeting to find the hall in an uproar. Helen Duncanon had declared herself to be in love with a man. And, as you know, the club is primarily for lesbians. I myself am exempt from the rule because you count as a woman. We expelled Helen and I spent the night at the Station Hotel. (*She swallows her drink.*)

NICHOLAS BECKETT *enters. He is a hotel page. He wears a page-boy's uniform.*

NICK (*to MRS PRENTICE*). If you'd care to check your baggage, madam. I'd like to return to my duties.

MRS PRENTICE (*to DR PRENTICE*). Cast your eye across my luggage, will you? Half of it has already been stolen by the hotel staff. (*She turns to the table and pours a drink.*) It's so difficult being a woman.

PRENTICE. Well, I'm sure you're the best judge of that.

He goes into the hall, disgruntled. MRS PRENTICE *puts ice in her drink and turns to* NICK, *a cold expression on her face.*

MRS PRENTICE. I'm not asking for my handbag back, or for the money you've stolen, but unless my dress and wig are returned I shall file a complaint with your employers. You have until lunchtime.

NICK. I've already sold the dress for a lump sum. I could get it back at a price. I've also found someone to take an option on the photographs.

MRS PRENTICE *stares.*

MRS PRENTICE. What photographs?

NICK. I had a camera concealed in the room.

MRS PRENTICE (*open-mouthed*). When I gave myself to you the contract didn't include cinematic rights.

NICK. I'd like a hundred quid for the negatives. You've got until lunchtime.

MRS PRENTICE. I shall complain to the manager.

NICK. It will do you no good. He took the photographs.

MRS PRENTICE. Oh, this is scandalous! I'm a married woman.

NICK. You didn't behave like a married woman last night.

MRS PRENTICE. I was upset. A lesbian friend of mine had just announced her engagement to a Member of Parliament.

NICK. You must be more careful in your choice of friends. I'd like to get out of the indecent photograph racket. It's so wearing on the nerves. Can you find me a worthwhile job? I had a hard boyhood.

MRS PRENTICE. What kind of job do you want?

NICK. I'm an expert typist. I was taught by a man in the printing trade.

MRS PRENTICE (*firmly*). I'm willing to pay for the photographs, but I can't possibly recommend your typing.

NICK. I want a hundred pounds and the post of secretary to your husband!

MRS PRENTICE. You put me in an impossible position.

NICK. No position is impossible when you're young and healthy.

MRS PRENTICE *turns to the desk. She pours herself a drink. Her hand trembles.* DR PRENTICE *enters from the hall. He carries an overnight case.* MRS PRENTICE *puts an empty whisky bottle aside and drops ice into her glass.*

PRENTICE (*to* NICK). She'll be sodden before long. (*He puts the case down.*)

NICK. Have you a family, sir?

PRENTICE. No. My wife said breast-feeding would spoil her shape. Though, from what I remember, it would've been improved by a little nibbling.

MRS PRENTICE *gives a nervy toss of her head and drinks whisky.*

PRENTICE. She's an example of in-breeding among the lobelia-growing classes. A failure in eugenics, combined with a taste for alcohol and sexual intercourse, makes it most un-desirable for her to become a mother.

MRS PRENTICE (*quietly*). I hardly ever have sexual intercourse

PRENTICE. You were born with your legs apart. They'll send you to the grave in a Y-shaped coffin.

MRS PRENTICE (*with a brittle laugh*). My trouble stems from your inadequacy as a lover! It's embarrassing. You must've learned your technique from a Christmas cracker. (*Her mouth twists into a sneer.*) Rejuvenation pills have no effect on you.

PRENTICE (*stuffily*). I never take pills.

MRS PRENTICE. You take them all the time during our love-making. The deafening sound of your chewing is the reason for my never having an orgasm.

DR PRENTICE *is stung by her remarks. He approaches closer.*

PRENTICE. How dare you say that! Your book on the climax in the female is largely autobiographical. (*Pause. He stares.*) Or have you been masquerading as a sexually responsive woman?

MRS PRENTICE. My uterine contractions have been bogus for some time!

She picks up her drink and triumphantly flounces into the ward carrying the overnight case.

PRENTICE (*looking after her*). What a discovery! Married to a mistress of the fraudulent climax. (*He pours himself a drink.*)

NICK (*after a pause*). My parents were divorced, sir. I missed the warmth of a happy family atmosphere.

PRENTICE. As a psychiatrist I do all I can to bring estranged couples together. (*He presses money into* NICK's *hand.*) Don't hesitate to call on me if you're mentally disturbed.

NICK *takes the money and goes into the hall.* DR PRENTICE *drink in hand, pulls the curtain on the couch aside and looks through.*

PRENTICE. It's no good lying there, Miss Barclay. My wife has returned.

GERALDINE *looks over the curtain.*

GERALDINE. Oh, good! She'll be able to help with your examination.

PRENTICE. The examination is cancelled until further notice. (*He picks up the underclothes from the chair.*) Get dressed!

MRS PRENTICE *enters from the ward. She has an empty glass in her hand.*

MRS PRENTICE (*going to the desk*). Has your new secretary arrived?

DR PRENTICE *holds the underwear behind his back.* GERAL-DINE *is concealed by the curtain.*

PRENTICE. Yes. I've got her particulars somewhere.

Unable to conceal the underclothes behind his back, he drops them into a wastepaper basket. MRS PRENTICE *opens a new bottle of whisky.*

MRS PRENTICE. Have you ever given thought to a male secretary?

PRENTICE. A man could never get used to the work.

MRS PRENTICE. My father had a male secretary. My mother said he was much better than a woman.

PRENTICE. I couldn't ask a young fellow to do overtime and then palm him off with a lipstick or a bottle of Yardley's. It'd be silk suits and Alfa Romeos if I so much as breathed on him.

MRS PRENTICE. Try a boy for a change. You're a rich man. You can afford the luxuries of life.

PRENTICE. What will become of Miss Barclay? I've already given her a preliminary interview.

MRS PRENTICE. You must explain the altered circumstances.

GERALDINE *looks over the curtain.* DR PRENTICE *motions her down. She disappears. He picks up the shorthand pad, scribbles a note on it, and tosses it over the curtain.* MRS PRENTICE *pours herself a drink.* DR PRENTICE *sees Geraldine's dress lying on the chair and picks it up. He is about to drop it into the wastepaper basket with the underwear when* MRS PRENTICE *turns, drink in hand.* DR PRENTICE *attempts to conceal the dress behind his back. It hangs down.*

MRS PRENTICE (*in a surprised tone*). What are you doing with that dress?

PRENTICE (*pause*). It's an old one of yours.

MRS PRENTICE. Have you taken up transvestism? I'd no idea our marriage teetered on the edge of fashion.

PRENTICE. Our marriage is like the peace of God – it passeth all understanding.

MRS PRENTICE *swallows her drink and holds out her hand.*

MRS PRENTICE. Give me the dress. I shall wear it.

PRENTICE (*reluctant*). May I have the one you're wearing in exchange?

MRS PRENTICE (*putting glass down*). I'm not wearing a dress.

She slips off her fur coat. Under it she is dressed only in a slip.
DR PRENTICE *cannot conceal his surprise.*

PRENTICE. Why aren't you wearing a dress? Are you following some extreme fashion?

MRS PRENTICE (*putting on* GERALDINE'S *dress*). I'm going to speak frankly and with complete candour. Please listen carefully and save your comments for later. (*She zips up the dress.*) My room at the hotel was small, airless and uncomfortable. A model of its kind. As I was dressing for dinner I noticed that the sheets on the bed were none too clean. I went to the linen cupboard, which I knew to be on the second floor, hoping to find a chambermaid. Instead I found a pageboy who enticed me into the cupboard and then made an indecent suggestion. When I repulsed him he attempted to rape me. I fought him off but not before he'd stolen my handbag and several articles of clothing.

PRENTICE. It doesn't sound the kind of behaviour one expects at a four-star hotel.

MRS PRENTICE. The boy has promised to return my dress. He's sold it to a friend who probably intends using it at sex orgies.

PRENTICE (*joining her at the desk*). Do you realize what would happen if your adventures became public? I'd be ruined. The doors of London society would be slammed in my face. (*He pours a whisky.*) Did you inform the authorities of this escapade?

MRS PRENTICE. No.

PRENTICE. Why not?

MRS PRENTICE. I saw in his youth the remnants of a natural goodness that had all but been destroyed by the pressures of society. I promised to find him employment.

PRENTICE. Is there a market for illegal entrance?

MRS PRENTICE. I don't propose to lead him into a dead-end job.

PRENTICE. What other qualifications has he?

MRS PRENTICE. He can type.

PRENTICE. There aren't many jobs for male typists.

MRS PRENTICE. No. He's been depressed by his failure in commerce. That's why he took to rape.

PRENTICE. How do you hope to employ him?

MRS PRENTICE. As your secretary. He'll be back in an hour. You can check his credentials at your leisure. Where is Miss Barclay?

PRENTICE. She's upstairs.

MRS PRENTICE. I shall inform her that the situation is no longer vacant.

DR PRENTICE *swallows his drink and puts the glass down.*

PRENTICE. Could I borrow one of your dresses for a while, my dear?

MRS PRENTICE. I find your sudden craving for women's clothing a dull and, on the whole, a rather distasteful subject.

She puts her glass down and goes into the hall. DR PRENTICE *passes a hand across his brow.*

PRENTICE. She'll bring my grey hairs in sorrow to the grave. (*He goes to the couch, pulls curtain aside, and looks through.*) Miss Barclay – the present situation is fraught with danger – my wife is under the impression that your dress belongs to her.

GERALDINE *looks over the curtain.*

GERALDINE. We must explain, as tactfully as possible, that she has made a mistake.

PRENTICE. I'm afraid that is impossible. You must be patient for a little longer.

GERALDINE. Doctor – I'm naked! You do realize that, don't you?

PRENTICE (*a tremor passing across his face*). Indeed I do, Miss

Barclay. I'm sure it must cause you acute embarrassment. I'll set about finding you suitable clothing.

He turns to the wastepaper basket, and is about to remove the underclothing when DR RANCE *enters from the garden.* DR PRENTICE *drops the clothing into the basket and puts the basket down.* GERALDINE *ducks behind the curtain out of sight.*

RANCE (*with a polite smile*). Good morning. (*He takes off his hat.*) Are you Dr Prentice?

PRENTICE. Yes. Have you an appointment?

RANCE. No. I never make appointments. (*He puts the hat and the brief-case aside and shakes hands.*) I'd like to be given details of your clinic. It's run, I understand, with the full knowledge and permission of the local hospital authorities? You specialize in the complete breakdown and its by-products?

PRENTICE. Yes. But it's highly confidential. My files are never open to strangers.

RANCE. You may speak freely in front of me. I represent Her Majesty's Government. Your immediate superiors in madness. I'm from the Commissioners.

PRENTICE (*worried, taking off his spectacles*). Which branch?

RANCE. The mental branch.

PRENTICE. Do you cover asylums proper? Or just houses of tentative madness?

RANCE. My brief is infinite. I'd have sway over a rabbit hutch if the inmates were mentally disturbed. (*He opens the brief-case, and takes out the notebook.*)

DR PRENTICE, *unsteadily, pours himself a whisky.*

PRENTICE. You're obviously a force to be reckoned with.

RANCE. I hope our relationship will be a pleasant one. Is this your consulting-room?

PRENTICE (*swallowing drink*). Yes.

RANCE. Why are there so many doors. Was the house designed by a lunatic?

PRENTICE. Yes. (*He pours another whisky.*) We have him here as a patient from time to time.

RANCE (*glancing upwards*). A skylight too? Is it functional?

PRENTICE. No. It's perfectly useless for anything – except to let light in.

DR RANCE *nods, gravely. He wanders round the room examining everything, watched by* DR PRENTICE.

RANCE (*by the couch*). Is your couch regulation size? It looks big enough for two.

PRENTICE (*with a wary smile*). I do double consultations. Toddlers are often terrified of a doctor. So I've taken to examining their mothers at the same time.

RANCE. Has the theory received much publicity?

PRENTICE. I don't approve of scientists who publicize their theories.

RANCE. I must say I agree with you. I wish more scientists would keep their ideas to themselves.

A piece of paper flutters from under the curtain.

RANCE (*picking up the paper*). Is this something to do with you, Prentice?

PRENTICE. It's a prescription, sir.

RANCE (*reading*). 'Keep your head down and don't make a sound'? (*Pause.*) Do you find your patients react favourably to such treatment?

PRENTICE. I can claim to have had some success with it.

RANCE (*drily*). Your ideas, I think, are in advance of the times.

He opens the curtains and closes them again, rapidly. He turns to DR PRENTICE, *startled.*

RANCE. There's a naked woman behind there.

PRENTICE. She's a patient, sir. I'd just managed to calm her down when you arrived.

RANCE. You were attacked by a naked woman?

PRENTICE. Yes.

RANCE. Well, Prentice, I don't know whether to applaud your daring or envy you your luck. Let's take a glance at her.

DR PRENTICE *goes to the curtains.*

PRENTICE. Miss Barclay, a gentleman wishes to speak to you.

GERALDINE (*looking over the curtain*). I can't meet anyone without my clothes on, doctor.

PRENTICE (*coolly, to* DR RANCE). Notice the obstinacy with which she clings to her suburban upbringing.

RANCE. Have you tried shock treatment?

PRENTICE. No.

RANCE. How long has she been a patient?

PRENTICE. The committal order hasn't yet been signed.

RANCE. Bring it here. I'll sign it.

DR PRENTICE *goes to the desk.* DR RANCE *turns to* GERAL- DINE, *and addresses her in a brusque manner.*

RANCE. Why did you take your clothes off? Did it never occur to you that your psychiatrist might be embarrassed by your behaviour?

GERALDINE. I'm not a patient. I'm from the Friendly Faces Employment Bureau.

RANCE (*over his shoulder to* DR PRENTICE). When did those delusions first manifest themselves?

PRENTICE (*returning with a document*). I've been aware of them for some time, sir.

RANCE (*to* GERALDINE). Do you imagine that any business- man would tolerate a naked typist in his office?

GERALDINE *smiles and, in a reasonable manner, attempts to explain.*

GERALDINE. Dr Prentice asked me to undress in order that he might discover my fitness for the tasks ahead. There was no suggestion of my working permanently without clothing.

RANCE (*to* DR PRENTICE). I shall take charge of this case. It appears to have the bizarre quality that makes for a fascinating thesis. (*He signs the document.*) Make the necessary entry in your register and alert the dispensary of my requirements.

DR PRENTICE *goes into the dispensary with the document.* DR RANCE *turns to* GERALDINE.

RANCE. Is there a history of mental illness in your family?

GERALDINE (*primly*). I find your questions irrelevant. I refuse to answer them.

RANCE. I've just certified you insane. You know that, don't you?

GERALDINE *gives a gasp of surprise, and draws back from* DR RANCE.

GERALDINE. What right have you to take such high-handed action?

RANCE. Every right. You've had a nervous breakdown.

GERALDINE. I'm quite sane!

RANCE. Pull yourself together. Why have you been certified if you're sane? Even for a madwoman you're unusually dense.

DR PRENTICE *enters from the dispensary wheeling a hospital trolley. On it is a rubber mattress, a pillow and a blanket. Over his arm* DR PRENTICE *carries a white hospital nightgown.* DR RANCE *takes this from him. He throws it over the curtain to* GERALDINE.

RANCE. Put that on!

GERALDINE (*to* DR RANCE). Oh, thank you. It's a great relief to be clothed again.

DR RANCE *draws* DR PRENTICE *aside.* GERALDINE *puts on the nightgown.*

RANCE. What is the background of this case? Has the patient any family?

PRENTICE. No, sir. Her step-mother died recently after

a remarkably intimate involvement with Sir Winston Churchill.

RANCE. What of the father?

PRENTICE. He appears to have been an unpleasant fellow. He made her mother pregnant at her place of employment.

RANCE. Was there any reason for such conduct?

PRENTICE. The patient is reticent on the subject.

RANCE. I find that strange. And very revealing. (*He opens the curtains on the couch. To* GERALDINE.) Lie on this trolley. (*To* DR PRENTICE.) Go and prepare a sedative.

DR PRENTICE *goes into the dispensary.* DR RANCE *helps* GERALDINE *from the couch.*

GERALDINE. Please ring for a taxi, sir. I wish to return home. I haven't the qualities required for this job.

RANCE (*lifting her on to the trolley and covering her with the blanket*). You're slowing down your recovery rate, Miss Barclay.

DR PRENTICE *enters from the dispensary with a kidney-shaped bowl, swabs and a hypodermic syringe.* DR RANCE *bares* GERALDINE'S *arm, and wipes it with a swab.*

GERALDINE (*appealing to* DR PRENTICE). Tell him the truth, doctor! I'm a fully qualified shorthand-typist!

DR RANCE *gives her an injection. She gasps, and bursts into tears.*

GERALDINE. This is intolerable! You're a disgrace to your profession! I shall ring the B.M.A. after lunch.

RANCE. Accept your condition without tears and without abusing those placed in authority. (*He puts the hypodermic aside, and goes to wash his hands.*)

MRS PRENTICE *enters from the hall.*

MRS PRENTICE (*anxious*). Miss Barclay is nowhere to be found.

RANCE. She's under strong sedation and on no account to be disturbed.

DR PRENTICE, *nervous, gives a fleeting smile in* DR RANCE'*s direction.*

PRENTICE. My wife is talking of my secretary, sir. She's been missing for some time.

GERALDINE. I'm Geraldine Barclay. Looking for part-time secretarial work. I've been certified insane.

RANCE (*to* MRS PRENTICE). Ignore these random reflections. They're an essential factor in the patient's condition. (*To* DR PRENTICE.) Does she have the same name as your secretary?

PRENTICE. She's taken my secretary's name as her 'nom-de-folie'. Although morally reprehensible, there's little we can do legally, I'm afraid.

RANCE (*drying his hands*). It seems a trifle capricious, but the insane are famous for their wild ways.

MRS PRENTICE. I shall contact the employment agency. Miss Barclay can't have vanished into thin air.

She goes into the hall. DR PRENTICE *pours himself a drink.*

PRENTICE. My wife is unfamiliar with the habits of young women, sir. I've known many who could vanish into thin air. And some who took a delight in doing so.

DR RANCE *puts on a white coat.*

RANCE. In my experience young women vanish only at midnight and after a heavy meal. (*He buttons the coat.*) Were your relations with your secretary normal?

PRENTICE. Yes.

RANCE. Well, Prentice, your private life is your own affair. I find it shocking none the less. Did the patient know of your liaison with Miss Barclay?

PRENTICE. She may have done.

RANCE. I see. A definite pattern is beginning to emerge.

He returns to the trolley and stands looking down at GERAL-DINE.

Under the influence of the drug I've administered, Miss
Barclay, you are relaxed and unafraid. I'm going to ask you
some questions which I want answered in a clear non-
technical style. (*To* DR PRENTICE.) She'll take that as an
invitation to use bad language. (*To* GERALDINE.) Who was
the first man in your life?

GERALDINE. My father.

RANCE. Did he assault you?

GERALDINE. No!

RANCE (*to* DR PRENTICE). She may mean 'Yes' when she says
'No'. It's elementary feminine psychology. (*To* GERALDINE.)
Was your step-mother aware of your love for your father?

GERALDINE. I lived in a normal family. I had no love for my
father.

RANCE (*to* DR PRENTICE). I'd take a bet that she was the
victim of an incestuous attack. She clearly associates violence
and the sexual act. Her attempt, when naked, to provoke
you to erotic response may have deeper significance. (*To*
GERALDINE.) Did your father have any religious beliefs?

GERALDINE. I'm sure he did.

RANCE (*to* DR PRENTICE). Yet she claims to have lived in a
normal family. The depth of her condition can be measured
from such a statement. (*To* GERALDINE.) Did your father's
church sanction rape? (*To* DR PRENTICE.) Some sects will
turn a blind eye to anything as long as it's kept within the
family circle. (*To* GERALDINE.) Was there a Church service
before you were assaulted?

GERALDINE. I can't answer these questions, sir. They seem
pointless and disgusting.

RANCE. I'm interested in rape, Miss Barclay, not the aesthetics
of cross-examination. Answer me, please! Were you molested
by your father?

GERALDINE (*with a scream of horror*). No, no, no!

DR RANCE *straightens up and faces* DR PRENTICE.

RANCE. The vehemence of her denials is proof positive of guilt.

It's a text-book case! A man beyond innocence, a girl aching for experience. The beauty, confusion and urgency of their passion driving them on. They embark on a reckless love-affair. He finds it difficult to reconcile his guilty secret with his spiritual convictions. It preys on his mind. Sexual activity ceases. She, who basked in his love, feels anxiety at its loss. She seeks advice from her priest. The Church, true to Her ancient traditions, counsels chastity. The result – madness.

He puts the swabs and the hypodermic into the kidney-shaped bowl.

PRENTICE. It's a fascinating theory, sir, and cleverly put together. Does it tie in with known facts?

DR RANCE picks up the bowl.

RANCE. That need not cause us undue anxiety. Civilizations have been founded and maintained on theories which refused to obey facts. As far as I'm concerned this child was un-naturally assaulted by her own father. I shall base my future actions upon that assumption.

He goes into the dispensary taking the bowl, swabs and hypo-dermic with him.

GERALDINE (*pause*). Am I mad, doctor?
PRENTICE. No.
GERALDINE. Are you mad?
PRENTICE. No.
GERALDINE. Is it the candid camera?
PRENTICE. There's a perfectly rational explanation for what is taking place. Keep calm. All will be well.

DR RANCE re-enters.

RANCE. It's also obvious to the meanest amateur, Prentice, that you resemble the patient's father. That is why she undressed herself. When I arrived on the scene she was about to re-enact the initial experience with her parent. The vexed question of motive is now clear. She was aware of the

understanding that exists between you and your secretary.
You represent her father. Her identification with Miss
Barclay completes the picture.

He releases the wheel-lock on the trolley.

PRENTICE. Perhaps there's a simpler explanation for the
apparent complexities of the case, sir.

RANCE. Simple explanations are for simple minds. I've no use
for either. (*He pushes the trolley towards the ward door.*) Open
the door. I shall supervise the cutting of the patient's hair.

DR PRENTICE *opens the ward door.* DR RANCE *wheels*
GERALDINE *into the ward.* DR PRENTICE *goes to the desk,
pours himself a drink and swallows it quickly. His glance falls
on to the wastepaper basket. He shakes out* GERALDINE's
underclothes, sees her shoes and stockings and picks them up.
MRS PRENTICE *enters from the hall.* DR PRENTICE *swings
round, turns his back on her and walks away, bent double in an
effort to conceal the clothing.*

MRS PRENTICE (*alarmed by this strange conduct*). What's the
matter? (*She approaches.*) Are you in pain?

PRENTICE (*his back to her, strangled*). Yes. Get me a glass of
water.

MRS PRENTICE *hurries into the dispensary.* DR PRENTICE
*stares about him in desperation. He sees a tall vase of roses. He
removes the roses and stuffs the underclothing and one shoe into
the vase. The second shoe won't go in. He pauses, perplexed.
He is about to replace the roses when* MRS PRENTICE *enters
carrying a glass of water.* DR PRENTICE *conceals the shoe
under his coat.* MRS PRENTICE *stares. He is holding the roses.
He gives a feeble smile and presents them to her with a flourish.*
MRS PRENTICE *is surprised and angry.*

MRS PRENTICE. Put them back at once!

The shoe slips and DR PRENTICE, *in an effort to retain it,
doubles up.*

Should I call a doctor?

PRENTICE. No. I'll be all right.

MRS PRENTICE (*offering him the glass*). Here. Drink this.

DR PRENTICE *backs away, still holding the roses and the shoe.*

PRENTICE. I wonder if you'd get another glass? That one is quite the wrong shape.

MRS PRENTICE (*puzzled*). The wrong shape?

PRENTICE. Yes.

MRS PRENTICE *stares hard at him, then goes into the dispensary.* DR PRENTICE *tries to replace the roses in the vase. They won't go in. He picks up a pair of scissors from his desk and cuts the stalks down to within an inch or so of the heads. He puts the roses into the vase and wraps the stalks in his handkerchief and puts it into his pocket. He looks for somewhere to conceal the second shoe. He gets on his knees and shoves the shoe between the space on top of the books on the lower shelf of the bookcase.* MRS PRENTICE *enters carrying another glass. She stops and stares.*

MRS PRENTICE. What are you doing now?

PRENTICE (*lifting his hands*). Praying.

MRS PRENTICE. This puerile behaviour ill accords with your high academic standards. (*She puts the glass of water down, and tosses her head.*) The youth I wish you to engage as your secretary has arrived.

PRENTICE (*drinking water*). Perhaps he'd call back later. I'm still feeling dicky.

MRS PRENTICE. I'll see what he says. He's an impatient young man.

PRENTICE. Is that why he took to rape?

MRS PRENTICE. Yes. He can't wait for anything.

She hurries away into the hall. DR PRENTICE *wipes his brow.*

PRENTICE. Two decades spent fighting her and a receding hairline! I've had just about enough of both.

DR RANCE *enters from the ward.*

RANCE. You'll have no trouble recognizing the patient, Prentice. I've clipped her hair to within an inch of the scalp.

PRENTICE (*shocked*). Was it quite wise to do that, sir? Is it in accord with the present enlightened approach to the mentally sick?

RANCE. Perfectly in accord. I've published a monograph on the subject. I wrote it at University. On the advice of my tutor. A remarkable man. Having failed to achieve madness himself he took to teaching it to others.

PRENTICE. And you were his prize pupil?

RANCE. There were some more able than I.

PRENTICE. Where are they now?

RANCE. In mental institutions.

PRENTICE. Running them?

RANCE. For the most part.

MRS PRENTICE *enters from the hall.*

MRS PRENTICE (*to* DR PRENTICE). He insists upon punctuality. He'll give you five minutes.

PRENTICE (*to* DR RANCE). A prospective employee, sir. It's useless to claim that Socialism has had no effect.

RANCE (*to* MRS PRENTICE). Is there no news of Miss Barclay?

MRS PRENTICE. None. I've checked with the Employment Bureau. Their clients have strict instructions to ring them immediately after an interview. Miss Barclay has failed to do so.

RANCE. A search party must be organized. (*To* DR PRENTICE.) What have you in the way of dogs?

PRENTICE. A spaniel and a miniature poodle.

RANCE. Let them be unleashed! Geraldine Barclay must be found or the authorities informed.

MRS PRENTICE. I'll contact the warden. He has charge of the gate and will know whether she left the building. (*She turns to go.*)

PRENTICE. No – don't do that. Miss Barclay is quite safe. She's downstairs. I've just remembered.

RANCE (*pause, surprised*). Why did you keep the fact from us?

PRENTICE. It'd slipped my memory.

RANCE. Have you suffered from lapses of memory before?

PRENTICE. I can't remember.

RANCE. Your memory plays you false even on the subject of its own inadequacy?

PRENTICE. I may have had a blackout. I don't recall having one on any other occasion.

RANCE. You might have forgotten. You admit your memory isn't reliable.

PRENTICE. I can only state what I know, sir. I can't be expected to remember things I've forgotten.

MRS PRENTICE. What's Miss Barclay doing downstairs?

PRENTICE. She's making white golliwogs for sale in colour-prejudice trouble-spots.

DR RANCE *and* MRS PRENTICE *exchange startled looks.*

RANCE. You claim, Prentice, that you forgot your secretary was manufacturing these monstrosities?

PRENTICE. Yes.

RANCE. I can hardly credit it. Once seen a white golliwog is not easily forgotten. What was the object in creating these nightmare creatures?

PRENTICE. I hoped it might promote racial harmony.

RANCE. These hellish white homuncules must be put out of their misery. I order you to destroy them before their baleful influence can make itself felt.

PRENTICE (*wearily*). I'll get Miss Barclay to carry out your orders, sir.

He goes out by the ward door. DR RANCE *turns to* MRS PRENTICE *and mops his brow.*

RANCE. The man's a second Frankenstein.

MRS PRENTICE *goes to the desk and pours herself a whisky.*

MRS PRENTICE (*with a half-smile*). My husband is a strange person, doctor. Is he a genius or merely a highly-strung fool?

RANCE. I'd like to know him better before I ventured an opinion. Have there been other schemes besides this golliwog scandal?

MRS PRENTICE (*drinking whisky*). His letters to the newspapers 're legion.

She takes her drink to the bookcase. She lifts, from the bottom ·nelf, a leather-bound cuttings book.

(*Opening the book and showing it to* DR RANCE.) From his first letter, at the age of twelve, complaining of inaccurate information given to him by a German child whilst they were playing 'mothers and fathers' – he speculates on the nature and extent of Nazi propaganda.

DR RANCE *stares hard at the book.* MRS PRENTICE *turns the pages.*

To his latest letter, published a month ago, in which he calls Gentlemen's Lavatories 'the last stronghold of male privilege . . .'

DR RANCE, *after reading, hands the book back.*

RANCE. Your husband's behaviour gives me cause for grave disquiet. Are you yourself convinced that his methods can result in a lessening of tension between the sane and the insane?

MRS PRENTICE. The purpose of my husband's clinic isn't to cure, but to liberate and exploit madness.

RANCE. In this he appears to succeed only too well. (*He faces her, candidly.*) Never have I seen matters conducted as they are in this house.

He takes a piece of paper from his pocket and hands it to her.

Read that.

MRS PRENTICE (*reading*). 'Keep your head down and don't make a sound'? (*Handing it back.*) What does it mean?

RANCE. Your husband is using dangerously unorthodox methods in his treatment of the insane. (*He goes to his brief-case and puts the note away.*)

MRS PRENTICE *frowns and puts the glass down.*

MRS PRENTICE. I hesitate to mention this, doctor – as a wife my loyalties are involved – but I must confess that only this morning my husband announced his intention of using Thomas Hardy to cure a disorder of the bladder.

RANCE (*grimly*). As a psychiatrist your husband seems not only ineffective, but also undesirable.

MRS PRENTICE *takes the cuttings book back to the bookcase and attempts to put the book away. She is unable to do so. She investigates. She discovers GERALDINE's shoe and looks at it in amazement.*

MRS PRENTICE. What a thing to find in a bookcase!

RANCE (*pause*). Is it yours?

MRS PRENTICE. No.

RANCE. Let me see it.

She hands him the shoe. He turns it over in his hand.

RANCE (*looking up, after a pause*). I must ask you to be honest with me, Mrs Prentice. Has Dr Prentice at any time given you cause to doubt his own sanity?

MRS PRENTICE *gives a quick gasp of fear, rising to her feet.*

MRS PRENTICE. He's a respected member of his profession. His work in all fields has been praised by numerous colleagues.

RANCE. Radical thought comes easily to the lunatic.

MRS PRENTICE (*pause*). You're quite right. (*She dabs at her nose with a handkerchief.*) I've known for some time that all was not well. I've tried to convince myself that my fears were groundless. All the while I knew I was cheating myself.

DR RANCE *leads her to a chair. She sits, overcome by shock.*

RANCE (*quietly*). What first aroused your suspicions?

MRS PRENTICE. Oh, I think his boorish attitude towards my mother. He used to ring her up and suggest painful ways of committing suicide. Worn out at last by his pestering she took his advice.

RANCE. And more recently, say from this morning, has there been an increase in his condition?

MRS PRENTICE. Oh, yes. Quite definitely, doctor. He had no sympathy for me when I complained of being assaulted by a page-boy at the Station Hotel.

RANCE. What was the object of the assault?

MRS PRENTICE. The youth wanted to rape me.

RANCE. He didn't succeed?

MRS PRENTICE. No.

RANCE (*shaking his head*). The service in these hotels is dreadful.

MRS PRENTICE. Shortly after my return my husband started having the most extraordinary ideas which I'd've been willing to indulge if they hadn't overstepped the bounds of good taste.

RANCE. Give me an example.

MRS PRENTICE. He has developed a craving for women's clothes.

RANCE (*picking up* GERALDINE's *shoe*). This confirms your story.

MRS PRENTICE. I refused to loan him any of mine and went in search of Miss Barclay. Some time later, in my presence, my husband had a kind of fit. He asked me to get him a drink. When I returned he presented me with a bouquet of flowers.

RANCE. He wished to congratulate you on your safe return.

MRS PRENTICE. I'd only been to the dispensary. And he'd taken the flowers from the vase. (*She points to the vase.*) I was angry and not a little frightened. At this point a spasm of

agony crossed his otherwise tranquil features. I offered him
the glass of water. He reacted in a violent manner. He said
the glass was the wrong shape.

RANCE. What a revealing phrase!

MRS PRENTICE. I returned to the dispensary. When I got back
he was on his knees praying.

RANCE. How shocking! His abnormal condition has driven
him to seek refuge in religion. Always the last ditch stand of
a man on the brink of disaster. (*He pats* MRS PRENTICE *on
the shoulder.*) I can't doubt that what you've told me has
great significance. We must also take into account his admitted lapse of memory, and the attempts to create alien
forms of life. (*He puts the shoe into his case.*) Say nothing of
our suspicions. Fancies grow like weeds in the unhealthy
soil of a sick brain.

MRS PRENTICE (*dabbing her eyes with a handkerchief*). Oh,
doctor, you've no idea what a relief it's been to talk to
someone like yourself.

RANCE. Why haven't you done so before?

MRS PRENTICE. A woman doesn't like facing the fact that the
man she loves is insane. It makes her look such a fool.

*She puts the handkerchief away, pours herself a drink and
drops ice into the glass.* DR PRENTICE *enters from the ward.*

RANCE (*turning to him*). Have you carried out my instructions?

PRENTICE. Yes.

RANCE. You guilty scientists will destroy the world with your
shameful secrets. (*He takes* GERALDINE's *shoe from his brief-
case.*) Does this belong to your secretary?

PRENTICE. No. (*Pause.*) It's mine.

DR RANCE *and* MRS PRENTICE *exchange looks.* DR RANCE
raises an eyebrow.

RANCE (*heavily, with irony*). Are you in the habit of wearing
women's footwear?

PRENTICE (*quickly, desperate*). My private life is my own. Society must not be too harsh in its judgements.

DR RANCE *puts the shoe aside.*

RANCE. Where is this secretary of yours? I've a few questions I'd like to put to her.

PRENTICE. I can't allow you to disturb her. She has work to do.

DR RANCE *gives a humourless smile.*

RANCE. I don't think you quite appreciate the position, Prentice. The powers vested in me by the Commissioners give the right to interview any member of your staff should occasion demand. Where is Geraldine Barclay?

PRENTICE. She's in the garden.

RANCE. Ask her to step this way.

PRENTICE. She's making a funeral pyre for the golliwogs. It would be wrong to disturb her.

RANCE. Very well. (*Tight-lipped.*) I shall seek her out myself. You may be sure, Prentice, your conduct won't go unreported!

He goes into the garden. DR PRENTICE *turns on his wife in cold fury.*

PRENTICE. What've you told him?

MRS PRENTICE. Nothing but the truth.

PRENTICE (*pouring a drink*). You've been spreading it around that I'm a transvestite, haven't you?

MRS PRENTICE. There was a woman's shoe hidden in the bookcase. What was it doing there?

PRENTICE. Why were you rooting among my books?

MRS PRENTICE. I was looking for the cuttings album. I showed it to Dr Rance.

PRENTICE. You'd no right to do that.

MRS PRENTICE. Are you ashamed of the fact that you write to strange men?

PRENTICE. There's nothing furtive in my relationship with the editor of *The Guardian*.

MRS PRENTICE *pours herself another drink.*

MRS PRENTICE. Dr Rance and I are trying to help you. We're not satisfied with your condition.

PRENTICE. Neither am I. It's impossible and you're to blame. I should've driven you out with ignominy years ago.

MRS PRENTICE *puts the empty whisky bottle aside and turns on* DR PRENTICE *resentfully.*

MRS PRENTICE. Whose fault is it if our marriage is on the rocks? You're selfish and inconsiderate. Don't push me too far. (*With a toss of her head.*) I might sleep with someone else.

PRENTICE. Who?

MRS PRENTICE. An Indian student.

PRENTICE. You don't know any.

MRS PRENTICE. New Delhi is full of them.

PRENTICE (*staring, aghast*). You can't take lovers in Asia! The air fare would be crippling.

MRS PRENTICE *drops ice into her glass and ignores* DR PRENTICE, *her nose in the air.* DR PRENTICE *stands beside her and shouts into her ear.*

Your irresponsible behaviour causes me untold anxiety. A man exposed himself to you last summer.

MRS PRENTICE (*without looking at him*). I didn't see anything.

PRENTICE. And your disappointment marred our holiday.

MRS PRENTICE. You've no psychological understanding of the difficulties I face. (*She drinks whisky.*)

PRENTICE (*pulling her round, white with rage*). Unless you're very careful you'll find yourself in a suitcase awaiting collection!

MRS PRENTICE *laughs, sharply.*

MRS PRENTICE. These veiled threats confirm the doubts I already have of your sanity.

She drinks the whisky and walks away from DR PRENTICE *who scowls at her.* NICK *enters from the hall. He carries a slim cardboard box with the words* 'STATION HOTEL' *printed on it.*

NICK (*to* MRS PRENTICE). If you'll hand over the money, madam, I'll let you have the photos. However, some guarantee of employment must be given before I part with the negatives.

DR PRENTICE, *puzzled, turns to* MRS PRENTICE.

PRENTICE. What's he talking about?
MRS PRENTICE. He has in his possession a series of pornographic studies of me. He took them last night without my knowledge.

DR PRENTICE *turns away, weary, almost in tears.*

PRENTICE. Oh, the damnable frivolity of the woman! I shall have to turn paederast to get her out of this mess. (*He passes a hand across his brow.*)

NICK *presents* MRS PRENTICE *with the box.*

NICK. I have to deliver this. It's from our two-hour cleaning service.

MRS PRENTICE *opens the box.*

MRS PRENTICE (*with delight*). My dress and wig!

DR PRENTICE *narrows his eyes and gives a brief exclamation.*

PRENTICE. A dress? I'll take possession of that. (*He takes the box from her.*)
MRS PRENTICE. I shall inform Dr Rance of your theft of one of my dresses. (*She spits the words into his astonished face.*)
PRENTICE. Don't raise your voice. Take a biscuit from the barrel and retire to your room.

MRS PRENTICE *tosses her head, picks a full bottle of whisky from the desk and flounces into the hall.*

NICK. I'm sorry if my behaviour last night caused your wife anxiety, but I've a burning desire to sleep with every woman I meet.

PRENTICE. That's a filthy habit and, in my opinion, very injurious to the health.

NICK. It is, sir. My health's never been the same since I went off stamp-collecting.

DR PRENTICE *puts the box on to the desk and pours himself a drink.*

PRENTICE. We have an overall moral policy in this clinic from which even I am not exempt. Whilst you're with us I shall expect you to show an interest in no one's sexual organs but your own.

NICK. I would miss a lot of fun that way.

PRENTICE. That is the object of the exercise.

DR RANCE *enters from the garden.*

RANCE. I can find no trace of your secretary. I might add, Prentice, that my patience is all but exhausted.

PRENTICE. She might be in the dispensary.

RANCE. Unless I discover her whereabouts within the next few minutes you'll find yourself in serious trouble.

He goes into the dispensary. MRS PRENTICE *enters from the hall.*

MRS PRENTICE. A policeman is at the door. He wishes to speak to some member of the household.

PRENTICE. Ask him to step this way.

MRS PRENTICE *goes into the hall.* NICK *stands and appeals to* DR PRENTICE, *emotional.*

NICK. Oh, sir! They've come to arrest me!

PRENTICE. This paranoia is uncalled-for. The officer has

probably called to ask me for the hand of my cook in marriage.

NICK. You're wrong, sir! They'll give me five years if I'm caught.

PRENTICE. Why are you in danger of arrest. You may be quite frank with me.

NICK. Well, sir, as your wife has already told you, I attempted last night to misbehave myself with her. I didn't succeed.

PRENTICE. I'm sure you didn't. Despite all appearances to the contrary, Mrs Prentice is harder to get into than the reading room at the British Museum.

NICK. Undeterred I took the lift to the third floor of the hotel where a party of schoolgirls were staying. Oh, sir, what lonely and aimless lives they lead!

PRENTICE (*with a frown*). Was there no mistress in attendance?

NICK. She occupied a room across the corridor.

PRENTICE. Did you disturb her?

NICK. No. And she'll never forgive me for it. It was she who reported the incident to the police. Oh, sir! Don't turn me over to the law.

DR RANCE *enters from the dispensary.*

RANCE. I warn you, Prentice, unless you're prepared to co-operate in finding Miss Barclay I shall call upon you to account for her disappearance. If you're unable to do so the police must be informed.

He goes into the ward.

NICK. Have you given a thought to my predicament?

PRENTICE. No. I'm obsessed by my own. (*He wipes his brow.*) We shall be sharing the same cell at this rate.

His eye lights on the cardboard box. He turns to NICK, *an idea dawning.*

(*Abruptly.*) Take your clothes off.

NICK (*pause*). Are you going to mess me about, sir?

PRENTICE. Certainly not! Is that what usually happens when men ask you to take your clothes off?

NICK. Yes. They give me five shillings.

PRENTICE. Five shillings! Good gracious the rate hasn't changed in thirty years. What can the unions be thinking of? (*He puts a hand on* NICK's *shoulder.*) Come along, strip!

NICK *tugs at a zip. The jacket opens from shoulder to hip. He takes it off, kicks away his shoes and drops his trousers.* DR PRENTICE *stares in admiration.*

PRENTICE. Remarkable. My last secretary couldn't better you. And she was a descendant of Houdini.

NICK *hands the clothes to* DR PRENTICE. *He is naked except for a pair of shorts. He is about to take them off when* DR PRENTICE *holds up his hand.*

Don't remove your drawers. My medical training has familiarized me with what is underneath.

MRS PRENTICE *enters from the hall. She stops in horror.*

MRS PRENTICE. What devilry are you up to now?

PRENTICE. I'm carrying out a medical examination.

MRS PRENTICE. But you're not a physician. Why do you need the child undressed?

PRENTICE (*smiling, with enormous patience*). My investigations upon his clothed body would be strictly 'unscientific' and, inevitably, superficial. In order to assure myself that he's going to be of use to me I must examine him fully. And skin-wise.

MRS PRENTICE. You ogre! Never, in my whole life, have I heard anything so lame and stupid. This folly will get you struck off the Register. (*Picking up* NICK's *uniform.*) Come with me, dear. You mustn't be left with this man.

She takes the uniform into the hall.

NICK. What do we do now, sir? If the law comes I can't even run for it.

DR PRENTICE picks up the cardboard box and takes out a leopard-spotted dress and a wig.

PRENTICE. I have an idea. I want you to impersonate my secretary. Her name is Geraldine Barclay. It will solve all our problems if you agree to my request.

He gives NICK the dress and wig.

It's of particular importance to convince Dr Rance that you're a woman. You should encounter no real difficulties there. He's an elderly man. I don't suppose he's checked with the original lately.

He takes NICK to the dispensary door.

After your meeting plead illness and leave the house. I'll be waiting with your own clothes. The operation completed you'll be given a sum of money and a ticket for any destination you choose. (*Pushing him into the dispensary.*) If you run into trouble I shall deny all knowledge of you. Dress in there.

He shuts the dispensary door, goes to the hall and calls in friendly tones:

Would you like to step this way, officer? I'm sorry to have kept you waiting.

He goes to the desk and opens a fresh bottle of whisky. NICK opens the dispensary door and looks through.

NICK. Shoes, sir!

DR PRENTICE swings round in alarm.

PRENTICE. Shoes! (*He puts the bottle down.*) One moment!

He takes GERALDINE's shoe from DR RANCE's brief-case and throws it to NICK. He goes to the vase and lifts the roses

quickly. He puts a hand into the vase, searching for the other shoe. SERGEANT MATCH *enters.* NICK *darts into the dispensary.* DR PRENTICE *puts the roses behind his back.*
(*In cold tones.*) Would you mind not entering my consulting room without permission?

MATCH (*a little put out*). You asked me to come in, sir.
PRENTICE. I don't believe I did. Wait outside.

SERGEANT MATCH *leaves the room.* DR PRENTICE *shakes* GERALDINE's *shoe from the vase. He hurries to the dispensary, throws the shoe inside and darts back to the vase. He is about to replace the flowers when* MRS PRENTICE *enters from the hall. She sees* DR PRENTICE *is holding the flowers and steps back in amazement.* DR PRENTICE *offers her the bunch of roses. Her face turns ashen. She is angry and a little frightened.*

MRS PRENTICE. Why do you keep giving me flowers?
PRENTICE. It's because I'm very fond of you, my dear.
MRS PRENTICE. Your actions grow wilder with every passing moment. Why were you rude to the policeman?
PRENTICE. He barged in without so much as a by-your-leave.
MRS PRENTICE. But you asked him to come in. Had you forgotten?
PRENTICE. Yes. (*Pause.*) My memory isn't what it was. Tell him I'll see him now.

MRS PRENTICE *goes into the hall.* DR PRENTICE *replaces the flowers, goes to his desk and pours a large whisky.* GERALDINE *enters from the ward. Her hair has been cut short. She is wearing the hospital nightgown.* DR PRENTICE *is considerably alarmed by her presence in the room.*

Miss Barclay! What are you doing here?
GERALDINE. Nothing would induce me to remain on your staff a moment longer, doctor. I wish to give notice.

SERGEANT MATCH *enters from the hall. His view of* GERAL-DINE *is obscured by the couch.*

MATCH. Sorry for the misunderstanding, sir.

PRENTICE (*turning, abrupt*). Please remain outside. I think I made myself plain.

MATCH (*pause*). You don't wish to see me?

PRENTICE. No.

SERGEANT MATCH, *somewhat perplexed by the situation, goes into the hall.* DR PRENTICE *takes* GERALDINE *by the arm.*

Your disclosures could ruin me. Give me a chance to get us out of this mess.

GERALDINE. You must put matters right by telling the truth.

PRENTICE (*pulls curtains round couch*). Hide behind here. Nothing unpleasant will happen. You have my word as a gentleman.

GERALDINE. We must tell the truth!

PRENTICE. That's a thoroughly defeatist attitude. (*He bundles her behind the curtain.*)

GERALDINE (*looking over the curtain*). At least give me back my clothes. I feel naked without them.

DR PRENTICE *removes the roses from the vase, takes out* GERALDINE's *underclothes and stockings and throws them to her.* MRS PRENTICE *and* SERGEANT MATCH *enter from the hall.* GERALDINE *ducks behind the curtain.* DR PRENTICE *has the roses in his hand.* MRS PRENTICE *clutches* SERGEANT MATCH's *arm.*

MRS PRENTICE. Oh, if he presents me with those flowers again I shall faint!

They watch in silence as DR PRENTICE *replaces the roses with an air of confidence. Without* GERALDINE's *clothes under them the stalks are too short. The flowers vanish into the vase.* MRS PRENTICE *cries out in surprise.*

MRS PRENTICE. He's cut the stalks off! His lunacy is beyond belief.

DR PRENTICE *picks up his drink and turns, blandly, to* SERGEANT MATCH.

PRENTICE. Excuse my wife's hysteria, sergeant. A man tried to molest her last night. Her recovery is far from complete.

MATCH. I understand that Mrs Prentice introduced the young man to you, sir?

PRENTICE. Yes. We shan't prefer charges.

MATCH. I believe your wife to be ill-advised in not repeating her experiences before a judge and jury. However, as it happens, I'm not concerned with this case. I'm interested in the youth's movements between midnight and seven a.m. During that period he is alleged to have misconducted himself with a party of schoolchildren.

MRS PRENTICE (*pouring a drink*). How vile and disgraceful!

MATCH. After carrying out a medical examination our lady doctor is up in arms. She can't wait to meet this fellow face to face.

PRENTICE. Well, sergeant, he isn't on the premises. If he turns up you'll be informed.

MRS PRENTICE (*shocked*). How dare you give misleading information to the police? (*To* SERGEANT MATCH.) He was here. I have his clothes outside.

MATCH. Very wise of you to confiscate his clothing, ma'am. If more women did the same the number of cases of rape would be halved.

PRENTICE (*at the desk*). Or doubled.

MRS PRENTICE. Disregard anything my husband says. I'll fetch the clothing.

She goes into the hall carrying her drink. SERGEANT MATCH *turns to* DR PRENTICE.

MATCH. I'm also anxious, sir, to trace the whereabouts of a young woman called Barclay. Can you help in my inquiries?

PRENTICE (*a spasm of anxiety crossing his face*). Why do you wish to see Miss Barclay?

MATCH. It's a matter of national importance. Miss Barclay's step-mother, a woman of otherwise unblemished character, died recently. Shortly before her death her name had been linked in a most unpleasant way with that of Sir Winston Churchill. Mrs Barclay's association with the great man gave offence in some circles. However, the local council, composed by and large of no-nonsense men and women of the 'sixties, decided in view of his war record to overlook Sir Winston's moral lapse. Under expert guidance he was to be reintegrated into society. The task accomplished it became clear that the great man was incomplete. When the true facts got out the die-hards were in uproar. The press took up the story and it snowballed out of all proportion. At last – with the full support of the Conservative and Unionist Party – the council decided to sue the heirs of Mrs Barclay for those parts of Sir Winston which an army-type medical had proved to be missing. The council's lawyers obtained an exhumation order. This morning the coffin was opened in the presence of the Lord Mayor and Lady Mayoress of this borough. Fainting women were held back as the official in charge searched high and low for council property. His efforts were not crowned with success. Mrs Barclay had taken nothing with her to the grave except those things which she ought to have done. At noon today the matter came to the attention of the police.

PRENTICE (*pouring whisky*). You suspect my secretary of having stolen certain parts of Sir Winston Churchill?

MRS PRENTICE enters with NICK's uniform.

MRS PRENTICE. Here is proof that the young man was in this room.

MATCH. He can't get far without clothing.

PRENTICE. His progress without clothing last night was enviable.

MATCH (*to* DR PRENTICE). You still claim, sir, that you have no knowledge of the youth's whereabouts?

PRENTICE. No.

MATCH. And what has become of Miss Barclay?

PRENTICE. I've no idea.

MRS PRENTICE. You told Dr Rance she was burning the golli-wogs.

SERGEANT MATCH looks from one to the other in amazement.

Was that a lie?

PRENTICE. It may have been. I can't remember.

MRS PRENTICE gives an impatient toss of her head.

MRS PRENTICE. You must talk to Dr Rance, sergeant. He may be able to account for my husband's unusual behaviour pattern.

MATCH. Where would the doctor be?

MRS PRENTICE. In the garden. Please tell him that his special-ized knowledge is urgently required.

SERGEANT MATCH goes into the garden. MRS PRENTICE turns to her husband and addresses him in unfamiliar tones of quietness and sympathy.

Now, darling, you've clearly lost the capacity to remember fresh items of information, to solve unaccustomed problems and to remain orientated. Don't let this worry you. I shall be at your side throughout the whole course of your illness. I'm even going to take notes on the progress of your break-down. So nothing will be wasted. Try to remember why you damaged the flowers in this vase. It may have a direct bearing on the case.

She gives a charming smile, picks up the vase and goes into the hall. GERALDINE pokes her head over the curtain.

GERALDINE. Tell the truth, sir. All your troubles spring from a lack of candour.

PRENTICE. My troubles spring from a misguided attempt to seduce you.

GERALDINE (*with a gasp*). You never told me you were seducing me. You said you were interested in my mind.

PRENTICE. That's like 'open sesame' – a formula for gaining entrance.

SERGEANT MATCH *appears in the french windows.* GERAL-DINE *ducks behind the curtain.*

MATCH. Are you sure that Dr Rance is out here, sir?

PRENTICE. Yes.

MATCH. Where would he be then?

PRENTICE. In the shrubbery. We've a naked elf on a bird-bath. We often have trouble with peeping-toms.

MATCH. I'd like you to accompany me, sir.

DR PRENTICE *shrugs and follows* SERGEANT MATCH *into the garden.* GERALDINE *steps down from the couch. She is wearing her panties and bra. She carries the nightgown. She picks up* NICK's *uniform. She drops the nightgown on to a chair and hurries to the dispensary. She retreats at once.*

GERALDINE. A strange woman!

She runs to the ward door, looks through and backs terrified.

Dr Rance! Oh, whatever shall I do?

She scurries to the hall, checks herself and scuttles back to the couch. She climbs behind the curtains. MRS PRENTICE *enters carrying the roses in a smaller vase.* NICK *enters from the dispensary. He is dressed in women's clothing and wears a blonde wig.* MRS PRENTICE *gives a gasp of surprise and puts the vase down.*

MRS PRENTICE. Are you Geraldine Barclay?

NICK. Yes. (*He speaks in low, cultured tones.*)

MRS PRENTICE. Where have you been?

NICK (*primly*). I've been attending to the thousand and one duties that occupy the average secretary during her working hours.

MRS PRENTICE. It doesn't take the whole morning to file your nails, surely?

NICK. I had to lie down. I was sick.

MRS PRENTICE. Are you pregnant?

NICK *tosses back a lock of hair.*

NICK. I can't discuss my employer's business with you.

MRS PRENTICE. What was your last job?

NICK. I was a hostess at the 'One, Two, Three' Club.

MRS PRENTICE *purses her lips in disapproval.*

MRS PRENTICE. It's obvious that you're unsuited to the work here. I shan't recommend you for employment.

DR PRENTICE *and* SERGEANT MATCH *enter from the garden.*

(*To* SERGEANT MATCH.) This is my husband's secretary, sergeant. She'll be pleased to help you in your inquiries.

MATCH (*to* NICK). Miss Barclay, I must ask you to produce or cause to be produced, the missing parts of Sir Winston Churchill.

NICK. What do they look like?

MATCH. You're claiming ignorance of the shape and structure of the objects sought?

NICK. I'm in the dark.

MATCH. You handled them only at night? We shall draw our own conclusions.

NICK. I'm not the kind of girl to be mixed-up in that kind of thing. I'm an ex-member of the Brownies.

MATCH. Are you concealing unlawful property about your person?

NICK. No.

MATCH. I'll have to call medical evidence to prove your story, miss. You must be thoroughly looked into.

PRENTICE. I'm a qualified doctor.

MATCH. Only women are permitted to examine female suspects.

PRENTICE. Doesn't that breed discontent in the force?

MATCH. Among the single men there's a certain amount of bitterness. Married men who are familiar with the country are glad to be let off extra map-reading.

MRS PRENTICE. I'll examine Miss Barclay. That will solve the problem.

MATCH. Thank you, ma'am. I accept your kind offer. Take the young lady into the dispensary and get her to submit to a medical examination.

MRS PRENTICE *leads* NICK *into the dispensary.* DR RANCE *enters from the ward, his face a mask of horror.*

RANCE. Prentice! The patient has escaped. Sound the alarm.

MATCH. How long has the patient been gone, sir?

RANCE. Only a few minutes.

MATCH. Any steps you feel may be necessary to recover your patient may be taken, sir.

DR RANCE *crosses, pulls the siren bell and hurries into the hall.*

She must've come through this room. You and I were in the garden. Mrs Prentice was in the hall. Escape would be impossible. She must still be in this room. (*He turns to* DR PRENTICE *in triumph.*) Only one hiding place is possible.

He pulls the curtain on the couch aside. GERALDINE *is revealed. She is wearing* NICK's *uniform, his hat and shoes. She has on* DR PRENTICE's *spectacles.*

MATCH (*taking in the picture at a glance*). Are you from the Station Hotel?

GERALDINE *answers in a scared voice.*

GERALDINE. Yes.
MATCH. I want a word with you, my lad. (*He takes out his notebook.*)

A siren begins to wail.

Curtain

[*Note:* Orton's original ending to the Act includes a final speech by PRENTICE, which is usually omitted in performance:

    MATCH. I want a word with you, my lad. (*He takes out his notebook.*)
    PRENTICE (*turning aside, wringing his hands*). This appalling situation is the result of my lax moral code. It's clean living and Teach Yourself Woodwork for me from now on!

    He picks up a whisky. A siren begins to wail. SERGEANT MATCH *opens his notebook.*

Curtain.]

Act Two

One minute later. The siren fades.

DR PRENTICE *opens another bottle of whisky.* GERALDINE *steps from the couch in relief.*

GERALDINE (*to* SERGEANT MATCH). You've no idea how glad I am to be arrested.

MATCH. Why?

GERALDINE. I'm in great danger.

MATCH. Who from?

GERALDINE. Dr Prentice. His conduct is scandalous. Take me to the police station. I shall prefer charges.

MATCH (*to* DR PRENTICE). Have you anything to say, sir?

PRENTICE. Yes. What this young woman claims is a tissue of lies.

SERGEANT MATCH *scratches his head.*

MATCH (*pause*). This is a boy, sir. Not a girl. If you're baffled by the difference it might be as well to approach both with caution. (*To* GERALDINE.) Let's hear what you've got to say for yourself.

GERALDINE. I came here for a job. On some pretext the doctor got me to remove my clothes. Afterwards he behaved in a strange manner.

MATCH. What did he do?

GERALDINE. He asked me to lie on that couch.

SERGEANT MATCH *glances at* DR PRENTICE *in disapproval.* DR PRENTICE *drinks whisky.* MATCH *turns to* GERALDINE.

MATCH (*quietly*). Did he, at any time, attempt to interfere with you?

PRENTICE (*putting the glass down*). You'll be disappointed, sergeant, if you imagine that boy has lost his virginity.

MATCH. I hope he'll be considerably more experienced before he loses that, sir. What reason had you for taking off his clothes?

PRENTICE. I wished to assure myself of his unquestioning obedience. I give a prize each year. I hope ultimately to tie it in with the Duke of Edinburgh's Award scheme.

MATCH. I'd prefer not to have Royalty mentioned in this context, sir. Have you been in trouble of this kind before?

PRENTICE. I'm not in trouble.

MATCH. You must realize this boy is bringing a serious charge against you?

PRENTICE. Yes. It's ridiculous. I'm a married man.

MATCH. Marriage excuses no one the freaks' roll-call.

PRENTICE. I'm a respected member of my profession. Your accusation is absurd.

MATCH. It's not for me to bring accusations in a matter I don't fully understand.

PRENTICE. The boy has an unsavoury reputation. Last night requires explaining before this morning.

GERALDINE. I had nothing to do with the disgraceful happenings at the Station Hotel.

MATCH. You deny that on the night of Thursday last you did behave in an obscene manner with a section of the Priory Road School for girls?

GERALDINE. Yes.

MATCH. Nicholas Beckett I warn you that anything you say will be taken down and may be used in evidence against you.

GERALDINE. My name isn't Nicholas Beckett.

MATCH (*pause, with a frown*). Then why d'you suppose I'd wish to arrest you?

GERALDINE. To safeguard my interests?

DR PRENTICE, *at the desk, pours whisky into a glass.*

PRENTICE. You imagine you'll be safe from acts of indecency in a police station?

GERALDINE. Of course.

PRENTICE. I wish I shared your optimism.

DR RANCE *enters from the hall.*

RANCE. Full security arrangements are in force. No one is to leave the clinic without written permission. Prentice, get your secretary to issue warrants to every member of the staff.

PRENTICE. I'll do that, sir, as soon as she's ready to resume her normal duties.

MATCH (*to* DR RANCE). Would you help us clear up a spot of bother, doctor? It's a matter of some urgency. Last night this youth assaulted a number of children. This morning he was assaulted in his turn.

RANCE (*with a shrug*). What can I say? It's an extreme case of 'be done by as you did'.

MATCH. The boy has made a serious charge against Dr Prentice. He claims he was forced to strip and lie on a couch.

RANCE (*to* DR PRENTICE). A complete list of your indiscretions would make a best-seller.

PRENTICE. It's all a dreadful mistake, sir.

RANCE. Now, Prentice, at the moment there's only one thing to advise. Absolute frankness. Have you behaved in an unseemly manner?

PRENTICE. No!

MATCH. The doctor said he wanted to put the boy in some kind of club.

RANCE. It's no good trying to do that. Boys cannot be put in the club. That's half their charm.

DR PRENTICE *passes a hand across his brow. An expression of desperate anxiety is on his face.*

PRENTICE. I'm sorry if my statement misled the sergeant. My nerves are on edge.

RANCE. You should consult a qualified psychiatrist.

PRENTICE. I am a qualified psychiatrist.

RANCE. You're a fool. That isn't quite the same thing. Though, in your case, the two may have much in common. (*To* SERGEANT MATCH.) Has the boy come to your notice before?

MATCH. Not on a case of this kind. That's why we have to be careful. As the doctor rightly says, he has an unsavoury reputation. It may be that he bears Dr Prentice a grudge.

RANCE (*to* DR PRENTICE). Perhaps this accusation springs from disappointment. It might have been wiser if you hadn't rejected the young fellow's blandishments.

PRENTICE. Unnatural vice can ruin a man.

RANCE. Ruin follows the accusation not the vice. Had you committed the act you wouldn't now be facing the charge.

PRENTICE. I couldn't commit the act. I'm a heterosexual.

RANCE. I wish you wouldn't use these Chaucerian words. It's most confusing. (*To* SERGEANT MATCH.) How do you propose to get to the bottom of this affair?

MATCH. A reputable person must examine the lad.

GERALDINE. I refuse to be examined!

MATCH. You can't refuse. You're under arrest.

GERALDINE. I'm not Nicholas Beckett. I want to be taken to prison.

MATCH. If you aren't Nicholas Beckett you can't go to prison. You're not under arrest.

GERALDINE (*pause, biting her lip*). I am Nicholas Beckett.

MATCH. Then you're under arrest. You'll submit to a medical examination.

RANCE. And I shall conduct it. The mind of the victim of this kind of assault must be considered equally with the body.

GERALDINE. I haven't been assaulted.

RANCE. Then why make such a foul accusation?

GERALDINE. I didn't accuse anyone. The sergeant made the accusation.

RANCE (*to* SERGEANT MATCH). Has Dr Prentice assaulted you too? (*To* DR PRENTICE.) Is it policemen or young boys you're after? At your age it's high time you came to a decision. (*To* SERGEANT MATCH.) Wait outside. I shall examine the boy and make my report. Afterwards I'll take a look at you.

MATCH (*stunned*). At me?

RANCE. Yes. We can't be too careful.

MATCH. It seems a bit unusual, sir.

RANCE (*with a bray of laughter*). You're in a madhouse. Unusual behaviour is the order of the day.

MATCH. Only for patients.

RANCE. We've no privileged class here. It's democratic lunacy we practise.

SERGEANT MATCH *goes into the hall, perplexed.* DR RANCE *turns to the sink, folds back his cuffs and rinses his hands.*

(*Over his shoulder.*) Take your clothes off, sonny. Lie on the couch. (*He returns to the sink.*)

GERALDINE *clutches* DR PRENTICE *by the arm.*

GERALDINE (*in a frantic whisper*). What are we to do now? I can't undress. He'd spot the deception at once.

PRENTICE. Keep calm! The situation, though desperate, is by no means lost.

DR RANCE *picks up a towel and dries his hands.*

GERALDINE. I shouldn't've behaved as I did, sir. I wasn't harmed.

RANCE. You enjoyed the experience? (*He puts the towel aside and pulls on rubber gloves.*) Would you enjoy normal intercourse?

GERALDINE. No. I might get pregnant – (*She realizes her mistake and attempts to cover up.*) – or be the cause of pregnancy in others.

DR RANCE, *quick to notice the error, turns to* DR PRENTICE.

RANCE. He's just given away a vital piece of information.

(*He advances on* GERALDINE.) Do you think of yourself as a girl?

GERALDINE. No.

RANCE. Why not?

GERALDINE. I'm a boy.

RANCE (*kindly*). Do you have the evidence about you?

GERALDINE (*her eyes flashing an appeal to* DR PRENTICE). I must be a boy. I like girls.

DR RANCE *stops and wrinkles his brow, puzzled.*

RANCE (*aside, to* DR PRENTICE). I can't quite follow the reasoning there.

PRENTICE. Many men imagine that a preference for women, is *ipso facto*, a proof of virility.

RANCE (*nodding, sagely*). Someone should really write a book on these folk-myths. (*To* GERALDINE.) Take your trousers down. I'll tell you which sex you belong to.

GERALDINE (*backing away*). I'd rather not know!

RANCE. You wish to remain in ignorance?

GERALDINE. Yes.

RANCE. I can't encourage you in such a self-indulgent attitude. You must face facts like the rest of us.

He forces GERALDINE *back to the couch.*

PRENTICE. You're forcing the boy to undergo a repetition of a traumatic experience, sir. He might go insane.

RANCE. This is a mental home. He couldn't choose a more appropriate place. (*To* GERALDINE.) Undress. My time is valuable.

GERALDINE, *unable to stand the ordeal any longer, cries out to* DR PRENTICE *in anguish.*

GERALDINE. I can't go on, doctor! I must tell the truth. (*To* DR RANCE.) I'm not a boy! I'm a girl!

RANCE (*to* DR PRENTICE). Excellent. A confession at last. He wishes to believe he's a girl in order to minimize the feelings of guilt after homosexual intercourse.

GERALDINE (*wild-eyed, desperate*). I pretended to be a boy. I did it to help Dr Prentice.

RANCE. How does it help a man if a girl pretends to be a boy?

GERALDINE. Wives are angry if they find their husbands have undressed and seduced a girl.

RANCE. But boys are fair game? I doubt whether your very personal view of Society would go unchallenged.

Provoked beyond endurance, GERALDINE *flings herself into* DR RANCE's *arms and cries hysterically.*

GERALDINE. Undress me then, doctor! Do whatever you like only prove that I'm a girl.

DR RANCE *pushes away and turns, frigidly to* DR PRENTICE.

RANCE. If he's going to carry on like this he'll have to be strapped down.

MRS PRENTICE *enters from the dispensary.*

MRS PRENTICE (*to* DR RANCE). Would you take a look at Miss Barclay, doctor? She refuses to undress in front of a woman.

RANCE. How about in front of a man?

MRS PRENTICE. I haven't sounded her on the subject.

RANCE. I wonder if I could tempt her. (*He chews his lip.*) I'll give it a try. She may be a nymphomaniac. (*To* DR PRENTICE.) If this lad becomes foul-mouthed keep him on the boil till I return.

He goes into the dispensary followed by MRS PRENTICE. GERALDINE *pulls herself together.*

GERALDINE. I'll go through the garden, doctor. I can get a taxi home.

PRENTICE. That isn't possible Strict security precautions are in force until the patient is recaptured.

GERALDINE. When she is recaptured can I go?

PRENTICE. No.
GERALDINE. Why not?
PRENTICE. You *are* the patient.

GERALDINE *gives a little cry of distress.* DR RANCE *re-enters from the dispensary removing his rubber gloves.*

RANCE. Your secretary is standing on a table fighting off any attempt to undress her. She seems incapable of conducting herself in a proper manner.

PRENTICE. She's given me no cause for complaint.

RANCE. But you expect a secretary to misbehave herself. It's a condition of employment. (*He faces* DR PRENTICE, *candidly.*) Do you realize the woman uses a razor?

PRENTICE. I see nothing remarkable in that. Mrs Prentice has occasion sometimes to remove unwanted hair.

RANCE. From her chin? (*He flings the rubber gloves aside.*) There are two sexes. The unpalatable truth must be faced. Your attempts at a merger can end only in heart-break.

MRS PRENTICE *enters from the dispensary leading a chastened* NICK *by the hand.*

MRS PRENTICE. Miss Barclay is calmer now, doctor. I've given her a sedative.

RANCE (*turning to* NICK, *shaking his head*). What an absorbing picture of the mind in decay.

PRENTICE. Miss Barclay is no more ill than I am.

RANCE. But your condition is worse than hers.

PRENTICE. I can't accept that.

RANCE. No madman ever accepts madness. Only the sane do that. (*To* NICK, *brusquely.*) Why won't you allow Mrs Prentice to undress you?

MRS PRENTICE. Her objections appear to be religious. She claims to be at one with God.

RANCE (*to* NICK). When were you first aware of a special relationship with the Almighty?

NICK. When I was presented with a copy of the Bible bound in calf.

RANCE. Was it an autographed copy?

NICK. I don't think God actually signed it.

RANCE. Well, of course, these things slip one's memory. Was there an inscription?

NICK. Yes.

RANCE. What did it say?

NICK. W. H. Smith & Sons.

RANCE. Oh, they count as God. You've clearly had a genuine religious experience. (*He nods to* GERALDINE.) Were you present when Dr Prentice used this youth unnaturally?

NICK. What is unnatural?

RANCE (*to* MRS PRENTICE). How disturbing the questions of the mad can be. (*To* NICK.) Suppose I made an indecent suggestion to you? If you agreed something might occur which, by and large, would be regarded as natural. If, on the other hand, I approached this child – (*He smiles at* GERALDINE.) – my action could result only in a gross violation of the order of things.

MRS PRENTICE (*nodding to* GERALDINE). Has my husband misbehaved with that boy?

RANCE. It's impossible to say with any degree of accuracy. He refuses to co-operate with a medical examination.

MRS PRENTICE (*to* DR PRENTICE). What happened to the other boy?

PRENTICE. Which boy?

MRS PRENTICE. The one you undressed.

RANCE. This is the boy he undressed.

MRS PRENTICE. No. He undressed the boy who made a nuisance of himself to me.

RANCE (*pause*). Isn't this the same one?

MRS PRENTICE. No.

RANCE (*staring, perplexed*). There's another boy?

MRS PRENTICE. He was being interviewed for a secretarial post. My husband made him undress.

RANCE (*coldly, to* DR PRENTICE). How long have you been a pervert?

PRENTICE. I'm not a pervert!

RANCE. How would you describe a man who mauls young boys, importunes policemen and lives on terms of intimacy with a woman who shaves twice a day?

PRENTICE. I'd say the man was a pervert.

RANCE. I'm glad you're beginning to face the realities of the situation. (*To* GERALDINE.) Who are you if you're not Nicholas Beckett?

GERALDINE *looks to* DR PRENTICE *and bites her lip.*

PRENTICE. His name is Gerald Barclay.

RANCE (*indicating* NICK). Is he this young woman's brother?

PRENTICE. No.

RANCE. What has happened then to Nicholas Beckett?

PRENTICE. He left an hour ago to resume his duties at the Station Hotel.

MRS PRENTICE. He can't have done! I took his uniform. He'd be naked.

PRENTICE. From what one hears of the Station Hotel the uniform is optional.

RANCE (*shaking his head, worried*). I hope we haven't lost another one. We'll be alone with our miracle drugs if many more go. (*To* MRS PRENTICE.) Find out whether the boy has returned to the hotel.

MRS PRENTICE *goes into the hall.* DR RANCE *turns to* DR PRENTICE.

Prepare the necessary papers. I'm certifying these two.

Cries of alarm come from NICK *and* GERALDINE.

NICK. Can't you do something about him, sir? He's off his head.

RANCE (*sternly*). I am a representative of order, you of chaos. Unless that fact is faced I can never hope to cure you.

(*To* DR PRENTICE.) Make out the committal orders for me to sign.

PRENTICE (*upset and angry*). I can't agree to such drastic action. We've no evidence of insanity.

RANCE. I'm relieving you of your post as head of this clinic. You'll do as I say from now on.

PRENTICE. I resent your handling of this affair, sir. I shall make my views known to the Commissioners.

RANCE. I doubt whether the views of a madman will carry much weight with the Commissioners.

PRENTICE. I'm not mad. It only looks that way.

RANCE. Your actions today would get the Archbishop of Canterbury declared non-compos.

PRENTICE. I'm not the Archbishop of Canterbury.

RANCE. That will come at a later stage of your illness.

PRENTICE. Your interpretation of my behaviour is misplaced and erroneous. If anyone borders on lunacy it's you yourself!

RANCE. Bearing in mind your abnormality that is a normal reaction. The sane appear as strange to the mad as the mad to the sane. Remain where you are. I shall give you a capsule.

He hurries into the dispensary.

GERALDINE (*with a sob*). Twice declared insane in one day! And they said I'd be working for a cheerful, well-spoken crowd. (*She blows her nose.*)

NICK. Why is he wearing my uniform?

PRENTICE. He isn't a boy. He's a girl.

GERALDINE. Why is she wearing my shoes?

PRENTICE. She isn't a girl. She's a boy. (*Pouring whisky.*) Oh, if I live to be ninety, I'll never again attempt sexual intercourse.

NICK. If we changed clothes, sir, we could get things back to normal.

PRENTICE. We'd then have to account for the disappearance of my secretary and the page-boy.

GERALDINE. But they don't exist!

PRENTICE. When people who don't exist disappear the account of their departure must be convincing.

NICK (*pause*). Is the sergeant corruptible?

PRENTICE. No.

NICK. I must have his uniform.

PRENTICE. Why?

NICK. To arrest myself.

DR PRENTICE *passes a hand across his forehead, dazed and weary.*

PRENTICE. I've been too long among the mad to know what sanity is.

NICK. Once I'm arrested we can write me off.

GERALDINE. You're multiplying our problems not dividing them.

NICK (*to* DR PRENTICE). Some glib pretext will get her out of the way. Then we can change clothes.

PRENTICE (*pause, uneasy*). The dangers of the cure may outweigh the disease.

DR RANCE *enters from the dispensary. He hands a bright red pill-box to* DR PRENTICE.

RANCE. Take two of these.

PRENTICE (*looking at the pill-box*). What are they?

RANCE. Dangerous drugs intended to relieve your pathologically elevated mood. Be careful not to exceed the stated dose. (*To* NICK.) Get a grip on yourself, young woman, and release those objects for which the police of five counties are searching. (*He takes* GERALDINE *by the arm.*) I'm putting this youth into a padded cell. Rampant hermaphroditism must be discouraged.

GERALDINE. Oh, I'm glad my parents are dead. This would've killed them.

DR RANCE *takes her into the ward.*

PRENTICE (*to* NICK). I'll get the sergeant to undress. I'm suspected of the offence, I might as well commit it.

NICK. Can't you give him a shot of something, sir? To damp him down?

PRENTICE. A mild tranquillizer wouldn't harm him, I suppose. You'll find a box of anti-depressants in my desk.

NICK *goes to the desk and takes a square, white pill-box from the drawer.* DR PRENTICE *opens the hall door.*

(*Calling, friendly.*) Would you step this way, sergeant?

NICK *hands* DR PRENTICE *the white pill-box and enters the dispensary.* SERGEANT MATCH *enters from the hall.*

MATCH. You wish to speak to me, doctor?

PRENTICE. Yes. I'd like you to undress and lie on that couch.

MATCH (*pause*). I haven't been interfered with.

PRENTICE. Never mind about that. Strip down to your underwear.

MATCH (*sitting on couch, unlacing boots*). If you make any attempt to arouse me, doctor, I shall call for help.

PRENTICE. It's easy to see why you've never been interfered with. You place too many obstacles in the way.

SERGEANT MATCH *takes off his boots.* NICK *appears in the doorway of the dispensary.* DR PRENTICE *hands him the boots.* NICK *takes them into the dispensary.* SERGEANT MATCH *takes off his tunic and hands it to* DR PRENTICE. NICK, *without his shoes and wig, appears in the doorway of the dispensary.* DR PRENTICE *hands him the* SERGEANT's *tunic.* NICK *turns.* DR PRENTICE *unzips his dress.* NICK *takes the tunic into the dispensary.* SERGEANT MATCH *takes off his shirt and tie.* NICK *wearing only his underpants, appears in the doorway of the dispensary.* DR PRENTICE *hands him the* SERGEANT's *shirt and tie.* NICK *goes into the dispensary.* SERGEANT MATCH *drops his trousers.* MRS PRENTICE *enters from the hall. Seeing the* SERGEANT *without his trousers, she screams loudly. Shocked and embarrassed* SERGEANT MATCH, *pulls up his trousers.*

MRS PRENTICE (*icily*). What were you doing with your trousers down, officer?

MATCH. The doctor is going to examine me.

MRS PRENTICE. Why?

MATCH. There's reason to suppose that I had a nasty experience a short time ago.

MRS PRENTICE. What kind of experience.

PRENTICE. He was meddled with.

MRS PRENTICE. By whom?

PRENTICE. Me.

MRS PRENTICE. And why are you examining him?

PRENTICE. To find out whether his story is true.

MRS PRENTICE. Don't you know?

PRENTICE. No. I didn't feel a thing.

MRS PRENTICE (*with a toss of her head*). Where is Dr Rance?

PRENTICE. He's just certified the hotel page. He's putting him in a padded cell.

MRS PRENTICE. I must speak to him. Things are getting out of control.

She hurries into the ward. DR PRENTICE *turns to* SERGEANT MATCH.

PRENTICE. Remove your trousers, sergeant, and we'll continue.

SERGEANT MATCH *takes off his trousers and hands them to* DR PRENTICE. *He is naked except for his underpants and socks. With a flourish* DR PRENTICE *takes the red pill-box from his pocket and hands it to the* SERGEANT.

(*Smiling.*) I'd like you to swallow these. Take as many as you like. They're quite harmless.

The SERGEANT *accepts the box.*

Now I want you to lie on this couch and concentrate on the closing chapters of your favourite work of fiction.

SERGEANT MATCH *lies on the couch.* DR PRENTICE *pulls the curtain around him and hurries to the dispensary with the trousers. He meets* NICK *in the doorway.* NICK *carries the* SERGEANT's *uniform.* DR PRENTICE *hands him the trousers.*

(*To* NICK.) In the garden you'll find a little summer house. You won't be disturbed in there.

NICK *goes into the garden with the clothes.* DR PRENTICE *goes to the desk and pours a whisky. He swallows it quickly.* NICK *appears, without the uniform, in the french windows.*

NICK. The helmet, sir!

DR PRENTICE *hurries to the couch.*

PRENTICE. The helmet, sergeant!
MATCH (*from behind the curtain*). In the hall, sir.
PRENTICE (*to* NICK). Where are Miss Barclay's clothes?
NICK. In the dispensary!

NICK *hurries into the hall.* DR PRENTICE *hurries into the dispensary.* MRS PRENTICE *enters from the ward.* NICK *re-enters from the hall wearing only underpants and the helmet. Upon seeing him* MRS PRENTICE *shrieks and backs away.* NICK *runs into the garden.*

MRS PRENTICE (*at the desk, weakly*). Oh, this place is like a madhouse!

DR RANCE *enters from the ward.* MRS PRENTICE *turns upon him, wildly.*

You must help me, doctor! I keep seeing naked men.
RANCE (*pause*). When did these delusions start?
MRS PRENTICE. They're not delusions. They're real.
RANCE (*with a bray of laughter*). Everyone who suffers from hallucinations imagines they are real. When did you last think you saw a naked man?
MRS PRENTICE. Just now. He was nude except for a policeman's helmet.

RANCE (*drily*). It's not difficult to guess what's on your mind, my dear. Are you having marital troubles?

MRS PRENTICE. Well, I do suffer from neuritis. My husband refuses to prescribe anything.

RANCE. A man shouldn't have to drug his wife in order to achieve a happy union.

MRS PRENTICE. I don't want drugs. I want account taken of my sexual nature.

She goes to the desk and pours whisky. DR RANCE *speaks to her gently yet with firmness.*

RANCE. Your depraved appetites may have contributed in part to your husband's breakdown. Where is Dr Prentice?

MRS PRENTICE (*putting ice into her glass*). I don't know. When I returned from telephoning the Station Hotel he was undressing the sergeant.

RANCE. How would you describe his relations with the sergeant?

MRS PRENTICE. Strange and, in many ways, puzzling. He's called him into this room on several occasions and then abruptly dismissed him.

RANCE. Playing the coquette, eh? Well, well, it adds spice to a love affair. What news of the patient?

MRS PRENTICE. None. Except that this looks like the nightgown she was wearing. (*She holds up* GERALDINE's *nightgown.*)

RANCE. She must be naked then?

MRS PRENTICE. Yes.

RANCE. And what's the report from the Station Hotel?

MRS PRENTICE. They state that they have no page called Gerald Barclay on their register. The youth you've certified insane must be an impostor.

RANCE. And what of Nicholas Beckett – the real page-boy?

MRS PRENTICE. He hasn't returned to the hotel. Yet when he disappeared his uniform was in my possession.

RANCE (*greatly concerned*). Two young people – one mad and

one sexually insatiable – both naked – are roaming this house. At all costs we must prevent a collision.

MRS PRENTICE. Oh, doctor! Does any of this make sense to you?

RANCE. It most certainly does. It's a human interest story. A respected member of the medical fraternity is married to a dazzlingly beautiful woman. Hopelessly in love but, through mutual distrust, refusing to admit it, there is little they can do to prevent a once-precious relationship turning sour. The doctor has a charming, but mentally unstable patient. She is the key to the mystery. At an early age she was the victim of a sexual attack. The assailant was her own father! An act of transference, common to the experience of any psychiatrist, allows her to identify the doctor as her parent. The demands of a nymphomaniac wife and patient, coupled with those of his torrid secretary, prove too much for his sanity. He turns, in his anguish, to assaulting young boys. Retaining, however, some vestiges of normal feelings, he persuades his minions to dress in women's clothes. This explains his desire for female garments. As his neurosis matures we'll better be able to decide whether he intended his boys to impersonate wife, patient or secretary.

MRS PRENTICE. And why did he assault the policeman?

RANCE. Pure madness. No other reason.

MRS PRENTICE. How long do you think my husband has been insane?

RANCE. I trace the origins of his illness as far back as that first letter to *The Guardian*. From the startling ideas of Dr Goebbels on the function of the male sexual organ we pass quite logically to white golliwogs. An attempt, in fact, to change the order of creation – homesexuality slots in here – dabbling in the black arts! The reported theft of the private parts of a well-known public figure ties in with this theory. We've phallic worship under our noses or I'm a Dutchman! (*With a neigh of laughter.*) When this is published I'll make my fortune. My 'documentary type' novelette will go into twelve record-breaking reprints. I'll be able to leave the service of the Commissioners and bask in the attentions of those who, like myself, find other people's iniquity puts money in their purse.

MRS PRENTICE (*drinking whisky with a shudder*). What a dreadful story. I'd condemn it in the strongest terms if it were fiction.

RANCE. I shan't now ask Dr Prentice to open our Mental Health Fair. (*Pressing his lips together.*) We'll have to fall back upon one of the saner members of the Cabinet.

MRS PRENTICE *picks a bright red pill-box from the floor near the couch.* DR RANCE *is quick to notice.*

What's that?

MRS PRENTICE. A pill-box, doctor. It's empty.

DR RANCE *seizes it and turns it over, with slowly growing horror.*

RANCE. He's taken an overdose! We have here terrible evidence of conflict. His tormented mind, seeking release, has led him to attempt to destroy himself.

MRS PRENTICE *gasps with shock and amazement.*

MRS PRENTICE. Suicide? This is so unexpected.

RANCE. Just when one least expects it, the unexpected always happens. We must find him before it's too late.

They part rapidly in opposite directions – MRS PRENTICE *into the hall,* DR RANCE *into the ward.* DR PRENTICE *and* NICK *enter simultaneously from the dispensary and the garden.* DR PRENTICE *carries the shoes and wig wrapped in the dress.* NICK *is wearing the* SERGEANT's *uniform.*

NICK (*urgent*). Miss Barclay is hanging from the window of the padded cell, doctor!

PRENTICE (*staring about the room*). Where can one hide a woman's dress in a doctor's consulting-room?

He picks up the vase. It is now too small to contain the dress. He looks around, quickly, desperate. The curtains of the couch part and SERGEANT MATCH *tumbles forward on the floor, drugged into insensibility.* DR PRENTICE *and* NICK *react to the* SERGEANT'S *condition.* DR PRENTICE *feels in his pocket and pulls out the square white pill-box. His eyes widen. He clutches his throat.*

(*With a strangled cry.*) My God! I've poisoned him!

NICK *runs to the sink, wets a towel and flicks it into the* SERGEANT'S *face.* DR PRENTICE *puts the dress down and attempts to drag* SERGEANT MATCH *to his feet. The* SERGEANT *moans, stares about him in a stupor and shivers uncontrollably.*

NICK (*holding the* SERGEANT'S *pulse*). He's frozen, sir.

PRENTICE. The effect of the drug. We find the same process at work in corpses.

NICK. Get some clothes on him and dump him outside. Let him sleep it off.

He picks up the dress.

PRENTICE (*wringing his hands*). How shall I explain the presence in my garden of the drugged body of a police sergeant?

NICK (*putting the dress on to* SERGEANT MATCH). You're guilty. You don't have to explain. Only the innocent do that.

He zips up the dress. DR PRENTICE *forces the* SERGEANT *to his feet.*

PRENTICE (*with a wail*). Oh, if this gets out I'll be reduced to selling matches!

They drag the semi-conscious SERGEANT MATCH *into the garden.* MRS PRENTICE *enters from the hall,* DR RANCE *from the ward.*

MRS PRENTICE. Someone has stolen the sergeant's helmet from the hall table. Do you suppose it could be my husband?

RANCE. Possibly. His behaviour is so ridiculous one might almost suspect him of being sane.

MRS PRENTICE, *at the french windows, suddenly cries out in alarm.*

What is it, my dear? You seem to express more emotion than is necessary at the mention of a policeman's helmet.

MRS PRENTICE. I've just seen my husband carrying a woman into the shrubbery.

RANCE. Was she struggling?

MRS PRENTICE. No.

RANCE. Then a new and frightening possibility presents itself. The drugs in this box – (*He lifts up the bright red pill-box.*) – may not have been used for suicide, but for murder. Your husband has made away with his secretary!

MRS PRENTICE *pours a whisky with a nervous laugh.*

MRS PRENTICE. Isn't that a little melodramatic, doctor?

RANCE. Lunatics *are* melodramatic. The subtleties of drama are wasted on them. The ugly shadow of anti-Christ stalks this house. Having discovered her Father/Lover in Dr Prentice the patient replaces him in a psychological re-shuffle by that archetypal Father-figure – the Devil himself. Everything is now clear. The final chapters of my book are knitting together: incest, buggery, outrageous women and strange love-cults catering for depraved appetites. All the fashionable bric-à-brac. A beautiful but neurotic girl has influenced the doctor to sacrifice a white virgin to propitiate the dark gods of unreason. 'When they broke into the evil-smelling den they found her poor body bleeding beneath the obscene and half-erect phallus.' (*To* MRS PRENTICE.) My 'unbiased account' of the case of the infamous sex-killer Prentice will undoubtedly add a great deal to our under-standing of such creatures. Society must be made aware of the growing menace of pornography. The whole treacherous avant-garde movement will be exposed for what it is – an instrument for inciting decent citizens to commit bizarre crimes against humanity and the state! (*He pauses, a little overcome and wipes his brow.*) You have, under your roof, my dear, one of the most remarkable lunatics of all time. We must institute a search for the corpse. As a transvestite, fetishist, bi-sexual murderer Dr Prentice displays considerable deviation overlap. We may get necrophilia too. As a sort of bonus.

DR PRENTICE *enters from the garden.*

(*Turning, and giving a disdainful stare.*) Would you confirm, Prentice, that your wife saw you carrying a body into the shrubbery?

PRENTICE. Yes. I have an explanation for my conduct.

RANCE. I'm not interested in your explanations. I can provide my own. Where is your secretary?

PRENTICE. I've given her the sack.

RANCE (*aside to* MRS PRENTICE). He killed her and wrapped her body in a sack. The word association is very clear.

PRENTICE. I haven't killed anyone!

RANCE. Your answer is in accord with the complex structure of your neurosis.

PRENTICE. The person my wife saw wasn't dead. They were asleep.

RANCE (*to* MRS PRENTICE). He hopes for a resurrection. We've a link here with primitive religion. (*To* DR PRENTICE.) Why have you turned your back on the God of your Fathers?

PRENTICE. I'm a rationalist.

RANCE. You can't be a rationalist in an irrational world. It isn't rational. (*Picking up the wig and shoes.*) Was it your intention to wear these for auto-erotic excitement?

PRENTICE. No, I'm a perfectly normal man.

RANCE (*to* MRS PRENTICE). His belief in normality is quite

abnormal. (*To* DR PRENTICE.) Was the girl killed before or after you took her clothes off?

PRENTICE. He wasn't a girl. He was a man.

MRS PRENTICE. He was wearing a dress.

PRENTICE. He was a man for all that.

RANCE. Women wear dresses, Prentice, not men. I won't be a party to the wanton destruction of a fine old tradition. Did you change clothes with your victim before it died?

PRENTICE. Nobody died! The person you saw me with was a policeman who'd taken an overdose of narcotics.

MRS PRENTICE. Why was he dressed as a woman?

PRENTICE. He was naked when I found him. The dress was readily to hand.

MRS PRENTICE. Where were his own clothes?

PRENTICE. A boy had stolen them.

DR RANCE *draws* MRS PRENTICE *aside, his face a mask of disapproval.*

RANCE. The time has come to call a halt to this Graeco-Roman hallucination. Is there a strait-jacket in the house?

MRS PRENTICE. Modern methods of treatment have rendered the strait-jacket obsolete.

RANCE. I'm well aware of that. We still use them none the less. Have you one in your possession?

MRS PRENTICE. The porter has a few.

RANCE. We can take no chances with your husband in his present condition.

He goes into the hall. DR PRENTICE, *at the desk, pouring whisky, spits his words venomously at his wife.*

PRENTICE. Is this another of your plots to undermine my reputation for sound judgement, you treacherous harpy?

MRS PRENTICE *makes no effort to reply. She smiles and puts a hand upon* DR PRENTICE's *shoulder.*

MRS PRENTICE (*gently*). You've caused a poor girl's death'

darling. You may be called upon to accept a period of restraint.

PRENTICE (*swallowing whisky*). Miss Barclay isn't dead!

MRS PRENTICE. Produce her then and your difficulties will be over.

PRENTICE. I can't.

MRS PRENTICE. Why not?

PRENTICE. You're wearing her dress. (*With a shrug of resignation.*) You surprised me this morning making an ill-timed attempt to seduce her.

MRS PRENTICE *smiles a smile of quiet disbelief.*

MRS PRENTICE. If we're to save our marriage, my dear, you must admit that you prefer boys to women. Dr Rance has explained the reasons for your aberration. You'll find me quite tolerant. In fact I know a number of charming youths. I could pass a few of the younger ones on to you. It would raise the tone of our marriage considerably.

DR PRENTICE *is stunned by her suggestion. He rounds on her in a fury.*

PRENTICE. I won't have you making scandalous allegations in a matter of which you know nothing.

MRS PRENTICE (*tossing her head*). The page at the hotel accused you of behaving in an indecent manner.

PRENTICE. That wasn't a boy. It was a girl.

MRS PRENTICE. Admit that you prefer your sex to mine. I've no hesitation in saying that I do.

PRENTICE. You filthy degenerate! Take your clothes off!

MRS PRENTICE *unzips her dress.*

MRS PRENTICE (*eagerly*). Are you going to beat me? Do if you wish. Your psychotic experiences are immensely valuable to you and should be encouraged rather than thwarted or repressed.

DR PRENTICE *seizes her, smacks her face and tears the dress from her. She struggles.*

MRS PRENTICE (*gasping as he slaps her*). Oh, my darling! This is the way to sexual adjustment in marriage.

DR PRENTICE *throws her from him. She crashes into the vase which topples to the floor.* DR RANCE *runs in from the hall with two strait-jackets.* DR PRENTICE *runs into the garden with his wife's dress.* MRS PRENTICE *sits among the overthrown flowers, her hair tousled, wearing only her underclothes.*

MRS PRENTICE (*rising, stumbling to the desk*). Oh, doctor, during your absence my husband became violent and struck me. (*She pours a whisky.*)
RANCE. Did you enjoy it?
MRS PRENTICE. At first. But the pleasures of the senses quickly pall.

She drinks the whisky. DR RANCE *stoops and picks up the vase and scattered flowers.*

RANCE. Was there an attempt to destroy these flowers?
MRS PRENTICE. They fell during the struggle.
RANCE. You're aware of the plant allegory? The rose is a common cipher for a woman. He intended to do you harm.
MRS PRENTICE. Yes. I was beaten until I was nearly senseless.
RANCE. Oh, that was a mere physical act with no special psychological significance. We must lose no time in putting Dr Prentice under restraint. We'll need help in the enterprise. Have you no brawny-youth upon whom you can call in times of stress?
MRS PRENTICE. I'm a married woman, doctor! Your suggestion is in the worst of taste.

NICK *enters from the garden dressed in the* SERGEANT's *uniform.*

NICK. I'd like a word with you, doctor, about my brother, Nicholas Beckett. I've just arrested him.

RANCE. Such a touching demonstration of brotherly love is quite in key with the spirit of the age. Why did you arrest him?

NICK. He'd broken the law.

RANCE. And because of that he's to be treated as a criminal? What's happened to the British love of fair play? Where is your brother now?

NICK. In gaol.

RANCE (*to* MRS PRENTICE). Your sleep won't be disturbed tonight, my dear.

MRS PRENTICE. Life is full of disappointments.

RANCE (*to* NICK). Where is Sergeant Match?

NICK. Keeping my brother company.

RANCE. Has he been charged?

NICK. He hasn't committed a crime.

RANCE (*to* MRS PRENTICE). When the punishment for guilt or innocence is the same it becomes an act of logic to commit the crime. (*To* NICK.) Was Dr Prentice in the garden?

NICK. No.

RANCE. You may have difficulty in recognizing him. He was probably dressed as a woman.

MRS PRENTICE. He has killed his secretary.

NICK (*horrified*). He can't've done. He's an O.B.E.

RANCE. These cabbalistic signs are of no more use in warding off evil than the moons and stars on a sorcerer's hat. We shall need your help in tracking down the mindless killer of young Geraldine Barclay.

NICK *stares at* DR RANCE.

NICK (*with a groan*). Oh, doctor, I'm obsessed by feelings of guilt. I have to make a confession.

RANCE. You must ring for an appointment. I can't listen to confessions off the cuff.

NICK. I am Nicholas Beckett. I've no right to wear this uniform. (*He takes off his helmet.*) I did it at the doctor's request never imagining that I was unwittingly assisting a psychopath.

RANCE. You have no brother? And Sergeant Match isn't in custody?

NICK. No. I'm a page-boy employed by the Station Hotel. I met Dr Prentice quite by chance. I took to him instantly. After a short conversation during which we discussed sex matters in an uninhibited and free-wheeling way, he asked me if I'd mind dressing up as a woman. I agreed to his suggestion having heard that transvestism is no longer held to be a dangerous debilitating vice. The doctor introduced me to his colleagues as 'Miss Barclay'. I was to be paid a sum of money. (*To* MRS PRENTICE.) That's why I objected to being undressed. It would've embarrassed me.

MRS PRENTICE (*to* DR RANCE). You understand what this means, doctor?

RANCE. Yes. Miss Barclay has been missing since this morning. (*To* NICK.) When Dr Prentice asked you to pose as a woman did he give a reason?

NICK. No.

MRS PRENTICE. Didn't you consider his request strange?

NICK. No.

RANCE. Have you aided other men in their perverted follies?

NICK. During my last term at school I was the slave of a corporal in the Welsh Fusiliers.

RANCE. Were you never warned of the dangers inherent in such relationships?

NICK. When he was posted abroad he gave me a copy of 'The Way to Healthy Manhood'.

RANCE (*drily, to* MRS PRENTICE). A case of opening the stable door after the horse is in. (*To* NICK.) Your life appears to have been spent among the more brutal and irresponsible members of society. You'd better help me to right the wrongs you've done.

NICK. What do you want me to do, sir? After my recent experiences I'm understandably suspicious.

RANCE. You'll find the demands of medicine easier to satisfy than those of the army. (*He picks up the strait-jacket.*) This is a strait-jacket. I require your help in persuading Dr Prentice to put it on. There may be violence. His body has a mind of its own. (*To* MRS PRENTICE.) Have you a gun?

MRS PRENTICE *opens a drawer in the desk and takes out two guns.*

MRS PRENTICE (*handing one to* DR RANCE). You will make sure before you fire that my husband isn't waving an olive branch?

RANCE. An olive branch can be used as an offensive weapon. If there's trouble I shall blow him from the floor.

NICK (*to* DR RANCE). You're going to flush him from his hiding-place, sir?

RANCE. Yes. Really we should hire beaters, but they'll expect to have their fares paid from Scotland. (*He goes to the french windows, shaking his head.*) I'm loath to certify a fellow psychiatrist. It causes such bad feelings within the profession.

He goes into the garden.

MRS PRENTICE (*to* NICK). Take no chances. Call for help immediately you see Dr Prentice. (*She goes to the hall door, waving the gun.*) Try not to break his arms or legs. It makes the job of adjusting the jacket doubly difficult.

She goes into the hall. NICK *opens the strait-jacket.* DR PRENTICE *enters from the ward carrying the dress taken from* MRS PRENTICE. *He looks harassed.*

PRENTICE. Miss Barclay has fallen from the window of the padded cell. When I asked her to undress she became hysterical.

NICK *nods, understandingly. He walks across to* DR PRENTICE *and takes him firmly by the shoulder.*

NICK. Come along now, doctor, I want you to put this on. (*He lifts the jacket.*)

PRENTICE (*hardly hearing*). I want you to co-operate with me in getting things back to normal in this house.

NICK (*soothingly*). You can rely on me, sir.

PRENTICE. It would help me considerably if you'd take your clothes off.

NICK (*pause*). If I do that, sir, will you put this on? (*He holds up the jacket.*)

PRENTICE (*angry, losing patience*). Of course not! That's a strait-jacket. I won't be a party to kinky capers. You've lived too long at the Station Hotel to know how decent people behave. Now do as I say and undress!

SERGEANT MATCH, *wearing the leopard-spotted dress appears in the french windows.*

MATCH (*swaying, unsteadily*). I'm ready to be examined when you are, doctor.

He stumbles into the dispensary, clutching the furniture, his face pale, his eyes staring. GERALDINE, wearing NICK's uniform, staggers in from the garden. Her face is bruised and smeared with soil. She is white with shock.

GERALDINE. They're combing the grounds for us, doctor! They've got guns. What shall we do?

PRENTICE. You must lose no time in getting undressed. (*He seizes her and attempts to unbutton her uniform.*)

GERALDINE (*tearful, beating him away*). You're behaving like a maniac!

NICK. He is a maniac. He's murdered a woman and hidden her body somewhere.

PRENTICE. Who is responsible for these vile stories?

NICK. Dr Rance is having you certified. (*Waving the jacket.*) I've got to get you into this!

He leaps upon DR PRENTICE and attempts to put him into the strait-jacket. DR PRENTICE pulls GERALDINE's trousers down. She beats him away, weeping profusely. She pulls her trousers up. DR PRENTICE *wards off* NICK *and tries to prevent* GERALDINE *pulling up her trousers.* SERGEANT MATCH *enters dizzily from the dispensary, stumbling across the room, crashing and upsetting furniture.*

MATCH. I'm ready when you are, doctor!

He reels out into the ward. DR PRENTICE *shakes* NICK *away, furiously.*

PRENTICE (*to* GERALDINE). Give this youth the clothes you're wearing. (*He lifts the dress.*) Put this on. (*To* NICK.) Let the sergeant have his uniform back. When he next passes through we can confiscate my wife's dress and our problems will be solved.

NICK *takes off his uniform.* GERALDINE *pulls down her trousers. A shot is heard from the ward.* SERGEANT MATCH *enters. Blood is pouring down his leg.*

MATCH. I was on the lavatory, doctor, when a man appeared and fired a gun at me. I'd like your opinion as to the extent of the damage.

He reels into the dispensary. A crash is heard. NICK *is now naked except for his underpants.* MRS PRENTICE *enters from the hall.* NICK *ducks behind the desk,* GERALDINE *is concealed from view by the couch.* MRS PRENTICE *advances on* DR PRENTICE.

MRS PRENTICE (*waving the gun*). Come with me and lie down!
PRENTICE. The woman is insatiable.
MRS PRENTICE. Unless you make love to me I shall shoot you.
PRENTICE. No husband can be expected to give his best at gun-point. (*Backing away.*)

MRS PRENTICE *fires.* DR PRENTICE *ducks and runs quickly from the room into the garden.* MRS PRENTICE *follows and fires again.* SERGEANT MATCH *runs out of the dispensary, terrified. Seeing him* MRS PRENTICE *screams.* SERGEANT MATCH *gives a bellow of fright and runs into the hall.* NICK *runs from behind the desk into the hall.* MRS PRENTICE *squeals with surprise.* GERALDINE, *wearing the top half of* NICK's *uniform and no trousers, runs into the dispensary.* MRS PRENTICE *runs to the ward door. As she reaches it a shot is heard and* NICK *re-enters, moaning and clutching his shoulder. Screaming with terror* MRS PRENTICE *fires wildly at* NICK *who gives a yelp of pain and runs into the garden.* DR RANCE *enters from the ward holding a smoking gun.* MRS PRENTICE *flings herself upon him.*

MRS PRENTICE. Doctor, doctor! The world is full of naked men running in all directions!

DR RANCE *grabs her arm.*

RANCE. Where do you keep your tranquillizers?

MRS PRENTICE *hurries into the dispensary. A cry and a crash are heard and* GERALDINE *runs out. She has taken off the uniform and wears her own panties and bra.*

RANCE (*with a bray of triumph*). At last we've caught the patient!

He points his gun at GERALDINE. MRS PRENTICE *runs from the dispensary with a strait-jacket and flings it over* GERALDINE.

GERALDINE. I'm not a patient. I'm telling the truth!
RANCE. It's much too late to tell the truth.

They drag the weeping girl to the couch and fasten her into the strait-jacket.

RANCE (*watching as* MRS PRENTICE *ties* GERALDINE *down*). These final harrowing scenes will be lavishly illustrated with graphs showing the effect of her downfall upon her poor tortured mind. Meanwhile, in his temple of love, the hideous

Dr Prentice and his acolyte are praying to their false gods unaware that the forces of reason have got their measure.

MRS PRENTICE *steps back.*

Fetch a syringe.

MRS PRENTICE *goes into the dispensary.*

GERALDINE (*trussed up, unable to move*). What have I done to deserve this? I've always led such a respectable life.

RANCE. Your mind has given way. You'll find the experience invaluable in your efforts to come to terms with twentieth-century living. Why did you persuade your father to kill Geraldine Barclay?

GERALDINE. I am Geraldine Barclay.

RANCE. You imagine you're a secretary. In fact you're the leading player in one of the most remarkable and sinister stories of recent history. The extent to which you influenced your employer and contributed to his breakdown has yet to be measured.

GERALDINE (*weeping, bitterly*). This is dreadful. Dreadful.

RANCE. I'm glad you're adopting a more responsible attitude. It's most encouraging. Where is the body?

GERALDINE. I don't know.

RANCE. Are you under the seal of the confessional? What black rites were you initiated into by that foul priest of the Unknown?

GERALDINE *sobs, unable to speak.* DR RANCE *abruptly throws himself on to her and holds her in his arms.*

Let me cure your neurosis! It's the only thing I want out of life.

MRS PRENTICE *enters from the dispensary carrying a hypodermic syringe and bowl.*

MRS PRENTICE. What is the meaning of this exhibition?

RANCE (*breaking away from* GERALDINE). It's a new and

hitherto untried type of therapy. I think it's viable under the circumstances.

MRS PRENTICE. Your treatment seems designed to plunge the patient deeper into lunacy rather than achieve any lasting cure.

DR RANCE *rounds on her with icy dignity.*

RANCE. Someone whose unconscious is as quirky as your own could hardly be expected to understand my methods.

MRS PRENTICE. What do you mean by that?

RANCE. I'm referring to those manifestations of the penis which you encounter with an increasing degree of frequency.

MRS PRENTICE. You've seen them too.

RANCE. What does that prove? Merely that you've given me your wretched disease. (*He takes the hypodermic from her.*)

MRS PRENTICE. Shall I swab the patient's arm?

RANCE. You don't imagine I'm wasting this stuff on her, do you? (*He rolls back his sleeve.*) At five guineas an ounce it would be criminal. (*He gives himself an injection.*) Go and call the police.

MRS PRENTICE *goes into the hall.* DR RANCE *puts the hypodermic aside.* MRS PRENTICE *re-enters, wild-eyed, her hands smeared with blood.*

MRS PRENTICE. There's a policeman outside. Naked and covered in blood.

RANCE. The bounds of decency have long been overstepped in this house. (*He slaps her face.*) Your subconscious cannot be encouraged in its skulduggery.

MRS PRENTICE (*desperate, showing her hands*). Is this blood real?

RANCE. No.

MRS PRENTICE. Can you see it?

RANCE. Yes.

MRS PRENTICE. Then what explanation is there?

RANCE. I'm a scientist. I state facts, I cannot be expected to

provide explanations. Reject any para-normal phenomena.
It's the only way to remain sane.

MRS PRENTICE. It seems real.

RANCE. Who are you to decide what reality is? Remain where
you are. I'll call the police.

He goes into the hall. MRS PRENTICE *pours herself a whisky.*
NICK *appears in the french windows, pale, swaying unsteadily
and bleeding from a wound on his shoulder. Blood oozes from
between his fingers.*

NICK (*anguished, fainting*). I'm in pain. I've been shot. Call a
doctor.

MRS PRENTICE (*dropping her glass, hiding her head in her hands*).
Oh, I'm losing my mind!

She sobs to herself. GERALDINE *calls to* NICK.

GERALDINE. Help me! I'm suffering untold anguish. Untie
me.

NICK. Why are you tied up?

GERALDINE. Dr Rance did it. He says I'm mad.

NICK. He's a psychiatrist, he must know. He wouldn't put you
in a strait-jacket if you were sane. He'd have to be mad.

GERALDINE. He is mad!

NICK *supports himself on the desk and stares at the sobbing*
MRS PRENTICE.

NICK (*to* GERALDINE). Is she mad?

GERALDINE. She thinks she is. She imagines you're a figment
of her imagination.

NICK (*to* MRS PRENTICE, *nodding to* GERALDINE). She can
see me. Doesn't that prove I'm real?

MRS PRENTICE. No. She's mad.

NICK. If you think I'm a phantom of your subconscious you
must be mad.

MRS PRENTICE (*with a hysterical shriek*). I am mad!

GERALDINE *bursts into tears.* NICK *hangs over the desk, blood pouring from his wound.* DR PRENTICE *hurries in from the garden.*

PRENTICE. My wife has shot at me. She thinks I'm mad!

NICK. You are mad! I've been told to put you into a strait-jacket.

He picks MRS PRENTICE'S *gun from the desk, lifts the strait-jacket and advances on* DR PRENTICE. MRS PRENTICE *covers her face with her hands.* DR RANCE *runs in from the hall carrying another strait-jacket. He flings it over* MRS PRENTICE. *They crash to the floor screaming and struggling.*

PRENTICE (*to* NICK). Put that gun down! (*To* DR RANCE.) A husband must be allowed to put his wife into a strait-jacket. It's one of the few pleasures left in modern marriage.

He makes a move. NICK *holds out the jacket with one hand and waves the gun with the other.*

You should have that wound attended to. Have you a handkerchief?

NICK. No.

PRENTICE. Borrow mine.

He pulls his handkerchief from his pocket. It is full of flower stalks. He tosses them into NICK'S *face.* NICK *is knocked off guard.* DR PRENTICE *flings himself on to him. They join* DR RANCE *and* MRS PRENTICE *in a struggling, grunting heap on the floor watched by the tearful* GERALDINE *from the couch.* DR PRENTICE *wrenches the gun from* NICK *and stands.* NICK *moans and crawls away, his wound streaming blood, his face white and ill.* DR RANCE *stands to his feet having tied* MRS PRENTICE *into a strait-jacket.*

PRENTICE (*waving his gun*). Stay where you are, doctor! Your conduct today has been a model of official irresponsibility and bloody-mindedness. I'm going to certify you.

RANCE (*quietly, with dignity*). No. I am going to certify you.

PRENTICE. I have the weapon. You have the choice. What is it to be? Either madness or death?

RANCE. Neither of your alternatives would enable me to continue to be employed by Her Majesty's Government.

PRENTICE. That isn't true. The higher reaches of the civil service are recruited entirely from corpses or madmen. Press the alarm!

DR RANCE goes to the wall and presses the alarm. A siren wails. Metal grilles fall over each of the doors. The lights go out. The siren wails to a stop. The room is lit only by the glare of a bloody sunset shining through the trees in the garden.

An overloading of the circuit! We're trapped.

RANCE (*drily*). I hope the security arrangements in the wards are as efficient as those in your consulting-room. We could starve to death.

PRENTICE. A fitting tribute to the effectiveness of our early warning system.

RANCE. Since neither of us can escape your deterrent is useless. Put it down.

DR PRENTICE puts the gun on to the desk. DR RANCE takes out his own and points it at the astonished DR PRENTICE.

RANCE (*holding DR PRENTICE at bay with one gun and picking up the other*). I'll have you in a jacket within the hour. It's a hat trick!

PRENTICE. Is this a record for you?

RANCE (*slipping DR PRENTICE's gun into his pocket*). By no means. I once put a whole family into a communal straitjacket.

PRENTICE. How proud your mother must've been.

RANCE. She wasn't, I'm afraid. It was my own family, you see. I've a picture of the scene at home. My foot placed squarely upon my father's head. I sent it to Sigmund Freud and had a charming postcard in reply.

NICK crawls, almost fainting, to a chair.

NICK. What about me, sir? I'm not mad.

RANCE (*with a smile*). You're not human.

NICK. I can't be an hallucination. (*He points to his bleeding shoulder.*) Look at this wound. That's real.

RANCE. It appears to be.

NICK. If the pain is real I must be real.

RANCE. I'd rather not get involved in metaphysical speculation.

PRENTICE. This young man is the page-boy from the Station Hotel. He misbehaved himself with my wife. He wasn't an hallucination when he did that.

RANCE. Your wife is subject to a type of nervous disorder which leads her to imagine she is being pursued by un-clothed male figures. This young man is one of them. If he is her assailant it follows that the assault was a fabrication of her diseased mind.

PRENTICE. But Sergeant Match wishes to arrest the young man.

RANCE. The sergeant too may not exist. According to your wife he also appeared to her naked. For all we know he could be a type of incubus employed by Scotland Yard. He ad-mitted that his brother was a figment of his imagination confirming my own law that the relations of apparitions are also apparitions. (*In a firm voice.*) What have you done with Geraldine Barclay?

GERALDINE (*feebly*). I'm here.

DR PRENTICE *goes to the desk and pours a large whisky.*

PRENTICE (*to* DR RANCE). The story you're about to hear is concerned solely with the heart: the mind and its mysteries could not have been further from my thoughts when, early this morning, I persuaded that young woman to take her clothes off. (*He drinks the whisky.*)

GERALDINE (*to* DR RANCE). Mrs Prentice mistook my dress for her own and, by an oversight, you mistook me for a patient. Dr Prentice asked me to keep quiet in order to protect his good name. What could I do? I was terrified of exposure.

RANCE. You were naked at the time?

GERALDINE. Yes. Under duress I agreed to help the doctor. I've never ceased reproaching myself. The whole day has been spent fighting to retain my self-respect.

DR RANCE *chews his lip and turns abruptly to* DR PRENTICE.

RANCE. Release her. And your wife. (*As* DR PRENTICE *does so he stares, baffled.*) I'd be willing to stake my professional reputation upon the fact that this girl has been the victim of an incestuous attack. I won't go back upon my diagnosis. My publishers will sue me for loss of royalties.

GERALDINE (*stepping from the couch*). I'm sure my typing speed has been affected by what I've suffered today. (*Tearful, to* DR PRENTICE.) And I wish to report the loss of my lucky elephant charm.

DR RANCE *takes a brooch from his pocket.*

RANCE. Is this the piece of jewellery to which you refer?

GERALDINE. Yes. It has great sentimental value.

DR RANCE *gives it to her.* NICK *picks up the trousers of his uniform.*

NICK. I've got a brooch like that. (*He shows* GERALDINE *a brooch.*) You see – they make a pair!

MRS PRENTICE, *released now from the strait-jacket, gives a cry of surprise.*

MRS PRENTICE. Let me see those pieces of jewellery. (*The two brooches are shown to her.*) A single brooch can be made of these two fragments. (*She fits the brooch together.*) Oh, my heart is beating like a wild thing!

DR RANCE *examines the brooch.*

RANCE. Two elephants carrying a richly engraved howdah in

which is seated a young and beautiful woman – perhaps a princess of the royal line – magnificent example of oriental craftsmanship. (*To* MRS PRENTICE.) How did you know this was a single piece?

MRS PRENTICE. It belonged to me once. Many years ago, when I was a young woman, I was raped in a linen cupboard on the second floor of the Station Hotel. As the man left me he pressed that brooch into my hands in part payment.

RANCE. How did these children come to be in possession of the separate halves?

MRS PRENTICE. I paid for my misdemeanour by conceiving twins. It was impossible for me to keep them – I was by then engaged to be married to a promising young psychiatrist. I decided to abandon them to their fate. I broke the brooch in half and pinned a separate piece to each babe. I then placed them at either end of the small country town in which I was resident. Some kind people must've brought the children up as their own. (*Weeping, hugging* NICK *and* GERALDINE.) Oh, children! I am your mother! Can you ever forgive me for what I did?

NICK. What kind of mother must you have been to stay alone at the Station Hotel?

MRS PRENTICE. I was employed as a chambermaid. I did it for a joke shortly after the war. The effect of a Labour Government on the middle-classes had to be seen to be believed.

GERALDINE. Was our father also employed by the Station Hotel?

MRS PRENTICE. I never saw your father. The incident occurred during a power-cut. I became pregnant as I waited for normal service to be resumed.

DR PRENTICE, *his face white with shock, comes forward.*

PRENTICE (*weakly, to* DR RANCE). You'll find an inscription on the back of the brooch, sir –

DR RANCE *turns the brooch over.*

PRENTICE.—'To Lillian from Avis. Christmas 1939'. I found that brooch many years ago. It was on the pavement outside a large department store.

RANCE. Who were Lillian and Avis?

PRENTICE. I've no idea. It fell from the collar of a pekinese. Lillian and Avis may have been the creature's owners. (*He stares about him in shame.*) I haven't seen it since I pressed it into the hand of a chambermaid whom I debauched shortly before my marriage.

MRS PRENTICE (*with a cry of recognition*). I understand now why you suggested that we spend our wedding night in a linen cupboard!

PRENTICE. I wished to recreate a moment that was very precious to me. If you'd given in to my request our marriage would never have foundered.

MRS PRENTICE From this time on we'll never make love except in a linen cupboard. It's the least I can do after the years of suffering I've caused you!

He embraces her and embraces NICK *and* GERALDINE.

RANCE (*to* PRENTICE, *wild with delight*). If you are this child's father my book can be written in good faith – she *is* the victim of an incestuous assault!

MRS PRENTICE. And so am I, doctor! My son has a collection of indecent photographs which prove beyond doubt that he made free with me in the same hotel – indeed in the same linen cupboard where his conception took place.

RANCE. Oh, what joy this discovery gives me! (*Embracing* MRS PRENTICE, GERALDINE *and* NICK.) Double incest is even more likely to produce a best-seller than murder – and this is as it should be for love *must* bring greater joy than violence.

Everyone embraces one another. The skylight opens, a rope ladder is lowered and, in a great blaze of glory, SERGEANT MATCH, *the leopard-spotted dress torn from one shoulder and streaming with blood, descends.*

We're approaching what our racier novelists term 'the climax'.

Reaching the floor SERGEANT MATCH *stares about him in bewilderment.*

MATCH. Will someone produce or cause to be produced the missing parts of Sir Winston Churchill?

RANCE. We have no knowledge of such things.

MATCH. I must ask for your co-operation in a matter of vital importance to this country. (*He sways, but hangs on to the rope ladder.*) Who was the last to see Mrs Barclay dead?

GERALDINE. The undertaker.

MATCH. Did he have no words of comfort for you as the only living descendant of a woman violated by the hero of 1940?

GERALDINE. He handed me a box.

MATCH. What did it contain?

GERALDINE. I assumed it held the clothes my step-mother wore on the day of her death. I was going to deliver them to some poor and needy person.

MATCH. Where is the box?

GERALDINE *picks up the box which she had upon entering the room. It has remained on the desk ever since.* SERGEANT MATCH *opens the box, looks inside, and gives a sigh.*

The Great Man can once more take up his place in the High Street as an example to us all of the spirit that won the Battle of Britain.

SERGEANT MATCH *takes from the box and holds up a section from a larger than life-sized bronze statue. Deep intakes of breath from everyone.*

RANCE (*with admiration*). How much more inspiring if, in those dark days, we'd seen what we see now. Instead we had to be content with a cigar – the symbol falling far short, as we all realize, of the object itself.

The dying sunlight from the garden and the blaze from above gild SERGEANT MATCH *as he holds high the nation's heritage.*

PRENTICE. Well, sergeant, we have been instrumental in uncovering a number of remarkable peccadilloes today. I'm sure you'll co-operate in keeping them out of the papers?

MATCH. I will, sir.

RANCE. I'm glad you don't despise tradition. Let us put our clothes on and face the world.

They pick up their clothes and weary, bleeding, drugged and drunk, climb the rope ladder into the blazing light.

Curtain

[*Note:* The bowdlerized ending runs as follows, after MATCH's speech, 'The Great Man can once more take up his place in the High Street as an example to us all of the spirit that won the Battle of Britain.':

RANCE *looks inside the box.*

RANCE (*with admiration*). How much more inspiring if, in those dark days, we'd seen what we see now. Instead we had to be content with a cigar – the symbol falling far short, as we all realize, of the object itself.

GERALDINE *looks inside the box.*

GERALDINE. But it is a cigar!

RANCE. Ah, the illusions of youth!

SERGEANT MATCH *loudly shuts the lid of the box and tucks it under his arm.*

PRENTICE. Well, sergeant, we have been instrumental ... etc.]